DANISH
VOCABULARY

ENGLISH-
DANISH

The most useful words
To expand your lexicon and sharpen
your language skills

9000 words

Danish vocabulary for English speakers - 9000 words

By Andrey Taranov

T&P Books vocabularies are intended for helping you learn, memorize, and revise foreign words. The dictionary is divided into themes, covering all major spheres of everyday activities, business, science, culture, etc.

The process of learning words using T&P Books' theme-based dictionaries gives you the following advantages:

- Correctly grouped source information predetermines success at subsequent stages of word memorization
- Availability of words derived from the same root allowing memorization of word units (rather than separate words)
- Small units of words facilitate the process of establishing associative links needed for consolidation of vocabulary
- Level of language knowledge can be estimated by the number of learned words

T&P Books Publishing
www.tpbooks.com

ISBN: 978-1-78071-307-6

This book is also available in E-book formats.
Please visit www.tpbooks.com or the major online bookstores.

DANISH VOCABULARY
for English speakers

T&P Books vocabularies are intended to help you learn, memorize, and review foreign words. The vocabulary contains over 9000 commonly used words arranged thematically.

- Vocabulary contains the most commonly used words
- Recommended as an addition to any language course
- Meets the needs of beginners and advanced learners of foreign languages
- Convenient for daily use, revision sessions, and self-testing activities
- Allows you to assess your vocabulary

Special features of the vocabulary

- Words are organized according to their meaning, not alphabetically
- Words are presented in three columns to facilitate the reviewing and self-testing processes
- Words in groups are divided into small blocks to facilitate the learning process
- The vocabulary offers a convenient and simple transcription of each foreign word

The vocabulary has 256 topics including:

Basic Concepts, Numbers, Colors, Months, Seasons, Units of Measurement, Clothing & Accessories, Food & Nutrition, Restaurant, Family Members, Relatives, Character, Feelings, Emotions, Diseases, City, Town, Sightseeing, Shopping, Money, House, Home, Office, Working in the Office, Import & Export, Marketing, Job Search, Sports, Education, Computer, Internet, Tools, Nature, Countries, Nationalities and more ...

T&P BOOKS' THEME-BASED DICTIONARIES

The Correct System for Memorizing Foreign Words

Acquiring vocabulary is one of the most important elements of learning a foreign language, because words allow us to express our thoughts, ask questions, and provide answers. An inadequate vocabulary can impede communication with a foreigner and make it difficult to understand a book or movie well.

The pace of activity in all spheres of modern life, including the learning of modern languages, has increased. Today, we need to memorize large amounts of information (grammar rules, foreign words, etc.) within a short period. However, this does not need to be difficult. All you need to do is to choose the right training materials, learn a few special techniques, and develop your individual training system.

Having a system is critical to the process of language learning. Many people fail to succeed in this regard; they cannot master a foreign language because they fail to follow a system comprised of selecting materials, organizing lessons, arranging new words to be learned, and so on. The lack of a system causes confusion and eventually, lowers self-confidence.

T&P Books' theme-based dictionaries can be included in the list of elements needed for creating an effective system for learning foreign words. These dictionaries were specially developed for learning purposes and are meant to help students effectively memorize words and expand their vocabulary.

Generally speaking, the process of learning words consists of three main elements:

- Reception (creation or acquisition) of a training material, such as a word list
- Work aimed at memorizing new words
- Work aimed at reviewing the learned words, such as self-testing

All three elements are equally important since they determine the quality of work and the final result. All three processes require certain skills and a well-thought-out approach.

New words are often encountered quite randomly when learning a foreign language and it may be difficult to include them all in a unified list. As a result, these words remain written on scraps of paper, in book margins, textbooks, and so on. In order to systematize such words, we have to create and continually update a "book of new words." A paper notebook, a netbook, or a tablet PC can be used for these purposes.

This "book of new words" will be your personal, unique list of words. However, it will only contain the words that you came across during the learning process. For example, you might have written down the words "Sunday," "Tuesday," and "Friday." However, there are additional words for days of the week, for example, "Saturday," that are missing, and your list of words would be incomplete. Using a theme dictionary, in addition to the "book of new words," is a reasonable solution to this problem.

The theme-based dictionary may serve as the basis for expanding your vocabulary.

It will be your big "book of new words" containing the most frequently used words of a foreign language already included. There are quite a few theme-based dictionaries available, and you should ensure that you make the right choice in order to get the maximum benefit from your purchase.

Therefore, we suggest using theme-based dictionaries from T&P Books Publishing as an aid to learning foreign words. Our books are specially developed for effective use in the sphere of vocabulary systematization, expansion and review.

Theme-based dictionaries are not a magical solution to learning new words. However, they can serve as your main database to aid foreign-language acquisition. Apart from theme dictionaries, you can have copybooks for writing down new words, flash cards, glossaries for various texts, as well as other resources; however, a good theme dictionary will always remain your primary collection of words.

T&P Books' theme-based dictionaries are specialty books that contain the most frequently used words in a language.

The main characteristic of such dictionaries is the division of words into themes. For example, the *City* theme contains the words "street," "crossroads," "square," "fountain," and so on. The *Talking* theme might contain words like "to talk," "to ask," "question," and "answer".

All the words in a theme are divided into smaller units, each comprising 3–5 words. Such an arrangement improves the perception of words and makes the learning process less tiresome. Each unit contains a selection of words with similar meanings or identical roots. This allows you to learn words in small groups and establish other associative links that have a positive effect on memorization.

The words on each page are placed in three columns: a word in your native language, its translation, and its transcription. Such positioning allows for the use of techniques for effective memorization. After closing the translation column, you can flip through and review foreign words, and vice versa. "This is an easy and convenient method of review – one that we recommend you do often."

Our theme-based dictionaries contain transcriptions for all the foreign words. Unfortunately, none of the existing transcriptions are able to convey the exact nuances of foreign pronunciation. That is why we recommend using the transcriptions only as a supplementary learning aid. Correct pronunciation can only be acquired with the help of sound. Therefore our collection includes audio theme-based dictionaries.

The process of learning words using T&P Books' theme-based dictionaries gives you the following advantages:

- You have correctly grouped source information, which predetermines your success at subsequent stages of word memorization

- Availability of words derived from the same root (lazy, lazily, lazybones), allowing you to memorize word units instead of separate words

- Small units of words facilitate the process of establishing associative links needed for consolidation of vocabulary

- You can estimate the number of learned words and hence your level of language knowledge

- The dictionary allows for the creation of an effective and high-quality revision process

- You can revise certain themes several times, modifying the revision methods and techniques

- Audio versions of the dictionaries help you to work out the pronunciation of words and develop your skills of auditory word perception

The T&P Books' theme-based dictionaries are offered in several variants differing in the number of words: 1.500, 3.000, 5.000, 7.000, and 9.000 words. There are also dictionaries containing 15,000 words for some language combinations. Your choice of dictionary will depend on your knowledge level and goals.

We sincerely believe that our dictionaries will become your trusty assistant in learning foreign languages and will allow you to easily acquire the necessary vocabulary.

TABLE OF CONTENTS

T&P Books' Theme-Based Dictionaries   4
Pronunciation guide   15
Abbreviations   17

BASIC CONCEPTS   18
Basic concepts. Part 1   18

1. Pronouns   18
2. Greetings. Salutations. Farewells   18
3. How to address   19
4. Cardinal numbers. Part 1   19
5. Cardinal numbers. Part 2   20
6. Ordinal numbers   21
7. Numbers. Fractions   21
8. Numbers. Basic operations   21
9. Numbers. Miscellaneous   22
10. The most important verbs. Part 1   22
11. The most important verbs. Part 2   23
12. The most important verbs. Part 3   24
13. The most important verbs. Part 4   25
14. Colors   26
15. Questions   27
16. Prepositions   27
17. Function words. Adverbs. Part 1   28
18. Function words. Adverbs. Part 2   30

Basic concepts. Part 2   31

19. Weekdays   31
20. Hours. Day and night   31
21. Months. Seasons   32
22. Time. Miscellaneous   34
23. Opposites   35
24. Lines and shapes   37
25. Units of measurement   38
26. Containers   39
27. Materials   40
28. Metals   40

HUMAN BEING 42
Human being. The body 42

29. Humans. Basic concepts 42
30. Human anatomy 42
31. Head 43
32. Human body 44

Clothing & Accessories 45

33. Outerwear. Coats 45
34. Men's & women's clothing 45
35. Clothing. Underwear 46
36. Headwear 46
37. Footwear 46
38. Textile. Fabrics 47
39. Personal accessories 47
40. Clothing. Miscellaneous 48
41. Personal care. Cosmetics 49
42. Jewelry 50
43. Watches. Clocks 50

Food. Nutricion 52

44. Food 52
45. Drinks 54
46. Vegetables 55
47. Fruits. Nuts 55
48. Bread. Candy 56
49. Cooked dishes 57
50. Spices 58
51. Meals 58
52. Table setting 59
53. Restaurant 59

Family, relatives and friends 61

54. Personal information. Forms 61
55. Family members. Relatives 61
56. Friends. Coworkers 62
57. Man. Woman 63
58. Age 64
59. Children 64
60. Married couples. Family life 65

Character. Feelings. Emotions 67

61. Feelings. Emotions 67

62. Character. Personality   68
63. Sleep. Dreams   69
64. Humour. Laughter. Gladness   70
65. Discussion, conversation. Part 1   70
66. Discussion, conversation. Part 2   72
67. Discussion, conversation. Part 3   73
68. Agreement. Refusal   74
69. Success. Good luck. Failure   74
70. Quarrels. Negative emotions   75

Medicine   78

71. Diseases   78
72. Symptoms. Treatments. Part 1   79
73. Symptoms. Treatments. Part 2   80
74. Symptoms. Treatments. Part 3   81
75. Doctors   82
76. Medicine. Drugs. Accessories   82
77. Smoking. Tobacco products   83

HUMAN HABITAT   84
City   84

78. City. Life in the city   84
79. Urban institutions   85
80. Signs   87
81. Urban transport   88
82. Sightseeing   89
83. Shopping   89
84. Money   90
85. Post. Postal service   91

Dwelling. House. Home   93

86. House. Dwelling   93
87. House. Entrance. Lift   94
88. House. Electricity   94
89. House. Doors. Locks   94
90. Country house   95
91. Villa. Mansion   95
92. Castle. Palace   96
93. Apartment   96
94. Apartment. Cleaning   97
95. Furniture. Interior   97
96. Bedding   98
97. Kitchen   98
98. Bathroom   100
99. Household appliances   100
100. Repairs. Renovation   101

101.	Plumbing	101
102.	Fire. Conflagration	102

HUMAN ACTIVITIES — 104
Job. Business. Part 1 — 104

103.	Office. Working in the office	104
104.	Business processes. Part 1	105
105.	Business processes. Part 2	106
106.	Production. Works	107
107.	Contract. Agreement	109
108.	Import & Export	109
109.	Finances	110
110.	Marketing	110
111.	Advertising	111
112.	Banking	112
113.	Telephone. Phone conversation	112
114.	Mobile telephone	113
115.	Stationery	114
116.	Various kinds of documents	114
117.	Kinds of business	115

Job. Business. Part 2 — 118

118.	Show. Exhibition	118
119.	Mass Media	119
120.	Agriculture	120
121.	Building. Building process	121
122.	Science. Research. Scientists	122

Professions and occupations — 124

123.	Job search. Dismissal	124
124.	Business people	124
125.	Service professions	126
126.	Military professions and ranks	126
127.	Officials. Priests	127
128.	Agricultural professions	128
129.	Art professions	128
130.	Various professions	129
131.	Occupations. Social status	130

Sports — 132

132.	Kinds of sports. Sportspersons	132
133.	Kinds of sports. Miscellaneous	133
134.	Gym	134

135.	Hockey	134
136.	Football	134
137.	Alpine skiing	136
138.	Tennis. Golf	137
139.	Chess	137
140.	Boxing	138
141.	Sports. Miscellaneous	138

Education 140

142.	School	140
143.	College. University	141
144.	Sciences. Disciplines	142
145.	Writing system. Orthography	142
146.	Foreign languages	144
147.	Fairy tale characters	145
148.	Zodiac Signs	145

Arts 146

149.	Theater	146
150.	Cinema	147
151.	Painting	148
152.	Literature & Poetry	149
153.	Circus	150
154.	Music. Pop music	150

Rest. Entertainment. Travel 152

155.	Trip. Travel	152
156.	Hotel	153
157.	Books. Reading	153
158.	Hunting. Fishing	155
159.	Games. Billiards	156
160.	Games. Playing cards	156
161.	Casino. Roulette	157
162.	Rest. Games. Miscellaneous	157
163.	Photography	158
164.	Beach. Swimming	159

TECHNICAL EQUIPMENT. TRANSPORT 161
Technical equipment 161

165.	Computer	161
166.	Internet. E-mail	162
167.	Electricity	163
168.	Tools	164

Transport 167

169.	Airplane	167
170.	Train	168
171.	Ship	169
172.	Airport	171
173.	Bicycle. Motorcycle	172

Cars 173

174.	Types of cars	173
175.	Cars. Bodywork	173
176.	Cars. Passenger compartment	174
177.	Cars. Engine	175
178.	Cars. Crash. Repair	176
179.	Cars. Road	177
180.	Traffic signs	178

PEOPLE. LIFE EVENTS 180
Life events 180

181.	Holidays. Event	180
182.	Funerals. Burial	181
183.	War. Soldiers	182
184.	War. Military actions. Part 1	183
185.	War. Military actions. Part 2	184
186.	Weapons	186
187.	Ancient people	187
188.	Middle Ages	188
189.	Leader. Chief. Authorities	190
190.	Road. Way. Directions	190
191.	Breaking the law. Criminals. Part 1	192
192.	Breaking the law. Criminals. Part 2	193
193.	Police. Law. Part 1	194
194.	Police. Law. Part 2	195

NATURE 197
The Earth. Part 1 197

195.	Outer space	197
196.	The Earth	198
197.	Cardinal directions	199
198.	Sea. Ocean	199
199.	Seas' and Oceans' names	200
200.	Mountains	201
201.	Mountains names	202
202.	Rivers	202
203.	Rivers' names	203

| 204. | Forest | 204 |
| 205. | Natural resources | 205 |

The Earth. Part 2

207

206.	Weather	207
207.	Severe weather. Natural disasters	208
208.	Noises. Sounds	208
209.	Winter	209

Fauna

211

210.	Mammals. Predators	211
211.	Wild animals	211
212.	Domestic animals	213
213.	Dogs. Dog breeds	214
214.	Sounds made by animals	214
215.	Young animals	215
216.	Birds	215
217.	Birds. Singing and sounds	216
218.	Fish. Marine animals	217
219.	Amphibians. Reptiles	218
220.	Insects	218
221.	Animals. Body parts	219
222.	Actions of animals	220
223.	Animals. Habitats	220
224.	Animal care	221
225.	Animals. Miscellaneous	221
226.	Horses	222

Flora

224

227.	Trees	224
228.	Shrubs	225
229.	Mushrooms	225
230.	Fruits. Berries	225
231.	Flowers. Plants	226
232.	Cereals, grains	227
233.	Vegetables. Greens	228

REGIONAL GEOGRAPHY
Countries. Nationalities

230
230

234.	Western Europe	230
235.	Central and Eastern Europe	232
236.	Former USSR countries	233
237.	Asia	234

238.	North America	236
239.	Central and South America	237
240.	Africa	238
241.	Australia. Oceania	238
242.	Cities	239
243.	Politics. Government. Part 1	240
244.	Politics. Government. Part 2	242
245.	Countries. Miscellaneous	243
246.	Major religious groups. Confessions	244
247.	Religions. Priests	245
248.	Faith. Christianity. Islam	245

MISCELLANEOUS 248

249.	Various useful words	248
250.	Modifiers. Adjectives. Part 1	249
251.	Modifiers. Adjectives. Part 2	252

MAIN 500 VERBS 255

252.	Verbs A-C	255
253.	Verbs D-G	257
254.	Verbs H-M	260
255.	Verbs N-S	262
256.	Verbs T-W	265

PRONUNCIATION GUIDE

Letter	Danish sample	T&P phonetics alphabet	English sample
Aa	Afrika, kompas	[æ], [ɑ], [ɑː]	man, father
Bb	barberblad	[b]	baby, book
Cc	cafe, creme	[k]	clock, kiss
Cc [1]	koncert	[s]	city, boss
Dd	direktør	[d]	day, doctor
Dd [2]	facade	[ð]	weather, together
Ee	belgier	[e], [ə]	medal, elm
Ee [3]	elevator	[ɛ]	man, bad
Ff	familie	[f]	face, food
Gg	mango	[g]	game, gold
Hh	høne, knurhår	[h]	home, have
Ii	kolibri	[i], [iː]	feet, Peter
Jj	legetøj	[j]	yes, New York
Kk	leksikon	[k]	clock, kiss
Ll	leopard	[l]	lace, people
Mm	marmor	[m]	magic, milk
Nn	natur, navn	[n]	name, normal
ng	omfang	[ŋ]	English, ring
nk	punktum	[ŋ]	English, ring
Oo	fortov	[o], [ɔ], [ɒ]	baught, drop
Pp	planteolie	[p]	pencil, private
Qq	sequoia	[k]	clock, kiss
Rr	seriøs	[r], [ʁ], [ɒ]	Rome, ripe
Ss	selskab	[s]	city, boss
Tt	strøm, trappe	[t]	tourist, trip
Uu	blæksprutte	[uː]	pool, room
Vv	børnehave	[ʊ]	vase, winter
Ww	whisky	[w]	vase, winter
Xx	Luxembourg	[ks]	box, taxi
Yy	lykke	[y], [ø]	fuel, eternal
Zz	Venezuela	[s]	city, boss
Ææ	ærter	[ɛ], [ɛː]	habit, bad
Øø	grønsager	[ø], [œ]	church, eternal
Åå	åbent, afgå	[ʌ], [ɔ]	sun, lucky

Comments

[1] before e, i
[2] after a stressed vowel
[3] at the beginning of words

ABBREVIATIONS
used in the vocabulary

ab.	-	about
adj	-	adjectif
adv	-	adverb
attr	-	attributive noun
e.g.	-	for example
etc.	-	et cetera
fem.	-	feminine
masc.	-	masculine
noun	-	noun
pl	-	plural
pron.	-	pronoun
sb	-	somebody
sing.	-	singular
sth	-	something
vi	-	intransitive verb
vi, vt	-	intransitive, transitive verb
vt	-	transitive verb
c	-	common gender
n	-	neuter
c pl	-	common gender plural
n pl	-	neuter plural
n, c	-	neuter, common gender

BASIC CONCEPTS

Basic concepts. Part 1

1. Pronouns

I, me	**jeg**	['jɑj]
you	**du**	[du]
he	**han**	[han]
she	**hun**	[hun]
it	**den, det**	[dɛn], [de]
we	**vi**	[vi]
you	**I**	[i]
they	**de**	[di]

2. Greetings. Salutations. Farewells

Hello! (familiar)	**Goddag!**	[goˈdæː]
Hello! (formal)	**Goddag!**	[goˈdæː]
Good morning!	**Godmorgen!**	[goˈmɒːɒn]
Good afternoon!	**Goddag!**	[goˈdæː]
Good evening!	**Godaften!**	[goˈɑfdən]
to say hello	**at sige goddag**	[at siːə goˈdæː]
Hi! (hello)	**Hej!**	[hɑj]
greeting (noun)	**hilsen** (c)	[ˈhilsən]
to greet (vt)	**at hilse**	[at ˈhilsə]
How are you?	**Hvordan går det?**	[vɒˈdan gɒː de]
What's new?	**Hvad nyt?**	[vað nyd]
Bye-Bye! Goodbye!	**Farvel!**	[fɑˈvɛl]
See you soon!	**på gensyn!**	[pɒ ˈgɛnsyːn]
Farewell! (to a friend)	**Farvel!**	[fɑˈvɛl]
Farewell (formal)	**Farvel!**	[fɑˈvɛl]
to say goodbye	**at sige farvel**	[at ˈsiːə fɑˈvɛl]
So long!	**Hej-hej!**	[hɑj-hɑj]
Thank you!	**Tak!**	[tɑk]
Thank you very much!	**Mange tak!**	[ˈmɑŋə tɑg]
You're welcome	**Velbekomme**	[ˈvɛlbəˈkʌmə]
Don't mention it!	**Det var så lidt**	[de vɑ sɒ led]
It was nothing	**Det var så lidt**	[de vɑ sɒ led]

| Excuse me! | **Undskyld!** | ['ɔn‚skyl] |
| to excuse (forgive) | **at undskylde** | [at 'ɔn‚skylə] |

to apologize (vi)	**at undskylde sig**	[at 'ɔn‚sgylə saj]
My apologies	**Undskyld mig**	['ɔn‚sgyl maj]
I'm sorry!	**Undskyld mig!**	['ɔn‚sgyl maj]
to forgive (vt)	**at tilgive**	[at 'tel‚giuə]
It's OK	**Det gør ikke noget**	[de gœɒ 'egə 'nɔəð]

| please (adv) | **værsgo** | ['væɒ'sgo] |
| Don't forget! | **Husk!** | [husk] |

Certainly!	**Selvfølgelig!**	[sɛl'føləli]
Of course not!	**Naturligvis ikke!**	[na'tuɒlivi:s 'egə]
OK! (I agree)	**OK!**	['o'kɔ]
That's enough!	**Så er det nok!**	[sɒaɒ de nɒk]

3. How to address

Mister, Sir	**Herren**	['hæːɒn]
Ma'am	**Frue**	['fʁuːə]
Miss	**Frøken**	['fʁœkən]

4. Cardinal numbers. Part 1

0 zero	**nul** (n)	[nɔl]
1 one	**en**	[en]
2 two	**to**	[toː]
3 three	**tre**	[tʁɛː]
4 four	**fire**	['fiːɒ]

5 five	**fem**	[fɛm]
6 six	**seks**	[sɛks]
7 seven	**syv**	['syw]
8 eight	**otte**	['ɔːdə]
9 nine	**ni**	[niː]

10 ten	**ti**	[tiː]
11 eleven	**elleve**	['ɛlvə]
12 twelve	**tolv**	[tɒl]
13 thirteen	**tretten**	['tʁadən]
14 fourteen	**fjorten**	['fjoɒdən]

15 fifteen	**femten**	['fɛmdən]
16 sixteen	**seksten**	['sajsdən]
17 seventeen	**sytten**	['sødən]
18 eighteen	**atten**	['adən]
19 nineteen	**nitten**	['nedən]

20 twenty	**tyve**	[ty:wə]
21 twenty-one	**enogtyve**	['e:nɒˌty:uə]
22 twenty-two	**toogtyve**	['to:ɒˌty:uə]
23 twenty-three	**treogtyve**	['tʁɛ:ɒˌty:uə]
30 thirty	**tredive**	['tʁaðvə]
31 thirty-one	**enogtredive**	['e:nɒˌtʁaðvə]
32 thirty-two	**toogtredive**	['to:ɒˌtʁaðvə]
33 thirty-three	**treogtredive**	['tʁɛ:ɒˌtʁaðvə]
40 forty	**fyrre**	['fœɒʌ]
41 forty-one	**enogfyrre**	['e:nɒˌfœɒ]
42 forty-two	**toogfyrre**	['to:ɒˌfœɒ]
43 forty-three	**treogfyrre**	['tʁɛ:ɒˌfœɒ]
50 fifty	**halvtreds**	[hal'tʁɛs]
51 fifty-one	**enoghalvtreds**	['e:nɒhalˌtʁɛs]
52 fifty-two	**tooghalvtreds**	['to:ɒhalˌtʁɛs]
53 fifty-three	**treoghalvtreds**	['tʁɛ:ɒhalˌtʁɛs]
60 sixty	**tres**	[tʁɛs]
61 sixty-one	**enogtres**	['e:nɒˌtʁɛs]
62 sixty-two	**toogtres**	['to:ɒˌtʁɛs]
63 sixty-three	**treogtres**	['tʁɛ:ɒˌtʁɛs]
70 seventy	**halvfjerds**	[hal'fjeɒs]
71 seventy-one	**enoghalvfjerds**	['e:nɒhalˌfjeɒs]
72 seventy-two	**tooghalvfjerds**	['to:ɒhalˌfjeɒs]
73 seventy-three	**treoghalvfjerds**	['tʁɛ:ɒhalˌfjeɒs]
80 eighty	**firs**	[fiɒs]
81 eighty-one	**enogfirs**	['e:nɒˌfiɒs]
82 eighty-two	**toogfirs**	['to:ɒˌfiɒs]
83 eighty-three	**treogfirs**	['tʁɛ:ɒˌfiɒs]
90 ninety	**halvfems**	[hal'fɛms]
91 ninety-one	**enoghalvfems**	['e:nɒhalˌfɛms]
92 ninety-two	**tooghalvfems**	['to:ɒhalˌfɛms]
93 ninety-three	**treoghalvfems**	['tʁɛ:ɒhalˌfɛms]

5. Cardinal numbers. Part 2

100 one hundred	**hundrede**	['hunʌðə]
200 two hundred	**tohundrede**	['tɒw ˌhunʌðə]
300 three hundred	**trehundrede**	['tʁɛ: ˌhunʌðə]
400 four hundred	**firehundrede**	['fi:huˌ'hunʌðə]
500 five hundred	**femhundrede**	['fɛmˌhunʌðə]
600 six hundred	**sekshundrede**	['sɛksˌhunʌðə]
700 seven hundred	**syvhundrede**	['sywˌhunʌðə]

800 eight hundred	**ottehundrede**	['ɔ:də ˌhunʌðə]
900 nine hundred	**nihundrede**	['niˌhunʌðə]
1000 one thousand	**tusind**	['tu:sən]
2000 two thousand	**totusind**	['to:ˌtu:sən]
3000 three thousand	**tretusind**	['tʁɛˌtu:sən]
10000 ten thousand	**titusind**	['tiˌtu:sən]
one hundred thousand	**hundredetusind**	['hunʌðə ˌtu:sə]
million	**million** (c)	[mili'o:n]
billion	**milliard** (c)	[mili'ɑ:d]

6. Ordinal numbers

first	**første**	['fœɒsdə]
second	**anden**	['anən]
third	**tredje**	['tʁɛðjə]
fourth	**fjerde**	['fjɛ:ɒ]
fifth	**femte**	['fɛmdə]
sixth	**sjette**	['ɕɛ:də]
seventh	**syvende**	['sywənə]
eighth	**ottende**	['ɔ:dənə]
ninth	**niende**	['ni:ənə]
tenth	**tiende**	['ti:ənə]

7. Numbers. Fractions

fraction	**brøk** (c)	[bʁœ:k]
one half	**halvdelen (af)**	['halde:lən]
one third	**tredjedel** (c)	['tʁɛðjəˌde:l]
one quarter	**fjerdedel** (c)	['fjɛ:ʌˌdel]
one eighth	**ottendedel** (c)	['ɔ:dənəˌde:l]
one tenth	**tiendedel** (c)	['ti:ənəˌdel]
two thirds	**to tredjedele**	[to: 'tʁɛðjəˌde:lə]
three quarters	**tre fjerdedele**	[tʁɛ: 'fjɛ:ʌˌdelə]

8. Numbers. Basic operations

subtraction	**fratrækning** (c)	[fʁɑ'tʁagnən]
to subtract (vi, vt)	**at subtrahere**	[at subtʁɑ'heʌ]
division	**division** (c)	[divi'ɕo:n]
to divide (vt)	**at dividere**	[at divi'deɒ]
addition	**addition** (c)	[adi'ɕo:n]
to add up (vt)	**at lægge sammen**	[at 'lɛgə 'samən]

to add (vi)	at lægge til	[at 'lɛgə tel]
multiplication	multiplikation (c)	[multiplika'ɕo:n]
to multiply (vi, vt)	at gange	[at 'gɑŋə]

9. Numbers. Miscellaneous

digit, figure	ciffer (n)	['sifʌ]
number	tal (n)	[tal]
numeral	talord (n)	[ta'lo:d]
minus	minus (n)	['mi:nus]
plus	plus (n)	[plus]
formula	formel (c)	[fɒ'məl]

calculation	beregning (c)	[be'ʁɑjnen]
to count (vi, vt)	at tælle	[at 'tɛlə]
to count up	at sammenregne	[at 'sɑmənʁɑjnə]
to compare (vt)	at sammenligne	[at 'sɑmən,li:nə]

How much?	Hvor meget?	[vɒ: 'mɑjəð]
How many?	Hvor mange?	[vɒ: 'mɑŋə]
sum, total	sum (c)	[sɔm]
result	resultat (n)	[ʁɛsul'tæ:d]
remainder	rest (c)	['ʁasd]

a few ...	nogle få ...	['noən fɔ:]
the rest	øvrig (n)	['øwʁi]
one and a half	halvanden	[hal'anən]
dozen	dusin (n)	[du'si:n]

in half	i to halvdele	[i 'to: 'hal,de:lə]
equally (evenly)	ligeligt	['liə,lid]
half	halvdel (c)	['halde:l]
time (instance)	gang (c)	[gɑŋ]

10. The most important verbs. Part 1

to advise (vt)	at råde	[at 'ʁɔ:ðə]
to agree (say yes)	at enes	[at 'e:nəs]
to answer (vi, vt)	at svare	[at 'svɑ:ɑ]
to apologize (vi)	at undskylde sig	[at 'ɔn,sgylə sɑj]
to arrive (vi)	at ankomme	[at 'an,kʌmə]

to ask (~ sb to do sth)	at bede om	[at 'be:ðə ɒm]
to ask (e.g., ~ oneself)	at spørge	[at 'sbœɒuə]
to be afraid	at frygte	[at 'fʁœgdə]

| to be hungry | at være sulten | [at 'vɛ:ɒ 'suldən] |
| to be interested in ... | at interessere sig (for ...) | [at entʁə'seʌ sɑj fɒ ...] |

to be necessary	at være nødvendig	[at 'vɛːɒ nøð'vɛndi]
to be surprised	at blive forbavset	[at 'bliːə fɒ'bausəð]
to be thirsty	at være tørstig	[at 'vɛːɒ 'tœɒsdi]

to begin (vi, vt)	at starte	[at 'sdɑːdə]
to belong to ...	at tilhøre	[at tel'høːɒ]
to boast (vi)	at prale	[at 'pʁɑːlə]
to break (split into pieces)	at brække	[at 'bʁakə]

to call (for help)	at tilkalde	[at 'tel‚kalə]
can (modal verb)	kunne	['kunə]
to catch (vt)	at fange	[at 'faŋə]
to change (vt)	at ændre	[at 'ɛndʁɒ]
to choose (select)	at vælge	[at 'vɛljə]

to come down	at stige ned	[at 'sdiːə neð]
to come in (enter)	at komme ind	[at 'kɒmə en]
to compare (vt)	at sammenligne	[at 'samən‚liːnə]
to complain (vi, vt)	at klage	[at 'klæːjə]
to continue (vi, vt)	at fortsætte	[at fʌ'dsɛdə]

to control (vt)	at kontrollere	[at kʌntʁo'leʌ]
to cook (dinner)	at lave	[at 'læːuə]
to cost (vt)	at koste	[at 'kɒsdə]
to count (add up)	at regne	[at 'ʁɑjnə]
to count on ...	at regne med ...	[at 'ʁɑjnə mɛð]
to create (vt)	at skabe	[at 'skæːbə]
to cry (weep)	at græde	[at 'gʁaðə]

11. The most important verbs. Part 2

to deceive (vi, vt)	at snyde	[at 'snyːðə]
to decorate (tree, street)	at pynte	[at 'pøndə]
to defend (a country etc.)	at forsvare	[at fʌ'svɑːɑ]
to demand (request firmly)	at kræve	[at 'kʁɛːuə]

to dig (vi, vt)	at grave	[at 'gʁɑːuə]
to direct (supervise)	at lede	[at 'leːðə]
to discuss (talk about)	at drøfte	[at 'dʁœfdə]
to do (vt)	at gøre	[at 'gœːɒ]
to doubt (have doubts)	at tvivle	[at 'tviulə]
to drop (let fall)	at tabe	[at 'tæːbə]

to exist (vi)	at eksistere	[at ɛksi'sdeɒ]
to expect (foresee)	at forudse	[at 'fɒuð‚se]
to explain (vi, vt)	at forklare	[at fʌ'klɑːɑ]

to fall (vi)	at falde	[at 'falə]
to find (vt)	at finde	[at 'fenə]
to finish (vt)	at afslutte	[at ɑu'sludə]

to fly (vi)	at flyve	[at 'fly:və]
to follow … (come after)	at følge efter …	[at 'føljə 'ɛfdʌ]
to forget (vi, vt)	at glemme	[at 'glɛmə]
to forgive (vt)	at tilgive	[at 'tel‚giuə]

to give (vt)	at give	[at gi:]
to go (to walk)	at gå	[at gɔ:]
to go for a swim	at bade	[at 'bæ:ðə]
to go out	at gå ud	[at gɔ: uð]
to guess right	at gætte	[at 'gɛdə]

to have (vt)	at have	[at 'hæ:və]
to have breakfast	at spise morgenmad	[at 'sbi:sə 'mɒ:ɒn‚mað]
to have dinner	at spise aftensmad	[at 'sbi:sə 'ɑfdəns‚mað]
to have lunch	at spise frokost	[at 'sbi:sə 'fʁɔkʌsd]

to hear (vi, vt)	at høre	[at 'hø:ɒ]
to help (assist, aid)	at hjælpe	[at 'jɛlbə]
to hide (vt)	at gemme	[at 'gɛmə]
to hint (vi)	at antyde	[at an'tyðə]
to hope (vi, vt)	at håbe	[at 'hɔ:bə]
to hunt (vi, vt)	at jage	[at 'jæ:jə]
to hurry (vi)	at skynde sig	[at 'sgønə sɑj]

12. The most important verbs. Part 3

to inform (vi, vt)	at informere	[at enfɒ'me:ɒ]
to insist (vi, vt)	at insistere (på …)	[at ensi'sdeʌ pɔ …]
to insult (vt)	at fornærme	[at fʌ'naɒmə]
to invite (vt)	at invitere	[at envi'te:ɒ]
to joke (vi)	at spøge	[at 'sbø:jə]

to keep (vt)	at beholde	[at be'hɒlə]
to keep silence	at tie	[at 'ti:ə]
to kill (vt)	at dræbe	[at 'dʁɛ:bə]
to know (sb)	at kende	[at 'kɛnə]
to know (sth)	at vide	[at 'vi:ðə]

to laugh (vi)	at grine	[at 'gʁi:nə]
to liberate (vt)	at befri	[at be'fʁi:]
to like (I like …)	at holde af …	[at 'hɒlə a]
to look for … (search)	at søge …	[at 'sø:ə]
to love sb	at elske	[at 'ɛlskə]

to make a mistake	at tage fejl	[at 'tæ:ə fɑjl]
to mean (signify)	at betyde	[at be'tyðə]
to mention (talk about)	at omtale	[at ɒm'tæ:lə]
to miss (school etc.)	at forsømme	[at fʌ'sœmə]
to mix up (confuse)	at blande sammen	[at 'blanə 'sɑmən]
to notice (see)	at bemærke	[at be'mæɒkə]

to object (vi, vt)	at indvende	[at en'vɛnə]
to observe (see)	at observere	[at ʌbsæɒ'vʌ]
to open (vt)	at åbne	[at 'ɔ:bnə]
to order (meal etc.)	at bestille	[at be'sdelə]
to order (military)	at beordre	[at be'ɒ:dʁɒ]
to own (possess)	at eje	[at 'ɑjə]
to participate (vi)	at deltage	[at 'delˌtæ]
to pay (vi, vt)	at betale	[at be'tæ:lə]
to permit (allow)	at tillade	[at 'teˌlæðə]
to plan (vi, vt)	at planlægge	[at 'plæ:nˌlɛ:gə]
to play (vi, vt)	at spille	[at 'sbelə]
to pray (vi, vt)	at bede	[at 'be:ðə]
to prefer (vt)	at foretrække	[at fɒ:ɒ'tʁakə]
to promise (vt)	at love	[at 'lo:uə]
to pronounce (say)	at udtale	[at 'uðˌtæ:lə]
to propose (vt)	at foreslå	[at fɒ:ɒ'slɔ:]
to punish (vt)	at straffe	[at 'sdʁɑfə]
to read (vi, vt)	at læse	[at 'lɛ:sə]
to recommend (vt)	at anbefale	[at anbe'fæ:lə]
to refuse (vi, vt)	at afslå	[at ɑu'slɔ:]
to regret (be sorry)	at fortryde	[at fʌ'tʁyðə]
to rent (of a tenant)	at leje	[at 'lɑjə]
to repeat (say again)	at gentage	[at gɛn'tæ:ə]
to reserve, to book	at reservere	[at ʁɛsaɒ've:ɒ]
to run (vi)	at løbe	[at 'lø:bə]

13. The most important verbs. Part 4

to save (rescue)	at redde	[at 'ʁɛðə]
to say (e.g., ~ thank you)	at sige	[at 'si:ə]
to scold (vt)	at skælde	[at 'skɛlə]
to see (vi, vt)	at se	[at se:]
to sell (goods)	at sælge	[at 'sɛljə]
to send (vt)	at afsende	[at ɑu'sɛnə]
to shoot (vi)	at skyde	[at 'sky:ðə]
to shout (vi)	at råbe	[at 'ʁɔ:bə]
to show (vi, vt)	at vise	[at 'vi:sə]
to sign (document)	at underskrive	[at 'ɒnɒˌskʁiuə]
to sit down (vi)	at sætte sig ned	[at 'sɛdə sɑj neð]
to smile (vi)	at smile	[at 'smi:lə]
to speak (vi, vt)	at tale	[at 'tæ:lə]
to steal (money, etc.)	at stjæle	[at 'sdjɛ:lə]
to stop (cease)	at standse	[at 'sdanse:]

to stop (vi)	at opholde sig	[at 'ʌbˌhʌlə sɑj]
to study (vt)	at studere	[at 'sdudeːɒ]
to swim (vi)	at svømme	[at 'svœmə]

to take (vt)	at tage	[at 'tæːə]
to think (vi, vt)	at tænke	[at 'tɛŋkə]
to threaten (vt)	at true	[at 'tʁuːə]
to touch (by hands)	at røre	[at 'ʁœːɒ]
to translate (word, text)	at oversætte	[at ɒuɒ'sɛdə]
to trust (vt)	at stole på	[at 'sdoːlə pɔ]
to try (attempt)	at prøve	[at 'pʁœːuə]
to turn (change direction)	at dreje	[at 'dʁɑjə]

to underestimate (vt)	at undervurdere	[at 'ɔnɑɒvuɒˌdeːɒ]
to understand (vi, vt)	at forstå	[at fʌ'sdɔː]
to unite (join)	at forene	[at fʌ'enə]

to wait (vi, vt)	at vente (på ...)	[at 'vɛndə pɔ]
to want (wish, desire)	at ville	[at 'vilə]
to warn (of the danger)	at advare	[at að'vɑːɑ]

to work (vi)	at arbejde	[at 'ɑːbɑjdə]
to write (vi, vt)	at skrive	[at 'skʁiuə]
to write down	at skrive ned	[at 'skʁiuə neð]

14. Colors

color	farve (c)	['fɑːuə]
shade (nuance)	nuance (c)	[ny'ɑŋsə]
tone	tone (c)	['toːnə]
rainbow	regnbue (c)	['ʁɑjnˌbuːə]

white	hvid	[við]
black	sort	['sɒːd]
gray	grå	[gʁɔː]

green	grøn	[gʁœn]
yellow	gul	[guːl]
red	rød	[ʁœð]

blue	blå	[blɔː]
light blue	lyseblå	['lysəˌblɔː]
pink	rosa	['ʁoːsa]
orange	orange-	[o'ʁɑŋɕə]
violet	violblå	[vi'oːlˌblɔː]
brown	brun	[bʁuːn]

golden	guld-	[gul]
silvery	sølv-	[søl]
beige	beige	['bɛːɕ]

cream	**cremefarvet**	['kʁɛm 'faːvəð]
turquoise	**turkis**	[tyɒ'kiːs]
cherry	**kirsebærrød**	['kiɒsəˌbæɒɶð]
lilac	**lilla**	['lela]
raspberry	**hindbærrød**	['henbæːɒˌɶð]
light	**lys**	[lyːs]
dark	**mørk**	['mɶɒk]
bright	**klar**	[klaː]
colored (pencils)	**farve-**	['faːuə]
black-and-white	**sort-hvid**	['sɒːdˌvið]
plain (one color)	**ensfarvet**	['eːnsˌfaːuəð]
multicolored	**kulørt**	[ku'lɶɒd]

15. Questions

Who?	**Hvem?**	[vɛm]
What?	**Hvad?**	[vað]
Where? (at, in)	**Hvor?**	[vɒː]
Where (to)?	**Hvorhen?**	[vɒ'hɛn]
Where ... from?	**Hvorfra?**	[vɒːˈfʁaː]
When?	**Hvornår?**	[vɒ'nɒ]
Why? (aim)	**Hvorfor?**	[vɔ'fɒ]
Why? (reason)	**Hvorfor?**	[vɔ'fɒ]
What for?	**For hvad?**	[fɒ 'vað]
How? (in what way)	**Hvordan?**	[vɒ'dan]
What? (which?)	**Hvilken?**	['vilkən]
Which?	**Hvilken?**	['vilkən]
To whom?	**Til hvem?**	[tel vɛm]
About whom?	**Om hvem?**	[ɒm vɛm]
About what?	**Om hvad?**	[ɒm vað]
With whom?	**Med hvem?**	[mɛð vɛm]
How many? How much?	**Hvor meget?**	[vɒː 'majəð]
Whose?	**Hvis?**	[ves]

16. Prepositions

with (accompanied by)	**med**	[mɛð]
without	**uden**	['uðən]
to (indicating direction)	**til**	[tel]
about (e.g., talking ~ ...)	**om**	[ɒm]
before (in time)	**før**	[fœɒ]
in front of ...	**foran ...**	['fɒan]
under (beneath, below)	**under**	['ɔnʌ]

above (in a higher position)	**over**	['ɒwʌ]
on (e.g., ~ the table)	**på**	[pɔ]
from (off, out of)	**fra**	[fʁɑ]
of (made from)	**af**	[a]
in (e.g., ~ ten minutes)	**om**	[ɒm]
over (across the top of)	**igennem**	[i'gɛnəm]

17. Function words. Adverbs. Part 1

Where? (at, in)	**Hvor?**	[vɒ:]
here	**her**	['hɛɒ]
there (in a particular place)	**derhenne**	[dɛɒ'hɛnə]
somewhere	**et sted**	[ed sdɛð]
nowhere (not anywhere)	**ingen steder**	['enŋən 'sdɛ:ðɒ]
by (near, beside)	**ved**	[veð]
by the window	**ved vinduet**	[veð 'vendu:əð]
Where (to)?	**Hvorhen?**	[vɒ'hɛn]
here (e.g., come ~!)	**herhen**	['hɛɒˌhɛn]
there (e.g., to go ~)	**derhen**	[dɛɒ'hɛn]
from here	**herfra**	['hɛɒˌfʁɑ:]
from there	**derfra**	['dɛɒfʁɑ:]
near (in space)	**nær**	['nɛɒ]
far (distant in space)	**langt**	[lɑŋd]
near (e.g., ~ Paris)	**nær**	['nɛɒ]
nearby	**i nærheden**	[i 'nɛɒhe:ðən]
not far	**ikke langt fra**	['egə lɑŋd fʁɑ]
left	**venstre**	['vɛnsdʁʌ]
on the left	**til venstre**	[tel 'vɛnsdʁɒ]
to the left	**til venstre**	[tel 'vɛnsdʁɒ]
right	**højre**	['hɒjʁɒ]
on the right	**til højre**	[tel 'hʌjʁʌ]
to the right	**til højre**	[tel 'hʌjʁʌ]
in front	**foran**	['fɒan]
front (attr)	**forrest**	['fɒɒsd]
ahead (in space)	**fremad**	['fʁamɑð]
behind	**bagved**	['bæ:veð]
from behind	**bagpå**	['bæ:pɔ:]
back (towards the rear)	**tilbage**	[te'bæ:jə]
middle	**midte** (c)	['medə]
in the middle	**i midten**	[i 'medən]

at the side	**på siden**	[pɔ ˈsiːðən]
everywhere	**overalt**	[ɒwʌˈald]
around (in all directions)	**rundt omkring**	[ˈʁɒnd ʌmˈkʁɛŋ]
from inside	**indefra**	[ˈenəˌfʁɑ]
somewhere (to go)	**et sted (at tage til)**	[ed sdɛð]
straight (directly)	**ligeud**	[ˈliːəˈuð]
back (e.g., come ~)	**tilbage**	[teˈbæːjə]
from anywhere	**et eller andet sted fra**	[et ɛlɒ ˈanɛð sdɛð fʁɑ]
from somewhere	**fra et sted**	[fʁɑ ed sdɛð]
firstly	**for det første**	[fɒ de ˈfœɒsdə]
secondly	**for det andet**	[fɒ de ˈanəð]
thirdly	**for det tredje**	[fɒ de ˈtʁɛðjə]
suddenly	**pludseligt**	[ˈplusəlid]
at first	**i begyndelsen**	[i beˈgønəlsən]
for the first time	**for første gang**	[fɒ ˈfœɒsdə gaŋ]
long before ...	**længe før ...**	[ˈlɛŋə fœɒ]
anew (over again)	**på ny**	[pɒ ˈnyː]
for good	**for altid**	[fɒ ˈaltið]
never	**aldrig**	[ˈaldʁi]
again	**igen**	[iˈgɛn]
now	**nu**	[nu]
often	**ofte**	[ˈʌfdə]
then	**dengang**	[ˈdɛngaŋ]
urgently (quickly)	**omgående**	[ɒmˈgɔːənə]
usually	**sædvanligvis**	[sɛðˈvæːnliviːs]
by the way, ...	**for resten ...**	[fɒ ˈʁasdən]
possible (e.g., that is ~)	**muligvis**	[ˈmuːliviːs]
probably	**sandsynligvis**	[sanˈsyːnliviːs]
maybe	**måske**	[mɔˈske]
besides ...	**ellers ...**	[ˈɛlɒs]
that's why ...	**derfor**	[ˈdɛɒfɒ]
in spite of ...	**uanset ...**	[ˈuanˌsed]
thanks to ...	**takket være ...**	[ˈtɑkəð ˌvɛːɒ]
what (pron.)	**hvad**	[vað]
that	**at**	[ad]
something	**noget**	[ˈnɔəð]
anything (something)	**et eller andet**	[ed ˈɛlɒ ˈanəð]
nothing	**ikke noget**	[ˈegə ˈnɔəð]
who (pron.)	**hvem**	[vɛm]
someone	**nogen**	[ˈnoən]
somebody	**nogen**	[ˈnoən]
nobody	**ingen**	[ˈennən]
nowhere (not to any place)	**ingen steder**	[ˈennən ˈsdɛːðɒ]

nobody's	**ingens**	['enŋəns]
somebody's	**en eller andens**	[en 'ɛlɒ 'anəns]
so (e.g., I'm ~ glad)	**så**	[sɒ]
also (as well)	**også**	['ɒusɒ]
too (as well)	**også**	['ɒusɒ]

18. Function words. Adverbs. Part 2

Why?	**Hvorfor?**	[vɒ'fɒ]
for some reason	**af en eller anden grund**	[a en 'ɛlɒ 'anən gʁɒn]
because …	**fordi …**	[fɒ'di:]
for some purpose	**af en eller anden grund**	[a en 'ɛlɒ 'anən gʁɒn]
and	**og**	[ʌ / ɒw]
or	**eller**	['ɛlɒ]
but	**men**	[mɛn]
for (e.g., ~ me)	**for, til**	[fɒ], [tel]
too (excessively)	**for**	[fɒ]
only (exclusively)	**kun**	[kɔn]
exactly	**præcis**	[pʁɛ'si:s]
about (more or less)	**cirka**	['sipka]
approximately	**cirka**	['sipka]
approximate	**omtrentlig**	[ʌm'tʁandli]
almost	**næsten**	['nɛsdən]
the rest	**øvrig**	['øwʁi]
other, another	**anden**	['anən]
each	**hver, hvert**	['vɛɒ], ['vɛɒd]
any (no matter which)	**enhver**	[en'vɛɒ]
many, much (a lot of)	**megen, meget**	['mɑjən], ['mɑjəð]
many people	**mange**	['mɑŋə]
all (everyone)	**alle**	['alə]
in exchange for …	**i bytte med …**	[i 'bydə mɛð]
in exchange	**i stedet for**	[i 'sdɛð fɒ]
by hand (made)	**i hånden**	[i 'hɒnən]
hardly (negative opinion)	**næppe**	['nɛbə]
probably	**vistnok**	['vesdnɒk]
on purpose	**forsætlig**	[fɒ:'sɛdli]
by accident	**tilfældigt**	[te'fɛldid]
very	**meget**	['mɑɑð]
for example	**for eksempel**	[fɒ ɛ'ksɛmbəl]
between	**imellem**	[i'mɛləm]
among	**mellem**	['mɛləm]
so much (such a lot)	**så meget**	[sɒ 'mɑjəð]
especially	**især**	[i'sɛɒ]

Basic concepts. Part 2

19. Weekdays

Monday	**mandag** (c)	['manda]
Tuesday	**tirsdag** (c)	['tiɒsda]
Wednesday	**onsdag** (c)	['ɔnsdæ:]
Thursday	**torsdag** (c)	['tɒ:sda]
Friday	**fredag** (c)	['fʁɛ:da]
Saturday	**lørdag** (c)	['lœɒda]
Sunday	**søndag** (c)	['sœnˌda]
today	**i dag**	[i dæ:]
tomorrow	**i morgen**	[i 'mɒ:ɒn]
the day after tomorrow	**i overmorgen**	[i 'ɒuɒˌmɒ:ɒn]
yesterday	**igår**	[i'gɒ:]
the day before yesterday	**i forgårs**	[i 'fɒ:gɒ:s]
day	**dag** (c)	[dæ:]
workday	**hverdag** (c)	['vɛɒˌdæ:]
holiday	**festdag** (c)	['fɛsdˌdæ:]
day off	**fridag** (c)	['fʁidæ:]
weekend	**weekend** (c)	['wiːˌkɛnd]
all day long	**hele dagen**	['he:lə 'dæ:ən]
next day	**næste dag**	['nɛsdə dæ:]
two days ago	**for to dage siden**	[fɒ to: 'dæ:ə 'si:ðən]
the day before	**dagen før**	['dæ:ən fœɒ]
daily	**daglig**	['dɑwli]
every day	**dagligt**	['dɑwlid]
week	**uge** (c)	['u:ə]
last week	**i sidste uge**	[i 'sisdə 'u:ə]
next week	**i næste uge**	[i 'nɛsdə 'u:ə]
weekly (adj)	**ugentlig**	['u:əndli]
every week	**ugentligt**	['u:əndlid]
twice a week	**to gange om ugen**	[to: 'gɒŋə ɒm 'u:ən]
every Tuesday	**hver tirsdag**	['vɛɒ ˌtiɒsda]

20. Hours. Day and night

morning	**morgen** (c)	['mɒ:ɒn]
in the morning	**om morgenen**	[ɒm 'mɒ:ɒnən]
noon, midday	**middag** (c)	['meda]

in the afternoon	i eftermiddag	[i 'ɛfdɒmeda]
evening	aften (c)	['ɑfdən]
in the evening	om aftenen	[ɒm 'ɑfdənən]
night	nat (c)	[nad]
at night	om natten	[ɒm 'naən]
midnight	midnat (c)	['miðnad]

second	sekund (n)	[se'kɔnd]
minute	minut (n)	[mi'nud]
hour	time (c)	['ti:mə]
half an hour	en halv time	[en hal 'ti:mə]
quarter of an hour	kvart (n)	['kvɑ:d]
fifteen minutes	femten minutter	['fɛmdən mi'nudɒ]
24 hours	døgn (n)	[dɒjn]

sunrise	solopgang (c)	['so:lˌɒbgɑŋ]
dawn	daggry (n)	['dɑugʁʏ:]
early morning	tidlig morgen (c)	['tiðli 'mɒ:ɒn]
sunset	solnedgang (c)	['so:lˌneðgɑŋ]

early in the morning	tidligt om morgenen	['tiðlid ɒm 'mɒ:ɒnən]
this morning	i morges	[i 'mɒ:ɒes]
tomorrow morning	i morgen tidlig	[i 'mɒ:ɒn 'tiðli]

this afternoon	i dag	[i dæ:]
in the afternoon	i eftermiddag	[i 'ɛfdɒmeda]
tomorrow afternoon	i morgen eftermiddag	[i 'mɒ:ɒn 'ɛfdʌmeˌdæ]

| tonight (this evening) | i aften | [i 'ɑfdən] |
| tomorrow evening | i morgen aften | [i 'mɒ:ɒn 'ɑfdən] |

at 3 o'clock sharp	klokken tre præcis	['klɒkən tʁɛ: pʁɛ'si:s]
about 4 o'clock	ved fire tiden	[veð 'fi:ɒ 'tiðən]
by 12 o'clock	ved 12-tiden	[veð 'tʌl 'tiðən]

in 20 minutes	om 20 minutter	[ɒm 'ty:və mi'nudɒ]
in an hour	om en time	[ɒm en 'ti:mə]
on time	i tide	[i 'ti:ðə]
term (end of period)	frist (c)	[fʁɛsd]

a quarter of …	kvart i …	['kvɑ:d i]
within an hour	indenfor en time	['enənˈfʌ en 'ti:mə]
every 15 minutes	hvert 15 minut	['vɛɒd 'fɛmdənə mi'nud]
round the clock	døgnet rundt	['dɒjneð ʁɒnd]

21. Months. Seasons

January	januar (c)	['januɑ:]
February	februar (c)	['febʁuɑ:]
March	marts (c)	[mɑ:ds]

April	april (c)	[ap'ʁi:l]
May	maj (c)	[mɑj]
June	juni (c)	['ju:ni]

July	juli (c)	['ju:li]
August	august (c)	[ɑu'gɔsd]
September	september (c)	[sɛb'tɛmbɒ]
October	oktober (c)	[ok'tobʌ]
November	november (c)	[no'vɛmbɒ]
December	december (c)	[de'sɛmbʌ]

spring	forår (n)	['fɒ:ˌɒ]
in spring	om foråret	[ɒm 'fɒ:ɒð]
spring (attr)	forårs-	['fɒ:ˌɒs]

summer	sommer (c)	['sɒmmʌ]
in summer	om sommeren	[ɒm 'sɒmɒn]
summer (attr)	sommer-	['sɒmmɒ]

fall	efterår (n)	['ɛfdʌˌɒ]
in the fall	om efteråret	[ɒm 'ɛfdɒɒ:ɒð]
fall (attr)	efterårs-	['ɛfdʌˌɒs]

winter	vinter (c)	['vendʌ]
in winter	om vinteren	[ɒm 'vendɒɒn]
winter (attr)	vinter-	['vendɒ]

month	måned (c)	['mɔ:nəð]
this month	i denne måned	[i 'dɛnə 'mɔ:nəð]
next month	næste måned	['nɛsdə 'mɔ:nəð]
last month	i sidste måned	[i 'sisdə 'mɔ:nəð]

a month ago	for en måned siden	[fɒ en 'mɔ:nəð 'si:ðən]
in a month	om en måned	[ɒm en 'mɔ:nəð]
in two months	om 2 måneder	[ɒm to 'mɔ:nəðɒ]
a whole month	hele måneden	['he:lə 'mɔ:nəðən]
all month long	hele måneden	['he:lə 'mɔ:nəðən]

monthly (~ magazine)	månedlig	['mɔ:nəðli]
monthly (adv)	månedligt	['mɔ:nəðlid]
every month	hver måned	['vɛɒ ˌmɔ:nəð]
twice a month	to gange om måneden	[to: 'gɑŋə ɒm 'mɔ:nəðən]

year	år (n)	[ɒ:]
this year	i år	[i ɒ:]
next year	næste år	['nɛsdə ɒ:]
last year	i fjor	[i 'fjoɒ]

a year ago	for et år siden	[fɒ ed ɒ: 'si:ðən]
in a year	om et år	[ɒm ed ɒ:]
in two years	om 2 år	[ɒm to ɒ:]
a whole year	hele året	['he:lə 'ɒ:ɒð]

all year long	hele året	['he:lə 'ɒ:ɒð]
every year	hvert år	['vɛɒd ɒ:]
annual (adj)	årlig	['ɒ:li]
annually	årligt	['ɒ:lid]
4 times a year	fire gange om året	['fi:ɒ 'gɑŋə ɒm 'ɒ:ɒð]

date (e.g., today's ~)	dato (c)	['dæ:to]
date (e.g., ~ of birth)	dato (c)	['dæ:to]
calendar (of dates)	kalender (c)	[ka'lɛndʌ]

half a year	et halvt år	[ed hald ɒ:]
six months	halvår (n)	['halvɒ:]
season (summer etc.)	sæson (c)	[sɛ'sɒŋ]
century	århundrede (n)	[ɒ'hunʁʌðə]

22. Time. Miscellaneous

time	tid (c)	[tið]
instant (noun)	øjeblik (n)	['ɒjə‚blek]
moment	øjeblik (n)	['ɒjə‚blek]
instant (adj)	øjeblikkelig	['ɒjə‚blegəli]
period (length of time)	tidsrum (n)	['tiðsʁɒm]
life	liv (n)	['liu]
eternity	evighed (c)	['e:viheð]

epoch	epoke (c)	[e'po:kə]
era	æra (c)	['ɛɒɑ]
cycle	cyklus (c)	['syklus]
period	tidsrum (n)	['tiðsʁɒm]
term (period)	periode (c)	[paɒi'o:ðə]

the future	fremtid (c)	['fʁamtið]
future (attr)	fremtidig	['fʁamtiði]
next time	næste gang	['nɛsdəgɑŋ]
the past	fortid (c)	['fɒ:tið]
past (recent)	forleden	[fɒ'le:ðən]
last time	sidste gang	['sisdə ‚gɑŋ]

later	senere	['se:nɒɒ]
after	efter	['ɛfdɒ]
nowadays	nu	[nu]
now	nu	[nu]
immediately	omgående	[ɒm'gɔ:ənə]
soon	snart	[snɑ:d]
in advance (beforehand)	på forhånd	[pɔ 'fɒ:‚hʌn]

a long time ago	for lang tid siden	[fɒ lɑŋ tið 'si:ðən]
recently	forleden	[fɒ'le:ðən]
destiny	skæbne (c)	['skɛ:bnə]
memories (recollection)	erindring (c)	[e'ʁɛndʁɛŋ]

archives	**arkiv** (n)	[ɑ'kiu]
during ...	**under ...**	['ɔnʌ]
long, a long time	**længe**	['lɛŋə]
not long	**ikke længe**	['egə lɛŋə]
early (in the morning)	**tidligt**	['tiðlid]
late (not early)	**sent**	[se:nd]

forever (for good)	**for evigt**	[fɒ 'e:vid]
to start (begin)	**at starte**	[at 'sdɑ:də]
to postpone (vt)	**at udsætte**	[at 'uð‚sɛdə]
at the same time	**samtidigt**	['sɑm‚tiðid]
permanently	**altid**	['altið]
constant (noise, pain)	**stadig**	['sdæ:ð]
temporary	**midlertidig**	['miðlʌ‚tiði]

sometimes	**af og til**	[a ɒu 'tel]
rarely	**sjældent**	['ɕɛlənd]
often	**ofte**	['ʌfdə]

23. Opposites

| rich | **rig** | [ʁi:] |
| poor | **fattig** | ['fadi] |

| ill, sick | **syg** | [sy:] |
| healthy | **rask** | [ʁɑsk] |

| big | **stor** | ['sdoɒ] |
| small | **lille** | ['lilə] |

| quickly | **hurtigt** | ['huɒdid] |
| slowly | **langsomt** | ['lɑŋsɒmd] |

| fast | **hurtig** | ['huɒdi] |
| slow | **langsom** | ['lɑŋsɒm] |

| cheerful | **glad** | [glað] |
| sad | **sørgelig** | ['sœɒwəli] |

| together | **sammen** | ['sɑmən] |
| separately | **særskilt** | ['sɛɒskeld] |

| aloud (read) | **højt** | [hɒjd] |
| silently | **for sig selv** | [fɒ sɑj sɛl] |

| tall | **høj** | [hɒj] |
| low | **lav** | ['læ:u] |

| deep | **dyb** | [dy:b] |
| shallow | **lille** | ['lilə] |

yes	**ja**	[ja]
no	**nej**	[nɑj]
distant	**fjern**	['fjaɒn]
nearby (adj)	**nær**	['nɛɒ]
far	**langt**	[lɑŋd]
nearby (adv)	**ved siden af**	[veð 'si:ðən a]
long	**lang**	[lɑŋ]
short	**kort**	[kɒːd]
kind	**god**	[goð]
evil	**vred**	[vʁɛð]
married	**gift**	[gifd]
single	**ugift**	['u,gifd]
to forbid (vt)	**at forbyde**	[at fʌ'byðə]
to permit (vi, vt)	**at tillade**	[at 'te,læðə]
end	**ende** (c)	['ɛnə]
beginning	**begyndelse** (c)	[be'gønəlsə]
left	**venstre**	['vɛnsdʁʌ]
right	**højre**	['hɒjʁɒ]
first	**første**	['fœɒsdə]
last	**sidste**	['sisdə]
crime	**forbrydelse** (c)	[fɒ'bʁyðəlsə]
punishment	**straf** (c)	[sdʁɑf]
to order (vi, vt)	**at beordre**	[at be'ɒːdʁɒ]
to obey (vi, vt)	**at underordne sig**	[at 'ɔnɒ,ɒːdnə sɑj]
straight	**lige**	['li:ə]
curved	**krum**	[kʁɔm]
Paradise	**paradis** (n)	['pɑːɑ,dis]
Hell	**helvede** (n)	['hɛlvəðə]
to be born	**at blive født**	[at 'bli:ə fø:d]
to die (vi, vt)	**at dø**	[at dø:]
strong	**kraftig**	['kʁɑfdi]
weak	**svag**	[svæ:]
old	**gammel**	['gɑməl]
young	**ung**	[ɔŋ]
old	**gammel**	['gɑməl]
new	**ny**	[ny:]

| hard | **hård** | [hɒ:] |
| soft | **blød** | [bløð] |

| warm | **varm** | [vɑ:m] |
| cold | **kold** | [kɒl] |

| fat | **tyk** | [tyk] |
| slim | **tynd** | [tøn] |

| narrow | **snæver** | ['snɛwʌ] |
| wide | **bred** | [bʁɛð] |

| good | **god** | [goð] |
| bad | **dårlig** | ['dɒ:li] |

| brave | **tapper** | ['tɑbɒ] |
| cowardly | **frygtsom** | ['fʁœgdsɒm] |

24. Lines and shapes

square	**firkant** (c)	[fiɒ'kand]
square (attr)	**firkantet**	[fiɒ'kandəð]
circle	**cirkel** (c)	['siɒkəl]
round	**rund**	[ʁɒn]
triangle	**trekant** (c)	['tʁɛ͵kand]
triangular	**trekantet**	['tʁɛ͵kandəð]

oval	**oval** (c)	[o'væ:l]
oval (attr)	**oval-**	[o'væ:l]
rectangle	**rektangel** (n)	['ʁag͵tɑŋəl]
rectangular	**retvinklet**	[ʁad'veŋkləð]

pyramid	**pyramide** (c)	[pyɒ'mi:ðə]
rhombus	**rombe** (c)	['ʁombə]
trapezoid	**trapez** (n)	[tʁɑ'pɛds]
cube	**terning** (c)	['tæɒneŋ]
prism	**prisme** (n)	['pʁismə]

circumference	**cirkel** (c)	['siɒkəl]
sphere	**sfære** (c)	['sfɛ:ɒ]
sphere (ball)	**kugle** (c)	['ku:lə]

diameter	**diameter** (c)	[dia'me:dʌ]
radius	**radius** (c)	['ʁɑdjus]
perimeter	**perimeter** (c)	[pɛɒi'me:dʌ]
center	**centrum** (n)	['sɛntʁɒm]
horizontal	**vandret**	['van͵ʁad]
vertical	**lodret**	['lʌð͵ʁad]
parallel (noun)	**parallel** (c)	[pɑɑ'lɛl]
parallel (adj)	**parallel**	[pɑɑ'lɛl]

line	**linje** (c)	['linjə]
stroke	**streg** (c)	[sdʁɑj]
straight line	**lige linje** (c)	['li:ə 'linjə]
curve	**kurve** (c)	['kuɒwə]
thin (layer)	**tynd**	[tøn]
contour (outline)	**kontur** (c)	[kʌn'tuɒ]
intersection	**skæring** (c)	['sgɛɒeŋ]
right angle (angle of 90°)	**ret vinkel** (c)	[ʁat 'veŋkəl]
segment	**segment** (n)	[seg'mɛnd]
sector	**sektor** (c)	['sɛktɒ]
side (of triangle)	**side** (c)	['si:ðə]
angle	**hjørne** (n)	['jœɒnə]

25. Units of measurement

weight	**vægt** (c)	[vɛgd]
length	**længde** (c)	['lɛŋdə]
width	**bredde** (c)	['bʁɛːdə]
height	**højde** (c)	['hɔjdə]
depth	**dybde** (c)	['dybdə]
volume	**rumfang** (n)	['ʁɔmfɑŋ]
area	**areal** (n)	[ˌɑe'æːl]
gram	**gram** (n)	[gʁɑm]
milligram	**milligram** (n)	['miliʁɑm]
kilogram	**kilogram** (n)	[kilo'gʁɑm]
ton	**ton** (c)	[tɒn]
pound (unit of weight)	**pund** (n)	[pun]
ounce	**ounce** (c)	['ɑwns]
meter	**meter** (c)	['medʌ]
millimeter	**millimeter** (c)	['milime:dʌ]
centimeter	**centimeter** (c)	[sɛnti'me:dʌ]
kilometer	**kilometer** (c)	[kilo'me:dʌ]
mile	**mil** (c)	[mi:l]
inch	**tomme** (c)	['tɒmə]
foot	**fod** (c)	[foð]
yard	**yard** (c)	['jɑ:d]
square meter	**kvadratmeter** (c)	[kva'dʁɑːdˌme:dʌ]
hectare	**hektar** (c)	[hɛk'tɑ]
liter	**liter** (c)	['lidʌ]
degree	**grad** (c)	[gʁɑ:ð]
volt	**volt** (c)	[vɒld]
ampere	**ampere** (c)	[ɑm'pɒɒ]
horsepower	**hestekraft** (c)	['hɛsdəˌkʁɑfd]
quantity	**mængde** (c)	['mɛŋdə]

a little bit of ...	**lidt ...**	['lid ...]
half	**halvdel** (c)	['halde:l]
dozen	**dusin** (n)	[du'si:n]
piece (item)	**stykke** (n)	['sdøkə]
size	**størrelse** (c)	['sdœɒlsə]
scale (of model, drawing)	**målestok** (c)	['mɔ:ləsdɒk]
minimum	**minimal-**	[mi:ni'mæ:l]
the smallest	**den allermindste**	[dɛn 'alɒˌmensdə]
medium	**middel**	['miðəl]
maximum	**maksimal**	[mɑksi'mæ:l]
the largest	**den/det største**	[dɛn/de 'sdœɒsdə]

26. Containers

jar (glass)	**glasdåse** (n)	['glasˌdɔ:sə]
can	**dåse** (c)	['dɔ:sə]
bucket	**spand** (c)	[sbʌn]
barrel	**tønde** (c)	['tønə]
basin (for washing)	**balje** (c)	['baljə]
tank (for liquid, gas)	**tank** (c)	[taŋk]
flask (for water, wine)	**lærke** (c), **flaske** (c)	['læɒkə], ['flaskə]
jerrycan	**dunk** (c)	[doŋk]
cistern (tank)	**cisterne** (c)	[si'sdæɒnə]
mug	**krus** (n)	[kʁu:s]
cup (of coffee etc.)	**kop** (c)	[kob]
saucer	**underkop** (c)	['ɔnɒkɒb]
glass (~ of water)	**glas** (n)	[glas]
glass (~ of vine)	**vinglas** (c)	['vi:nglas]
stew pot	**kasserolle** (c)	[kasə'ʁʌlə]
bottle (e.g., ~ of wine)	**flaske**	['flaskə]
neck (of the bottle)	**flaskehals** (c)	['flaskəˌhals]
carafe	**karaffel** (c)	[kɑ'ʁɑfəl]
pitcher (earthenware)	**krukke** (c)	['kʁɔkə]
vessel (container)	**beholder** (c)	[be'hɒlʌ]
pot (crock)	**potte** (c)	['pɒdə]
vase	**vase** (c)	['væ:sə]
bottle (e.g., ~ of perfume)	**flakon** (c)	[fla'kɒn]
vial, small bottle	**lille flaske** (c)	['lilə 'flaskə]
tube (of toothpaste)	**tube** (c)	['tu:bə]
sack (bag)	**sæk** (c)	[sɛk]
bag (paper, plastic)	**pose** (c)	['po:sə]
package (small parcel)	**pakke** (c)	['pɑkə]

pack (of cigarettes etc.)	**pakke** (c)	['pɑkə]
pack	**pakke** (c)	['pɑkə]
box (e.g., shoebox)	**æske** (c)	['ɛskə]
box (for transportation)	**kasse** (c)	['kasə]
basket (for carrying)	**kurv** (c)	['kuɒw]

27. Materials

material	**materiale** (c)	[mateɒi'æ:lə]
wood	**træ** (n)	[tʁɛ:]
wooden	**træ-**	[tʁɛ:]
glass (noun)	**glas** (n)	[glas]
glass (attr)	**glas-**	[glas]
stone (noun)	**sten** (c)	[sde:n]
stone (attr)	**sten-**	[sde:n]
plastic (noun)	**plastic** (n)	['plasdig]
plastic (attr)	**plastic-**	['plasdig]
rubber (noun)	**gummi** (n, c)	['gomi]
rubber (attr)	**gummi-**	['gomi]
material, fabric (noun)	**stof** (n)	[sdɒf]
fabric (attr)	**af stof**	[a sdɒf]
paper (noun)	**papir** (n)	[pa'piɒ]
paper (attr)	**papir-**	[pa'piɒ]
cardboard (noun)	**karton** (c)	[kɑ'tɒŋ]
cardboard (attr)	**karton-**	[kɑ'tɒŋ]
polythene	**polyætylen** (n, c)	[polyɛdy:'lən]
cellophane	**cellofan** (n)	[sɛlo'fan]
linoleum	**linoleum** (n)	[li'no:leɔm]
plywood	**finer** (c)	[fi'nʌ]
porcelain (noun)	**porcælen** (n)	[pɒsɛ'lən]
porcelain (attr)	**af porcælen**	[a pɒsɛ'lən]
clay (noun)	**ler** (n)	[leʌ]
clay (attr)	**ler-**	[leɒ]
ceramics (noun)	**keramik** (c)	[keʁɑ'mik]
ceramic (attr)	**keramik-**	[keʁɑ'mik]

28. Metals

metal (noun)	**metal** (n)	[me'tal]
metal (attr)	**metal-**	[me'tal]

alloy (noun)	**legering** (c)	[le'geɒeŋ]
gold (noun)	**guld** (n)	[gul]
gold, golden	**guld-**	[gul]
silver (noun)	**sølv** (n)	[søl]
silver (attr)	**sølv**	[søl]
iron (noun)	**jern** (n)	['jæɒn]
iron, made of iron	**jern-**	['jæɒn]
steel (noun)	**stål** (n)	[sdɔ:l]
steel (attr)	**stål-**	[sdɔ:l]
copper (noun)	**kobber** (n)	['kɒwʌ]
copper (attr)	**kobber-**	['kɒwʌ]
aluminum (noun)	**aluminium** (n)	[alu'mi:niɔm]
aluminum (attr)	**aluminiums-**	[alu'mi:niɔms]
bronze (noun)	**bronze** (c)	['bʁɒŋsə]
bronze (attr)	**bronze-**	['bʁɒŋsə]
brass	**messing** (n)	['mɛseŋ]
nickel	**nikkel** (n)	['nekəl]
platinum	**platin** (n)	[pla'ti:n]
mercury	**kviksølv** (n)	['kvik‚søl]
tin	**tin** (n)	[ti:n]
lead	**bly** (n)	[bly:]
zinc	**zink** (n, c)	[seŋk]

HUMAN BEING

Human being. The body

29. Humans. Basic concepts

human, human being	**menneske** (n)	['mɛnəskə]
man (adult male)	**mand** (c)	[man]
woman	**kvinde** (c)	['kvenə]
child	**barn** (n)	[bɑːn]
girl	**pige** (c)	['piːə]
boy	**dreng** (c)	['dʁaŋ]
teenager	**teenager** (c)	['tiːnˌɛjdɢʌ]
old man	**gamling** (c)	['gɑmleŋ]
old woman	**gammel dame** (c)	['gɑməl 'dæːmə]

30. Human anatomy

organism	**organisme** (c)	[ɒgɑ'nismə]
heart	**hjerte** (n)	['jæɒdə]
blood	**blod** (n)	[bloð]
artery	**arterie** (c)	[ɑː'teɒjə]
vein	**åre** (c)	['ɒːɒ]
brain	**hjerne** (c)	['jæɒnə]
nerve	**nerve** (c)	['næɒvə]
nerves	**nerver** (pl)	['næɒvʌ]
vertebra	**ryghvirvel** (c)	['ʁœgˌviɒwel]
spine	**rygrad** (c)	['ʁœgˌʁɑːð]
stomach (organ)	**mavesæk** (c)	['mæːvə,mæːuəsɛk]
intestines	**tarmkanal** (c)	['tɑːmkaˌnæːl]
intestine	**tarm** (c)	[tɑːm]
liver	**lever** (c)	['leːvʌ]
kidney	**nyre** (c)	['nyːɒ]
bone	**ben** (n)	[beːn]
skeleton	**skelet** (n)	[ske'lɛd]
rib	**ribben** (n)	['ʁibeːn]
skull	**kranium** (n)	['kʁɑːnɔm]
muscle	**muskel** (c)	['muskəl]
biceps	**biceps** (c)	['bisɛbs]

triceps	triceps (c)	['tʁi:sɛbs]
tendon	sene (c)	['se:nə]
joint	led (n)	[leð]
lungs	lunger (pl)	['lɔŋʌ]
genitals	kønsdele (pl)	['kœn̩sde:lə]
skin	hud (c)	[huð]

31. Head

head	hoved (n)	['ho:əð]
face	ansigt (n)	['ansegd]
nose	næse (c)	['nɛ:sə]
mouth	mund (c)	[mɔn]

eye	øje (c)	['ɒjə]
eyes	øjne (pl)	['ɒjnə]
pupil	pupil (c)	[pu'pel]
eyebrow	øjenbryn (n)	['ɒjən̩bʁy:n]
eyelash	øjenvippe (c)	['ɒjən̩vebə]
eyelid	øjenlåg (n)	['ɒjən̩lɒu]

tongue	tung (c)	[tɔŋ]
tooth	tand (c)	[tan]
lips	læber (pl)	['lɛ:bʌ]
cheekbones	kindben (n)	['kend̩be:n]
gum	tandkød (n)	['tankøð]
palate	gane (c)	['gæ:nə]

nostrils	næsebor (pl)	['nɛ:sə̩bɔɒ]
chin	hage (c)	['hæ:jə]
jaw	kæbe (c)	['kɛ:bə]
cheek	kind (c)	[ken]

forehead	pande (c)	['panə]
temple	tinding (c)	['teneŋ]
ear	øre (n)	['ø:ɒ]
back of the head	nakke (c)	['nɑkə]
neck	hals (c)	[hals]
throat	hals (c)	[hals]

hair	hår (n)	[hɒ:]
hairstyle	frisure (c)	[fʁi'sy:ɒ]
haircut	klipning (c)	['klebneŋ]
wig	paryk (c)	[pɑ'ʁœk]

mustache	overskæg (n)	['ɒwʌsgɛ:g]
beard	skæg (n)	[sgɛ:g]
to have (a beard etc.)	at have (skæg)	[at 'hæ:və]
braid	fletning (c)	['flɛdneŋ]
sideburns	bakkenbart (c)	['bɑkən̩bɑd]

red-haired	**rødhåret**	['ʁœðˌhɒːɒð]
gray (hair)	**gråhåret**	['gʁɒhɒːɒð]
bald	**skaldet**	['skaləð]
bald patch	**skaldet plet** (c)	['skaləðˌplɛð]
ponytail	**hestehale** (c)	['hɛsdəˌhæːlə]
bangs	**pandehår** (n)	['panəˌhɒː]

32. Human body

hand	**håndrod** (c)	['hɒnˌʁoð]
arm	**arm** (c)	[ɑːm]
finger, toe	**finger** (c)	['feŋʌ]
thumb	**tommelfinger** (c)	['tɒmməlˌfeŋʌ]
little finger	**lillefinger** (c)	['liləˌfeŋʌ]
nail	**negl** (c)	[nɑjl]
fist	**knytnæve** (c)	['knydˌnɛːuə]
palm	**håndflade** (c)	['hɒnˌflæːðə]
wrist	**håndled** (n)	['hɒnˌleð]
forearm	**underarm** (c)	['ɔnɒˌɑːm]
elbow	**albue** (c)	[al'buːə]
shoulder	**skulder** (c)	['skulʌ]
leg	**ben** (n)	[beːn]
foot	**fod** (c)	[foð]
knee	**knæ** (n)	[knɛː]
calf (part of leg)	**læg** (c)	[lɛːg]
hip	**lår** (n)	[lɒː]
heel	**hæl** (c)	[hɛːl]
body	**krop** (c)	[kʁɒb]
stomach (abdomen)	**mave** (c)	['mæːvə]
chest	**bryst** (n)	[bʁœsd]
breast	**barm** (c)	[bɑm]
side (of the body)	**side** (c)	['siːðə]
back	**ryg** (c)	[ʁœg]
lower back	**lænd** (c)	[lɛn]
waist	**talje** (c)	['taljə]
navel	**navle** (c)	['nɑulə]
buttocks	**baller** (pl)	['balɒ]
behind	**bagdel** (c)	['bɑuˌdeːl]
beauty mark	**modermærke** (n)	['moːðɒˌmaɒkə]
birthmark	**modermærke** (n)	['moːðɒˌmaɒkə]
tattoo	**tatovering** (c)	[tato'veːʁɐŋ]
scar	**ar** (n)	[ɑː]

Clothing & Accessories

33. Outerwear. Coats

clothes	**tøj** (n)	[tɒj]
outer clothing	**overtøj** (n)	[ˈɒwʌˌtɒj]
winter clothing	**vintertøj** (n)	[ˈvendɒˌtɒj]
overcoat	**frakke** (c)	[ˈfʁakə]
fur coat	**pelskåbe** (c)	[ˈpɛlsˌkɔːbə]
fur jacket	**kort pelsjakke** (c)	[ˈkɒːd ˈpɛlsˌjagə]
down coat	**dynejakke** (c)	[ˈdyːnəˌjakə]
jacket (e.g., leather ~)	**jakke** (c)	[ˈjakə]
raincoat	**regnfrakke** (c)	[ˈʁajnˌfʁagə]
waterproof	**vandtæt**	[ˈvantɛd]

34. Men's & women's clothing

shirt	**skjorte** (c)	[ˈskjɒɒdə]
pants	**bukser** (pl)	[ˈbɔksʌ]
jeans	**jeans** (pl)	[ˈdjiːns]
jacket (of man's suit)	**jakke** (c)	[ˈjakə]
suit	**jakkesæt** (n)	[ˈjakəˌsɛd]
dress (frock)	**kjole** (c)	[ˈkjoːlə]
skirt (garment)	**nederdel** (c)	[ˈneðɒdeːl]
blouse	**bluse** (c)	[ˈbluːsə]
knitted jacket	**trøje** (c)	[ˈtʁɒjə]
jacket (of woman's suit)	**cardigan** (c)	[ˈkɑːdigan]
shawl	**sjal** (n)	[ɕæːl]
T-shirt	**T-shirt** (c)	[ˈtiːˌɕœːd]
shorts (short trousers)	**shorts** (pl)	[ˈɕɒːds]
tracksuit	**træningsdragt** (c)	[ˈtʁɛːnɛŋˌsdʁagd]
bathrobe	**badekåbe** (c)	[ˈbæːðəˌkɔːbə]
pajamas	**pyjamas** (c)	[pyˈjæːmas]
sweater	**sweater** (c)	[ˈswɛdʌ]
pullover	**pullover** (c)	[pulˈɔwvʌ]
vest	**vest** (c)	[vɛsd]
tailcoat	**kjolesæt** (n)	[ˈkjoːləˌsɛd]
tuxedo	**smoking** (c)	[ˈsmɔwkeŋ]

uniform	uniform (c)	[uni'fɔ:m]
workwear	arbejdstøj (n)	['ɑ:bɑjds,tɒj]
overalls	kedeldragt (c)	['ke:ðəl,dʁagd]
coat (e.g., doctor's ~)	kittel (c)	['kidəl]

35. Clothing. Underwear

underwear	undertøj (tøj) (n)	['ɔnɒ,tɒj]
undershirt (underwear)	undertrøje (c)	['ɔnɒ,tʁɒjə]
socks	sokker (pl)	['sɒkʌ]

nightgown	natkjole (c)	['nad,kjo:lə]
bra	BH (c)	[be'hɔ]
knee highs	knæstrømper (pl)	['knɛ,sdʁœmbʌ]
pantyhose	strømpebukser (pl)	['sdʁœmbə,bɒksʌ]
stockings	strømper (pl)	['sdʁœmbʌ]
bathing suit	badedragt (c)	['bæ:ðə,dʁagd]

36. Headwear

hat	hue (c)	['hu:ə]
fedora	hat (c)	[had]
baseball cap	baseballkasket (c)	['bɛjs,bɒ:l ka'skɛd]
flatcap	kasket (c)	[ka'skɛd]

beret	baskerhue (n)	['bɑ:skɒ,hu:ə]
hood	hætte (c)	['hɛdə]
panama	panamahat (c)	['panamɑ:,had]
knitted hat	strikhue (c)	['sdʁɛk,hue]

headscarf	hovedtørklæde (n)	['ho:əð dœɒ,klɛ:ðə]
women's hat	hat (c)	[had]
scarf (headscarf)	tørklæde (n)	['tœɒ,klɛ:ðə]

hard hat	hjelm (c)	[jɛlm]
garrison cap	skråhue (c)	['skʁɒ,hu:ə]
helmet	hjelm (c)	[jɛlm]

| derby | bowlerhat (c) | ['bɔwlʌhad] |
| top hat | høj hat (c) | [hɒj 'had] |

37. Footwear

footwear	sko (c)	[sko:]
ankle boots	sko (pl)	[sko:]
shoes (wingtip shoes)	sko (pl)	[sko:]

boots (e.g., cowboy ~)	**støvler** (pl)	['sdœulʌ]
slippers	**hjemmesko** (pl)	['jɛməˌsko:]
tennis shoes	**kondisko** (pl)	['kʌndiˌsko:]
sneakers	**sportssko** (pl)	['sbɒ:dsˌsko:]
sandals	**sandaler** (pl)	[san'dæ:lʌ]
cobbler	**skomager** (c)	['sgoˌmæjʌ]
heel (of shoe)	**hæl** (c)	[hɛ:l]
pair (of shoes)	**par** (n)	['pɑ]
shoestring	**snørebånd** (n)	['snœɒ'bɒn]
to lace (vt)	**at snøre**	[at snœɒ]
shoehorn	**skohorn** (n)	['sko:ˌhoɒn]
shoe polish	**skocreme** (c)	['skoˌkʁɛ:m]

38. Textile. Fabrics

cotton (noun)	**bomuld** (c)	['bɒmul]
cotton (attr)	**af bomuld**	[a b'ɒmul]
flax (noun)	**hør** (c)	[høɒ]
flax (attr)	**af hør**	[a høɒ]
silk (noun)	**silke** (c)	['selkə]
silk (attr)	**silke-**	['selkə]
wool (noun)	**uld** (c)	[ul]
woolen	**uld-**	[ul]
velvet	**fløjl** (n)	[flɒjl]
suede	**ruskind** (n)	['ʁusken]
corduroy	**fløjl** (n)	[flɒjl]
nylon (noun)	**nylon** (n, c)	['nɑjlɒn]
nylon (attr)	**af nylon**	[a 'nɑjlɒn]
polyester (noun)	**polyester** (n)	[poly'ɛsdʌ]
polyester (attr)	**polyester-**	[poly'ɛsdɒ]
leather (noun)	**læder** (n)	['lɛðʌ]
leather (attr)	**af leder**	[a 'le:ðɒ]
fur (noun)	**pels** (c)	[pɛls]
fur (e.g., ~ coat)	**pels-**	[pɛls]

39. Personal accessories

gloves	**handsker** (pl)	['hanskʌ]
mittens	**vanter** (c pl)	['vandə]
scarf (long)	**halstørklæde** (n)	['halstœɒˌklɛ:ðə]
glasses	**briller** (pl)	['bʁɛlʌ]

frame (for spectacles)	**indfatning** (c)	[en'fadneŋ]
umbrella	**paraply** (c)	[pɑɑ'ply:]
walking stick	**spadserestok** (c)	[sba'seʌ sdɒk]
hairbrush	**hårbørste** (c)	['hɒːˌbœɒsdə]
fan (accessory)	**vifte** (c)	['vefdə]
necktie	**slips** (n)	[slebs]
bow tie	**butterfly** (c)	['bɒdɒflly:]
suspenders	**seler** (pl)	['se:lɒ]
handkerchief	**lommetørklæde** (n)	['lʌməˌtœɒklɛːðə]
comb (for hair)	**kam** (c)	[kɑm]
barrette	**hårspænde** (n)	['hɒːˌsbɛnə]
hairpin	**hårnål** (n)	['hɒːˌnɔl]
buckle	**spænde** (n)	['sbɛnə]
belt	**bælte** (n)	['bɛldə]
shoulder strap	**rem** (c)	[ʁɛm]
bag (handbag)	**taske** (c)	['taskə]
purse	**dametaske** (c)	['dæːmeˌtaskə]
backpack	**rygsæk** (c)	['ʁœgˌsɛg]

40. Clothing. Miscellaneous

fashion	**mode** (c)	['moːðə]
in vogue	**moderigtig**	['moːðæˌʁɛgdi]
fashion designer	**modedesigner** (c)	['moːðə di'sɑjnʌ]
collar	**krave** (c)	['kʁɑːuə]
pocket	**lomme** (c)	['lʌmə]
pocket (e.g., ~ camera)	**lomme-**	['lʌmə]
sleeve	**ærme** (n)	['aɒmə]
hanging tab (loop)	**strop** (c)	[sdʁɒb]
fly (on trousers)	**gylp** (c)	[gyːlb]
zipper (fastener)	**lynlås** (c)	['lyːnˌlɔːs]
fastener	**hægte** (c)	['hɛgdə]
button	**knap** (c)	[knɑb]
buttonhole	**knaphul** (n)	['knɑbˌhɔl]
to come off (ab. button)	**at løsrive sig**	[at 'løsˌʁiuə sɑj]
to sew (vi, vt)	**at sy**	[at syː]
to embroider (vi, vt)	**at brodere**	[at bʁo'deʌ]
embroidery	**broderi** (n)	[bʁoːdə'ʁiː]
sewing needle	**synål** (c)	[sø'nɔːl]
thread	**tråd** (c)	[tʁɔð]
seam	**søm** (c)	[sœm]
to get dirty (vi)	**at blive beskidt**	[at 'bliːə be'skid]
stain (mark, spot)	**plet** (c)	[plɛð]

to crease, crumple (vi)	at krølles	[at 'kʁœləs]
to tear (vt)	at rive i stykker	[at 'ʁiːuə i 'sdøkə]
clothes moth	møl (n)	[møl]

41. Personal care. Cosmetics

toothpaste	tandpasta (c)	['tanˌpasda]
toothbrush	tandbørste (c)	['tanˌbœɒsdə]
to brush one's teeth	at børste tænder	[at 'bœɒsdə 'tɛnɒ]
razor	barbermaskine (c)	[bɑ'beɒ maˈskiːnə]
shaving cream	barbercreme (c)	[bɑ'beɒ ˌkʁɛːm]
to shave (vi)	at barbere sig	[at bɑ'beːɒ sɑj]
soap	sæbe (c)	['sɛːbə]
shampoo	shampoo (c)	['ɕæːmˌpuː]
scissors	saks (pl)	[sɑks]
nail file	neglefil (c)	['nɑjləˌfiːl]
nail clippers	neglesaks (c)	['nɑjləˌsɑgs]
tweezers	pincet (c)	[pin'sɛd]
cosmetics	kosmetik (c)	[kɒsme'tik]
face mask	maske (c)	['maskə]
manicure	manicure (c)	[maniˈkyːʌ]
to have a manicure	at få manicure	[at fɔː maniˈkyːʌ]
pedicure	fodpleje (c)	['foðˌplɑjə]
make-up bag	kosmetiktaske (c)	[kɒsmeˈtikˌtaskə]
powder (for face)	pudder (n)	['puðʌ]
powder compact	pudderdåse (c)	['puðɒˌdɔːsə]
blusher	rouge (c)	['ʁuːɕ]
perfume (bottled)	parfume (c)	[pɑ'fyːmə]
toilet water	eau de toilette (n)	[eː di toa'lɛdə]
lotion	lotion (c)	['lowɕən]
cologne	eau de cologne (c)	[eː di ko'lɒunə]
eyeshadow	øjenskygge (pl)	['ɒjənˌsgygə]
eyeliner	eyeliner (c)	['ɑːjˌlɑjnʌ]
mascara	mascara (c)	[ma'sgɑːɑ]
lipstick	læbestift (c)	['lɛːbəˌsdefd]
nail polish, enamel	neglelak (c)	['nɑjləˌlɑg]
hair spray	hårspray (n)	['hɒːˌspʁɛj]
deodorant	deodorant (c)	[deodo'ʁand]
cream	creme (c)	[kʁɛːm]
face cream	ansigts creme (c)	['ansegds kʁɛːm]
hand cream	håndcreme (c)	['hɒnˌkʁɛːm]

anti-wrinkle cream	antirynke creme (c)	[antə'ʁɶŋkə kʁɛ:m]
day (attr)	dag-	[dæ:]
night (attr)	nat-	[nad]

tampon	tampon (c)	[tɑm'pɒn]
toilet paper	toiletpapir (n)	[toa'lɛdpaˌpiɒ]
hair dryer	hårtørrer (c)	['hɒːˌtœɒʌ]

42. Jewelry

jewelry	juveler (pl)	[juvə'lɒə]
precious (e.g., ~ stone)	ædel	['ɛ:ðəl]
hallmark	stempel (n)	['sdɛmbəl]

ring	ring (c)	[ʁɛŋ]
wedding ring	vielsesring (c)	['vi:əlsəsˌʁɛŋ]
bracelet	armbånd (n)	['ɑːmˌbɒn]

earrings	øreringe (pl)	['ø:ɒˌʁɛŋə]
necklace (~ of pearls)	halskæde (c)	['halsˌkɛ:ðə]
crown	krone (c)	['kʁo:nə]
beads (necklace)	halssmykke (n)	['halssmøkkə]

diamond	diamant (c)	[dia'mand]
emerald	smaragd (c)	[smɑ'ʁɑwd]
ruby	rubin (c)	[ʁu'bi:n]
sapphire	safir (c)	[sa'fiɒ]
pearl	perler (pl)	['pæɒlʌ]
amber	rav (c)	['ʁɑw]

43. Watches. Clocks

watch (wristwatch)	armbåndsur (n)	['ɑːmbɒnˌsuɒ]
dial	urskive (c)	['uɒˌski:və]
hand (of clock, watch)	viser (c)	['vi:sʌ]
bracelet	armbånd (n)	['ɑːmˌbɒn]
watch strap	urrem (c)	['uɒˌʁɛm]

battery	batteri (n)	[badə'ʁi:]
to be dead (battery)	at være fladt	[at 'vɛ:ɒ flat]
to change a battery	at skifte et batteri	[at 'skifdə ed badʌ'ʁi]
to run fast	at gå for hurtigt	[at gɔ: fo 'hoɒdid]
to run slow	at gå for langsomt	[at gɔ: fo 'laŋsɒmd]

wall clock	vægur (n)	['vɛ:gˌuɒ]
hourglass	timeglas (n)	['tɑjməˌglas]
sundial	solur (n)	['so:lˌuɒ]
alarm clock	vækkeur (n)	['vɛkəˌuɒ]

| watchmaker | **urmager** (c) | ['uɒˌmæːʌ] |
| to repair (vt) | **at reparere** | [at ʁɛpɑˈʁɛːɑ] |

Food. Nutricion

44. Food

meat	**kød** (n)	[køð]
chicken	**hønsekød** (n)	['hœnsə̩køð]
young chicken	**kylling** (c)	['kyleŋ]
duck	**and** (c)	[an]
goose	**gås** (c)	[gɔːs]
game	**fuglevildt** (n)	['fuːləvild]
turkey	**kalkun** (c)	[kal'kuːn]
pork	**flæsk** (n)	[flɛsk]
veal	**kalvekød** (n)	['kalvə̩køð]
lamb	**fårekød** (n)	['fɒːɒ̩køð]
beef	**oksekød** (n)	['ʌksə̩køð]
rabbit	**kanin** (c)	[ka'niːn]
sausage (salami etc.)	**pølse** (c)	['pølsə]
hot dog (frankfurter)	**pølse** (c)	['pølsə]
bacon	**bacon** (c)	['bɛjkʌn]
ham	**skinke** (c)	['skeŋkə]
gammon (ham)	**skinke** (c)	['skeŋkə]
pâté	**postej** (c)	[po'sdɑj]
liver	**lever** (c)	['leːvʌ]
lard	**fedt** (n)	[fed]
ground beef	**fars** (c)	[fɑːs]
tongue	**tung** (c)	[toŋ]
egg	**æg** (n)	[ɛːg]
eggs	**æg** (pl)	[ɛːg]
egg white	**protein** (n)	[pʁotə'in]
egg yolk	**æggeblomme** (c)	[ɛgə'blɒmə]
fish	**fisk** (c)	[fesk]
seafood	**fisk og skaldyr**	[fesg ɒu 'sgaldyɒ]
crustaceans	**krebsdyr** (pl)	['kʁabs̩dyɒ]
caviar	**kaviar** (c)	['kaviɑː]
crab	**krabbe** (c)	['kʁɑbə]
shrimp	**reje** (c)	['ʁɑjə]
oyster	**østers** (c)	['øsdɒs]
spiny lobster	**languster** (c)	[lɑ'gɔsdʌ]
octopus	**blæksprutte** (c)	['blɛk̩sbʁudə]
squid	**blæksprutte** (c)	['blɛk̩sbʁudə]

sturgeon	**stør** (c)	['sdøɒ]
salmon	**laks** (c)	[lɑks]
halibut	**hellefisk** (c)	[hɛlə'fesk]
cod	**torsk** (c)	[tɒːsk]
mackerel	**makrel** (c)	[mɑ'kʁal]
tuna	**tunfisk** (c)	['tuːnˌfesk]
eel	**ål** (c)	[ɔːl]
trout	**forel** (c)	[fo'ʁal]
sardine	**sardin** (c)	[sɑ'din]
pike	**gedde** (c)	['geðə]
herring	**sild** (c)	[sil]
bread	**brød** (n)	[bʁœð]
cheese	**ost** (c)	[ɔsd]
sugar	**sukker** (n)	['sɔkʌ]
salt	**salt** (n)	[sald]
rice	**ris** (c)	[ʁiːs]
pasta	**makaroni** (pl)	[mɑkə'ʁʌni]
noodles	**nudel** (c)	['nuːðəl]
butter	**smør** (n)	['smœɒ]
vegetable oil	**planteolie** (c)	['plandəˌoːljə]
sunflower oil	**solsikkeolie** (c)	['soːlsekəˌoːljə]
margarine	**margarine** (c)	[mɑgɑ'ʁiːnə]
olives	**oliven** (c)	[o'livən]
olive oil	**olivenolie** (c)	[o'livənˌoːljə]
milk	**mælk** (c)	['mɛlk]
condensed milk	**dåsemælk** (c)	['dɔːsəˌmɛlk]
yogurt	**jogurt** (c)	['joˌguɒd]
sour cream	**cremefraiche** (c)	[kʁɛm'fʁɛːɕ]
cream (of milk)	**fløde** (c)	['fløːðə]
mayonnaise	**mayonnaise** (c)	[mɑjo'nɛːs]
cream (filling for biscuits)	**creme** (c)	[kʁɛːm]
cereal grains	**gryn** (n)	[gʁyːn]
flour	**mel** (n)	[meːl]
canned food	**dåsemad** (c)	['dɔːsəˌmɑð]
cornflakes	**popcorn** (pl)	['pʌbˌkoɒn]
honey	**honning** (c)	['hɒneŋ]
jelly (e.g., strawberry ~)	**marmelade** (c)	[mɑmə'læːðə]
chewing gum	**tyggegummi** (n, c)	['tygəˌgomi]

45. Drinks

water	vand (n)	[van]
drinking water	drikkevand (n)	['dʁɛkəˌvan]
mineral water	mineralvand (n)	[minə'ʁɑːlˌvan]
still	uden kulsyre	['uðən 'kɔlˌsyːʌ]
carbonated	med brus	[mɛð bʁuːs]
sparkling	med brus	[mɛð bʁuːs]
ice	is (c)	[iːs]
with ice	med isterninger	[mɛð 'isdɒneŋɒ]
non-alcoholic	alkoholfri	[alko'hɒlfʁiː]
soft drink	alkoholfri drik (c)	[alko'hɒlfʁiː dʁɛk]
cool soft drink	læskedrik (c)	['lɛskəˌdʁɛk]
lemonade	limonade (c)	[limo'næːðə]
liquor	alkoholiske drikke (pl)	[alko'holiskə 'dʁɛkə]
wine	vin (c)	[viːn]
white wine	hvidvin (c)	['viðviːn]
red wine	rødvin (c)	['ʁœðˌviːn]
liqueur	likør (c)	[li'køɒ]
champagne	champagne (c)	[ɕam'panjə]
vermouth	vermouth (c)	['væɒmud]
whisky	whisky (c)	['wiski]
vodka	vodka (c)	['vʌdka]
gin	gin (c)	[djen]
cognac	cognac (c)	['kʌnjɑg]
rum	rom (c)	[ʁɒm]
coffee	kaffe (c)	['kɑfə]
black coffee	sort kaffe (c)	['soːd 'kɑfə]
coffee with milk	kaffe (c) med mælk	['kɑfə mɛð mɛlk]
cappuccino	kaffe (c) med fløde	['kɑfə mɛð 'fløːðə]
instant coffee	pulverkaffe (c)	['pɔlvɒɒˌkɑfə]
milk	mælk (c)	['mɛlk]
cocktail	cocktail (c)	['kʌkˌtɛjl]
milk shake	milkshake (c)	['milkˌɕɛjk]
juice	saft (c)	[sɑfd]
tomato juice	tomatjuice (c)	[to'mæːtˌdjuːs]
orange juice	appelsinjuice (c)	[apəl'sinjajuːs]
freshly squeezed juice	friskpresset juice (n)	['fʁɛskˌpʁasəð 'djuːs]
beer	øl (n)	[øl]
light beer	pilsner (n, c)	['pilsnʌ]
dark beer	mørkt øl (n)	['mœɒkdˌøl]
tea	te (c)	[teː]

| black tea | sort te (c) | ['sɒːd teː] |
| green tea | grøn te (c) | [gʁœn teː] |

46. Vegetables

| vegetables | grønsager (pl) | ['gʁœnˌsæːʌ] |
| greens | grønt (n) | [gʁœnd] |

tomato	tomat (c)	[to'mæːd]
cucumber	agurk (c)	[a'guɒg]
carrot	gulerod (c)	['guleˌʁoð]
potato	kartoffel (c)	[kɑ'tɒfəl]
onion	løg (n)	[lɒj]
garlic	hvidløg (n)	['viðˌlɒj]

cabbage	kål (c)	[kɔːl]
cauliflower	blomkål (c)	['blʌmˌkɔl]
Brussels sprouts	rosenkål (c)	['ʁoːsənˌkɔːl]
broccoli	broccoli (c)	['bʁɒkoli]

beet	rødbede (c)	['ʁɶðˌbeːðə]
eggplant	aubergine (c)	[obæɒ'ɕiːnə]
zucchini	squash (c)	['sgwʌɕ]
pumpkin	græskar (n)	['gʁasgɑ]
turnip	roe (c)	['ʁoːə]

parsley	persille (c)	[paɒ'silə]
dill	dild (c)	[dil]
lettuce	salat (c)	[sa'læːd]
celery	selleri (c)	[sɛlə'ʁiː]
asparagus	asparges (c)	[a'sbɑːɑəs]
spinach	spinat (c)	[sbi'næːd]

pea	ærter (pl)	['aɒdʌ]
beans	bønner (c pl)	['bœnʌ]
corn (maize)	majs (c)	[mɑjs]
kidney bean	bønne (c)	['bœnə]

bell pepper	peber (n)	['pewʌ]
radish	radiser (c)	[ʁɑ'disə]
artichoke	artiskok (c)	[ɑti'skɒk]

47. Fruits. Nuts

fruit	frugt (c)	[fʁɔgd]
apple	æble (n)	['ɛːblə]
pear	pære (c)	['pɛːɒ]
lemon	citron (c)	[si'tʁoːn]

orange	**appelsin** (c)	[ɑpəl'si:n]
strawberry	**jordbær** (n)	['joɒ̯ˌbɑɒ̯]
mandarin	**mandarin** (c)	[mandɑ'ʁi:n]
plum	**blomme** (c)	['blɒmə]
peach	**fersken** (c)	['faɒskən]
apricot	**abrikos** (c)	[ɑbʁi'ko:s]
raspberry	**hindbær** (n)	['henbaɒ̯]
pineapple	**ananas** (c)	['ananas]
banana	**banan** (c)	[ba'næ:n]
watermelon	**vandmelon** (c)	['vanmeˌlo:n]
grapes	**vindrue** (c)	['vi:nˌdʁu:ə]
cherry (sour cherry)	**kirsebær** (n)	['kiɒsəˌbæɒ̯]
cherry (sweet cherry)	**morel** (c)	[mo:'ɒl]
melon	**honningmelon** (c)	['hɒneŋmeˌlo:n]
grapefruit	**grapefrugt** (c)	['gʁɑpəˌfʁɔgd]
avocado	**avokado** (c)	[avo'kæ:do]
papaya	**papaja** (c)	[pa'pɑja]
mango	**mango** (c)	['mɑŋgo]
pomegranate	**granatæble** (n)	[gʁɑ'naˌdɛ:blə]
redcurrant	**ribs** (n)	[ʁɛbs]
blackcurrant	**solbær** (n)	['so:lˌbæɒ̯]
gooseberry	**stikkelsbær** (n)	['sdekəlsˌbæɒ̯]
bilberry	**blåbær** (n)	['blɒbaɒ̯]
blackberry	**brombær** (n)	['bʁɔmbaɒ̯]
raisin	**rosin** (c)	[ʁo'si:n]
fig	**figen** (c)	['fi:ən]
date	**daddel** (c)	['daðəl]
peanut	**jordnødder** (pl)	['joɒ̯ˌdnøðʌ]
almond	**mandel** (c)	['manəl]
walnut	**valnød** (c)	['valˌnøð]
hazelnut	**hasselnød** (c)	['hasəlˌnøð]
coconut	**kokosnød** (c)	['kokɔsnøð]
pistachios	**pistacienødder** (pl)	[pi'sdæːçənøðʌ]

48. Bread. Candy

confectionery (pastry)	**konditorvarer** (pl)	[kʌn'didʌˌvɑːɑ]
bread	**brød** (n)	[bʁœð]
cookies	**småkager** (pl)	['smɔˌkæ:jʌ]
chocolate (noun)	**chokolade** (c)	[çoko'læ:ðə]
chocolate (attr)	**chokolade-**	[çoko'læ:ðə]
candy	**konfekt** (c)	[kɔn'fɛkd]
cake (e.g., cupcake)	**kage** (c)	['kæ:jə]

cake (e.g., birthday ~)	lagkage (c)	[ˈlɑwˌkæːjə]
pie (e.g., apple ~)	kage (c)	[ˈkæːjə]
filling (for cake, pie)	fyld (n)	[fyl]

jam	syltetøj (n)	[ˈsyldəˌtɒj]
marmalade	marmelade	[mɑməˈlæːðə]
wafer	vaffel (c)	[ˈvɑfəl]
ice-cream	is (c)	[iːs]
pudding	budding (c)	[ˈbuðeŋ]

49. Cooked dishes

course, dish	ret (c), anretning (c)	[ʁad], [ˈanˌʁadnen]
cuisine	national køkken (n)	[nɑɕoˈnæːl ˈkøkən]
recipe	opskrift (c)	[ʌbˈskʁɛfd]
portion	portion (c)	[pɒˈɕoːn]

| salad | salat (c) | [saˈlæːd] |
| soup | suppe (c) | [ˈsɔbə] |

clear soup (broth)	bouillon (c)	[bulˈjʌn]
sandwich (bread)	smørrebrød (n)	[ˈsmœɐˌbʁœð]
fried eggs	spejlæg (n)	[ˈsbɑjlˌɛːg]

cutlet	frikadelle (c)	[fʁikaˈdɛlə]
hamburger (beefburger)	burger (c)	[ˈbœːgʌ]
beefsteak	bøf (c)	[bøf]
roast meat	steg (c)	[ˈsdɑj]

side dish	tilbehør (n)	[ˈtelbeˌhøɒ]
spaghetti	spaghetti (c)	[sbaˈgɛdi]
mashed potatoes	kartoffelmos (c)	[kɑˈtofəlmoːs]
pizza	pizza (c)	[ˈpidsa]
porridge (oatmeal, etc)	grød (c)	[gʁœð]
omelet	omelet (c)	[ɔməˈleð]

boiled (e.g., ~ beef)	kogt	[kɒgd]
smoked	røget	[ˈʁɒjəð]
fried	stegt	[sdɛgd]
dried	tørret	[ˈtœɒð]
frozen	frossen	[ˈfʁɔən]
pickled	marineret	[mɑʁiˈneːɒð]

sweet (in taste)	sød	[søð]
salty	saltet	[ˈsaldəð]
cold	kold	[kɒl]
hot	varm	[vɑːm]
bitter	bitter	[ˈbedɒ]
tasty	lækker	[ˈlɛkɒ]
to cook (vt)	at lave	[at ˈlæːuə]

to cook (vi)	at lave	[at 'læ:uə]
to fry (vt)	at stege	[at 'sdɑjə]
to heat up (food)	at varme op	[at 'vɑ:mə ɒb]
to salt (vt)	at salte	[at 'saldə]
to pepper (vt)	at pebre	[at 'pəbʁɒ]
to grate (vt)	at rive	[at 'ʁi:və]
peel (noun)	skræl (c)	[skʁal]
to peel (vt)	at skrælle	[at 'skʁallə]

50. Spices

salt	salt (n)	[sald]
salty	saltet	['saldəð]
to salt (vt)	at salte	[at 'saldə]
black pepper	sort peber (n)	['sɒ:d 'pewʌ]
red pepper	paprika (c)	['pɑpʁika]
mustard	sennep (c)	['senɒb]
horseradish	peberrod (c)	['pewʌˌʁoð]
seasoning (condiment)	krydderi (n)	[kʁyðə'ʁi:]
spice	krydderi (n)	[kʁyðə'ʁi:]
sauce	sovs (c)	['sɒws]
vinegar	eddike (c)	['ɛðikə]
anise	anis (c)	['anis]
basil	basilikum (c)	[ba'silikɒm]
cloves	nellike (c)	['nelikə]
ginger	ingefær (c)	['eŋəfɛɒ]
coriander	koriander (c)	[kɒi'andʌ]
cinnamon	kanel (n, c)	[ka'ne:l]
sesame	sesam (c)	[se:'sɑm]
bay leaf	laurbærblad (n)	['lɑwʌbæɒ ˌblað]
paprika	paprika (c)	['pɑpʁika]
caraway	kommen (c)	['kɒmən]
saffron	safran (c)	['sɑfʁɑn]

51. Meals

food (noun)	mad (c)	[mað]
to eat (vi, vt)	at spise	[at 'sbi:sə]
breakfast	morgenmad (c)	['mɒːɒnˌmað]
to have breakfast	at spise morgenmad	[at 'sbi:sə 'mɒːɒnˌmað]
lunch	frokost (c)	['fʁokɒsd]
to have lunch	at spise frokost	[at 'sbi:sə 'fʁɔkʌsd]

dinner (evening meal)	**aftensmad** (c)	['ɑfdənsmɑð]
to have dinner	**at spise aftensmad**	[at 'sbi:sə 'ɑfdəns‚mɑð]
appetite	**appetit** (c)	[ɑbə'tid]
Enjoy your meal!	**Velbekomme!**	['vɛlbə'kʌmə]
to open (e.g., ~ a bottle)	**at åbne**	[at 'ɔ:bnə]
to spill (liquid)	**at spilde**	[at 'sbilə]
to spill out (vi)	**at spildes**	[at 'sbiləs]
to boil (vi)	**at koge**	[at 'kɔ:uə]
to boil (vt)	**at give et opkog**	[at gi: ed 'ɒbkɔu]
boiled	**kogt**	[kɒgd]
to cool (vt)	**at afkøle**	[at ɑu'kø:lə]
to cool down (vi)	**at afkøles**	[at ɑu'kø:ləs]
taste, flavor	**smag** (c)	['smæj]
aftertaste	**bismag** (c)	['bismæ:]
to be on a diet	**at tabe sig**	[at 'tæ:bə sɑj]
diet	**diæt** (c)	[di'ɛ:d]
vitamin	**vitamin** (n)	[vita'mi:n]
calorie	**kalorie** (c)	[ka'lo:ʁiə]
vegetarian (noun)	**vegetar** (c)	[vegə'tɑ:]
vegetarian (adj)	**vegetar-**	[vegə'tɑ:]
fats (nutrient)	**fedt** (c)	[fed]
proteins	**proteiner** (pl)	[pʁote'i:nʌ]
carbohydrates	**kulhydrater** (pl)	['kɔlhy‚dʁɑ:dʌ]
slice (of lemon, ham)	**skive** (c)	['ski:və]
piece (of cake, pie)	**stykke** (n)	['sdøkə]
crumb (of bread)	**krumme** (c)	['kʁɔmə]

52. Table setting

spoon	**ske** (c)	[ske:]
knife	**kniv** (c)	['kniu]
fork	**gaffel** (c)	['gɑfəl]
cup (of coffee)	**kop** (c)	[kɒb]
dinner plate	**tallerken** (c)	[ta'læʁkən]
saucer	**underkop** (c)	['ɔnɒkɒb]
napkin (on table)	**serviet** (c)	[sæɒvi'ɛd]
toothpick	**tandstikker** (c)	['tan‚sdekʌ]

53. Restaurant

restaurant	**restaurant** (c)	[ʁɛsdo'ʁɑŋ]
café	**cafe** (c)	[ka'fe]

coffee house	**kaffebar** (c)	['kɑfə,bɑː]
pub, bar	**bar** (c)	[bɑː]
tearoom	**tesalon** (c)	['tɛ sa'lʌŋ]

waiter	**tjener** (c)	['tjɛːnʌ]
waitress	**servitrice** (c)	[saɒviʼtʁiːsə]
bartender	**bartender** (c)	['bɑː,tɛndʌ]

menu	**menu** (c), **menukort** (n)	[meʼny], [meʼny,kɒːd]
wine list	**vinkort** (n)	['ven,kɒɒd]
to book a table	**at bestille et bord**	[at besdelə ed 'boɒ]

course, dish	**ret** (c), **anretning** (c)	[ʁad], ['an,ʁadneŋ]
to order (meal)	**at bestille**	[at beʼsdelə]
to make an order	**at bestille**	[at beʼsdelə]
aperitif	**aperitif** (c)	[æːbʁiʼtef]
appetizer	**forret** (c)	['foʁað]
dessert	**dessert** (c)	[dɛʼsɛɒd]

check	**regning** (c)	['ʁɑjneŋ]
to pay the check	**at betale**	[at beʼtæːlə]
to give change	**at give penge tilbage**	[at giː ʼpɛŋə teʼbæːjə]
tip	**drikkepenge** (pl)	['dʁɛgə,pɛŋə]

Family, relatives and friends

54. Personal information. Forms

name, first name	**navn** (n)	['nɑun]
family name	**efternavn** (n)	['ɛfdɒ‚nɑun]
date of birth	**fødselsdato** (c)	['føsəls‚dæ:to]
place of birth	**fødested** (n)	['fø:ðəsdɛð]
nationality	**nationalitet** (c)	[naɕonali'te:d]
place of residence	**bopæl** (n)	[bo'pɛ:l]
country	**land** (n)	[lan]
profession (occupation)	**fag** (n)	['fæj]
gender, sex	**køn** (n)	[kœn]
height	**højde** (c)	['hɒjdə]
weight	**vægt** (c)	[vɛgd]

55. Family members. Relatives

mother	**mor** (c), **moder** (c)	['moʌ], ['mo:ðʌ]
father	**far** (c), **fader** (c)	[fɑ:], ['fæ:ðʌ]
son	**søn** (c)	[sœn]
daughter	**datter** (c)	['dadʌ]
younger daughter	**yngste datter** (c)	['øŋsdə 'dadʌ]
younger son	**yngste søn** (c)	['øŋsdə sœn]
elder daughter	**ældste datter** (c)	['ɛlsdə 'dadʌ]
elder son	**ældste søn** (c)	['ɛlsdə sœn]
brother	**bror** (c)	[bʁɒɒ]
sister	**søster** (c)	['søsdʌ]
cousin (masc.)	**fætter** (c)	['fɛdʌ]
cousin (fem.)	**kusine** (c)	[ku'si:nə]
mom	**mor** (c)	['moɒ]
dad, daddy	**far** (c)	[fɑ:]
parents	**forældre** (pl)	[fɒ'ɛldʁɒ]
child (boy or girl)	**barn** (n)	[bɑ:n]
children	**børn** (pl)	['bœɒn]
grandmother	**bedstemor** (c)	['bɛsdə‚moɒ]
grandfather	**bedstefar** (c)	['bɛsdə‚fɑ:]
grandson	**barnebarn** (n)	['bɑ:nə‚bɑ:n]

granddaughter	**barnebarn** (n)	['bɑːnəˌbɑːn]
grandchildren	**børnebørn** (pl)	['bœɒnəˌbœɒn]
uncle	**onkel** (c)	['ɔŋkəl]
nephew	**nevø** (c)	[ne'vø]
niece	**niece** (c)	[ni'ɛːsə]
mother-in-law	**svigermor** (c)	['sviːɒˌmoɒ]
father-in-law	**svigerfar** (c)	['sviːɒˌfɑː]
son-in-law	**svigersøn** (c)	['sviːɒˌsœn]
stepmother	**stedmor** (c)	['sdɛðˌmoɒ]
stepfather	**stedfar** (c)	['sdɛðˌfɑː]
baby (infant)	**spædbarn** (n)	['sbɛðˌbɑːn]
infant	**spædbarn** (n)	['sbɛðˌbɑːn]
little boy, kid	**lille barn** (n)	['lilə bɑːn]
wife	**kone** (c)	['koːnə]
husband	**ægtemand** (c)	[ɛgdə'man]
spouse (husband)	**ægtemand** (c)	[ɛgdə'man]
spouse (wife)	**hustru** (c)	['husdʁu]
married (man)	**gift**	[gifd]
married (woman)	**gift**	[gifd]
single (unmarried)	**ugift**	['uˌgifd]
bachelor	**ungkarl** (c)	['ɔŋkæːl]
divorced (man)	**fraskilt**	['fʁɑsˌkeld]
widow	**enke** (c)	['ɛŋkə]
widower	**enkemand** (c)	['ɛŋkəˌman]
relative	**slægtning** (c)	['slɛgdneŋ]
close relative	**nær slægtning** (c)	[nɛɒ 'slɛgdneŋ]
distant relative	**fjern slægtning** (c)	['fjaɒn 'slɛgdneŋ]
relatives	**slægtninge** (pl)	['slɛgdneŋə]
orphan (boy or girl)	**forældreløst barn** (n)	[fɒˈɛldʁəløːsd bɑːn]
guardian (of minor)	**formynder** (c)	[fɒːˈmønʌ]
to adopt (a boy)	**at adoptere**	[at adɒbˈteːɒ]
to adopt (a girl)	**at adoptere**	[at adɒbˈteːɒ]

56. Friends. Coworkers

friend (man)	**ven** (c)	[vɛn]
friend (girlfriend)	**veninde** (c)	[vɛˈnenə]
friendship	**venskab** (n)	['vɛnskæːb]
to be friends	**at være venner**	[at 'vɛːɒ vɛnɒ]
buddy (man)	**ven** (c)	[vɛn]
buddy (woman)	**veninde** (c)	[vɛˈnenə]
comrade (politics)	**kammerat** (c)	[kɑməˈʁɑːd]

| partner | **partner** (c) | ['pɑːdnʌ] |
| business partner | **samarbejdspartner** (c) | ['sɑmɑbɑjds̩pɑːdnʌ] |

chief (boss)	**chef** (c)	[ɕɛːf]
boss, superior	**chef** (c)	[ɕɛːf]
subordinate	**underordnet** (c)	['ɔnɒˌɒːdnəð]
colleague	**kollega** (c)	[ko'leːga]

acquaintance (person)	**bekendt** (c)	[bekɛnd]
fellow traveler	**medrejsende** (c)	['mɛðˌʁɑjsənə]
classmate	**skolekammerat** (c)	['skoːlə kɑməˈʁɑːd]

neighbor (man)	**nabo** (c)	['næːbo]
neighbor (woman)	**naboerske** (c)	['næːboːɒskə]
neighbors	**naboer** (pl)	['næːboːʌ]

57. Man. Woman

woman	**kvinde** (c)	['kvenə]
girl (young woman)	**pige** (c)	['piːə]
bride	**brud** (c)	[bʁuð]

beautiful	**skøn**	[skœn]
tall	**høj**	[hɒj]
slender	**slank**	['slɑŋk]
short	**ikke ret høj**	['ekə ʁat hɒj]

| blonde (noun) | **lyshåret kvinde** (c) | ['lysˌhɒːɒð kvenə] |
| brunette (noun) | **mørkhåret kvinde** (c) | ['mœɒkhɒːɒð 'kvenə] |

ladies'	**dame-**	['dæːmə]
virgin (girl)	**jomfru** (c)	['jʌmfʁu]
pregnant	**gravid**	[gʁɑˈvið]

man (adult male)	**mand** (c)	[man]
blond (noun)	**lyshåret mand** (c)	['lysˌhɒːɒð man]
brunet (noun)	**mørkhåret mand** (c)	['mœɒkhɒːɒð man]
tall	**høj**	[hɒj]
short	**ikke ret høj**	['ekə ʁat hɒj]

rude (rough)	**grov**	['gʁɒu]
stocky	**tætbygget**	['tɛdˌbygəð]
robust	**fast**	[fasd]
strong	**kraftig**	['kʁɑfdi]
strength (physical power)	**kraft** (c)	[kʁɑfd]

stout, fat	**tyk**	[tyk]
swarthy	**mørklødet**	['mœɒklɒːðət]
well-built	**slank**	['slɑŋk]
elegant	**elegant**	[eleˈgand]

58. Age

age	**alder** (c)	['alʌ]
youth (young age)	**ungdom** (c)	['ɔŋdɒm]
young	**ung**	[ɔŋ]
younger	**yngre**	['øŋʁʌ]
older	**ældre**	['ɛldʁɒ]
young man	**ung mand** (c)	['ɔŋ man]
teenager	**teenager** (c)	['ti:n‚ɛjdɕʌ]
guy, fellow	**fyr** (c)	[fyɒ]
old man	**gamling** (c)	['gɑmleŋ]
old woman	**gammel dame** (c)	['gɑməl 'dæ:mə]
adult	**voksen** (c)	['vɒksən]
middle-aged	**midaldrende**	['miδ‚alʁʌnə]
elderly	**ældre**	['ɛldʁɒ]
old	**gammel**	['gɑməl]
to retire (from job)	**at gå på pension**	[at gɔ: pɔ pɑŋ'ɕon]
retiree	**pensionist** (c)	[pɑŋɕo'nisd]

59. Children

child (boy or girl)	**barn** (n)	[bɑ:n]
children	**børn** (pl)	['bœɒn]
twins	**tvillinger** (c)	['tvileŋʌ]
cradle (for baby)	**vugge** (c)	['vɔgə]
rattle (for baby)	**rangle** (c)	['ʁɑŋlə]
diaper	**ble** (c)	[ble:]
pacifier	**sut** (c)	[sud]
baby carriage	**barnevogn** (c)	['bɑ:nə‚vɒwn]
kindergarten	**børnehave** (c)	['bœɒnə‚hæ:uə]
babysitter	**barnepige** (c)	['bɑ:nə‚pi:ə]
childhood	**barndom** (c)	['bɑ:n‚dɒm]
doll	**dukke** (c)	['dɔkə]
toy	**legetøj** (n)	['lɑjə‚tɒj]
construction set	**byggelegetøj** (n)	['bygəlɑjə‚tɒj]
well-bred	**velopdragen**	['vɛlʌb‚dʁɑwən]
ill-bred	**uopdragen**	[uʌb'dʁɑwən]
spoiled	**forkælet**	[fɒ'kɛ:ləð]
to be naughty	**at være fræk**	[at 'vɛ:ɒ fʁak]
naughty	**overstadig**	['ɒwʌ‚sdæði]

| naughtiness | kådhed (c) | ['kɒðheð] |
| naughty boy | spilopmager (c) | [sbi'lʌb‚mæjʌ] |

| obedient | artig | ['ɑdi] |
| disobedient | opsætsig | [ʌb'sɛdsi] |

docile	fornuftig	[fɒ'nɔfdi]
clever (smart)	klog	['klɔu]
child prodigy	vidunderbarn (n)	['viðɒnɒ‚bɑ:n]

60. Married couples. Family life

family (noun)	familie (c)	[fa'miljə]
family (attr)	familie-	[fa'miljə]
couple	par (n)	['pɑ]
marriage (state)	ægteskab (n)	['ɛgdəsgæ:b]
hearth (home)	hjemmets arne (c)	['jɛmeðs 'ɑ:nə]
dynasty	dynasti (n)	[dynas'di:]

| date | stævnemøde (n) | ['sdɛwnə‚mø:ðə] |
| kiss | kys (n) | [køs] |

love (for sb)	kærlighed (c)	['kɑɒli‚heð]
to love (sb)	at elske	[at 'ɛlskə]
beloved	elskede	['ɛlskəðə]

tenderness	ømhed (c)	['œmheð]
tender (affectionate)	blid	[blið]
faithfulness	troskab (n)	['tʁoskæ:b]
faithful	trofast	['tʁofasd]
care (attention)	omsorg (c)	[ʌm'sɒ:u]
caring (thoughtful)	omsorgsfuld	['ʌmsɒwsful]

newlyweds	de nygifte	[di 'ny‚gifdə]
honeymoon	hvedebrødsdage (pl)	['ve‚ðəbʁœðs‚dæ:ə]
to get married (woman)	at gifte sig	[at 'gifdə sɑj]
to get married (man)	at gifte sig	[at 'gifdə sɑj]

wedding	bryllup (n)	['bʁœlʌb]
golden wedding	guldbryllup (n)	['gul‚bʁœlɒb]
anniversary	årsdag (c)	['ɒ:s‚dæ]

| lover (man) | elsker (c) | ['ɛlskʌ] |
| mistress | elskerinde (c) | [ɛlskʌ'enə] |

adultery	utroskab (n)	['utʁo‚skæb]
to commit adultery	at svigte	[at 'svegdə]
jealous (fearful of rivals)	jaloux	[ɕa'lu]
to be jealous	at være jaloux	[at 'vɛ:ɒ ɕa'lu]
divorce	skilsmisse (c)	['skels‚misə]

to divorce (vi)	**at blive skilt**	[at 'bliːə skeld]
to quarrel (vi)	**at skændes**	[at 'skɛnəs]
to become reconciled	**at blive venner igen**	[at 'bliːə 'vɛnɒ i'gɛn]
together	**sammen**	['samən]
sex (sexual activity)	**sex** (c)	[sɛs]
happiness	**lykke** (c)	['løkə]
happy	**lykkelig**	['løgəli]
misfortune (accident)	**ulykke** (n)	['uˌløkə]
unhappy	**stakkels**	['sdɑkəls]

Character. Feelings. Emotions

61. Feelings. Emotions

feeling (emotion)	**følelse** (c)	['føːləlsə]
feelings	**følelser** (pl)	['føːləlsʌ]
to feel (vt)	**at føle**	[at 'føːlə]
hunger	**sult** (c)	[suld]
to be hungry	**at være sulten**	[at 'vɛːɒ 'suldən]
thirst	**tørst** (c)	['tœɒsd]
to be thirsty	**at være tørstig**	[at 'vɛːɒ 'tœɒsdi]
sleepiness	**søvnighed** (c)	['sɶwniˌheð]
to feel sleepy	**at være søvnig**	[at 'vɛːɒ 'sɶuni]
tiredness	**træthed** (c)	['tʁadˌheð]
tired	**træt**	[tʁad]
to get tired	**at være træt**	[at 'vɛːɒ tʁat]
mood (humor)	**stemning** (c)	['sdɛmneŋ]
boredom	**kedsomhed** (c)	['keðsɒmˌheð]
to be bored	**at kede sig**	[at 'keːðə sɑj]
seclusion	**ensomhed** (c)	['eːnsɒmheð]
to seclude oneself	**at isolere sig**	[at iso'leːɒ sɑj]
to worry (make anxious)	**at bekymre**	[at be'kømɒ]
to be worried	**at bekymre sig**	[at be'kømɒ sɑj]
anxiety	**bekymring** (c)	[be'kømʁɛŋ]
preoccupied	**bekymret**	[be'kømʁʌð]
to be nervous	**at være nervøs**	[at 'vɛːɒ nɑɒ'vøːs]
to panic (vi)	**at skabe panik**	[at 'skæːbə pa'nik]
hope	**håb** (n)	[hɔːb]
to hope (vi, vt)	**at håbe**	[at 'hɔːbə]
certainty	**sikkerhed** (c)	['sekʌˌheð]
certain, sure	**sikker**	['sekɒ]
uncertainty	**usikkerhed** (c)	['usekɒˌheð]
uncertain	**usikker**	['uˌsekʌ]
drunk	**fuld**	[ful]
sober	**ædru**	['ɛːdʁuː]
weak	**svag**	[svæː]
lucky	**heldig**	['hɛldi]
to scare (vt)	**at forskrække**	[at fʌ'skʁakə]
fury (madness)	**raseri** (n)	[ʁɑsə'ʁiː]

rage (fury)	**galskab** (n)	['galsgæ:b]
depression	**depression** (c)	[depʁɛ'ɕɔn]
discomfort (unease)	**ubehag** (n)	['ubeˌhæj]
comfort	**komfort** (c)	[kʌm'fɔ:], [kʌm'fɒ:d]
to regret (be sorry)	**at fortryde**	[at fʌ'tʁyðə]
regret	**beklagelse** (c)	[be'klæ:əlsə]
bad luck	**uheld** (n)	['uˌhɛl]
sadness	**bekymring** (c)	[be'kømʁɛŋ]
shame (feeling)	**skam** (c)	[skɑm]
merriment	**munterhed** (c)	['mɔndɒheð]
enthusiasm	**entusiasme** (c)	[ɑŋtu'ɕasmə]
enthusiast	**entusiast** (c)	[ɑŋtu'ɕasd]
to show enthusiasm	**at vise begejstring**	[at 'vi:sə be'gɑjsdʁɛŋ]

62. Character. Personality

character	**karakter** (c)	[kɑɑk'teʌ]
character flaw	**mangel** (c)	['mɑŋəl]
mind (intellect)	**fornuft** (c)	[fɒ'nɔfd]
conscience	**samvittighed** (c)	['sɑmˌvidiheð]
habit (custom)	**vane** (c)	['væ:nə]
ability	**evne** (c)	['ɛunə]
can (e.g., ~ swim)	**kunne**	['kunə]
patient	**tålmodig**	[tʌl'moði]
impatient	**utålmodig**	[utʌl'moði]
curious (inquisitive)	**nysgerrig**	['nysˌgɑɒi]
curiosity	**nysgerrighed** (c)	['nysˌgɑɒiheð]
modesty	**beskedenhed** (c)	[be'ske:ðənheð]
modest	**beskeden**	[be'ske:ðən]
immodest	**ubeskeden**	['ubeˌske:ðən]
lazy	**doven**	['dɒuən]
lazy person (masc.)	**dovenkrop** (c)	['dɒuənˌkʁɒb]
cunning (noun)	**list** (c)	[lesd]
cunning (attr)	**listig**	['lesdi]
distrust	**mistillid** (c)	['misteˌlið]
distrustful	**mistroisk**	['misˌtʁoisk]
generosity	**gavmildhed** (c)	['gɑumilˌheð]
generous	**gavmild**	['gɑumil]
talented	**begavet**	[be'gæ:uəð]
talent	**talent** (n)	[ta'lɛnd]
courageous	**dristig**	['dʁɛsdi]
courage	**dristighed** (c)	['dʁɛsdiheð]

| honest | **ærlig** | ['aɒli] |
| honesty | **ærlighed** (c) | ['aɒliheð] |

careful (cautious)	**forsigtig**	[fɒ'segdi]
brave	**dristig**	['dʁɛsdi]
serious	**seriøs**	[seɒi'øːs]
strict (severe, stern)	**streng**	[sdʁaŋ]

determined (resolute)	**fast**	[fasd]
indecisive	**ubeslutsom**	['ube͜sludsɒm]
shy, timid	**genert**	[ɕe'neɒd]
shyness, timidity	**generthed** (c)	[ɕe'neɒd͜heð]

trust (confidence)	**tillid** (c)	['te͜lið]
to trust (vt)	**at stole på**	[at 'sdoːlə pɒ]
trusting (naïve)	**tillidsfuld**	['te͜liðsful]

sincerely	**oprigtigt**	[ʌb'ʁɛgdid]
sincere	**oprigtig**	[ʌb'ʁɛgdi]
sincerity	**oprigtighed** (c)	[ʌb'ʁɛgdiheð]

calm	**rolig**	['ʁoːli]
frank, sincere	**åbenhjertig**	[ɔːbən'jaɒdi]
naive	**naiv**	[na'iu]
absent-minded	**fraværende**	[fʁɑ'vɛːɒnə]
funny (amusing)	**morsom**	['moɒsɒm]

greed	**grådighed** (c)	['gʁɔːðiheð]
greedy	**grådig**	['gʁɔːði]
evil	**vred**	[vʁɛð]
stubborn	**stædig**	['sdɛːði]
unpleasant (person)	**ærgerlig**	['aɒɒli]

selfish person (masc.)	**egoist** (c)	[ego'isd]
selfish	**egoistisk**	[ego'isdisg]
coward	**bangebuks** (c)	['baŋəbɒgs]
cowardly	**frygtsom**	['fʁɶgdsɒm]

63. Sleep. Dreams

to sleep (vi)	**at sove**	[at 'sɒwə]
sleep, sleeping	**søvn** (c)	['sɶwn]
dream	**drøm** (c)	[dʁɶm]
to dream (in sleep)	**at drømme**	[at 'dʁɶmə]
sleepy (person)	**søvnig**	['sɶwni]

bed	**seng** (c)	[sɛŋ]
mattress	**madras** (c)	[ma'dʁɑs]
blanket (e.g., comforter)	**tæppe** (n)	['tɛbə]
pillow	**pude** (c)	['puːðə]

sheet (for bed)	**lagen** (n)	['læ:ən]
insomnia	**søvnløshed** (c)	['sœwnløsˌheð]
sleepless	**søvnløs**	['sœwnˌløːs]
sleeping pill	**sovemiddel** (n)	['sɒweˌmiðəl]
to take a sleeping pill	**at tage en sovepille**	[at 'tæːə en 'sɒuəˌpelə]

to feel sleepy	**at være søvnig**	[at 'vɛːɒ 'sœuni]
to yawn (vi)	**at gabe**	[at 'gæːbə]
to go to bed	**at gå i seng**	[at gɔː i sɛŋ]
to make up the bed	**at rede sengen**	[at 'ʁɛːðe 'sɛŋən]
to fall asleep	**at falde i søvn**	[at 'falə i sœun]

nightmare	**mareridt** (n)	['mɑːɑˌʁid]
snoring	**snorken** (c)	['snɒːkən]
to snore (vi)	**at snorke**	[at 'snɒːkə]

alarm clock	**vækkeur** (n)	['vɛkəˌuɒ]
to wake (vt)	**at vække**	[at 'vɛkə]
to wake up (vi)	**at vågne op**	[at 'vɔunə ɒb]
to get up (vi)	**at stå op**	[at sdɔː ɒb]
to wash up (vi)	**at vaske sig**	[at 'vasgə sɑj]

64. Humour. Laughter. Gladness

humor (wit, fun)	**humor** (c)	['huːmɒ]
sense (of humor)	**humorsans** (c)	['huːmɒɒˌsans]
to have fun	**at more sig**	[at 'moːɒ sɑj]
merry, cheerful	**munter**	['mɔndɒ]
merriment	**sjov** (n)	['ɕɒw]

smile	**smil** (n)	[smiːl]
to smile (vi)	**at smile**	[at 'smiːlə]
to start laughing	**at bryde ud i latter**	[at 'bʁyðə uð i 'ladʌ]
to laugh (vi)	**at grine**	[at 'gʁiːnə]
laugh, laughter	**latter** (c)	['ladʌ]
anecdote	**anekdote** (c)	[anɛk'doːdə]
funny (amusing)	**sjov**	['ɕɒw]
funny (odd)	**sjov**	['ɕɒw]
to joke (vi)	**at spøge**	[at 'sbøːjə]
joke (verbal)	**sjov** (n)	['ɕɒw]
joy (such a ~)	**glæde** (c)	['glɛːðə]
to be glad	**at glæde sig**	[at 'glɛːðə sɑj]
glad, cheerful	**glad**	[glað]

65. Discussion, conversation. Part 1

| communication | **omgang** (c) | ['ʌmˌgɑŋ] |
| to communicate | **at omgås** | [at ɒm'gɔːs] |

conversation	**samtale** (c)	['sɑmˌtæːlə]
dialog	**dialog** (c)	[diaˈloː]
discussion (debate)	**diskussion** (c)	[diskuˈɕoːn]
debate	**debatter** (c)	[deˈbadʌ]
to debate (vi)	**at diskutere**	[at diskuˈteːɒ]
interlocutor	**samtalepartner** (c)	['sɑmˌtæːlə ˈpɑːdnʌ]
topic (theme)	**emne** (n)	['ɛmnə]
point of view	**synspunkt** (n)	['syːnsˌpɔŋd]
opinion (viewpoint)	**mening** (c)	['meːnen]
speech (talk)	**tale** (c)	['tæːlə]
discussion (of report etc.)	**drøftelse** (c)	['dʁœfdəlsə]
to discuss (proposal etc.)	**at drøfte**	[at 'dʁœfdə]
talk (conversation)	**samtale** (c)	['sɑmˌtæːlə]
to talk (vi)	**at tale sammen**	[at 'tæːlə 'sɑmən]
meeting	**møde** (n)	['møːðə]
to meet (vi, vt)	**at mødes**	[at 'møːðəs]
proverb	**ordsprog** (n)	['oɒˌsbʁou]
saying	**talemåde** (n)	['tæːləˌmɔːðə]
riddle (poser)	**gåde** (c)	['gɔːðə]
to ask a riddle	**at lave en gåde**	[at 'læːuə en 'gɔːðə]
password	**kodeord** (n)	['koːðəˌoɒ]
secret	**hemmelighed** (c)	['hɛməliˌheð]
oath (vow)	**ed** (c)	[eð]
to swear (an oath)	**at sværge (på ...)**	[at 'svɑɒuə pɔ]
promise	**løfte** (n)	['løfdə]
to promise (vt)	**at love**	[at 'lɔːuə]
advice (counsel)	**råd** (n)	[ʁɔð]
to advise (vt)	**at råde**	[at 'ʁɔːðə]
to listen (vi)	**at lytte til ... råd**	[at 'lydə tel ... ʁɔð]
news	**nyhed** (c)	['nyheð]
sensation (news)	**sensation** (c)	[sɛnsaˈɕoːn]
information (facts)	**oplysninger** (pl)	['ʌblyːsnenʌ]
conclusion (decision)	**konklusion** (c)	[kʌŋkluˈɕoːn]
voice	**stemme** (c)	['sdɛmə]
compliment	**kompliment** (c)	[kɒmpliˈmɑnd]
kind (nice)	**venlig**	['vɛnli]
word	**ord** (n)	['oɒ]
phrase	**frase** (c)	['fʁɑːsə]
answer	**svar** (n)	[svɑː]
response	**svar** (n)	[svɑː]
truth (true facts)	**sandhed** (c)	['sanheð]
lie (untruth)	**løgn** (c)	['lɔjn]
thought	**tanke** (c)	['tɑŋkə]
idea (plan, inspiration)	**ide** (c)	[iˈdeː]
fantasy	**fantasi** (c)	[fantaˈsiː]

66. Discussion, conversation. Part 2

respected	æret	[ˈɛːɒð]
to respect (vt)	at agte	[at ˈɑgdə]
respect	agtelse (c)	[ˈɑgdəlsə]
Dear ...	Ærede ...	[ˈɛːɒðə ...]
to introduce (present)	at gøre bekendt	[at ˈgœːɒ beˈkɛnd]
intention	hensigt (c)	[ˈhɛnsegd]
to intend (have in mind)	at have i sinde	[at ˈhæːvə i ˈsenə]
wish	ønske (n)	[ˈønskə]
to wish (~ good luck)	at ønske	[at ˈønskə]
surprise (astonishment)	forbavselse (c)	[fʌˈbɑwsəlsə]
to surprise (amaze)	at forundre	[at fʌˈɔndʁʌ]
to be surprised	at blive forbavset	[at ˈbliːə foˈbɑusəð]
to give (vt)	at give	[at giː]
to take (get hold of)	at tage	[at ˈtæːə]
to give back (vt)	at returnere	[at ʁɛtuɒˈneːɒ]
to return (give back)	at aflevere	[at ˈɑuleˌveːɒ]
to apologize (vi)	at undskylde sig	[at ˈɔnˌsgylə saj]
apology	undskyldning (c)	[ˈɔnˌsgylneŋ]
to forgive (vt)	at tilgive	[at ˈtelˌgiuə]
to talk (speak)	at tale sammen	[at ˈtæːlə ˈsɑmən]
to listen (vi)	at lytte	[at ˈlydə]
to hear sb out	at lytte efter	[at ˈlydə ˈɛfdɒ]
to understand (vt)	at forstå	[at fʌˈsdɔː]
to show (display)	at vise	[at ˈviːsə]
to look at ...	at kigge på ...	[at ˈkigə pɔ]
to call (with one's voice)	at kalde	[at ˈkalə]
to disturb (vt)	at forstyrre	[at fʌˈsdyɒɒ]
to pass (to hand sth)	at overrække	[at ɒuɒˈʁakə]
request (demand)	anmodning (c)	[ˈanˌmoðneŋ]
to request (ask)	at bede om	[at ˈbeːðə ɒm]
demand (firm request)	krav (n)	[ˈkʁɑːu]
to demand (request firmly)	at kræve	[at ˈkʁɛːuə]
to tease sb	at drille	[at ˈdʁɛlə]
to mock (deride)	at håne, at spotte	[at ˈhɔːnə], [at ˈsbʌdə]
mockery, derision	spot (c)	[sbɒd]
nickname	øgenavn (n)	[ˈøːəˌnɑun]
hint (indirect suggestion)	antydning (c)	[ˈanˌtyðneŋ]
to hint (vi)	at antyde	[at anˈtyðə]
to mean (what do you ~ ?)	at mene	[at ˈmeːnə]
description	beskrivelse (c)	[beˈskʁiːuəlsə]

to describe (vt)	**at beskrive**	[at be'skʁiuə]
praise (compliments)	**ros** (c)	[ʁoːs]
to praise (vt)	**at rose**	[at 'ʁoːsə]

disappointment	**skuffelse** (c)	['skɔfəlsə]
to disappoint (vt)	**at skuffe**	[at 'skɔfə]
to be disappointed	**at blive skuffet**	[at 'bliːə 'skɔfəð]

supposition	**formodning** (c)	[fɔ'moðnen]
to suppose (assume)	**at forudsætte**	[at fʌ:uð'sɛdə]
warning (caution)	**advarsel** (n)	[að'vɑːsəl]
to warn	**at advare**	[at að'vɑːɑ]

67. Discussion, conversation. Part 3

| to talk into (persuade) | **at overtale** | [at 'ɒuɒˌtæːlə] |
| to calm down (vt) | **at berolige** | [at be'ʁoːliə] |

silence (~ is golden)	**tavshed** (c)	['tɑwsˌheð]
to keep silent	**at tie**	[at 'tiːə]
to whisper (vt)	**at hviske**	[at 'veskə]
whisper	**hvisken** (c)	['veskən]

| frankly, sincerely | **åbenhjertigt** | [ɔːbən'jɑɒdid] |
| in my opinion … | **efter min mening ...** | ['ɛfdɒ min 'meːnen] |

detail (of the story)	**detalje** (c)	[de'taljə]
detailed	**omstændelig**	[ʌm'sdɛnəli]
in detail	**i detaljer**	[i de'taljə]

| hint, clue | **hint** (n) | [hend] |
| to give a hint | **at give et hint** | [at giː ed hend] |

look (glance)	**blik** (n)	[blek]
to have a look	**at kaste et blik**	[at 'kasdə ed blek]
fixed (look)	**stift**	[sdifd]
to blink (vi)	**at blinke**	[at 'blenkə]
to wink (vi)	**at blinke**	[at 'blenkə]
to nod (in assent)	**at nikke**	[at 'nekə]

sigh	**suk** (n)	[sɔk]
to sigh (vi)	**at sukke**	[at 'sɔkə]
to shudder (vi)	**at skælve**	[at 'skɛlvə]
gesture	**gestus** (c)	['gesdus]
to touch (one's arm etc.)	**at røre**	[at 'ʁœːɒ]
to seize (by the arm)	**at fatte**	[at 'fadə]
to tap (on the shoulder)	**at klappe**	[at 'klɑbə]

| Look out! | **Pas på!** | [pas 'pɔ] |
| Really? | **Virkelig?** | ['viɒgəli] |

Are you sure?	**Er du sikker?**	[aɒ du ˈsekɒ]
Good luck!	**Held og lykke!**	[hɛl ɒu ˈløɡə]
I see!	**Helt klart!**	[hɛld klɑːd]
It's a pity!	**Det var synd!**	[de vɑ søn]

68. Agreement. Refusal

agreement	**samtykke** (n)	[ˈsɑmˌtykə]
to agree (say yes)	**at enes**	[at ˈeːnəs]
approval	**godkendelse** (c)	[ɡoðˈkɛnəlsə]
to approve (vt)	**at godkende**	[at ɡoðˈkɛnə]
refusal	**afslag** (n)	[ɑuˈslæː]
to refuse (vi, vt)	**at afslå**	[at ɑuˈslɔː]

Great!	**Fint!**	[fiːnd]
All right!	**Godt nok!**	[ɡɒd nɒɡ]
OK! (I agree)	**OK!**	[ˈoˈkɔ]
That's wrong!	**Det er forkert!**	[de aɒ fɒˈkeɒd]

forbidden	**forbudt**	[fɒːˈbud]
it's forbidden	**forbudt**	[fɒːˈbud]
it's impossible	**umuligt**	[uˈmuːlid]
incorrect (adj)	**fejlagtig**	[ˈfɑjlˌɑɡdi]

to reject (~ a demand)	**at afvise**	[at ɑuˈviːsə]
to support (cause, idea)	**at støtte**	[at ˈsdødə]
to accept (~ an apology)	**at acceptere**	[at ɑɡsɛbˈteːɒ]

to confirm (vt)	**at bekræfte**	[at beˈkʁafdə]
confirmation	**bekræftelse** (c)	[beˈkʁafdəlsə]
permission	**lov** (c)	[ˈlɒw]
to permit (allow)	**at tillade**	[at ˈteˌlæðə]
decision	**beslutning** (c)	[beˈsludnəŋ]
to say nothing	**at tie stille**	[at tiːə ˈsdelə]

condition (term)	**betingelse** (c)	[beˈteŋəlsə]
excuse (pretext)	**påskud** (n)	[pɔːˈskuð]
praise (compliments)	**ros** (c)	[ʁoːs]
to praise (vt)	**at rose**	[at ˈʁoːsə]

69. Success. Good luck. Failure

success	**succes** (c)	[syɡˈse]
successfully	**med succes**	[mɛ syɡˈse]
successful	**vellykket**	[ˈvɛlˌløkəð]

| good luck | **held** (n) | [hɛl] |
| Good luck! | **Held og lykke!** | [hɛl ɒu ˈløɡə] |

lucky (e.g., ~ day)	**vellykket**	[ˈvɛlˌløkəð]
lucky (fortunate)	**heldig**	[ˈhɛldi]
failure (lack of success)	**uheld** (n)	[ˈuˌhɛl]
bad luck (failure)	**uheld** (n)	[ˈuˌhɛl]
misfortune (bad luck)	**uheld** (n)	[ˈuˌhɛl]
unsuccessful (attempt)	**uheldig**	[ˈuˌhɛldi]
catastrophe	**katastrofe** (c)	[kataˈsdʁoːfə]
pride	**stolthed** (c)	[ˈsdɒldˌheð]
proud	**stolt**	[sdɒld]
to be proud	**at være stolt**	[at ˈvɛːɒ ˈsdɒld]
winner (of competition)	**sejrherre** (c)	[ˈsɑjʌˌhæːɒ]
to win (vi)	**at sejre**	[at ˈsɑjʁʌ]
to lose (not win)	**at tabe**	[at ˈtæːbə]
try	**forsøg** (n)	[fɒˈsøː]
to try (vi)	**at prøve**	[at ˈpʁœːuə]
chance (opportunity)	**chance** (c)	[ˈɕɑŋsə]

70. Quarrels. Negative emotions

shout (scream)	**skrig** (n)	[sgʁiː]
to shout (vi)	**at råbe**	[at ˈʁoːbə]
to cry out (yell)	**at begynde at skrige**	[at beˈgønə at ˈsgʁiːə]
quarrel	**strid** (c)	[sdʁið]
to quarrel (vi)	**at skændes**	[at ˈskɛnəs]
fight (argument)	**skandale** (c)	[skanˈdæːlə]
to have a fight	**at lave ballade**	[at ˈlæːuə baˈlæːðə]
conflict	**konflikt** (c)	[kʌnˈflikd]
misunderstanding	**misforståelse** (c)	[misfʌˈsdɒəlsə]
insult	**fornærmelse** (c)	[fɒˈnaɒməlsə]
to insult (vt)	**at fornærme**	[at fʌˈnaɒmə]
insulted	**fornærmet**	[fɒˈnaɒməð]
offense (e.g., to take ~)	**fornærmelse** (c)	[fɒˈnaɒməlsə]
to offend (sb)	**at fornærme**	[at fʌˈnaɒmə]
to take offense	**at blive fornærmet**	[at ˈbliːə fɒˈnaɒməð]
indignation	**forargelse** (c)	[fʌˈɑwəlsə]
to be indignant	**at være forarget**	[at ˈvɛːɒ ˈfɒɑːuəð]
complaint	**klage** (c)	[ˈklæːə]
to complain (vi, vt)	**at klage**	[at ˈklæːjə]
apology	**undskyldning** (c)	[ˈɔnˌsgylnen]
to apologize (vi)	**at undskylde sig**	[at ˈɔnˌsgylə sɑj]
to beg pardon	**at bede om undskyldning**	[at ˈbeːðə ɒm ˈɔnˌsgylnen]
criticism	**kritik** (c)	[kʁiˈtik]

to criticize (vt)	at kritisere	[at kʁitiˈseːɒ]
accusation	beskyldning (c)	[beˈsgylneŋ]
to accuse (vt)	at beskylde	[at beˈskylə]
revenge	hævn (c)	[ˈhɛwn]
to avenge (vt)	at hævne	[at ˈhɛunə]
to pay back	at hævne	[at ˈhɛunə]
disdain	foragt (c)	[fɒˈɑgd]
to despise (vt)	at foragte	[at fɒˈɑgdə]
hatred, hate	had (n)	[ha ð]
to hate (vt)	at hade	[at ˈhæːðə]
nervous	nervøs	[næɒˈvøːs]
to be nervous	at være nervøs	[at ˈvɛːɒ naɒˈvøːs]
angry (mad)	vred	[vʁɛ ð]
to make angry	at ærgre	[at ˈæɒwʁʌ]
humiliation	ydmygelse (c)	[ˈyðˌmyəlsə]
to humiliate (vt)	at ydmyge	[at ˈyðˌmyə]
to humiliate oneself	at ydmyge sig	[at ˈyðˌmyə sɑj]
shock	chok (n)	[ɕɒk]
to shock (vt)	at chokere	[at ɕoˈkeɒ]
trouble (e.g., to be in ~)	ærgrelse (c)	[ˈæɒwʁʌlsə]
unpleasant	ærgerlig	[ˈɑɒuɒli]
fear (dread)	angst (c)	[ɑŋsd]
terrible (storm, heat)	frygtelig	[ˈfʁœgdəli]
scary (e.g., ~ story)	forfærdelig	[fɒˈfɑɒdəli]
horror	rædsel (c)	[ˈʁaðsəl]
awful (crime, news)	forfærdelig	[fɒˈfɑɒdəli]
to begin to tremble	at ryste	[at ˈʁœsdə]
to cry (weep)	at græde	[at ˈgʁaðə]
to start crying	at briste i gråd	[at ˈbʁɛsdə i gʁɔð]
tear	tåre (c)	[ˈtɒːɒ]
fault	fejl (n)	[fɑjl]
guilt (feeling)	skyld (c)	[skyl]
disgrace (dishonor)	skam (c)	[skɑm]
protest	protest (c)	[pʁoˈtɛsd]
stress (nervous tension)	stress (n, c)	[sdʁɛs]
to disturb (vt)	at forstyrre	[at fʌˈsdyɒɒ]
to be angry (with ...)	at blive vred (på ...)	[at ˈbliːə vʁɛð pɒ ...]
mad, angry	vred	[vʁɛ ð]
to end (e.g., relationship)	at afbryde	[at ɑuˈbʁyðə]
to be scared	at blive bange	[at ˈbliːə ˈbɑŋə]
to hit (strike with hand)	at slå	[at slɔː]

to fight (vi)	**at slås**	[at slɒs]
to settle (a conflict)	**at regulere**	[at ʁɛgu'leːɒ]
discontented	**utilfreds**	['uteˌfʁɛs]
furious (look)	**rasende**	['ʁɑːsənə]
It's not good!	**Det er ikke godt!**	[de aɒ 'egə 'gɒd]
It's bad!	**Det er dårligt!**	[de aɒ 'dɒːlid]

Medicine

71. Diseases

sickness	**sygdom** (c)	['sy:dɒm]
to be sick	**at være syg**	[at 'vɛ:ɒ sy:]
health	**sundhed** (c)	['sɔn̩heð]
runny nose	**snue** (c)	['snuə]
tonsillitis	**halsbetændelse** (c)	['halsbe̩tɛnəlsə]
cold	**forkølelse** (c)	[fɒ'kø:ləlsə]
to catch a cold	**at blive forkølet**	[at 'bli:ə fɒ'kø:ləð]
bronchitis	**bronkitis** (c)	[bʁɒŋ'kitis]
pneumonia	**lungebetændelse** (c)	['lɔŋəbe̩tɛnəlsə]
flu, influenza	**influenza** (c)	[enflu'ɛnsa]
near-sighted	**nærsynet**	['nɛɒsy:nəð]
far-sighted	**langsynet**	['laŋ̩sy:nəð]
strabismus	**skeløjethed** (c)	['skelʌjəð heð]
cross-eyed	**skeløjet**	['skelʌjəð]
cataract	**katarakt** (c), **stær** (c)	[kata'ʁakd], ['sdɛɒ]
glaucoma	**glaukom** (c)	[glɑu'kɒm]
stroke	**hjerneblødning** (n)	['jæɒnə̩blø:ðnəŋ]
heart attack	**infarkt** (c)	[en'fɑːkd]
myocardial infarction	**hjerteinfarkt** (n, c)	['jæɒdə en'fɑːkd]
paralysis	**lammelse** (c)	['lɑməlsə]
to paralyze (vt)	**at lamme**	[at 'lɑmə]
allergy	**allergi** (c)	[alɑɒ'gi:]
asthma	**astma** (c)	['asdma]
diabetes	**sukkersyge** (c)	['sɔgɒ̩sy:ə]
toothache	**tandpine** (c)	['tan̩pi:nə]
caries	**karies** (c)	['kɑiəs]
diarrhea	**diarre** (c)	[dia'ʁɛ]
constipation	**forstoppelse** (c)	[fʌ'sdʌbəlsə]
stomach upset	**dårlig mave** (c)	[dɒ:li 'mæːuə]
food poisoning	**forgiftning** (c)	[fɒ'gifdnəŋ]
arthritis	**artritis** (c)	[ɑ:'tʁitis]
rickets	**rakitis** (c)	[ʁa'kidis]
rheumatism	**reumatisme** (c)	[ʁʌjma'tismə]
atherosclerosis	**arterieforkalkning** (c)	[ɑ:'teɒi:əfɒ̩kalgnen]

gastritis	gastritis (c)	[ga'sdʁitis]
appendicitis	appendicit (c)	[apɛndi'sid]
cholecystitis	galdeblærebetændelse (c)	['galəblɒbe,tɛnəlsə]
ulcer	sår (n)	['sɒ:]

measles	mæslinger (pl)	['mɛ:slenʌ]
German measles	røde hunde (c)	['ʁɶ:ðə 'hunə]
jaundice	gulsot (c)	['gul,sod]
hepatitis	hepatitis (c)	[heba'tidis]

schizophrenia	skizofreni (c)	[skisofʁɒ'ni:]
hydrophobia, rabies	rabies (c)	['ʁɑ:bjəs]
neurosis	neurose (c)	[nœu'ʁo:sə]
concussion	hjernerystelse (c)	['jæɒnə,ʁɶsdəlsə]

cancer	kræft (c)	[kʁafd]
sclerosis	sklerose (c)	[sklə'ʁo:sə]
multiple sclerosis	dissemineret sklerose (c)	[disemi:'ne:ɒð sklə'ʁo:sə]

alcoholism	alkoholisme (c)	[alkoho'lismə]
alcoholic (noun)	alkoholiker (c)	[alko'ho:likʌ]
syphilis	syfilis (c)	['syfilis]
AIDS	AIDS (c)	[ɛjds]

tumor	svulst (c)	[svulsd]
fever	feber (c)	['fe:bʌ]
malaria	malaria (c)	[ma'lɑ:ia]
gangrene	koldbrand (c)	[kɒl'bʁɑn]
seasickness	søsyge (c)	['sø,sy:ə]
epilepsy	epilepsi (c)	[epi:lə'bsi:]

epidemic	epidemi (c)	[epide'mi:]
typhus	tyfus (c)	['tyfus]
tuberculosis	tuberkuløse (c)	[tu:bæɒku'løs]
cholera	kolera (c)	['ko:ləʁɑ]
plague (bubonic ~)	pest (c)	[pɛsd]

72. Symptoms. Treatments. Part 1

symptom	symptom (n)	[sym'to:m]
temperature	temperatur (c)	[tɛmbəʁɑ'tuɒ]
high temperature	feber (c)	['fe:bʌ]
pulse	puls (c)	[puls]

giddiness	svimmelhed (c)	['sveməl,heð]
hot	febril	[fe'bʁɛl]
shivering	kuldegysning (c)	['kule,gy:sneŋ]
pale (e.g., ~ face)	bleg	['blɑj]
cough	hoste (c)	['ho:sdə]
to cough (vi)	at hoste	[at 'ho:sdə]

to sneeze (vi)	at nyse	[at 'nysə]
faint	besvimelse (c)	[be'svi:məlsə]
to faint (vi)	at besvime	[at be'svi:mə]

bruise	blå mærke (n)	[blɔ: 'mæɒkə]
bump (lump)	bule (c)	['bu:lə]
to bruise oneself	at slå sig på ...	[at slɔ: saj pɔ]
bruise	kvæstelse (c)	['kvɛsdəlsə]
to get bruised	at støde sig	[at 'sdø:ðə saj]

to limp (vi)	at halte	[at 'haldə]
dislocation	forstuvning (c)	[fɒ'sdu:nen]
to dislocate (vt)	at forstuve	[at fʌ'sdu:ə]
fracture	brud (n)	[bʁuð]
to get a fracture	at få et brud	[at fɔ:ed bʁuð]

cut (e.g., on the finger)	snitsår (n)	['snidsɔ:]
to cut oneself	at skære sig	[at 'sgɛ:ɒ saj]
bleeding	blødning (c)	['blø:ðnen]

| burn (injury) | forbrænding (c) | [fɒ'bʁanen] |
| to burn oneself | at brænde sig | [at 'bʁanə saj] |

to prick (vt)	at stikke	[at 'sdekə]
to prick oneself	at stikke sig	[at 'sdegə saj]
to injure (vt)	at skade	[at 'skæ:ðə]
injury	skade (c)	['skæ:ðə]
wound	sår (n)	['sɔ:]
trauma	traume (c)	['tʁawmə]

to be delirious	at tale i vildelse	[at 'tæ:lə i 'vile:lsə]
to stutter (vi)	at stamme	[at 'sdamə]
sunstroke	solstik (n)	['so:lˌsdek]

73. Symptoms. Treatments. Part 2

| pain (physical) | smerte (c) | ['smæɒdə] |
| splinter (in foot, finger) | splint (c) | [sblend] |

sweat (perspiration)	sved (c)	['sveð]
to sweat (perspire)	at svede	[at 'sve:ðə]
vomiting	opkastning (c)	['ʌbkasdnen]
convulsions	kramper (pl)	['kʁambʌ]

pregnant	gravid	[gʁa'við]
to be born	at blive født	[at 'bli:ə fø:d]
delivery, labor	fødsel (c)	['føsəl]
to be in labor	at føde	[at 'fø:ðə]
abortion	abort (c)	[a'bɒ:d]
respiration	åndedrag (n)	['ɒnə'dʁɑ:u]

inhalation	**indånding** (c)	[e'nɒnen]
exhalation	**udånding** (c)	['u̩ðɒnen]
to breathe out	**at udånde**	[at 'uð̩ɒnə]
to breathe in	**at indånde**	[at e'nɒnə]
disabled person	**invalid** (c)	[enva'lið]
cripple	**krøbling** (c)	['kʁœblen]
drug addict	**narkoman** (c)	[nɑko'mæn]
deaf	**døv**	['døu]
dumb	**stum**	[sdɔm]
deaf-and-dumb	**døvstum**	['døw̩sdɔm]
mad, insane	**sindssyg**	['sen̩sy:]
to go insane	**at blive vanvittig**	[at 'bli:ə 'van̩vidi]
gene	**gen** (n)	[ge:n]
immunity	**immunitet** (c)	[imuni'te:d]
hereditary	**arvelig**	['ɑ:uəli]
congenital	**medfødt**	['mɛðfø:d]
virus	**virus** (n, c)	['vi:ʁus]
microbe	**mikrobe** (c)	[mi'kʁo:bə]
· bacterium	**bakterie** (c)	[bɑk'teɒjə]
infection	**infektion** (c)	[enfɛ'kɕo:n]

74. Symptoms. Treatments. Part 3

hospital	**hospital** (n), **sygehus** (n)	[hɔsbi'tæ:l], ['sye̩hu:s]
patient	**patient** (c)	[pa'ɕɛnd]
diagnosis	**diagnose** (c)	[dia'gno:sə]
cure, treatment	**behandling** (c)	[be'hanlen]
treatment	**behandling** (c)	[be'hanlen]
to get treatment	**at lade sig behandle**	[at 'læ:ðə saj be'hanlə]
to treat (vt)	**at pleje**	[at 'plɑjə]
to nurse (look after)	**at pleje**	[at 'plɑjə]
care (treatment)	**pleje** (c)	['plɑjə]
operation, surgery	**operation** (c)	[o:bɐʁa'ɕo:n]
to bandage (head, limb)	**at forbinde**	[at fɒ'benə]
bandaging	**forbinding** (c)	[fɒ'benen]
vaccination	**vaccination** (c)	[vɑgsina'ɕo:n]
to vaccinate (vt)	**at vaccinere**	[at vɑgsi:'ne:ɒ]
injection, shot	**indsprøjtning** (c)	[en'spʁɒjdnen]
to give an injection	**at injicere**	[at enji'seʌ]
attack (of illness, epilepsy)	**anfald** (n)	[an'fal]
amputation	**amputation** (c)	[ɑmputa'ɕo:n]

to amputate (vt)	at amputere	[at ɑmpu'teʌ]
coma	koma (c)	['ko:ma]
to be in a coma	at ligge i koma	[at 'legə i 'ko:ma]
intensive care	genoplivning (c)	[gɛnɒ'bliunen]

to recover (~ from flu)	at blive rask	[at 'bli:ə ʁɑsk]
state (patient's ~)	tilstand (c)	['tel,sdan]
consciousness	bevidsthed (c)	[be'vesdheð]
memory (faculty)	hukommelse (c)	[hu'kʌməlsə]

to extract (tooth)	at trække ... ud	[at 'tʁɑke ... uð]
filling (in tooth)	tandfyldning (c)	['tan,fylnen]
to fill (a tooth)	at plombere	[at plɒm'beɒ]

| hypnosis | hypnose (c) | [hyb'no:sə] |
| to hypnotize (vt) | at hypnotisere | [at hybnoti'se:ɒ] |

75. Doctors

doctor	læge (c)	['lɛ:jə]
nurse (in hospital)	sygeplejerske (c)	['syə,plɒjɒsgə]
private physician	privat læge (c)	[pʁi'væ:d 'lɛ:jə]
children's doctor	børnelæge (c)	['bœɒnə,lɛ:jə]

dentist	tandlæge (c)	['tan,lɛ:jə]
ophthalmologist	øjenlæge (c)	['ɒjən,lɛ:ə]
internist	terapeut (c)	[teɒ'pœwd]
surgeon	kirurg (c)	[ki'ʁuɒw]

psychiatrist	psykiater (c)	[syki'ædʌ]
pediatrician	børnelæge (c)	['bœɒnə,lɛ:jə]
psychologist	psykolog (c)	[sygo'lo:]
gynecologist	kvindelæge (c)	['kvenə,lɛ:jə]
cardiologist	hjertelæge (c)	['jæɒdə 'lɛ:jə]

76. Medicine. Drugs. Accessories

medicine, drug	medicin (c)	[medi'si:n]
remedy	middel (n)	['miðəl]
to prescribe (vt)	time (c)	['ti:mə]
prescription	recept (c)	[ʁɛ'sɛbd]

tablet, pill	tablet (c), pille (c)	[tɑb'lɛd], ['pelə]
ointment	salve (c)	['salvə]
ampule	ampul (c)	[ɑm'pul]
mixture	mikstur (c)	[miks'duɒ]
syrup	sirup (c)	[si:'ʁɔb]
pill	pille (c)	['pilə]

powder	**pulver** (n)	['pɔlvʌ]
bandage	**bind** (n)	[ben]
cotton wool	**vat** (n)	[vad]
iodine	**jod** (n, c)	['joð]
Band-Aid	**plaster** (n)	['plasdʌ]
eyedropper	**pipette** (c)	[pi'pɛdə]
thermometer	**termometer** (n)	[taɒmo'me:dʌ]
syringe	**sprøjte** (c)	['sbʁʌjdə]
wheelchair	**kørestol** (c)	['kø:ɒˌsdo:l]
crutches	**krykker** (pl)	['kʁœkʌ]
painkiller	**smertestillende medicin** (n)	['smæɒdə ˌsdelənə medi'si:n]
laxative	**afføringsmiddel** (n)	['ɑwføɒeŋs'miðəl]
spirit	**sprit** (c)	[sbʁid]
medicinal herbs	**lægeurter** (pl)	['lɛ:jəˌuɒdʌ]
herbal	**græs-**	[gʁas]

77. Smoking. Tobacco products

tobacco	**tobak** (c)	[to'bɑk]
cigarette	**cigaret** (c)	[sigə'ʁad]
cigar	**cigar** (c)	[si'gɑ:]
pipe	**pibe** (c)	['pi:bə]
pack (of cigarettes)	**pakke** (c)	['pɑkə]
matches	**tændstikker** (pl)	['tɛnˌsdekʌ]
matchbox	**tændstikæske** (c)	['tɛnˌsdekɛskə]
lighter	**lighter** (c)	['lɑjdʌ]
ashtray	**askebæger** (n)	['asgəˌbɛ:ʌ]
cigarette case	**cigaretetui** (n)	[sigɑ'ʁat ətuˌi:]
cigarette holder	**mundstykke** (n)	[mɔn'sdøkə]
filter	**filter** (n)	['fildʌ]
to smoke (vi, vt)	**at ryge**	[at 'ʁy:ə]
to light a cigarette	**at ryge**	[at 'ʁy:ə]
smoking	**rygning** (c)	['ʁy:neŋ]
smoker	**ryger** (c)	[ʁy:ʌ]
stub, butt (of cigarette)	**skod** (n)	[skɒð]
smoke	**røg** (c)	[ʁɒj]
ash	**aske** (c)	['askə]

HUMAN HABITAT

City

78. City. Life in the city

city, town	**by** (c)	[by:]
capital	**hovedstad** (c)	['ho:əð ,sdað]
village (e.g., fishing ~)	**landsby** (c)	['lansby:]
small town	**bebyggelse** (c)	[be'bygəlsə]
city map	**bykort** (n)	['bykɒ:d]
downtown	**centrum** (n) **af byen**	['sɛntʁɔm a 'by:ən]
suburb	**forstad** (c)	['fɒsdað]
suburban	**forstads-**	['fɒsdæ:s]
outskirts	**udkant** (c)	['uðkand]
environs (suburbs)	**omegn** (pl)	[ɒ'majn]
district (of city)	**bydel** (c)	['byde:l]
block	**kvarter** (n)	[kvɑ'teʌ]
residential block	**boligkvarter** (n)	['bo:likvɑ'teʌ]
traffic	**færdsel** (c), **trafik** (c)	['faɒsɛl], [tʁɑ'fik]
traffic lights	**lyskurv** (n)	['lys,kuɒu]
public transportation	**offentlig transport**	['ɒfəndli 'tʁɑnsbɒ:d]
intersection	**gadekryds** (n)	['gæ:ðə,kʁys]
crosswalk	**fodgængerovergang** (c)	['foðgɛŋ 'ɒwʌ,gɑŋ]
pedestrian underpass	**underjordisk overgang** (c)	['ɒnɒ,jɒɒdisg 'ɒwʌ,gɑŋ]
to cross (vt)	**at gå over**	[at gɔ: 'ɒuɒ]
pedestrian	**fodgænger** (c)	['foð,gɛŋʌ]
sidewalk	**fortov** (n)	[fɒ:'tɒu]
bridge	**bro** (c)	[bʁo:]
bank, quay	**kaj** (c)	[kɑj]
alley (in park, garden)	**alle** (c)	['alə]
park	**park** (c)	[pɑ:k]
boulevard	**boulevard** (c)	[bulə'vɑ:d]
square	**plads** (c)	[plas]
avenue (wide street)	**avenue** (c)	[avə'ny]
street	**gade** (c)	['gæ:ðə]
lane	**sidegade** (n)	['si:ðə,gæ:ðə]
dead end	**blindgyde** (c)	['blen,gy:ðə]
house	**hus** (n)	[hu:s]

building	**bygning** (c)	['bygnen]
skyscraper	**skyskraber** (c)	['sky,skʁɑːbʌ]

facade	**facade** (c)	[fa'sæːðə]
roof	**tag** (n)	[tæː]
window	**vindue** (n)	['vendu]
arch	**hvælving** (c)	['vɛlven]
column	**søjle** (c)	['sʌjlə]
corner	**hjørne** (n)	['jœɒnə]

store window	**udstillingsvindue** (n)	['uð,sdeleŋs 'vendu]
sign (on shop, bar etc.)	**skilt** (c)	[skeld]
poster	**annonce** (c)	[a'nɒŋsə]
advertising poster	**reklameplakat** (c)	[ʁɛ'klæːmə,plakæːd]
billboard	**reklameskilt** (n)	[ʁɛ'klæːmə,skeld]

garbage, trash	**affald** (n)	[ɑu'fal]
garbage can	**skraldespand** (c)	['skʁɑlə,sban]
to litter (vi)	**at smide affald**	[at 'smiːðə 'ɑw,fal]
garbage dump	**losseplads** (c)	['lɒsə,plas]

phone booth	**telefonboks** (c)	[telə'foːn,bɒks]
lightpost	**lygtepæl** (c)	['løgdə,pɛːl]
bench (park ~)	**bænk** (c)	[bɛŋk]

policeman	**politibetjent** (c)	[poli'tibe,tjɛnd]
police	**politi** (n)	[poli'tiː]
beggar	**tigger** (c)	['tegʌ]
homeless, bum	**hjemløs** (c)	['jɛm,lØːs]

79. Urban institutions

store	**forretning** (c)	[fɒ'ʁadnen]
drugstore, pharmacy	**apotek** (n)	[ɑpo'teːk]
optical store	**optik** (c)	[ʌb'tik]
shopping mall	**indkøbscenter** (n)	['enkØbs,sɛndʌ]
supermarket	**supermarked** (n)	['suːbɒ,mɑːkəð]

bakery	**bageri** (n)	[bæjʌ'ʁi]
baker	**bager** (c)	['bæːʌ]
confectionery	**konditori** (n)	[kʌndidʌ'ʁi]
grocery store	**kolonialforretning** (c)	[koloni'æːl fʌ'ʁadnen]
butcher shop	**slagterforretning** (c)	['slɑgdʌ fʌ'ʁadnen]

produce store	**grønthandel** (c)	['gʁœnd,hanəl]
market	**marked** (n)	['mɑːkəð]

coffee house	**cafe** (c)	[ka'fe]
restaurant	**restaurant** (c)	[ʁɛsdo'ʁɑŋ]
pub	**ølstue** (c)	['ølsduːə]

pizzeria	**pizzeria** (n)	[pidseːˈʁia]
hair salon	**frisørsalon** (c)	[fʁiˈsøʊsaˌlɒn]
post office	**postkontor** (n)	[ˈpɒsd kɔnˈtoɒ]
dry cleaners	**renseri** (n)	[ʁansəˈʁiː]
photo studio	**fotoatelier** (n)	[ˈfotoæːˌtəljejʌ]
shoe store	**skotøjsforretning** (c)	[ˈsgotɒjs fʌˈʁadneŋ]
bookstore	**boghandel** (c)	[ˈbouˌhanəl]
sporting goods store	**sportsforretning** (c)	[ˈsbɒːdsfɒˌʁadneŋ]
clothes repair	**reparation** (c) **af tøj**	[ʁɛbʁaˈɕon a ˈtɒj]
formal wear rental	**udlejning** (c) **af tøj**	[ˈuðˌlajneŋ aˌtɒj]
movie rental store	**filmleje** (c)	[ˈfilmˌlajə]
circus	**cirkus** (n)	[ˈsiɒkus]
zoo	**zoologisk have** (c)	[sooˈloːisg ˈhæːvə]
movie theater	**biograf** (c)	[bioˈgʁaːf]
museum	**museum** (n)	[muˈsɛːɔm]
library	**bibliotek** (n)	[biblioˈteːk]
theater	**teater** (n)	[teˈædʌ]
opera house	**operahus** (n)	[ˈoːbɐʁaˌhuːs]
nightclub	**natklub** (c)	[ˈnadˌklub]
casino	**kasino** (n)	[kaˈsiːno]
mosque	**moske** (c)	[moˈske]
synagogue	**synagoge** (c)	[synaˈgoːə]
cathedral	**katedral** (c)	[kadəˈdʁaːl]
temple	**tempel** (n)	[ˈtɛmbəl]
church	**kirke** (c)	[ˈkiɒkə]
institute	**institution** (c)	[ensдituˈɕoːn]
university	**universitet** (n)	[univæɒsiˈteːd]
school	**skole** (c)	[ˈskoːlə]
prefecture	**præfektur** (n)	[pʁɛfɛˈkduɒ]
city hall	**byråd** (n)	[ˈbyˌʁɔð]
hotel	**hotel** (n)	[hoˈtɛl]
bank	**bank** (c)	[baŋk]
embassy	**ambassade** (c)	[ɑmbaˈsæːðə]
travel agency	**rejsebureau** (n)	[ˈʁajsəbyˌʁo]
information office	**informationskontor** (n)	[enfɒmaˈɕoːns kɒnˌtoɒ]
money exchange	**vekselkontor** (n)	[ˈvɛksəl kɒnˈtoɒ]
subway	**metro** (c)	[ˈmetʁoː]
hospital	**hospital** (n), **sygehus** (n)	[hɔsbiˈtæːl], [ˈsyəˌhuːs]
gas station	**tankstation** (c)	[ˈtɑŋk sdaˈɕon]
parking lot	**parkeringsplads** (c)	[pɑˈkeːʁeŋsˌplas]

80. Signs

sign (on shop, bar etc.)	**skilt** (c)	[skeld]
inscription (plaque etc.)	**indskrift** (c)	[ˈenskʁɛfd]
poster	**poster** (c)	[ˈpowsdʌ]
direction sign	**vejviser** (c)	[ˈvɑjviːsʌ]
arrow (direction sign)	**viser** (c)	[ˈviːsʌ]
caution	**advarsel** (n)	[aðˈvɑːsəl]
warning	**advarsel** (c)	[aðˈvɑːsəl]
to warn (of the danger)	**at advare**	[at aðˈvɑːɑ]
day off	**fridag** (c)	[ˈfʁidæ:]
timetable (schedule)	**fartplan** (c)	[ˈfɑːdplæːn]
opening hours	**åbningstid** (c)	[ˈɔːbneŋstið]
WELCOME!	**VELKOMMEN!**	[ˈvɛlˌkʌmən]
ENTRANCE	**INDGANG**	[ˈengɑŋ]
EXIT	**UDGANG**	[ˈuðgɑŋ]
PUSH	**TRYK**	[tʁœk]
PULL	**TRÆK**	[tʁak]
OPEN	**ÅBENT**	[ˈɔːbənd]
CLOSED	**LUKKET**	[ˈlɔkəð]
WOMEN	**KVINDE**	[ˈkvenə]
MEN	**MAND**	[man]
DISCOUNTS	**TILBUD, RABAT**	[ˈtelbuð], [ʁɑˈbad]
SALE	**UDSALG**	[ˈuðsalj]
NEW!	**NYHED!**	[ˈnyheð]
FREE	**GRATIS**	[ˈgʁatiːs]
ATTENTION!	**PAS PÅ!**	[pas ˈpɔ]
NO VACANCIES	**INGEN LEDIGE PLADSER**	[ˈenŋən ˈleːðiə ˈplasɒ]
RESERVED	**RESERVERET**	[ʁɛsæɒˈveːɒð]
ADMINISTRATION	**ADMINISTRATION**	[aðminisdʁɑˈɕoːn]
STAFF ONLY	**KUN FOR PERSONALE**	[kɔn fɒ pæɒsoˈnæːlə]
BEWARE OF THE DOG!	**HER VOGTER JEG**	[hɛɒ ˈvɒgdɒ ˈjɑj]
NO SMOKING	**RYGNING FORBUDT**	[ˈʁyːneŋ fɒˈbud]
DO NOT TOUCH!	**MÅ IKKE BERØRES!**	[mɔ ˈekə beˈʁœʌs]
DANGEROUS	**FARLIG**	[ˈfɑːli]
DANGER	**FARE**	[fɑːɑ]
HIGH TENSION	**HØJSPÆNDING**	[ˈhʌjˌsbɛneŋ]
NO SWIMMING!	**BADNING FORBUDT**	[ˈbæːðneŋ fɒˈbud]
OUT OF ORDER	**UDE AF DRIFT**	[ˈuːðə a dʁɛfd]
FLAMMABLE	**BRANDFARLIG**	[ˈbʁanˌfɑːli]

FORBIDDEN	**FORBUDT**	[fɒ:ˈbud]
NO TRESPASSING!	**ADGANG FORBUDT**	[ˈɒdgɑŋ fɒ:ˈbud]
WET PAINT	**NYMALET**	[nyˈmæ:ləð]

81. Urban transport

bus	**bus** (c)	[bus]
streetcar	**sporvogn** (c)	[ˈsbɒɒˌvɒwn]
trolley	**trolleybus** (c)	[ˈtʁʌliˌbus]
route (of bus)	**rute** (c)	[ˈʁu:də]
number (e.g., bus ~)	**nummer** (n)	[ˈnɔmʌ]
to go by ...	**at køre ...**	[at ˈkø:ɒ]
to get on (~ the bus etc.)	**at stå på ...**	[at sdɒ: pɒ]
to get off ...	**at stå af ...**	[at sdɒ: a]
to get out (vi)	**at stå af ...**	[at sdɒ: a]
stop (e.g., bus ~)	**busstoppested** (n)	[ˈbus ˌsdɒbəsdɛð]
next stop	**næste station** (c)	[ˈnɛsdə sdaˈɕo:n]
terminus	**endestation** (c)	[ˈɛnəsdaˌɕo:n]
schedule	**fartplan** (c)	[ˈfɑ:dplæ:n]
to wait (vi, vt)	**at vente (på ...)**	[at ˈvɛndə pɒ]
ticket	**billet** (c)	[biˈlɛd]
fare (charge for bus etc.)	**billetpris** (c)	[biˈlɛd ˌpʁi:s]
cashier	**kasserer** (c)	[kaˈseʌ]
ticket inspection	**kontrol** (c)	[kʌnˈtʁɔl]
conductor	**billettør** (c)	[bileˈtøɒ]
to be late (for ...)	**at skynde sig**	[at ˈsgønə sɑj]
to miss ... (the train etc.)	**at ikke nå ...**	[at ˈekə nɔ:]
to be in a hurry	**at skynde sig**	[at ˈsgønə sɑj]
taxi, cab	**taxa** (c)	[ˈtɑgsa]
taxi driver	**taxachauffør** (c)	[ˈtɑgsaɕoˌføɒ]
by taxi	**i taxa**	[i ˈtɑsa]
taxi stand	**taxaholdeplads** (c)	[ˈtɑgsa ˈhʌləˌplas]
to call a taxi	**at bestille en taxa**	[at beˈsdelə en ˈtɑgsa]
to take a taxi	**at tage en taxa**	[at ˈtæːə en ˈtɑsa]
traffic	**færdsel** (c), **trafik** (c)	[ˈfaɒsɛl], [tʁɑˈfik]
traffic jam	**trafikprop** (c)	[tʁɑˈfikˌpʁɒb]
rush hour	**myldretid** (c)	[ˈmylʁʌtið]
to park (vi)	**at parkere**	[at pɑˈke:ɒ]
to park (vt)	**at parkere**	[at pɑˈke:ɒ]
parking lot	**parkeringsplads** (c)	[pɑˈke:ʁeŋsˌplas]
subway	**metro** (c)	[ˈmetʁo:]
station	**station** (c)	[sdaˈɕo:n]

to take the subway	**at køre med metroen**	[at ˈkøːɒ mɛð ˈmetʁoːən]
train	**tog** (n)	[ˈtɔw]
train station	**banegård** (c)	[ˈbæːnəˌɡɒː]

82. Sightseeing

monument	**mindesmærke** (n)	[ˈmenəsˌmæɒkə]
fortress	**fæstning** (c)	[ˈfɛsdneŋ]
palace	**palads** (n)	[paˈlas]
castle	**slot** (n)	[slɒd]
tower	**tårn** (n)	[tɒːn]
mausoleum	**mausoleum** (n)	[mɑwsoˈlɛːɔm]

architecture	**arkitektur** (c)	[ɑkitɛkˈtuɒ]
medieval	**middelalderlig**	[ˈmiðəlˌalʌli]
ancient	**gammel**	[ˈɡɑməl]
national	**national**	[naɕoˈnæːl]
famous	**kendt**	[kɛnd]

tourist	**turist** (c)	[tuˈʁisd]
guide (person)	**guide** (c)	[ˈɡɑjd]
excursion (organized trip)	**udflugt** (c)	[ˈuðflɒɡd]
to show (vt)	**at vise**	[at ˈviːsə]
to tell (vi, vt)	**at fortælle**	[at fʌˈtɛlə]

to find (vt)	**at finde**	[at ˈfenə]
to get lost	**at fare vild**	[at ˈfɑːɑ vil]
map (e.g., subway ~)	**kort** (n)	[kɒːd]
map (e.g., city ~)	**bykort** (n)	[ˈbykɒːd]

souvenir, gift	**souvenir** (c)	[suvəˈniɒ]
gift shop	**souvenirforretning** (c)	[suvəˈniɒ fʌˈʁadneŋ]
to take pictures	**at fotografere**	[at fotoɡʁɑːˈfeːɒ]
to be photographed	**lade sig fotografere**	[ˈlæːðə sɑj fotoɡʁɑːˈfeːɒ]

83. Shopping

to buy (purchase)	**at købe**	[at ˈkøːbə]
purchase	**indkøb** (n)	[ˈenkøːb]
to go shopping	**at gå på indkøb**	[at ɡɔ pɔ ˈenˌkøb]
shopping	**shopping** (c)	[ˈɕʌbeŋ]

| to be open | **at være åben** | [at ˈvɛːɒ ˈɔːbən] |
| to be closed | **at blive lukket** | [at ˈbliːə ˈlɔkəð] |

footwear	**sko** (c)	[skoː]
clothes, clothing	**tøj** (n)	[tɒj]
cosmetics	**kosmetik** (c)	[kɒsmeˈtik]

food	**madvare** (c)	['maðvɑːɑ]
gift, present	**gave** (c)	['gæːvə]
salesman	**ekspedient** (c)	[ɛksbe'djɛnd]
saleswoman	**ekspeditrice** (c)	[ɛksbədi'tʁiːsə]
check out, cash desk	**kasse** (c)	['kasə]
mirror	**spejl** (n)	['sbɑjl]
counter (in shop)	**disk** (c)	[disk]
fitting room	**prøverum** (n)	['pʁɶːwɛˌʁɔm]
to try on	**at prøve**	[at 'pʁɶːuə]
to fit (about dress etc.)	**at passe**	[at 'pasə]
to like (I like ...)	**at holde af ...**	[at 'hɒlə a]
price	**pris** (c)	[pʁiːs]
price tag	**prismærke** (n)	['pʁisˌmaɒkə]
to cost (vt)	**at koste**	[at 'kɒsdə]
How much?	**Hvor meget?**	[vɒ: 'mɑjəð]
discount	**rabat** (c)	[ʁɑ'bad]
inexpensive	**billig**	['bili]
cheap (inexpensive)	**billig**	['bili]
expensive	**dyr**	['dyɒ]
It's expensive	**Det er dyrt**	[de aɒ 'dyɒd]
rental (noun)	**leje** (c)	['lɑjə]
to rent (~ a tuxedo)	**at leje**	[at 'lɑjə]
credit	**kredit** (c)	[kʁɛ'did]
on credit	**på afbetaling**	[pɔ 'ɑubetæːleŋ]

84. Money

money	**penge** (pl)	['pɛŋə]
exchange	**ombytning** (c)	[ɒm'bydneŋ]
exchange rate	**kurs** (c)	[kuɒs]
ATM	**pengeautomat** (c)	['pɛŋə awto'mæd]
coin	**mønt** (c)	[mønd]
dollar	**dollar** (c)	['dɒlɑ]
euro	**euro** (c)	['œwʁo]
lira (currency)	**lire** (c)	['liːʌ]
Deutschmark	**mark** (c)	[mɑːk]
franc	**franc** (c)	[fʁɑŋg]
pound sterling	**engelske pund** (n)	['ɛŋəlsgə pun]
yen	**yen** (c)	['yːən]
debt	**gæld** (c)	[gɛl]
debtor	**debitor** (c)	['debitɒ]

to lend (money)	**at låne**	[at 'lɔːnə]
to borrow (vi, vt)	**at låne**	[at 'lɔːnə]
bank	**bank** (c)	[baŋk]
account	**bankkonto** (c)	['baŋkˌkɒnto]
to make a deposit	**at indbetale**	[at 'enbeˌtælə]
to withdraw (vt)	**at hæve fra kontoen**	[at 'hɛːuə fʁɑ 'kɒntoːən]
credit card	**kreditkort** (n)	[kʁɛ'didˌkoːd]
cash	**kontanter** (pl)	[kɔn'tandʌ]
check	**check** (c)	['ɕɛk]
to write a check	**at skrive en check**	[at 'skʁiuə en 'ɕɛk]
checkbook	**checkhæfte** (n)	['ɕɛkˌhɛfdə]
wallet	**tegnebog** (c)	['tajnəˌbow]
change purse	**pung** (c)	[pɔŋ]
safe	**pengeskab** (n)	['pɛŋəsgæːb]
heir	**arving** (c)	['ɑːveŋ]
inheritance	**arv** (c)	['ɑːu]
fortune (wealth)	**formue** (c)	['fɒːˌmuːə]
lease, rent	**leje** (c)	['lajə]
rent money	**husleje** (c)	['husˌlajə]
to rent (of a tenant)	**at leje**	[at 'lajə]
price	**pris** (c)	[pʁiːs]
cost	**værdi** (c)	[vaɒ'diː]
sum (amount of money)	**beløb** (n)	[be'løːb]
to spend (vi, vt)	**at bruge**	[at 'bʁuə]
expenses	**udgifter** (pl)	['uðˌgifdʌ]
to economize (vi, vt)	**at spare**	[at 'sbɑːɑ]
economical	**sparsommelig**	[sbɑ'sʌməli]
to pay (vi, vt)	**at betale**	[at be'tæːlə]
payment	**betaling** (c)	[be'tæːleŋ]
change (give the ~)	**byttepenge** (pl)	['bydəˌpɛŋə]
tax	**skat** (c)	[skad]
fine	**bøde** (c)	['bøːðə]
to fine	**at straffe med bøde**	[at 'sdʁɑfə mɛð 'bøːðə]

85. Post. Postal service

post office	**postkontor** (n)	['pɒsd kɔn'toɒ]
mail (letters etc.)	**post** (c)	[pɒsd]
mailman	**postbud** (n)	['pɒsdˌbuð]
working hours	**åbningstid** (c)	['ɔːbneŋstið]
letter	**brev** (n)	['bʁɛu]

registered letter	**anbefalet brev** (n)	[ˈanbefæːləð ˈbʁɛu]
postcard	**postkort** (n)	[ˈpɒsdˌkɒːd]
telegram	**telegram** (n)	[teləˈgʁɑm]
parcel	**postpakke** (c)	[ˈpɒsdˌpɑkə]
money transfer	**pengeoverførsel** (c)	[ˈpɛŋə ˈɒwʌˌføɒsəl]
to receive (vt)	**at få**	[at fɔː]
to send (vt)	**at afsende**	[at ɑuˈsɛnə]
sending	**afsendelse** (c)	[ɑuˈsɛnəlsə]
address	**adresse** (c)	[adˈʁɑsə]
ZIP code	**indeks** (c)	[ˈendɛks]
addressee	**adressat** (c)	[adʁɛˈsæd]
sender	**afsender** (c)	[ɑuˈsɛnʌ]
receiver, addressee	**modtager** (c)	[ˈmoðtæːʌ]
name	**navn** (n)	[ˈnɑun]
family name	**efternavn** (n)	[ˈɛfdɒˌnɑun]
rate (of postage)	**tarif** (c)	[tɑˈʁif]
ordinary	**sædvanlig**	[sɛðˈvæːnli]
standard (adj)	**økonomisk**	[økonoˈmisk]
weight	**vægt** (c)	[vɛgd]
to weigh up (vt)	**at veje**	[at ˈvɑjə]
envelope	**konvolut** (c)	[kɒnvoˈlud]
postage stamp	**frimærke** (n)	[ˈfʁiˌmæɒkə]

Dwelling. House. Home

86. House. Dwelling

house	**hus** (n)	[hu:s]
at home	**hjemme**	[ˈjɛmə]
courtyard	**gård** (c)	[gɒ:]
railings (fence)	**hegn** (n)	[hɑjn]
brick (noun)	**mursten** (c)	[ˈmuɒsdən]
brick (building)	**mursten-**	[ˈmuɒsdən]
stone (noun)	**sten** (c)	[sde:n]
stone (made of stone)	**sten-**	[sde:n]
concrete (noun)	**beton** (c)	[beˈtɒŋ]
concrete (attr)	**beton-**	[beˈtɒŋ]
new	**ny**	[ny:]
old	**gammel**	[ˈgɑməl]
decrepit (house)	**faldefærdig**	[ˈfaləˌfæɒdi]
modern	**moderne**	[moˈdæɒnə]
multistory	**fleretages-**	[ˈfleˌtæɕʌs]
high	**høj**	[hɒj]
floor, story	**etage** (c)	[eˈtæɕə]
single-story	**enetages**	[ˈe:neˌtæɕəs]
ground floor	**stue** (c)	[ˈsdu:ə]
top floor	**øverste etage** (c)	[ˈø:vɒsdə eˈtæ:ɕə]
roof (of building)	**tag** (n)	[tæ:]
chimney	**skorsten** (c)	[ˈskɒːˌsdən]
tiles (for roof)	**tegl, teglsten** (n pl)	[tɑjl], [ˈtɑjlˌsden]
tiled	**tegl-, teglsten-**	[tɑjl], [ˈtɑjlˌsden]
loft (attic)	**loft** (n)	[lɒfd]
window	**vindue** (n)	[ˈvendu]
glass	**glas** (n)	[glas]
window ledge	**vindueskarm** (c)	[ˈvendusˌkɑ:m]
shutters	**vinduesskodder** (pl)	[ˈvendusˌskɒðʌ]
wall	**væg** (c)	[vɛ:g]
balcony	**altan** (c)	[alˈtæ:n]
downspout	**nedløbsrør** (n)	[ˈneðløbsˌʁœɒ]
upstairs (to be ~)	**oppe**	[ˈʌbə]
to go upstairs	**at stige op**	[at ˈsdi:ə ɔp]
to come down	**at stige ned**	[at ˈsdi:ə neð]
to move (to new premises)	**at flytte**	[at ˈflødə]

87. House. Entrance. Lift

entrance	**indgang** (c)	['engɑn]
stairs (stairway)	**trappe** (c)	['tʁɑbə]
stairs (steps)	**trin** (n)	[tʁin]
banisters	**gelænder** (n)	[ge'lɛnʌ]
lobby (e.g., hotel ~)	**hall** (c)	[hal]

mailbox	**postbrevkasse** (c)	['pɒsd͜bʁɛ:wkasə]
trash can	**skraldebøtte** (c)	['skʁalə͜bødə]
trash chute	**affaldsskakt** (c)	[ɑu'falsskɑkd]

elevator	**elevator** (c)	[elə'væ:tɒ]
freight elevator	**godselevator** (c)	['gɔslə͜væ:tɒ]
elevator cage	**elevatorstol** (c)	[elə'væ:tɒ sdo:l]
to take the elevator	**at tage elevatoren**	[at 'tæ:ə elə'væ:tɒɒn]

apartment	**lejlighed** (c)	['lɑjliheð]
tenants	**beboere** (c)	[be'boɒɒ]
neighbors	**naboer** (pl)	['næ:bo:ʌ]

88. House. Electricity

electricity	**elektricitet** (c)	[elɛktʁisi'ted]
light bulb	**elektrisk pære** (c)	[e'lɛktʁisk 'pɛ:ɒ]
switch (for light)	**afbryder** (c)	[ɑu'bʁyðʌ]
fuse	**sikring** (c)	['segʁɛŋ]

cable, wire (electric ~)	**ledning** (c)	['leðnen]
wiring	**elinstallation** (c)	['e:l ensdala'ɕo:n]
electricity meter	**elektricitetsmåler** (c)	[elɛgtʁisi'ted 'mɔ:lʌ]
readings	**udslag** (n)	['uð͜slæj]

89. House. Doors. Locks

door	**dør** (c)	[dœɒ]
gate (of villa etc.)	**port** (c)	['pɒɒd]
handle, doorknob	**dørgreb** (n)	['dœɒˌgʁɛ:b]
to unlock (unbolt)	**at låse op**	[at 'lɔ:sə ɔp]
to open (vi, vt)	**at åbne**	[at 'ɔ:bnə]
to close (vt)	**at lukke**	[at 'lɔkə]

key	**nøgle** (c)	['nɒjlə]
bunch (of keys)	**nøgleknippe** (n)	['nɒjlə͜knebə]
to creak (door hinge)	**at knirke**	[at 'kniɒkə]
creak	**knirken** (c)	['kniɒkən]
hinge (of door)	**hængsel** (n)	['hɛŋsəl]

doormat	**dørmåtte** (c)	['dɶɒˌmʌdə]
lock	**lås** (c)	[lɔ:s]
keyhole	**nøglehul** (n)	['nɒjləˌhɔl]
bolt (big sliding bar)	**slå** (c)	[slɔ:]
bolt (small latch)	**skyder** (c)	['skyðʌ]
padlock	**hængelås** (c)	['hɛŋəˌlɔ:s]
to ring (~ the door bell)	**at ringe**	[at 'ʁɛŋə]
ringing (sound)	**ringning** (c)	['ʁɛŋnɛŋ]
doorbell	**ringeklokke** (c)	['ʁɛŋəˌklɒgə]
button	**knap** (c)	[knɑb]
knock (at the door)	**banken** (c)	['bɑŋkən]
to knock (vi)	**at banke**	[at 'bɑŋkə]
code	**kode** (c)	['ko:ðə]
code lock	**kodelås** (c)	['ko:ðəˌlɔ:s]
door phone	**dørtelefon** (c)	['dɶɒdeləˌfo:n]
number (on the door)	**nummer** (n)	['nɔmʌ]
nameplate	**skilt** (n)	[skeld]
peephole	**kighul** (n)	['kiˌhɔl]

90. Country house

village	**landsby** (c)	['lansby:]
vegetable garden	**køkkenhave** (c)	['køkənˌhæ:uə]
fence	**stakit** (n)	[sdɑ'kid]
paling	**hegn** (n)	[hɑjn]
wicket gate	**låge** (c)	['lɔ:wə]
granary	**lade** (c)	['læ:ðə]
cellar	**kælder** (c)	['kɛlʌ]
shed (in garden)	**skur** (n)	['skuɒ]
well (for water)	**brønd** (c)	[bʁɶn]
stove (for heating)	**ovn** (c)	['ɒwn]
to stoke	**at fyre**	[at 'fy:ɒ]
firewood	**brænde** (pl)	['bʁanə]
log (firewood)	**brændeknude** (c)	['bʁanəˌknu:ðə]
veranda, stoop	**veranda** (c)	[ve'ʁɑnda]
terrace (patio)	**terrasse** (c)	[ta'ʁɑsə]
front steps	**trappe** (c)	['tʁabə]
swing (hanging seat)	**gynge** (c)	['gøŋə]

91. Villa. Mansion

country house	**sommerhus** (n)	['sɒmɒˌhu:s]
villa (by sea)	**villa** (c)	['vila]

wing (of building)	**fløj** (c)	[flɒj]
garden	**have** (c)	['hæːvə]
park	**park** (c)	[pɑːk]
greenhouse (tropical ~)	**drivhus** (n)	['dʁiːuˌhuːs]
to look after (garden etc.)	**at passe**	[at 'pasə]
swimming pool	**svømmebassin** (n)	['svœməbaˌsɛn]
gym	**sportshal** (c)	['sbɒːdshal]
tennis court	**tennisbane** (c)	['tɛnisˌbæːnə]
home theater room	**biograf** (c)	[bio'gʁɑːf]
garage	**garage** (c)	[gɑ'ʁɑːɕə]
private property	**privat ejendom** (c)	[pʁi'væːd 'ɑjəndɒm]
private land	**privat eje** (n)	[pʁi'væːd 'ɑjə]
warning (caution)	**advarsel** (c)	[að'vɑːsəl]
warning sign	**advarselsskilt** (n)	[að'vɑːsəls'skeld]
security	**sikkerhedsvagt** (c)	['segʌˌheðs'vɑgd]
security guard	**sikkerhedsvagt** (c)	['segʌˌheðs'vɑgd]
burglar alarm	**alarm(system)** (n)	[a'lɑːm sy'sdem]

92. Castle. Palace

castle	**slot** (n)	[slɒd]
palace	**palads** (n), **palæ** (n)	[pa'las], [pa'lɛː]
fortress	**fæstning** (c)	['fɛsdnen]
wall (round castle)	**mur** (c)	['muɒ]
tower	**tårn** (n)	[tɒːn]
main tower, donjon	**hovedtårn** (n)	['hoːəð ˌdɒːn]
portcullis	**faldgitter** (n)	['falˌgidʌ]
underground passage	**underjordisk gang** (c)	['ɔnɒˌjoɒdisg gaŋ]
moat	**grøft** (c)	[gʁœfd]
chain	**kæde** (c)	['kɛːðə]
arrow loop	**skydeskår** (n)	['skyːðəˌskɒː]
magnificent	**pragtfuld**	['pʁagdful]
majestic	**majestætisk**	[majə'sdɛdisk]
impregnable	**utilgængelig**	[ute'gɛŋəli]
knight's	**ridder-**	['ʁiðɒ]
medieval	**middelalderlig**	['miðəlˌalʌli]

93. Apartment

apartment	**lejlighed** (c)	['lɑjliheð]
room	**værelse** (n)	['væːɒlsə]

bedroom	**soveværelse** (n)	['sɒwə‚væːɒlsə]
dining room	**spisestue** (c)	['sbisə‚sduːə]
living room	**dagligstue** (c)	['dɑwli‚sduːə]
study	**arbejdsværelse** (n)	['ɑːbɑjds‚væːlsə]

entry room	**entre** (c), **forstue** (c)	[ɑŋ'tʁɒ], ['fɒː‚sduːə]
bathroom	**badeværelse** (n)	['bæː‚ðə‚væːɒlsə]
half bath	**toilet** (n)	[toa'lɛd]

ceiling	**loft** (n)	[lɒfd]
floor	**gulv** (n)	[gɔl]
corner (inside room)	**hjørne** (n)	['jœɒnə]

94. Apartment. Cleaning

| to clean (vi, vt) | **at rydde op** | [at 'ʁyðə ɒb] |
| to put away (vt) | **at tage bort** | [at 'tæːə bɒːd] |

dust	**støv** (n)	['sdøu]
dusty	**støvet**	['sdøːuəð]
to dust (vt)	**at tørre støv af**	[at 'tœɒ sdøu a]
vacuum cleaner	**støvsuger** (c)	['sdøw‚suʌ]
to vacuum (vt)	**at støvsuge**	[at 'sdøw‚suə]

to sweep (vi, vt)	**at feje (op)**	[at 'fɑjə ɔp]
sweepings	**snavs** (n)	['snɑus]
order	**orden** (c)	['ɒdən]
disorder, mess	**uorden** (c)	['u‚ɒdən]

mop	**svaber** (c)	['svæːbʌ]
dust cloth	**klud** (c)	[kluð]
broom	**riskost** (c)	['ris‚kɔsd]
dustpan	**fejeblad** (n)	['fɑjə‚blað]

95. Furniture. Interior

furniture (for house)	**møbler** (pl)	['møblʌ]
table	**bord** (n)	['boɒ]
chair	**stol** (c)	[sdoːl]
bed	**seng** (c)	[sɛŋ]
couch, sofa	**sofa** (c)	['soːfa]
armchair	**lænestol** (c)	['lɛːnə‚sdoːl]

bookcase	**bogskab** (n)	['bɔu‚sgæːb]
shelf	**boghylde** (c)	['bɔuhylə]
set of shelves	**reol** (c)	[ʁɛ'oːl]
wardrobe	**klædeskab** (n)	['klɛː‚ðə‚skæːb]
coat rack	**knagerække** (c)	['knæːə‚ʁagə]

coat stand	**stumtjener** (c)	['sdɔm,tjɛ:nʌ]
chest of drawers	**kommode** (c)	[ko'mo:ðə]
coffee table	**sofabord** (n)	['so:fa,boɒ]

mirror	**spejl** (n)	['sbɑjl]
carpet	**tæppe** (n)	['tɛbə]
rug, small carpet	**lille tæppe** (n)	['lilə 'tɛbə]

fireplace	**pejs** (c)	['pɑjs]
candle	**lys** (n)	[ly:s]
candlestick	**lysestage** (c)	['ly:sə,sdæ:ə]

kitchen curtains	**køkkengardiner** (pl)	['køggəgɑ,di:nʌ]
drapes	**gardiner** (pl)	[gɑ'di:nʌ]
wallpaper	**tapet** (n)	[ta'pe:d]
blinds (jalousie)	**persienne** (c)	[pæɒ'ɕɛnə]

table lamp	**bordlampe** (c)	['boɒ,lɑmbə]
wall lamp	**lampe** (c)	['lɑmbə]
floor lamp	**standerlampe** (c)	['sdanɒ,lɑmbə]
chandelier	**lysekrone** (c)	['lysə,kʁo:nə]

leg (of chair, table)	**ben** (n)	[be:n]
armrest	**armlæn** (n)	['ɑ:m,lɛ:n]
back	**ryglæn** (n)	['ʁœg,lɛ:n]
drawer	**skuffe** (c)	[skɔfə]

96. Bedding

bedclothes	**sengetøj** (n)	['sɛŋə,tɒj]
pillow	**pude** (c)	['pu:ðə]
pillowcase	**pudebetræk** (n)	['pu:də,betʁak]
blanket (comforter)	**tæppe** (n)	['tɛbə]
sheet	**lagen** (n)	['læ:ən]
bedspread	**sengetæppe** (n)	['sɛŋə,tɛbə]

97. Kitchen

kitchen	**køkken** (n)	['køkən]
gas	**gas** (c)	[gas]
gas stove	**gaskomfur** (n)	['gasgɒm,fuɒ]
electric stove	**elkomfur** (n)	['ɛlkɒm,fuɒ]
oven	**bageovn** (c)	['bæ:əɒun]
microwave oven	**mikrobølgeovn** (c)	['mikʁobøljə,ɒun]

fridge	**køleskab** (n)	['kø:lə,skæ:b]
freezer	**dybfryser** (c)	['dyb,fʁy:sʌ]
dishwasher	**opvaskemaskine** (c)	[ʌb'vaskəma,ski:nə]

meat grinder	**kødhakkemaskine** (c)	['køð,hakɛma'ski:nə]
juicer	**saftpresser** (c)	['safd,pʀasʌ]
toaster	**brødrister** (c)	['bʀœð,ʀɛsdʌ]
mixer	**mikser** (c)	['miksʌ]

coffee maker	**kaffemaskine** (c)	['kafə ma,ski:nə]
coffee pot	**kaffekande** (c)	['kafə,kanə]
coffee grinder	**kaffekværn** (c)	['kafə,kvaɒn]

kettle	**tekedel** (c)	['te:,kəðəl]
teapot	**tekande** (c)	['te:,kanə]
lid	**låg** (n)	['lɔu]
tea strainer	**tesi** (c)	['tɛsi:]

spoon	**ske** (c)	[ske:]
teaspoon	**teske** (c)	['te:,skə]
tablespoon	**spiseske** (c)	['sbisə,skə]
fork	**gaffel** (c)	['gafəl]
knife	**kniv** (c)	['kniu]

tableware	**spisestel** (n pl)	['sbi:sə,sdɛl]
plate	**tallerken** (c)	[ta'læɒkən]
saucer	**underkop** (c)	['ɔnɒkɒb]

small wineglass	**glas** (n)	[glas]
glass (e.g., ~ of water)	**glas** (n)	[glas]
cup	**kop** (c)	[kɒb]

sugar bowl	**sukkerdåse** (c)	['sɔkaɒ,dɔ:sə]
salt shaker	**saltbøsse** (c)	['sald,bøsə]
pepper shaker	**peberbøsse** (c)	['pewʌ,bøsə]
butter dish	**smørskål** (c)	['smœɒ,skɔ:l]

saucepan	**kasserolle** (c)	[kasə'ʀʌlə]
frying pan	**pande** (c)	['panə]
ladle	**potageske** (c)	[po'tæ:çəsgə]
colander	**dørslag** (n)	['dœɒ,slæj]
tray	**bakke** (c)	['bakə]

bottle	**flaske**	['flaskə]
jar (glass)	**glas** (n)	[glas]
can	**dåse** (c)	['dɔ:sə]

bottle opener	**oplukker** (c)	['ʌblɔkʌ]
can opener	**dåseåbner** (c)	['dɔ:sə ,ɔ:bnʌ]
corkscrew	**proptrækker** (c)	['pʀʌb,tʀakʌ]

filter	**filter** (n)	['fildʌ]
to filter (vt)	**at filtrere**	[at fil'tʀɛ:ɒ]

trash	**skrald** (n)	[skʀal]
trash can	**skraldespand** (c)	['skʀalə,sban]

98. Bathroom

bathroom	**badeværelse** (n)	['bæːðəˌvæːɒlsə]
water	**vand** (n)	[van]
tap, faucet	**hane** (c)	['hæːnə]
hot water	**varmt vand** (n)	['vɑːmd van]
cold water	**koldt vand** (n)	[kɒld van]
toothpaste	**tandpasta** (c)	['tanˌpasda]
to brush one's teeth	**at børste tænder**	[at 'bɶɒsdə 'tɛnɒ]
to shave (vi)	**at barbere sig**	[at bɑ'beːɒ sɑj]
shaving foam	**barberskum** (n)	[bɑ'bɒ ˌskɔm]
razor	**barbermaskine** (c)	[bɑ'bɒ ma'skiːnə]
to wash (clean)	**at vaske**	[at 'vaskə]
to take a bath	**at vaske sig**	[at 'vasgə sɑj]
shower	**brusebad** (n)	['bʁusəˌbað]
to take a shower	**at tage brusebad**	[at 'tæːə 'bʁusəbað]
bathtub	**badekar** (n)	['bæːðəˌkɑː]
toilet	**wc-kumme** (c)	['veˌse 'kɔmə]
sink	**vask** (c)	[vask]
soap	**sæbe** (c)	['sɛːbə]
soap dish	**sæbekop** (c)	['sɛːbəˌkɒb]
sponge	**svamp** (c)	[svɑmb]
shampoo	**shampoo** (c)	['ɕæːmˌpuː]
towel	**håndklæde** (n)	['hɒnˌklɛːðə]
bathrobe	**badekåbe** (c)	['bæːðəˌkɔːbə]
laundry (process)	**vask** (c)	[vask]
washing machine	**vaskemaskine** (c)	['vaskəmaˌskiːnə]
to do the laundry	**at vaske**	[at 'vaskə]
laundry detergent	**vaskepulver** (n)	['vaskəˌpʊlvʌ]

99. Household appliances

TV set	**fjernsyn** (n)	['fjaɒnˌsyːn]
tape recorder	**båndoptager** (c)	['bɒnˌɒbtæːʌ]
video, VCR	**videobåndoptager** (c)	['viːdeobɒnˌɒbtæːʌ]
radio	**radio** (n)	['ʁɑːdio]
player (CD, MP3 etc.)	**afspiller** (c)	['ɑuˌsbelʌ]
video projector	**videoprojektor** (c)	['viːdeo pʁo'ɕɛktʌ]
home movie theater	**hjemmebio** (c)	['jɛməˌbiːo]
DVD player	**DVD afspiller** (c)	[deve'de ɑu'sbelʌ]
amplifier	**forstærker** (c)	[fɒ'sdaɒkʌ]

video game console	spillekonsol (c)	['sbelǝkɔn'sʌl]
video camera	videokamera (n)	['vi:deo‚kæ:mǝʀa]
camera (photo)	fotografiapparat (n)	[fotogʀa'fiɑpɑʀɑ:d]
digital camera	digital kamera (n)	[digi'tæ:l 'kæ:mǝʀa]

vacuum cleaner	støvsuger (c)	['sdøw‚suʌ]
iron (e.g., steam ~)	strygejern (n)	['sdʀyǝjɑɒn]
ironing board	strygebræt (n)	['sdʀyǝ‚bʀad]

telephone	telefon (c)	[telǝ'fo:n]
mobile phone	mobiltelefon (c)	[mo'bi:l telǝ'fo:n]
typewriter	skrivemaskine (c)	['skʀi:vǝ ma'ski:nǝ]
sewing machine	symaskine (c)	['syma‚ski:nǝ]

microphone	mikrofon (c)	[mikʀo'fo:n]
headphones	hovedtelefoner (pl)	['ho:ǝð delǝ‚fo:nʌ]
remote control (TV)	fjernbetjener (c)	['fjaɒn‚betjɛ:nʌ]

compact disc, CD	cd (c)	[se'de]
cassette	kassette (c)	[ka'sɛdǝ]
record (vinyl LP)	plade (c)	['plæ:ðǝ]

100. Repairs. Renovation

renovations	renovering (c)	[ʀɛno've:ʀeŋ]
to renovate (vt)	at renovere	[at ʀɛno'veʌ]
to repair (vt)	at reparere	[at ʀɛpɑ'ʀɛ:ɑ]
to put in order	at bringe i orden	[at 'bʀeŋǝ i 'ɒ:dn]
to redo (vt)	at lave om	[at 'læ:uǝ ɒm]

paint	maling (c)	['mæ:leŋ]
to paint (e.g., ~ a wall)	at male	[at 'mæ:lǝ]
house painter	maler (c)	['mæ:lʌ]
brush	pensel (c)	['pɛnsǝl]

| whitewash | hvidtekalk (c) | ['vitǝ‚kalk] |
| to whitewash (vt) | at hvidte | [at 'vidǝ] |

wallpaper	tapet (n)	[ta'pe:d]
to put up wallpaper	at tapetsere	[at tape'dse:ɒ]
varnish	fernis (c)	['faɒnis]
to varnish (vt)	at lakere	[at la'ke:ɒ]

101. Plumbing

water	vand (n)	[van]
hot water	varmt vand (n)	['vɑ:md van]
cold water	koldt vand (n)	[kɒld van]

tap, faucet	**hane** (c)	['hæ:nə]
drop (of water)	**dråbe** (c)	['dʁɔ:bə]
to drip (vi)	**at dryppe**	[at 'dʁœbə]
to leak (about pipe)	**at flyde**	[at 'fly:ðə]
leak (in pipe)	**læk** (c)	[lɛk]
puddle	**pyt** (c)	[pyd]

pipe	**vandrør** (n)	['van,ʁœɐ]
valve	**ventil** (c)	[vɛn'ti:l]
to be clogged up	**at blive tilstoppet**	[at 'bli:ə tel'sdɒbəð]

tools	**værktøj** (pl)	['væɒk,tɒj]
adjustable wrench	**skiftenøgle** (c)	['sgifdə,nɒjlə]
to unscrew (vt)	**at skrue af**	[at 'skʁu:ə a]
to screw (tighten)	**at skrue fast**	[at 'skʁu:ə fasd]

to unclog (vt)	**at rense**	[at 'ʁansə]
plumber	**blikkenslager** (c)	['blegən,sla:ʌ]
basement	**kælder** (c)	['kɛlʌ]
sewerage (system)	**kloaksystem** (n)	[klo'ɑg sy,sde:m]

102. Fire. Conflagration

fire (e.g., to catch ~)	**ild** (c)	[il]
flame	**flamme** (c)	['flɑmə]
spark	**gnist** (c)	[gnisd]
smoke (from fire)	**røg** (c)	[ʁɒj]
torch (flaming stick)	**fakkel** (c)	['fakəl]
campfire	**bål** (n)	[bɔ:l]

gas, gasoline	**benzin** (c)	[bɛn'si:n]
kerosene (for aircraft)	**petroleum** (n)	[pe'tʁo:leɔm]
flammable	**brændbar**	['bʁan,bɑ]
explosive	**eksplosiv**	['ɛksblo,siw]
NO SMOKING	**RYGNING FORBUDT**	['ʁy:neŋ fɒ:'bud]

safety	**sikkerhed** (c)	['sekʌ,heð]
danger	**fare** (c)	['fɑ:ɑ]
dangerous	**farlig**	['fɑ:li]

to catch fire	**at antændes**	[at an'tɛnəs]
explosion	**eksplosion** (c)	[ɛksblo'çon]
to set fire	**at sætte ild**	[at 'sɛdə il]
incendiary (arsonist)	**brandstifter** (c)	['bʁan,sdefdʌ]
arson	**brandstiftelse** (c)	['bʁan,sdefdəlsə]

to blaze (vi)	**at blusse**	[at 'blusə]
to burn (be on fire)	**at brænde**	[at 'bʁanə]
to burn down	**at brænde ned**	[at 'bʁanə neð]
to call the fire department	**at tilkalde brandvæsenet**	[at 'tel,kalə 'bʁan,vɛ:snəð]

fireman	**brandmand** (c)	['bʁɑnˌman]
fire truck	**brandbil** (c)	['bʁɑnˌbiːl]
fire department	**brandkorps** (n)	['bʁɑnˌkɒːbs]
fire truck ladder	**redningsstige**	['ʁɛðneŋsˌsdie]
fire hose	**slange** (c)	['slɑŋe]
fire extinguisher	**brandslukker** (c)	['bʁɑnˌslɔkʌ]
helmet	**hjelm** (c)	[jɛlm]
siren	**sirene** (c)	[si'ʁɛːne]
to shout (vi)	**at råbe**	[at 'ʁɔːbe]
to call for help	**at tilkalde hjælp**	[at 'telˌkale jɛlb]
rescuer	**redder** (c)	['ʁɛðʌ]
to rescue (vt)	**at redde**	[at 'ʁɛðe]
to arrive (vi)	**at ankomme**	[at 'anˌkʌme]
to extinguish (vt)	**at slukke**	[at 'slɔke]
water	**vand** (n)	[van]
sand	**sand** (n)	[san]
ruins (destruction)	**ruiner** (pl)	[ʁu'iːnʌ]
to collapse (building, roof)	**at styrte sammen**	[at 'sdyɒde 'samen]
to fall down	**at styrte ned**	[at 'sdyɒde neð]
to cave in (ceiling, floor)	**at styrte sammen**	[at 'sdyɒde 'samen]
fragment (piece of wall etc.)	**brudstykke** (n)	['bʁuðˌsdøke]
ash	**aske** (c)	['aske]
to suffocate (die)	**at blive forpustet**	[at 'bliːe fɒ'puːsdeð]
to be killed (perish)	**at omkomme**	[at ɒm'kɒme]

HUMAN ACTIVITIES

Job. Business. Part 1

103. Office. Working in the office

office (of firm)	kontor (n)	[kɔn'toɒ]
office (of director etc.)	kontor (n)	[kɔn'toɒ]
front desk (in the office)	reception (c)	[ʁɛsəb'ɕon]
secretary	sekretær (c)	[sekʁɛ'tɛɒ]
director	direktør (c)	[diɒek'tøɒ]
manager (employee)	manager (c)	['manidjʌ]
accountant	bogholder (c)	['bɒuˌhɒlʌ]
employee	medarbejder (c)	['mɛðaˌbɑjdʌ]
furniture	møbler (pl)	['møblʌ]
desk	bord (n)	['boɒ]
desk chair	lænestol (c)	['lɛːnəˌsdoːl]
chest of drawers	kommode (c)	[ko'moːðə]
coat stand	stumtjener (c)	['sdɔmˌtjɛːnʌ]
computer	computer (c)	[kɔm'pjuːdʌ]
printer	printer (c)	['pʁɛndʌ]
fax machine	fax (c)	[fɑs]
photocopier	kopimaskine (c)	[ko'pimaˌskiːnə]
paper	papir (n)	[pa'piɒ]
office supplies	kontorartikler (pl)	[kɔn'toɒˌɑtiklɒ]
mouse pad	musemåtte (c)	['museˌmɒdə]
sheet (of paper)	ark (n)	[ɑːk]
folder, binder	mappe (c)	['mɑbə]
catalog	katalog (n, c)	[kada'lo]
phone book	håndbog (c)	['hɒnˌbɒu]
documentation	dokumentation (c)	[dokumɛnta'ɕoːn]
booklet	hæfte (n)	['hɛfdə]
leaflet	løbeseddel (c)	['løːbəˌsɛðəl]
sample	vareprøve (c)	['vɑːɑ ˌpʁœːwə]
training meeting	træning (c)	['tʁɛːneŋ]
meeting (of managers)	møde (n)	['møːðə]
lunch time	spisepause (c)	['sbiseˌpɑwsə]
to copy (photocopy)	at kopiere	[at ko'pjeʌ]
to make copies	at kopiere	[at ko'pjeʌ]

| to receive a fax | at modtage en fax | [at 'moð̥ˌtæːə en faks] |
| to send a fax | at sende en faks | [at 'sɛnə en faks] |

to call (telephone)	at ringe	[at 'ʁɛŋə]
to answer (vi, vt)	at svare	[at 'svaːɑ]
to put through	at sætte i forbindelse	[at 'sɛdə i fʌ'benəlsə]

to arrange (organize, plan)	at arrangere	[at ɑɑŋ'ɕeʌ]
to show (to display)	at demonstrere	[at demɒn'sdʁɛːɒ]
to be absent	at være fraværende	[at 'vɛːɒ fʁɑ'vɛːɒ nə]
absence	forsømmelse (c)	[fɒ'sœməlsə]

104. Business processes. Part 1

occupation	fag (n)	['fæj]
firm	firma (n)	['fiɒma]
company	selskab (n)	['sɛlˌskæːb]
corporation	korporation (c)	[kɒbɒʁɑ'ɕon]
enterprise	foretagende (n)	['foːɒˌtæjənə]
agency	agentur (n)	[agɛn'tuɒ]

agreement (contract)	aftale (c)	[ɑu'tæːlə]
contract	kontrakt (c)	[kɔn'tʁɑkd]
deal	overenskomst (c)	[ɒwʌ'ensˌkʌmsd]
order (to place an ~)	ordre (c)	['ɒːdʁɒ]
term (of contract)	betingelse (c)	[be'teŋəlsə]

wholesale (adv)	en gros	[en 'gʁo]
wholesale (adj)	engros-	[ɑŋ'gʁo]
wholesale (noun)	engroshandel (c)	[ɑŋ'gʁosˌhanəl]
retail (adj)	detail-	[de'tɑjl]
retail (noun)	detailhandel (c)	[de'tɑjlˌhanəl]

competitor	konkurrent (c)	[kʌŋko'ʁand]
competition	konkurrence (c)	[kʌŋko'ʁɑŋsə]
to compete (vi)	at konkurrere	[at kʌŋko'ʁɛʌ]

| partner (associate) | medstifter (c) | ['mɛð̥ˌsdefdʌ] |
| partnership | partnerskab (n) | ['paːdnʌˌskæb] |

crisis	krise (c)	['kʁiːsə]
bankruptcy	fallit (c)	[fa'lid]
to go bankrupt	at gå fallit	[at gɔ: fa'lid]
difficulty	vanskelighed (c)	['vanskəliˌheð]
problem	problem (n)	[pʁo'bleːm]
catastrophe	katastrofe (c)	[kata'sdʁoːfə]

economy	økonomi (c)	[økono'miː]
economic (e.g., ~ growth)	økonomisk	[økono:'misk]
economic recession	økonomisk nedgang (c)	[økono:'misg 'neð̥gɑŋ]

| goal (aim) | **mål** (n) | [mɔ:l] |
| task | **opgave** (c) | [ˈʌbˌgæ:və] |

to trade (vi)	**at handle**	[at ˈhanlə]
network (distribution ~)	**netværk** (n)	[nɛdˈvɛrk]
stock	**lager** (n)	[ˈlæjʌ]
assortment	**sortiment** (n)	[sɒtiˈmɑnd]

leader	**leder** (c)	[ˈle:ðʌ]
big, large	**stor**	[ˈsdoɒ]
monopoly	**monopol** (n)	[monoˈpo:l]

theory	**teori** (c)	[teoˈʁi]
practice	**praksis** (c)	[ˈpʁaksis]
experience (in my ~)	**erfaring** (c)	[aɒˈfɑ:eŋ]
trend (tendency)	**tendens** (c)	[tɛnˈdɛns]
development	**udvikling** (c)	[ˈuðvegleŋ]

105. Business processes. Part 2

| profit (benefit) | **fordel** (c) | [ˈfɒde:l] |
| profitable | **fordelagtig** | [ˈfɒdelˌagdi] |

delegation (group)	**delegation** (c)	[delegaˈɕo:n]
salary	**løn** (c)	[lœn]
to correct (vt)	**at rette**	[at ˈʁadə]
business trip	**tjenesterejse** (c)	[ˈtjɛ:nəsde:ˌʁajsə]
commission	**kommission** (c)	[kɒmiˈɕo:n]

to control (vt)	**at kontrollere**	[at kʌntʁoˈleʌ]
conference	**konference** (c)	[kʌnfəˈʁɑŋsə]
license	**licens** (c)	[liˈsɛns]
reliable (trustworthy)	**pålidelig**	[pʌˈliðəli]

initiative (new project etc.)	**foretagende** (n)	[ˈfɒːɒˌtæjənə]
norm (standard)	**standard** (c)	[sdanˈdɑ:d]
circumstance	**omstændighed** (c)	[ʌmˈsdɛndiheð]
duty (of employee)	**pligt** (c)	[ˈplegd]
enterprise	**organisation** (c)	[ɒganisaˈɕo:n]

organization (process)	**organisering** (c)	[ɒganiˈse:ɒeŋ]
organized	**organiseret**	[ɒganiˈse:ɒð]
cancellation (calling off)	**annullering** (c)	[annɔˈljɒeŋ]
to cancel (call off)	**at annullere**	[at anuˈleʌ]
report (e.g., official ~)	**rapport** (c)	[ʁɑˈpɒ:d]

patent	**patent** (n)	[paˈtɛnd]
to patent (obtain patent)	**at patentere**	[at patɛnˈte:ɒ]
to plan (vi, vt)	**at planlægge**	[at ˈplæːnˌlɛ:gə]
bonus (money)	**pris** (c)	[pʁi:s]

| professional | **professionel** | [pʁoˈfɛɕoˌnɛl] |
| procedure | **procedure** (c) | [pʁosəˈdyːʌ] |

to examine (contract etc.)	**at undersøge**	[at ˈɔnɒˌsøːə]
calculation	**beregning** (c)	[beˈʁajneŋ]
reputation	**reputation** (c)	[ʁɛpjuːtaˈɕoːn]
risk	**risiko** (c)	[ˈʁisiko]

to manage (business etc.)	**at lede**	[at ˈleːðə]
information	**oplysninger** (pl)	[ˈʌblyːsneŋʌ]
property	**ejendom** (c)	[ˈajəndɒm]
union (association, group)	**forbund** (n)	[fɒˈbɒn]

life insurance	**livsforsikring** (c)	[ˈliusfɒˌsegʁɛŋ]
to insure (vt)	**at forsikre**	[at fʌˈsekʁɒ]
insurance	**forsikring** (c)	[fɒˈsegʁɛŋ]

auction	**auktion** (c)	[awkˈɕon]
to notify (inform)	**at meddele**	[at ˈmɛðˌdeːlə]
management (process)	**ledelse** (c)	[ˈleːðəlsə]
service (in shop, hotel)	**tjeneste** (c)	[ˈtjɛːnəsdə]

forum	**forum** (n)	[ˈfoːʁɒm]
to function (vi)	**at fungere**	[at foŋˈgeʌ]
stage (phase)	**etape** (c)	[eˈtabə]
legal	**juridisk**	[juˈʁiðisk]
lawyer (legal expert)	**jurist** (c)	[juˈʁisd]

106. Production. Works

plant	**fabrik** (c)	[faˈbʁɛk]
factory	**fabrik** (c)	[faˈbʁɛk]
workshop	**afdeling** (c)	[auˈdeːleŋ]
production site	**virksomhed** (c)	[ˈviɒksɒmˌheð]

industry	**industri** (c)	[enduˈsdʁi]
industrial	**industriel**	[enduˈsdʁiˈl]
heavy industry	**sværindustri** (c)	[ˈsvɛɒɒnduˌsdʁi]
light industry	**let industri** (c)	[ˌlɒt enduˈsdʁi]

products	**produktion** (c)	[pʁodukˈɕoːn]
to produce (vt)	**at producere**	[at pʁoduˈseːɒ]
raw materials	**råstoffer** (pl)	[ˈʁɒˌsdɒfʌ]

foreman	**sjakbajs** (c)	[ˈɕakˌbajs]
workers team	**sjak** (n)	[ɕak]
worker	**arbejder** (c)	[ˈɑːˌbajdʌ]

| workday | **arbejdsdag** (c) | [ˈɑːbajdsˌdæː] |
| pause | **pause** (c) | [ˈpɑusə] |

| meeting | **møde** (n), **forsamling** (c) | ['mø:ðə], [fʌ'samleŋ] |
| to discuss (~ a problem) | **at drøfte** | [at 'dʁœfdə] |

plan	**plan** (c)	[plæ:n]
to fulfill the plan	**at overholde planen**	[at 'ɒuɒhɒlə 'plæ:nən]
rate (of output)	**norm** (c)	[nɒ:m]
quality	**kvalitet** (c)	[kvali'te:d]
checking (control)	**kontrol** (c)	[kʌn'tʁɔl]
quality control	**kontrol** (c)	[kʌn'tʁɔl]

| safety of work | **arbejdssikkerhed** (c) | ['ɑ:bɑjds‚sekɒheð] |
| discipline | **disciplin** (c) | [disip'li:n] |

| violation (of rules) | **overtrædelse** (c) | ['ɒwʌ‚tʁaðəlsə] |
| to violate (vt) | **at krænke** | [at 'kʁaŋkə] |

| strike | **strejke** (c) | ['sdʁɑjkə] |
| striker | **strejkende** (c) | ['sdʁɑjkɛnə] |

| to be on strike | **at strejke** | [at 'sdʁɑjkə] |
| labor union | **fagforening** (c) | ['fɑwfʌ‚eneŋ] |

to invent (machine etc.)	**at opfinde**	[at 'ʌb‚fenə]
invention	**opfindelse** (c)	[ɒb'fenəlsə]
research	**forskning** (c)	['fɒ:sgneŋ]
to improve (make better)	**at forbedre**	[at fʌ'bɛðʁʌ]

| technology | **teknologi** (c) | [tɛgnolo'gi:] |
| technical drawing | **teknisk tegning** (c) | ['tɛgnisg 'tɑjneŋ] |

load, cargo	**last** (c)	[lasd]
loader (person)	**lastearbejder** (c)	['lasdə‚ɑ:bɑjdʌ]
to load (vehicle etc.)	**at laste**	[at 'lasdə]
loading (process)	**ladning** (c)	['laðneŋ]

| to unload (vi, vt) | **at læsse af** | [at 'lɛsə a] |
| unloading | **aflæsning** (c) | [ɑu'lɛ:sneŋ] |

transportation	**transport** (c)	[tʁɑns'pɒ:d]
transportation company	**transportfirma** (n)	[tʁɑns'pɒ:d‚fiɒma]
to transport (vt)	**at transportere**	[at tʁɑnsbɒ'te:ɒ]

freight car	**godsvogn** (c)	['gɔs 'vɒwn]
cistern	**tank** (c)	[tɑŋk]
truck	**lastbil** (c)	['lasd‚bi:l]

| machine tool | **værktøjsmaskine** (c) | ['væɒg‚tʌj ma'sgi:nə] |
| mechanism | **mekanisme** (c) | [meka'nismə] |

industrial waste	**affald** (n)	[ɑu'fal]
packing (process)	**pakning** (c)	['pɑgneŋ]
to pack (vt)	**at pakke**	[at 'pɑkə]

107. Contract. Agreement

contract	**kontrakt** (c)	[kɔn'tʁakd]
agreement	**overenskomst** (c)	[ɒwʌ'ens,kʌmsd]
addendum	**tillæg** (n)	['te,lɛg]
to sign a contract	**at indgå kontrakt**	[at en'gɔ: kɔn'tʁagd]
signature	**underskrift** (c)	['ɔnɒ,skʁɛfd]
to sign (vt)	**at underskrive**	[at 'ɔnɒ,skʁiuə]
stamp (on document)	**segl** (n)	['sɑjl]
subject (of contract)	**aftalens genstand** (n)	[ɑu'tæ:ləns gɛn'sdan]
clause	**paragraf** (c)	[pɑɑ'gʁaf]
parties (in contract)	**part** (c)	[pɑ:d]
legal address	**juridisk adresse** (c)	[ju'ʁiðisk a'dʁasə]
to break the contract	**at bryde kontrakten**	[at 'bʁyðə kɔn'tʁakdən]
commitment	**forpligtelse** (c)	[fɒ'plegdəlsə]
responsibility	**ansvar** (n)	['ansvɑ:]
force majeure	**force majeure**	[,fɔ:sma'ɕɶ:ɒ]
dispute	**strid** (c)	[sdʁið]
penalties	**straffeforanstaltning** (c)	['sdʁɑfə fʌan'sdaldnen]

108. Import & Export

import (activity)	**import** (c)	[em'pɒ:d]
importer	**importør** (c)	[empɒ'tøɒ]
to import (vt)	**at importere**	[at empɒ'te:ɒ]
import (e.g., ~ goods)	**import-**	[em'pɒ:d]
exporter	**eksportør** (c)	[ɛksbɒ'tøɒ]
to export (vi, vt)	**at eksportere**	[at ɛksbɒ'te:ɒ]
goods	**vare** (c)	['vɑ:ɑ]
load (e.g., carload)	**parti** (n)	[pɑ'ti:]
weight	**vægt** (c)	[vɛgd]
volume	**omfang** (n)	['ɒmfaŋ]
cubic meter	**kubikmeter** (c)	[ku'bik,me:dʌ]
manufacturer	**producent** (c)	[pʁodu'sɛnd]
transportation company	**transportfirma** (n)	[tʁans'pɒ:d,fiɒma]
container (for cargo)	**container** (c)	[kɒn'tɛjnʌ]
border (boundary)	**grænse** (c)	['gʁansə]
customs	**told** (c)	[tɒl]
customs duty	**toldafgift** (c)	['tɒl 'ɑw,gifd]
customs officer	**toldbetjent** (c)	['tɒl be'tjɛnd]
smuggling	**smugleri** (n)	[smulə'ʁi:]
contraband (goods)	**smuglergods** (pl)	['smu:lʌɒ,gɔs]

109. Finances

share, stock	aktie (c)	['akɕə]
bond (certificate)	obligation (c)	[ɒbliga'ɕo:n]
bill of exchange	veksel (c)	['vɛksəl]

| stock exchange | børs (c) | ['bœɒs] |
| stock price | aktiekurs (c) | ['akɕeˌkuɒs] |

| to become cheaper | at falde i pris | [at 'falə i pʁi:s] |
| to rise in price | at stige i pris | [at 'sdi:ə i 'pʁis] |

controlling interest	aktiemajoritet (c)	['akɕə majʌi'ted]
investment	investeringer (pl)	[envɛ'sde:ʁeŋʌ]
to invest (vi, vt)	at investere	[at envə'sdeʌ]
percent	procent (c)	[pʁo'sɛnd]
interest (on investment)	rente (c)	['ʁandə]

profit	profit (c)	[pʁo'fid]
profitable	profitabel	[pʁofi'tæ:bəl]
tax	skat (c)	[skad]

currency (foreign ~)	valuta (c)	[va'luta]
national	national	[naɕo'næ:l]
exchange (of currency)	udveksling (c)	['uðvɛgsleŋ]

| accountant | bogholder (c) | ['bouˌhɒlʌ] |
| accounts department | bogholderi (c) | [bɔwhʌlʌ'ʁi] |

collapse, crash	fallit (c)	[fa'lid]
ruin	fallit (c)	[fa'lid]
to be ruined	at gå fallit	[at gɒ: fa'lid]
inflation	inflation (c)	[enfla'ɕo:n]
devaluation	devaluering (c)	[devalu'eʁen]

capital	kapital (c)	[kapi'tæ:l]
income	indkomst (c)	['enkɒmsd]
turnover	omsætning (c)	[ʌm'sɛdneŋ]
resources	ressourcer (pl)	[ʁɛ'suɒsʌ]
monetary resources	pengemidler (pl)	['pɛŋəˌmiðlʌ]

| overhead | omkostninger (pl) | ['ʌmˌkɒsdneŋʌ] |
| to reduce (expenses) | at reducere | [at ʁɛdu'se:ɒ] |

110. Marketing

marketing	marketing (c)	['mɑ:gəteŋ]
market	marked (n)	['mɑ:kəð]
market segment	markedssegment (n)	['mɑ:gəðs seg'mɛnd]

| product | produkt (n) | [pʁo'dɔkd] |
| goods | vare (c) | ['va:ɑ] |

trademark	handelsmærke (n)	['hanels,mɑɒkə]
logotype	firmamærke (n)	['fiɒma,mɑɒkə]
logo	logo (n, c)	['lo:go]

demand	efterspørgsel (c)	['ɛfdʌ,sbœɒsəl]
offer	tilbud (n)	['telbuð]
need	fornødenhed (c)	[fʌ'nøðən,heð]
consumer	forbruger (c)	[fɒ'bʁu:ʌ]

analysis	analyse (c)	[ana'ly:sə]
to analyze (vt)	at analysere	[at analy'seʌ]
positioning	positionering (c)	[posiço:'ne:ʁeŋ]
to position (product)	at positionere	[at posiço'neʌ]

price	pris (c)	[pʁi:s]
pricing policy	prispolitik (c)	['pʁispoli'tik]
pricing	prisdannelse (c)	['pʁis,danəlsə]

111. Advertising

advertising	reklame (c)	[ʁɛ'klæ:mə]
to advertise (vt)	at reklamere	[at ʁɛklæ:'me:ɒ]
budget	budget (n)	[by'ɕɛd]

ad, advertisement	annonce (c)	[a'nɒŋsə]
TV advertising	tv-reklame (c)	['te,ve ʁɛklæ:mə]
radio advertising	radioreklame (c)	['ʁɑdjo ʁɛ'klæ:mə]
outdoor advertising	udendørs reklame (c)	['uðən,dœɒs ʁɛ'klæ:mə]

mass media	massemedier (pl)	['mase,me:diʌ]
periodical (noun)	tidsskrift (n)	['tiðs,skʁɛfd]
image (public appearance)	image (n)	['imidɕ]
slogan	slagord (n)	['slæj,ɒɒ]
motto (maxim)	motto (c)	['mʌto]

campaign	kampagne (c)	[kɑm'panjə]
advertising campaign	reklamekampagne (c)	[ʁɛ'klæ:məkɑm'panjə]
target group	målgruppe (c)	['mɔ:l,gʁubə]

business card	visitkort (n)	[vi'sid,kɒ:d]
leaflet	reklameblad (n)	[ʁɛ'klæ:mə,blað]
brochure	folder (c)	['fɒlʌ]
pamphlet	folder (c)	['fɒlʌ]
newsletter	bulletin (c)	[bulə'ti:n]
sign (on shop, bar etc.)	facadeskilt (n)	[fa'sæ:ðə 'skeld]
poster	plakat (n)	[pla'kæ:d]
billboard	reklameskilt (n)	[ʁɛ'klæ:mə,skeld]

112. Banking

bank	**bank** (c)	[baŋk]
branch (of bank etc.)	**afdeling** (c)	[ɑu'de:leŋ]
consultant	**konsulent** (c)	[kʌnsu'lɛnd]
manager (boss)	**bestyrer** (c)	[be'sdyʌ]
banking account	**bankkonto** (c)	['baŋkˌkɒnto]
account number	**kontonummer** (n)	['kʌntɒˌnɔmʌ]
checking account	**checkkonto** (c)	['ɕɛkˌkɒnto]
savings account	**opsparingskonto** (c)	['ʌbsbɑːeŋˌskɒnto]
to open an account	**at åbne**	[at 'ɔ:bnə]
to close the account	**at lukke**	[at 'lɔkə]
to deposit (vt)	**at indbetale**	[at 'enbeˌtælə]
to withdraw (vt)	**at hæve fra kontoen**	[at 'hɛ:uə fʁɑ 'kɒnto:ən]
deposit	**indskud** (n)	['enskuð]
to make a deposit	**at indbetale**	[at 'enbeˌtælə]
wire transfer	**overførelse** (c)	[ɒwʌ'fø:ɒlsə]
to wire (money)	**at oversætte**	[at ɒuɒ'sɛdə]
sum (amount of money)	**beløb** (n)	[be'lø:b]
How much?	**Hvor meget?**	[vɒ: 'majeð]
signature	**underskrift** (c)	['ɒnɒˌskʁɛfd]
to sign (vt)	**at underskrive**	[at 'ɒnɒˌskʁiuə]
credit card	**kreditkort** (n)	[kʁɛ'didˌkɒ:d]
code	**kode** (c)	['ko:ðə]
credit card number	**nummer** (n)	['nɔmʌ]
ATM	**pengeautomat** (c)	['pɛŋə ɑwto'mæd]
check	**check** (c)	['ɕɛk]
to write a check	**at skrive en check**	[at 'skʁiuə en 'ɕɛk]
checkbook	**checkhæfte** (n)	['ɕɛkˌhɛfdə]
loan (bank ~)	**kredit** (c)	[kʁɛ'did]
to ask for a loan	**at ansøge om kredit**	[at 'anˌsø:ə ɒm kʁɛ'did]
to take a loan	**at få kredit**	[at fɔ: 'kʁɛdid]
to grant a credit	**at yde kredit**	[at y:ðə kʁɛ'did]
guarantee	**garanti** (n)	[gɑɑn'ti:]

113. Telephone. Phone conversation

telephone	**telefon** (c)	[telə'fo:n]
mobile phone	**mobiltelefon** (c)	[mo'bi:l telə'fo:n]
answering machine	**telefonsvarer** (c)	[telə'fo:nsˌvɑːɑ]

to call (telephone)	**at ringe op**	[at ˈʁɛŋə ɒb]
phone call	**opringning** (c)	[ʌbˈʁɛŋnen]
to dial a number	**at taste et nummer**	[at ˈtasdə ed ˈnɔmɒ]
Hello!	**Hallo!**	[haˈlo]
to ask (vi, vt)	**at spørge**	[at ˈsbœɒuə]
to answer (vi, vt)	**at svare**	[at ˈsvɑːɑ]
to hear (vi, vt)	**at høre**	[at ˈhøːɒ]
well	**godt**	[gɒd]
not good, bad (adv)	**dårligt**	[ˈdɒːlid]
noises	**støj**	[sdɒj]
receiver	**telefonrør** (n)	[teləˈfoːnˌʁɶɒ]
to pick up (~ the phone)	**at tage telefonen**	[at ˈtæːə teləˈfoːnən]
to hang up (~ the phone)	**at lægge på**	[at ˈlɛgə pɔ]
busy	**optaget**	[ˈʌbˌtæj]
to ring (about phone)	**at ringe**	[at ˈʁɛŋə]
telephone book	**telefonbog** (c)	[teləˈfoːnˌbɔw]
local	**lokal**	[loˈkæːl]
long distance (e.g., ~ call)	**mellembys**	[ˈmɛləmˌbyːs]
international	**international**	[ˈentʌnaɕoˌnæl]

114. Mobile telephone

mobile phone	**mobiltelefon** (c)	[moˈbiːl teləˈfoːn]
display	**display** (n)	[disˈplɛj]
button	**knap** (c)	[knɑb]
SIM card	**SIM-kort** (n)	[ˈsimˌkɒːd]
battery	**batteri** (n)	[badeˈʁiː]
to be dead (battery)	**at være afladet**	[at ˈvɛːɒ ˈɑulæːðəð]
charger	**oplader** (c)	[ˈʌblæːðʌ]
menu	**menu** (c)	[meˈny]
settings	**indstillinger** (pl)	[enˈsdeleŋʌ]
tune (melody)	**melodi** (c)	[meloˈdiː]
to choose (select)	**at vælge**	[at ˈvɛljə]
calculator	**lommeregner** (c)	[ˈlʌməˌʁɑjnʌ]
answering machine	**telefonsvarer** (c)	[teləˈfoːnsˌvɑːɑ]
alarm clock	**vækkeur** (n)	[ˈvɛkəˌuɒ]
contacts	**telefonbog** (c)	[teləˈfoːnˌbɔw]
SMS (text message)	**SMS-besked** (c)	[ɛsɛmˈɛs beˈskeð]
subscriber	**abonnent** (c)	[aboˈnɛnd]

115. Stationery

ballpoint pen	**kuglepen** (c)	['ku:lə͵pən]
fountain pen	**fyldepen** (c)	['fylə͵pən]
pencil	**blyant** (c)	['blyand]
highlighter	**markør** (c)	[mɑːˈkøɒ]
felt-tip pen	**filtpen** (c)	['fild͵pən]
notepad	**skriveblok** (c)	['skʁi:və͵blɒk]
datebook	**kalender** (c)	[kaˈlɛndʌ]
ruler	**lineal** (c)	[lineˈæːl]
calculator	**regnemaskine** (c)	['ʁɑjnəma͵sgi:nə]
eraser	**viskelæder** (n)	['veskə͵lɛðʌ]
thumbtack	**tegnestift** (c)	['tɑjnə͵sdefd]
paper clip	**klips** (n)	[klebs]
glue	**lim** (c)	[li:m]
stapler	**hæftemaskine** (c)	['hɛfdama͵ski:nə]
hole punch	**hullemaskine** (c)	['hɔlə maˈsgi:nə]
pencil sharpener	**blyantspidser** (c)	['blyand͵spesʌ]
pointer	**pegepind** (c)	['pɑjəpen]
card index	**kartotek** (n)	[kɑtoˈte:k]
label	**etiket** (c)	[etiˈkɛd]

116. Various kinds of documents

account (report)	**rapport** (c)	[ʁɑˈpɒːd]
agreement	**overenskomst** (c)	[ɒwʌˈens͵kʌmsd]
application form	**ansøgningsskema** (n)	['ansøːneŋsˈsge:ma]
authentic	**ægte**	['ɛgdə]
badge (identity tag)	**badge** (c)	['badɕ]
business card	**visitkort** (n)	[viˈsid͵kɒːd]
certificate (~ of quality)	**certifikat** (n)	[sɑɒdifiˈkæːd]
check (e.g., draw a ~)	**check** (c)	['ɕɛk]
check (in restaurant)	**regning** (c)	['ʁɑjneŋ]
constitution	**forfatning** (c)	[foˈfadneŋ]
contract	**aftale** (c)	[ɑuˈtæːlə]
copy	**kopi** (c)	[koˈpi:]
copy (of contract etc.)	**eksemplar** (n)	[ɛksɛmˈplɑ:]
declaration	**deklaration** (c)	[deklɑɑˈɕon]
document	**dokument** (n)	[dokuˈmɛnd]
driver's license	**kørekort** (n)	['kø:ɒ͵kɒːd]
attachment (to the contract)	**bilag** (n)	['bi͵læj]

form	**spørgeskema** (n)	['sbœʊwəˌsge:ma]
identity card, ID	**legitimation** (c)	[legitima'ɕo:n]
inquiry (request)	**forespørgsel** (n)	['fɔːɒsbœɒsəl]
invitation	**indbydelseskort** (n)	[en'byðəlsəsˌkɒ:d]
invoice	**regning** (c)	['ʁɑjneŋ]
law	**lov** (c)	['lɒw]
letter (mail)	**brev** (n)	['bʁɛu]
letterhead	**blanket** (c)	[blɑŋ'kɛd]
list (of names etc.)	**liste** (c)	['lesdə]
manuscript	**manuskript** (n)	[manu'skʁɛbd]
newsletter	**informationsbulletin** (c)	[enfɒma'ɕo:ns buəˌti:n]
note (short letter)	**memo** (n)	['memo:]
pass (for worker, visitor)	**adgangskort** (n)	[að'gɑŋskɒ:d]
passport	**pas** (n)	[pas]
permit	**skriftlig tilladelse** (c)	['sgʁɛfdli 'teˌlæðəlsə]
résumé	**CV** (c), **curriculum vitæ** (c)	[se've], [ku'ʁikulɒm 'vi:ˌtɛ]
debt note, iou	**kvittering** (c)	[kvi'te:ʁeŋ]
receipt (for purchase etc.)	**kvittering** (c)	[kvi'te:ʁeŋ]
sales slip (receipt)	**kassebon** (c)	['kasəˌbɒn]
report	**rapport** (c)	[ʁɑ'pɒ:d]
to show (ID etc.)	**at forevise**	[at 'fɔːɒˌvisə]
to sign (vt)	**at underskrive**	[at 'ɔnɒˌskʁiuə]
signature	**underskrift** (c)	['ɔnɒˌskʁɛfd]
stamp (on document)	**segl** (n)	['sɑjl]
text	**tekst** (c)	[tɛksd]
ticket (for entry)	**billet** (c)	[bi'lɛd]
to cross out	**at overstrege**	[at ɒuɒ'sdʁɑjə]
to fill out (~ a form etc.)	**at udfylde**	[at 'uðˌfylə]
waybill	**fragtbrev** (n)	['fʁɑgdbʁɛu]
will	**testamente** (n)	[tɛsda'mɛndə]

117. Kinds of business

accounting services	**bogføringsservice** (c)	['bɒufø:ʁeŋs ˌsɒvis]
advertising	**reklame** (c)	[ʁɛ'klæ:mə]
advertising agency	**reklamebureau** (n)	[ʁɛ'klæ:məbyˌʁo]
air-conditioners	**klimaanlæg** (n pl)	['kli:manˌlɛ:g]
airline	**luftfartsselskab** (n)	['lɒfdfɑds 'sɛlˌskæb]
alcoholic drinks	**alkoholiske drikke** (pl)	[alko'holiskə 'dʁɛkə]
antiques	**antikvitet** (c)	[antikvi'te:d]
art gallery	**galleri** (n)	[galə'ʁi:]
audit services	**revisions kontor** (n)	[ʁɛvi'ɕo:ns kɒn'toɒ]
banks	**bankvæsen** (n)	['bɑŋkˌvɛ:sən]
bar	**bar** (c)	[bɑ:]

beauty parlor	skønhedssalon (c)	['skœnheðs sa'lʌŋ]
bookstore	boghandel (c)	['bou̯ˌhanəl]
brewery	bryggeri (n)	[bʁygə'ʁi:]
business center	forretningscenter (n)	[fɒ'ʁadneŋ ˌsɛndʌ]
business school	handelsskole (c)	['hanəlsˌsko:lə]

casino	kasino (n)	[ka'si:no]
construction	byggeri (n)	[bygə'ʁi:]
consulting	rådgivning (c)	['ʁɒðˌgivneŋ]

dentistry	tandlæge (c)	['tanˌlɛ:jə]
design	design (n)	[de'sɑjn]
drugstore, pharmacy	apotek (n)	[ɑpo'te:k]
dry cleaners	renseri (n)	[ʁansə'ʁi:]
employment agency	arbejdsformidling (c)	['ɑ:bɑjdsfɒˌmiðleŋ]

financial services	finansielle tjenesteydelser (pl)	[finan'ɕɛlə 'tjɛ:nəsdəˌy:ðəlsʌ]
food (industry)	fødevarer (pl)	['fø:ðəvaˌɑ]
funeral home	begravelseskontor (n)	[be'gʁɑːuəlsəsˌgɒntoɒ]
furniture (for house)	møbler (pl)	['møblʌ]
garment	konfektion (c)	[kʌnfək'ɕon]
hotel	hotel (n)	[ho'tɛl]

ice-cream	is (c)	[i:s]
industry	industri (c)	[endu'sdʁi:]
insurance	forsikring (c)	[fɒ'segʁɛŋ]
Internet	Internet (n)	['entʌˌnɛd]
investment	investeringer (pl)	[envɛ'sde:ʁeŋʌ]

jeweler	guldsmed (c)	['gulˌsmeð]
jewelry	juvelervarer (pl)	[juvə'loə ˌva:ɑ]
laundry (room, shop)	vaskeri (c)	[vaskə'ʁi:]
legal advisor	juridisk service (c)	[ju'ʁiðisk 'sœ:vis]
light industry	let industri (c)	[ˌlət endu'sdʁi:]

magazine	journal (c)	[ɕuɒ'næ:l]
mail-order selling	postordresalg (n)	['pɒsdˌɒːdʁɒsalj]
medicine	medicin (c)	[medi'si:n]
movie theater	biograf (c)	[bio'gʁɑ:f]
museum	museum (n)	[mu'sɛ:ɒm]

news agency	nyhedsbureau (n)	['nyheðsbyˌʁo]
newspaper	avis (c)	[a'vi:s]
nightclub	natklub (c)	['nadˌklub]

oil (petroleum)	råolie (c)	['ʁɒˌo:ljə]
parcels service	kurertjeneste (c)	[ku'ʁɛɒ 'tjɛ:nəsdə]
pharmaceuticals	farmaci (c)	[fɑma'si:]
printing (industry)	trykkeri (n)	[tʁœkə'ʁi:]
publishing house	forlag (n)	['fɒlæ:]
radio	radio (c)	['ʁɑ:dio]

real estate	**fast ejendom** (c)	[fasd ˈɑjəndɒm]
restaurant	**restaurant** (c)	[ʁɛsdoˈʁɑn]
security agency	**sikkerhedsselskab** (n)	[ˈsekʌˌheðsˈsɛlˌskæb]
sports	**sport** (c)	[sbɒːd]
stock exchange	**børs** (c)	[ˈbœɒs]
store	**forretning** (c)	[foˈʁadneŋ]
supermarket	**supermarked** (n)	[ˈsuːbɒˌmɑːkəð]
swimming pool	**svømmebassin** (n)	[ˈsvœməbaˌsɛŋ]
tailors	**skrædderi** (n)	[skʁaðəˈʁiː]
television	**fjernsyn** (n), **tv** (n)	[ˈfjɑɒnˌsyːn], [ˈteˌve]
theater	**teater** (n)	[teˈædʌ]
trade	**handel** (c)	[ˈhanəl]
transportation	**transport** (c)	[tʁɑnsˈpɒːd]
travel	**turisme** (c)	[tuˈʁismə]
veterinarian	**dyrlæge** (c)	[ˈdyɒ ˈlɛːjə]
warehouse	**lager** (n)	[ˈlæjʌ]
waste management	**affalds indsamling** (c)	[ˈɑwˌfals ˈenˌsɑmleŋ]

Job. Business. Part 2

118. Show. Exhibition

exhibition, show	**udstilling** (c)	['uðsdeleŋ]
trade show	**handelsmesse** (c)	['hanels 'mɛsə]
participation	**deltagelse** (c)	['delˌtæjəlsə]
to participate (vi)	**at deltage**	[at 'delˌtæ]
participant	**deltager** (c)	['delˌtæːʌ]
director	**direktør** (c)	[diɒɛk'tøɒ]
organizer's office	**arrangør** (n)	[ɑɑŋ'ɕøːɒ]
organizer	**organisator** (c)	[ɒɡani'sæːtʌ]
to organize (vt)	**at organisere**	[at ɒɡani'seʌ]
participation form	**ansøgningsskema** (n)	['ansøːneŋs'sgeːma]
to fill out (vt)	**at udfylde**	[at 'uðˌfylə]
details	**detalje** (c)	[de'taljə]
information	**information** (c)	[enfɒma'ɕoːn]
price	**pris** (c)	[pʁiːs]
including	**inklusive**	['enkluˌsiuə]
to include (vt)	**at inkludere**	[at enklu'deːɒ]
to pay (vi, vt)	**at betale**	[at be'tæːlə]
registration fee	**registreringsindskud** (n)	[ʁɛgi'sdʁɛɒeŋ 'enˌsguð]
entrance	**indgang** (c)	['engɑŋ]
pavilion, hall	**pavillon** (c)	[pavil'jɒŋ]
to register (vt)	**at registrere**	[at ʁɛgi'sdʁɛːɒ]
badge (identity tag)	**badge** (c)	['badɕ]
booth, stand	**stand** (c)	[sdan]
to reserve, to book	**at reservere**	[at ʁɛsaɒ've:ɒ]
display case	**vitrine** (c)	[vi'tʁiːnə]
spotlight	**lampe** (c)	['lɑmbə]
design	**design** (n)	[de'sɑjn]
to place (put, set)	**at placere**	[at pla'se:ɒ]
to be placed	**at blive placeret**	[at 'bliːə pla'se:ɒð]
distributor	**distributør** (c)	[disdʁibu'tøɒ]
supplier	**leverandør** (c)	[leːvɛʁan'døɒ]
to supply (vt)	**at levere**	[at leː'veːɒ]
country	**land** (n)	[lan]
foreign	**udenlandsk**	['uðənˌlansk]

product	**produkt** (n)	[pʁo'dɔkd]
association (grouping)	**forening** (c)	[fo'e:nen]
conference hall	**konferencesal** (c)	[kʌnfe'ʁɑnsɛˌsæ:l]
congress	**kongres** (c)	[kʌn'gʁas]
contest (competition)	**konkurrence** (c)	[kʌnko'ʁɑŋsə]

visitor	**besøgende** (c)	[be'sø:jənə]
to visit (vi, vt)	**at besøge**	[at be'sø:ə]
customer	**kunde** (c)	['kɔnə]

119. Mass Media

newspaper	**avis** (c)	[a'vi:s]
magazine	**tidsskrift** (n)	['tiðsˌskʁɛfd]
press (printed media)	**presse** (c)	['pʁasə]
radio	**radio** (c)	['ʁɑ:dio]
radio station	**radiostation** (c)	['ʁɑ:diosdaˌço:n]
television	**fjernsyn** (n), **tv** (n)	['fjaɒnˌsy:n], ['teˌve]

anchorman	**studievært** (c)	['sdu:djəˌvæɒd]
newscaster	**speaker** (c)	['sbi:kʌ]
commentator	**kommentator** (c)	[kɔmən'tæ:tʌ]

journalist	**journalist** (c)	[çuɒna'lisd]
correspondent (reporter)	**korrespondent** (c)	[kɒɒsbʌn'dɛnd]
press photographer	**pressefotograf** (c)	['pʁasə fotoˌgʁɑ:f]
reporter	**reporter** (c)	[ʁɛ'pɒ:dʌ]

| editor | **redaktør** (c) | [ʁɛdɑk'tøɒ] |
| editor-in-chief | **chefredaktør** (c) | ['çɛ:f ʁɛdɑk'tøɒ] |

to subscribe to ...	**at abonnere**	[at abo'ne:ɒ]
subscription	**abonnement** (n)	[abonə'maɳd]
subscriber	**abonnent** (c)	[abo'nɛnd]
to read (vi, vt)	**at læse**	[at 'lɛ:sə]
reader	**læser** (c)	['lɛ:sʌ]

circulation (of newspaper)	**oplag** (n)	['ʌbˌlæj]
monthly	**månedlig**	['mɔ:nəðli]
weekly (adj)	**ugentlig**	['u:əndli]
issue (edition)	**nummer** (n)	['nɔmʌ]
recent (new)	**ny**	[ny:]

headline	**overskrift** (c)	['ɒwʌskʁɛfd]
short article	**notits** (c)	[no'tids]
column (regular article)	**rubrik** (c)	[ʁub'ʁɛk]
article	**artikel** (c)	[ɑ'tikəl]
page	**side** (c)	['si:ðə]
reportage, report	**reportage** (c)	[ʁɛpɒ'tæ:çə]
event	**begivenhed** (c)	[be'givənˌheð]

sensation (news)	**sensation** (c)	[sɛnsaˈɕoːn]
scandal	**skandale** (c)	[skanˈdæːlə]
scandalous	**skandaløs**	[skandaˈløːs]
great (e.g., ~ scandal)	**stor**	[ˈsdoɒ]
program	**tv-program** (n)	[ˈteˌve pʁoˈgʁɑm]
interview	**interview** (n)	[endɒˈvju]
live broadcast	**direkte udsendelse** (c)	[diˈʁakdə ˈuðˌsɛnəlsə]
channel	**kanal** (c)	[kaˈnæːl]

120. Agriculture

agriculture	**landbrug** (n)	[ˈlanˌbʁuː]
peasant (man)	**bonde** (c)	[ˈbɔnə]
peasant (woman)	**bondekone** (c)	[ˈbɔnəˌkoːnə]
farmer	**bonde** (c)	[ˈbɔnə]
tractor	**traktor** (c)	[ˈtʁɑktɒ]
combine, harvester	**mejetærsker** (c)	[ˈmɑjəˌtæɒskʌ]
plow	**plov** (c)	[plɒuu]
to plow (vi, vt)	**at pløje**	[at ˈplɒjə]
plowland	**pløjemark** (c)	[ˈplʌjəˌmɑːk]
furrow (in field)	**plovfure** (c)	[ˈplɒwˌfuːɒ]
to sow (vi, vt)	**at så**	[at sɒ]
seeder	**såmaskine** (c)	[ˈsɔːmaˌskiːnə]
sowing (process)	**såning** (c)	[ˈsɔːneŋ]
scythe	**le** (c)	[leː]
to mow, to scythe	**at slå græs**	[at slɔː gʁas]
shovel (tool)	**spade** (c)	[ˈsbæːðə]
to dig (vi, vt)	**at grave**	[at ˈgʁɑːuə]
hoe	**lugejern** (n)	[ˈluːəˌjæɒn]
to hoe, to weed	**at luge**	[at ˈluːə]
weed (plant)	**ukrudt** (n)	[ukˈʁud]
watering can	**vandkande** (c)	[ˈvankanə]
to water (plants)	**at vande**	[at ˈvanə]
watering (act)	**vanding** (c)	[ˈvaneŋ]
pitchfork	**greb** (c)	[gʁɛːb]
rake	**rive** (c)	[ˈʁiːuə]
fertilizer	**gødning** (c)	[ˈgøðneŋ]
to fertilize (vt)	**at gøde**	[at ˈgøːðə]
manure (fertilizer)	**gødning** (c)	[ˈgøðneŋ]
field	**mark** (c)	[mɑːk]

meadow	**eng** (c)	[ɛŋ]
vegetable garden	**køkkenhave** (c)	['køkən,hæ:uə]
orchard (e.g., apple ~)	**have** (c)	['hæ:və]

to herd (livestock)	**at vogte**	[at 'vɒgdə]
herdsman	**hyrde** (c)	['hyɒdə]
pastureland	**græsgang** (c)	['gʁasgɑŋ]

| cattle breeding | **kvægavl** (c) | ['kvɛj,aul] |
| sheep farming | **fåreavl** (c) | ['fɒːɒ,aul] |

plantation	**plantage** (c)	[plan'tæ:çə]
row (garden bed ~s)	**havebed** (n)	['hæ:və,beð]
greenhouse	**drivbænk** (c)	['dʁiu,bɛŋk]
hothouse	**drivhus** (n)	['dʁi:u,hu:s]

| drought (lack of rain) | **tørke** (c) | ['tœɒkə] |
| dry (~ summer) | **tør** | ['tœɒ] |

| cereal plants | **korn** (pl) | ['koɒn] |
| to harvest, to gather | **at høste** | [at 'høsdə] |

miller (person)	**møller** (c)	['mølʌ]
mill (e.g., gristmill)	**mølle** (c)	[mølə]
to grind (grain)	**at male**	[at 'mæ:lə]
flour	**mel** (n)	[me:l]
straw	**strå** (n)	[sdʁɔ:]

121. Building. Building process

construction site	**byggeplads** (c)	['bygə,plas]
to build (vt)	**at bygge**	[at 'bygə]
construction worker	**bygningsarbejder** (c)	['bygneŋs ,ɑ:bɑjdʌ]

project	**projekt** (n)	[pʁo'çɛkd]
architect	**arkitekt** (c)	[ɑki'tɛkd]
worker	**bygningsarbejder** (c)	['bygneŋs ,ɑ:bɑjdʌ]

foundation (of building)	**fundament** (n)	[fɔnda'mɛnd]
roof	**tag** (n)	[tæ:]
pile (foundation ~)	**pæl** (c)	[pɛ:l]
wall	**mur** (c)	['muɒ]

| reinforcing bars | **armering** (c) | [ɑ'meɒeŋ] |
| scaffolding | **stillads** (n) | [sde'læs] |

concrete	**beton** (c)	[be'tɒŋ]
granite	**granit** (c)	[gʁɑ'nid]
stone	**sten** (c)	[sde:n]
brick	**mursten** (c)	['muɒsdən]

sand	**sand** (n)	[san]
cement	**cement** (c)	[se'mɛnd]
plaster (for walls)	**pudsekalk** (c)	['pusə‚kalk]
to plaster (vt)	**at pudse**	[at 'puse:]
paint	**maling** (c)	['mæ:leŋ]
to paint (e.g., ~ a wall)	**at male**	[at 'mæ:lə]
barrel	**tønde** (c)	['tønə]
crane	**kran** (c)	[kʁɑ:n]
to lift (vt)	**at løfte**	[at 'løfdə]
to lower (vt)	**at hejse ned**	[at 'hajsə neð]
bulldozer	**bulldozer** (c)	['bul‚do:sʌ]
excavator	**gravemaskine** (c)	['gʁɑ:uə ma'sgi:nə]
scoop, bucket	**graveskovl** (c)	['gʁɑ:uə ‚sgoul]
to dig (excavate)	**at grave**	[at 'gʁɑ:uə]
hard hat	**hjelm** (c)	[jɛlm]

122. Science. Research. Scientists

science	**videnskab** (c)	['viðən‚skæb]
scientific	**videnskabelig**	['vi:ðən‚sgæ:bəli]
scientist	**forsker** (c)	['fɔ:skʌ]
theory	**teori** (c)	[teo'ʁi]
axiom	**aksiom** (n)	[ɑk'ɕom]
analysis	**analyse** (c)	[ana'ly:sə]
to analyze (vt)	**at analysere**	[at analy'seʌ]
argument (reasoning)	**argument** (n)	[ɑgu'mɛnd]
substance (matter)	**stof** (n)	[sdɒf]
hypothesis	**hypotese** (c)	[hybo'te:sə]
dilemma	**dilemma** (n)	[di'lɛma]
dissertation	**afhandling** (c)	[ɑu'hanleŋ]
dogma	**dogme** (n)	['dɒumə]
doctrine	**doktrin** (c)	[dɒk'tʁin]
research	**forskning** (c)	['fɔ:sgneŋ]
to do research	**at forske**	[at 'fɔ:skə]
testing	**test** (c)	[tɛsd]
laboratory	**laboratorium** (n)	[laboʁɑ'toɒjɔm]
method	**metode** (c)	[me'to:ðə]
molecule	**molekyle** (n)	[mole'ky:lə]
monitoring	**overvågning** (c)	['ɒwʌ‚vɒwneŋ]
discovery (act, event)	**opdagelse** (c)	['ʌb‚dæjəlsə]
postulate	**postulat** (n)	[pɒsdu'lad]
principle	**princip** (n)	[pʁin'sib]
forecast	**prognose** (c)	[pʁo'no:sə]

to forecast (vt)	**at prognosticere**	[at pʁognɒsdi'se:ɒ]
synthesis	**syntese** (c)	[syn'te:sə]
trend (tendency)	**tendens** (c)	[tɛn'dɛns]
theorem	**teorem** (n)	[teo'ʁɛm]
teachings	**lærne** (pl)	['lɛ:ɒnə]
fact	**faktum** (n)	['fɑktɔm]
expedition (to go on an ~)	**ekspedition** (c)	[ɛksbədi'ɕo:n]
experiment	**eksperiment** (n)	[ɛkspeɒi'mɛnd]
academician	**akademimedlem** (n)	[akade:mi:'mɛðlɛm]
bachelor (e.g., ~ of Arts)	**bachelor** (c)	['badɕəlʌ]
doctor (PhD)	**doktor** (c)	['dɒkdɒ]
Associate Professor	**docent** (c)	[do'sɛnd]
Master (e.g., ~ of Arts)	**magister** (c)	[ma'gisdʌ]
professor	**professor** (c)	[pʁo'fɛsɒ]

Professions and occupations

123. Job search. Dismissal

job	**job** (n)	[djɒb]
personnel, staff	**personale** (n)	[paɒso'næ:lə]
career	**karriere** (c)	[kɑi'ɛ:ɒ]
prospect	**perspektiv** (n)	[pæɒsbək'tiw]
skills (expertise)	**kunnen** (c)	['kunən]
selection (for job)	**udvalg** (n)	['uðvalj]
employment agency	**arbejdsformidling** (c)	['a:bɑjdsfɒˌmiðleŋ]
résumé	**CV** (c), **curriculum vitæ** (c)	[se've], [ku'ʁikulɔm 'vi:ˌtɛ]
interview (for job)	**samtale** (c)	['samˌtæ:lə]
vacancy, opening	**ledig stilling** (c)	['le:ði 'sdeleŋ]
salary, pay	**løn** (c)	[lœn]
fixed pay	**løn** (c)	[lœn]
pay, compensation	**betaling** (c)	[be'tæ:leŋ]
position (job)	**stilling** (c)	['sdeleŋ]
duty (of employee)	**pligt** (c)	['plegd]
range of duties	**arbejdsområde** (n)	['a:ˌbɑjds 'ʌmˌʁɔ:ðə]
busy	**travl**	[tʁɑwl]
to fire (dismiss)	**at afskedige**	[at ɑu'sgeðiə]
dismissal	**afskedigelse** (c)	[ɑu'sgeði:əlsə]
unemployment	**arbejdsløshed** (c)	['a:bɑjdsˌlø:sheð]
unemployed (noun)	**arbejdsløs** (c)	['a:bɑjdslø:s]
retirement	**pension** (c)	[paŋ'ɕo:n]
to retire (from job)	**at gå på pension**	[at gɔ: pɔ paŋ'ɕon]

124. Business people

director	**direktør** (c)	[diɒek'tøɒ]
manager (director)	**forretningsfører** (c)	[fɒ'ʁadneŋs ˌfø:ʌ]
boss	**leder** (c)	['le:ðʌ]
superior	**chef** (c)	[ɕɛ:f]
management	**ledelse** (c)	['le:ðəlsə]
president	**præsident** (c)	[pʁɛsi'dɛnd]
chairman	**formand** (c)	['fɒman]
deputy (substitute)	**stedfortræder** (c)	['sdɛðfʌˌtʁɛðʌ]

assistant	**assistent** (c)	[asi'sdɛnd]
secretary	**sekretær** (c)	[sekʁɛ'tɛɒ]
personal assistant	**privatsekretær** (c)	[pʁi'væːd sekʁə'tɛɒ]
businessman	**forretningsmand** (c)	[fɒ'ʁadneŋs ˌman]
entrepreneur	**iværksætter** (c)	[i'væɒɡˌsɛdʌ]
founder	**stifter** (c)	['sdefdʌ]
to found (vt)	**at stifte**	[at 'sdefdə]
associate	**stifter** (c)	['sdefdʌ]
partner	**partner** (c)	['pɑːdnʌ]
shareholder	**aktionær** (c)	[ɑkɕo'nɛɒ]
millionaire	**millionær** (c)	[miljo'nɛɒ]
billionaire	**milliardær** (c)	[miljɑ'dɛɒ]
owner	**ejer** (c)	['ɑjʌ]
landowner	**jordbesidder** (c)	['joɒbeˌsiðʌ]
customer	**kunde** (c)	['kɔnə]
client	**kunde** (c)	['kɔnə]
regular client	**fast kunde** (c)	[fasd 'kɔnə]
buyer (customer)	**køber** (c)	['køːbʌ]
visitor	**besøgende** (c)	[be'søːjənə]
professional (noun)	**professionel** (c)	[pʁo'fɛɕoˌnɛl]
expert	**ekspert** (c)	[ɛks'pænd]
specialist	**specialist** (c)	[sbeɕa'lisd]
banker	**bankier** (c)	[bɑŋ'kje]
broker	**mægler** (c)	['mɛjlʌ]
cashier, teller	**kasserer** (c)	[ka'seʌ]
accountant	**bogholder** (c)	['bɔuˌhɒlʌ]
security guard	**sikkerhedsvagt** (c)	['seɡʌˌheðs'vɑgd]
investor	**investor** (c)	[en'vɛsdɒ]
debtor	**skyldner** (c)	['skylnʌ]
creditor	**långiver** (c)	['lɔːnˌgiːvʌ]
borrower	**låntager** (c)	['lɔːnˌtæːjʌ]
importer	**importør** (c)	[empɒ'tøɒ]
exporter	**eksportør** (c)	[ɛksbɒ'tøɒ]
manufacturer	**producent** (c)	[pʁodu'sɛnd]
distributor	**distributør** (c)	[disdʁibu'tøɒ]
middleman	**mellemhandler** (c)	['mɛləmˌhanlʌ]
consultant	**konsulent** (c)	[kʌnsu'lɛnd]
representative	**repræsentant** (c)	[ʁɛpʁɛsən'tand]
agent	**agent** (c)	[a'ɡɛnd]
insurance agent	**forsikringsagent** (c)	[fɒ'seɡʁɛŋs a'ɡɛnd]

125. Service professions

cook	kok (c)	[kɒk]
chef	køkkenchef (c)	['køkənˌɕɛːf]
baker	bager (c)	['bæːʌ]

bartender	bartender (c)	['bɑːˌtɛndʌ]
waiter	tjener (c)	['tjɛːnʌ]
waitress	servitrice (c)	[sɑɒviˈtʁiːsə]

lawyer, attorney	advokat (c)	[aðvoˈkæːd]
lawyer (legal expert)	jurist (c)	[juˈʁisd]
notary	notar (c)	[noˈtɑː]

electrician	elektriker (c)	[eˈlɛktʁikʌ]
plumber	blikkenslager (c)	['blegənˌslɑːʌ]
carpenter	tømrer (c)	['tœmʁʌ]

masseur	massør (c)	[maˈsøɒ]
masseuse	massøse (c)	[maˈsøːsə]
doctor	læge (c)	['lɛːjə]

taxi driver	taxachauffør (c)	['tɑgsaɕoˌføɒ]
driver	chauffør (c)	[ɕoˈføɒ]
courier	kurer (c)	[kuˈʁɛʌ]

chambermaid	stuepige (c)	['sduəˌpiːə]
security guard	sikkerhedsvagt (c)	['segʌˌheðsˈvɑgd]
flight attendant	stewardesse (c)	[sdjuɑˈdɛsə]

teacher (in primary school)	lærer (c)	['lɛːʌ]
librarian	bibliotekar (c)	[biblioteˈkɑː]
translator	tolk (c), oversætter (c)	[tɒlk], ['ɒwʌˌsɛdʌ]
interpreter	tolk (c)	[tɒlk]
guide (person)	guide (c)	['gɑjd]

hairdresser	frisør (c)	[fʁiˈsøɒ]
mailman	postbud (n)	['pɒsdˌbuð]
salesman	ekspedient (c)	[ɛksbeˈdjɛnd]

gardener	gartner (c)	['gɑdnʌ]
servant (in household)	tjener (c)	['tjɛːnʌ]
maid	tjenestepige (c)	['tjɛːnəsdəˌpiːə]
cleaner (cleaning lady)	rengøringsdame (c)	['ʁɛːnˌgœːʁeŋs 'dæːmə]

126. Military professions and ranks

| private | menig (c) | ['meːni] |
| sergeant | sergent (c) | [sæɒˈɕand] |

lieutenant	**løjtnant** (c)	['lʌjd̩nand]
captain	**kaptajn** (c)	[kɑb'tɑjn]
major	**major** (c)	[ma'joɒ]
colonel	**oberst** (c)	['o:bɒsd]
general	**general** (c)	[genə'ʁɑ:l]
marshal	**marskal** (c)	['mɑ:sal]
admiral	**admiral** (c)	[aðmi'ʁɑ:l]
military man	**militær** (n)	[mili'tɛɒ]
soldier	**soldat** (c)	[sɔl'dæ:d]
officer	**officer** (c)	[ɒfi'seʌ]
commander	**befalingsmand** (c)	[be'fæ:leŋs̩man]
border guard	**grænsesoldat** (c)	['gʁansə ˌsɔldæ:d]
radio operator	**radiooperatør** (c)	['ʁɑ:dio o:bəʁɑ'tøɒ]
scout (searcher)	**spejder** (c)	['sbɑjdʌ]
pioneer (sapper)	**pioner** (c)	[pio'neʌ]
marksman	**skytte** (c)	['skødə]
navigator	**styrmand** (c)	['sdyɒˌman]

127. Officials. Priests

king	**konge** (c)	['kʌŋə]
queen	**dronning** (c)	['dʁɒneŋ]
prince	**prins** (c)	[pʁɛns]
princess	**prinsesse** (c)	[pʁɛn'sɛsə]
tsar, czar	**tsar** (c)	[sɑ:]
czarina	**tsarina** (c)	[sa'ʁi:na]
president	**præsident** (c)	[pʁɛsi'dɛnd]
Secretary (~ of State)	**minister** (c)	[mi'nisdʌ]
prime minister	**statsminister** (c)	['sdæ:ds mi'nisdʌ]
senator	**senator** (c)	[se'natɒ]
diplomat	**diplomat** (c)	[diplo'mad]
consul	**konsul** (c)	['kʌnˌsul]
ambassador	**ambassadør** (c)	[ambasa'døɒ]
councelor, advisor	**rådgiver** (c)	['ʁɒðˌgivʌ]
official (civil servant)	**embedsmand** (c)	['ɛmbeðsˌman]
prefect	**præfekt** (c)	[pʁɛ'fɛkd]
mayor	**borgmester** (c)	[bɒw'mɛsdʌ]
judge	**dommer** (c)	['dɒmʌ]
district attorney	**statsadvokat** (c)	['sdæ:d aðvo'kæd]
missionary	**missionær** (c)	[miɕo'nɛɒ]
monk	**munk** (c)	[mɔŋk]

| abbot | **abbed** (c) | ['abəð] |
| rabbi | **rabbiner** (c) | [ʁaˈbiːnʌ] |

vizier	**vesir** (c)	[vɛˈsiɒ]
shah	**shah** (c)	[sha]
sheikh	**sheik** (c)	[ˈɕɑjk]

128. Agricultural professions

beekeeper	**biavler** (c)	[ˈbiɑulʌ]
herdsman	**hyrde** (c)	[ˈhyɒdə]
agronomist	**agronom** (c)	[æˈgʁoˈnoːm]
cattle breeder	**kvægavler** (c)	[ˈkvɛjˌɑulʌ]
veterinarian	**dyrlæge** (c)	[ˈdyɒ ˈlɛːjə]

farmer	**bonde** (c)	[ˈbɔnə]
winemaker	**vinavler** (c)	[ˈviːnˌɑwlʌ]
potter	**pottemager** (c)	[ˈpʌdəˌmæjʌ]
zoologist	**zoolog** (c)	[sooˈloː]
cowboy	**cowboy** (c)	[ˈkɒwˌbʌj]

129. Art professions

| actor | **skuespiller** (c) | [ˈskuəˌsbelʌ] |
| actress | **skuespillerinde** (c) | [ˌskuːəsbelʌˈenə] |

| singer (man) | **sanger** (c) | [ˈsɑŋʌ] |
| singer (woman) | **sangerinde** (c) | [sɑŋʌˈenə] |

| dancer (man) | **danser** (c) | [ˈdansʌ] |
| dancer (woman) | **danserinde** (c) | [dansɒˈenə] |

| performing artist (masc.) | **skuespiller** (c) | [ˈskuəˌsbelʌ] |
| performing artist (fem.) | **skuespillerinde** (c) | [ˌskuːəsbelʌˈenə] |

musician	**musiker** (c)	[ˈmusikʌ]
pianist	**klaverspiller** (c)	[klaˈveɒˌsbelʌ]
guitar player	**guitarist** (c)	[gitaˈʁisd]

conductor (of musicians)	**dirigent** (c)	[diɒiˈgɛnd]
composer	**komponist** (c)	[kɒmpoˈnisd]
impresario	**impresario** (c)	[empʁəˈsɑio]

movie director	**filminstruktør** (c)	[ˈfilm ensdʁukˈtøɒ]
producer	**producer** (c)	[pʁoˈdjuːsʌ]
scriptwriter	**manuskriptforfatter** (c)	[manuˈskʁɛbd fʌˈfadʌ]
critic	**kritiker** (c)	[ˈkʁitikʌ]
writer	**forfatter** (c)	[fɒˈfadʌ]

poet	**digter** (c)	['degdʌ]
sculptor	**billedhugger** (c)	['beləðˌhɔgʌ]
artist (painter)	**kunstmaler** (c)	['kɔnsdˌmæːlʌ]

juggler	**jonglør** (c)	[ɕɒŋg'løɒ]
clown	**klovn** (c)	['klɒwn]
acrobat	**akrobat** (c)	[akʁo'bad]
magician	**tryllekunstner** (c)	['tʁyləˌkɔnsdnʌ]

130. Various professions

doctor	**læge** (c)	['lɛːjə]
nurse (in hospital)	**sygeplejerske** (c)	['syəˌplɑjɒsgə]
psychiatrist	**psykiater** (c)	[syki'æːdʌ]
dentist	**tandlæge** (c)	['tanˌlɛːjə]
surgeon	**kirurg** (c)	[ki'ʁuɒw]

astronaut	**astronaut** (c)	[asdʁo'nɑud]
astronomer	**astronom** (c)	[asdʁo'noːm]
pilot	**pilot** (c)	[pi'loːd]

driver (of car, taxi etc.)	**chauffør** (c)	[ɕo'føɒ]
engineer (train driver)	**togfører** (c)	['tɔwˌføːʌ]
mechanic	**mekaniker** (c)	[me'kænikʌ]

miner	**minearbejder** (c)	['minəˌɑːbɑjdʌ]
worker	**arbejder** (c)	['ɑːˌbɑjdʌ]
metalworker	**maskinarbejder** (c)	[ma'skinˌɑːbɑjdʌ]
joiner, carpenter	**snedker** (c)	['sneːkʌ]
turner	**drejer** (c)	['dʁɑjʌ]
construction worker	**bygningsarbejder** (c)	['bygneŋs ˌɑːbɑjdʌ]
welder	**svejser** (c)	['svɑjsʌ]

professor	**professor** (c)	[pʁo'fɛsɒ]
architect	**arkitekt** (c)	[aki'tɛkd]
historian	**historiker** (c)	[hi'sdoɒikʌ]
scientist	**forsker** (c)	['fɒːskʌ]
physicist	**fysiker** (c)	['fysikʌ]
chemist (scientist)	**kemiker** (c)	['kemikʌ]

archeologist	**arkæolog** (c)	[ˌɑːkɛo'lo]
geologist	**geolog** (c)	[geo'loː]
researcher	**forsker** (c)	['fɒːskʌ]

| babysitter | **barnepige** (c) | ['bɑːnəˌpiːə] |
| teacher | **pædagog** (c) | [pɛda'goː] |

editor	**redaktør** (c)	[ʁɛdak'tøɒ]
editor-in-chief	**chefredaktør** (c)	['ɕɛːf ʁɛdak'tøɒ]
correspondent	**korrespondent** (c)	[kɒɒsbʌn'dɛnd]

typist (woman)	**maskinskriverske** (c)	[ma'ski:n 'skʁi:vʌskə]
designer	**designer** (c)	[de'sajnʌ]
computer expert	**computer-ekspert** (c)	[kɒm'pju:dɒ ɛks'pæɒd]
programmer	**programmør** (c)	[pʁogʁa'møɒ]
engineer (designer)	**ingeniør** (c)	[enɕən'jøɒ]

seaman	**sømand** (c)	['søman]
sailor	**matros** (c)	[ma'tʁos]
rescuer	**livredder** (c)	['li:u̯ʁɛðʌ]

fireman	**brandmand** (c)	['bʁɑn,man]
policeman	**politibetjent** (c)	[poli'tibe,tjɛnd]
watchman	**vagt** (c)	[vɑgd]
detective	**opdager** (c)	['ʌb,dæjʌ]

customs officer	**toldbetjent** (c)	['tɒl be'tjɛnd]
bodyguard	**livvagt** (c)	['li:u̯,vɑgd]
prison guard	**fangevogter** (c)	['faŋə,vɒgdʌ]
inspector	**inspektør** (c)	[ensbɛk'tøɒ]

sportsman	**sportsmand** (c)	['sbɒ:dsman]
trainer, coach	**træner** (c)	['tʁɛ:nʌ]
butcher	**slagter** (c)	['slɑgdʌ]
cobbler	**skomager** (c)	['sgo,mæjʌ]
businessman	**handelsmand** (c)	['hanels,man]
loader (person)	**lastearbejder** (c)	['lasdə,a:bajdʌ]

| fashion designer | **modedesigner** (c) | ['mo:ðə di'sajnʌ] |
| model (woman) | **model** (c) | [mo'dɛl] |

131. Occupations. Social status

| schoolboy | **skoleelev** (c) | ['sko:løe'lew] |
| student (college ~) | **studerende** (c) | [sdu'deʌnə] |

philosopher	**filosof** (c)	[filo'sɒf]
economist	**økonom** (c)	[øko'no:m]
inventor	**opfinder** (c)	['ʌb,fenʌ]

unemployed (noun)	**arbejdsløs** (c)	['a:bajdslø:s]
retiree	**pensionist** (c)	[paŋɕo'nisd]
spy, secret agent	**spion** (c)	[sbi'o:n]

prisoner	**fange** (c)	['faŋə]
striker	**strejkende** (c)	['sdʁajkɛnə]
bureaucrat	**bureaukrat** (c)	[byʁo'kʁa:d]
traveler	**rejsende** (c)	['ʁajsənə]

| homosexual | **bøsse** (c) | ['bøsə] |
| hacker | **hacker** (c) | ['hakʌ] |

hippie	**hippie** (c)	['hibi]
bandit	**bandit** (c)	[ban'did]
hit man, killer	**lejemorder** (c)	['lɑjə ˌmoͻdʌ]
drug addict	**narkoman** (c)	[nɑko'mæn]
drug dealer	**narkohandler** (c)	['nɑːkoˌhanlʌ]
prostitute (woman)	**prostitueret** (c)	[pʁosditu'eʌð]
pimp	**alfons** (c)	[al'foŋs]

sorcerer	**troldmand** (c)	['tʁɒlman]
sorceress	**troldkvinde** (c)	['tʁɒlˌkvenə]
pirate	**pirat** (c)	[pi'ʁɑːd]
slave	**slave** (c)	['slæːvə]
samurai	**samurai** (c)	[samu'ʁɑj]
savage (primitive)	**vildmand** (c)	['vilˌman]

Sports

132. Kinds of sports. Sportspersons

sportsman	**sportsmand** (c)	['sbɒːdsman]
kind of sports	**sportsgren** (c)	['sbɒːdsˌgʁɛːn]
basketball	**basketball** (c)	['baːskədˌbɒːl]
basketball player	**basketballspiller** (c)	['baːskədˌbɒːl ˌsbelʌ]
baseball	**baseball** (c)	['bɛjsˌbɒːl]
baseball player	**baseballspiller** (c)	['bɛjsˌbɒːl ˌsbelʌ]
soccer	**fodbold** (c)	['foðbɒld]
soccer player	**fodboldspiller** (c)	['foðbɒldˌsbelʌ]
goalkeeper	**målmand** (c)	['mɔːlman]
hockey	**ishockey** (c)	['isˌhʌki]
hockey player	**hockeyspiller** (c)	['hʌki ˌsbelʌ]
volleyball	**volleyball** (c)	['vʌliˌbɒːl]
volleyball player	**volleyballspiller** (c)	['vʌliˌbɒːl 'sbelʌ]
boxing	**boksning** (c)	['bɒgsneŋ]
boxer	**bokser** (c)	['bɒksʌ]
wrestling	**brydning** (c)	['bʁyðneŋ]
wrestler	**bryder** (c)	['bʁyðʌ]
karate	**karate** (c)	[kɑ'ʁɑːdə]
karate fighter	**karatedyrker** (c)	[kɑ'ʁɑːdə ˌdyɒkʌ]
judo	**judo** (c)	['juːdo]
judo athlete	**judokæmper** (c)	['juːdo 'kɛmbʌ]
tennis	**tennis** (c)	['tɛnis]
tennis player	**tennisspiller** (c)	['tɛnisˌsbelʌ]
swimming	**svømning** (c)	['svœmneŋ]
swimmer	**svømmer** (c)	['svœmʌ]
fencing	**fægtning** (c)	['fɛgdneŋ]
fencer	**fægter** (c)	['fɛgdʌ]
chess	**skak** (c)	[skɑk]
chess player	**skakspiller** (c)	['skɑkˌsbelʌ]

alpinism	**alpinisme** (c)	[alpi:'nismə]
alpinist	**bjergbestigning** (c)	['bjɑɒubeˌsdi:neŋ]
running	**løb** (n)	[lø:b]
runner	**løber** (c)	['lø:bʌ]
athletics	**atletik** (c)	[adlə'tik]
athlete	**atlet** (c)	[ad'led]
horseback riding	**ridesport** (c)	['ʁi:ðeˌsbɒ:d]
rider	**rytter** (c)	['ʁydʌ]
figure skating	**kunstskøjteløb** (n)	['kɔnsdˌskɒjdələ:b]
figure skater (man)	**kunstskøjteløber** (c)	['kɔnsdˌskɒjdələ:bʌ]
figure skater (woman)	**kunstskøjteløber** (c)	['kɔnsdˌskɒjdələ:bʌ]
weightlifting	**vægtløftning** (c)	['vɛgdˌløfdneŋ]
weightlifter	**vægtløfter** (c)	['vɛgdˌløfdʌ]
car racing	**motorløb** (n)	['mo:tʌlø:b]
racing driver	**racerkører** (c)	['ʁɛ:sɒˌkø:ʌ]
cycling	**cykelsport** (c)	['sykəlˌsbɒ:d]
cyclist	**cyklist** (c)	[syk'lisd]
broad jump	**længdespring** (n)	['lɛŋdeˌsbʁeŋ]
pole vault	**stangspring** (n)	['sdɑŋˌspʁeŋ]
jumper	**springer** (c)	['sbʁeŋʌ]

133. Kinds of sports. Miscellaneous

football	**amerikansk fodbold** (c)	[ameɒi'kæ:nsk 'foðbɒld]
badminton	**badminton** (c)	['badmentʌn]
biathlon	**skiskydning** (c)	['sgiˌsgyðneŋ]
billiards	**billard** (n)	['biliˌɑd]
bobsled	**bobslæde**	['bɒbslɛ:ðə]
bodybuilding	**bodybuilding** (c)	['bɒdiˌbilden]
water polo	**vandpolo** (c)	['van 'po:lo]
handball	**håndbold** (c)	['hɒnˌbold]
golf	**golf** (c)	[gɒlf]
rowing	**roning** (c)	['ʁo:neŋ]
diving	**dykning** (c)	['døgneŋ]
cross-country skiing	**skiløb** (n)	['skilø:b]
ping-pong	**bordtennis** (c)	['bɒɒˌtɛnis]
sailing	**sejlsport** (c)	['sɑjlˌsbɒ:d]
rally	**rally** (n)	['ʁɑli]
rugby	**rugby** (c)	['ʁʌgbi]

| snowboarding | **snowboard** (n) | ['snɔw,bɒːd] |
| archery | **bueskydning** (c) | ['buːə ˌskyðneŋ] |

134. Gym

| barbell | **vægtstang** (c) | ['vɛgd,sdɑŋ] |
| dumbbells | **håndvægt** (c) | ['hɒnvɛgd] |

training machine	**træningsmaskine**	['tʁɛːneŋsmaˌsgiːnə]
bicycle trainer	**motionscykel** (c)	[moˈɕoːnsˌsykəl]
treadmill	**løbebånd** (n)	['løːbəˌbʌn]

horizontal bar	**reck** (c)	[ʁɛk]
parallel bars	**barre** (c)	['bɑːɑ]
vaulting horse	**hest** (c)	[hɛsd]
mat (in gym)	**måtte** (c)	['mʌdə]

jump rope	**sjippetov** (n)	['ɕibəˌtɒw]
aerobics	**aerobic** (c)	[ɛˈʁʌbig]
yoga	**yoga** (c)	['joːga]

135. Hockey

hockey	**ishockey** (c)	['isˌhʌki]
hockey player	**hockeyspiller** (c)	['hʌki ˌsbelʌ]
to play hockey	**at spille hockey**	[at 'sbelə 'hʌki]
ice	**is** (c)	[iːs]

puck	**puck** (c)	[puk]
hockey stick	**kølle** (c)	['køllə]
ice skates	**skøjter** (pl)	['skɒjdʌ]

board	**barriere** (c)	[bɑiˈɛːʌ]
shot	**skud** (n)	[skuð]
goaltender	**målmand** (c)	['mɔːlman]
goal (score)	**mål** (n)	[mɔːl]
to score a goal	**at score et mål**	[at 'sgoːɒ ed mɔːl]

period	**periode** (c)	[paɒiˈoːðə]
second period	**anden periode**	['anən paɒiˈoːðə]
substitutes bench	**udskiftningsbænk** (c)	['uðˌsgifdneŋsˌbɛŋg]

136. Football

| soccer | **fodbold** (c) | ['foðbɒld] |
| soccer player | **fodboldspiller** (c) | ['foðbɒldˌsbelʌ] |

to play soccer	at spille fodbold	['sbelə 'foðbɒld]
major league	superliga (c)	['suˌbɒˌliːga]
soccer club	fodboldklub (c)	['foðbɒldˌklub]
coach	træner (c)	['tʁɛːnʌ]
owner	ejer (c)	['ajʌ]
team	hold (n)	[hɒl]
team captain	anfører (c)	['anˌføːʌ]
player	spiller (c)	['sbelʌ]
substitute	udskiftningsspiller (c)	['uðˌsgifdneŋsˌsbelʌ]
forward	angriber (c)	['anˌgʁiːbʌ]
center forward	centerforward (c)	['sɛndɒ 'foːˌvad]
striker, scorer	målscorer (c)	['mɔːlˌsgoːʌ]
defender, back	forsvarer (c)	['fɒsvaːa]
halfback	midtbanespiller (c)	['medbæːneˌsbelɒ]
match	kamp (c)	[kamb]
to meet (vi, vt)	at mødes	[at 'møːðəs]
final	finale (c)	[fi'næːlə]
semi-final	semifinale (c)	['semifiˌnæːlə]
championship	mesterskab (n)	['mɛsdʌˌskæːb]
period, half	halvleg (c)	['haˌlaj]
first period	første halvleg (c)	['fœʁsdə 'haˌlaj]
half-time	pause (c)	['pausə]
goal	mål (n)	[mɔːl]
goalkeeper	målmand (c)	['mɔːlman]
goalpost	stang (c)	[sdɑŋ]
crossbar	overligger (c)	['ɒwʌˌlegʌ]
net	net (n)	[nɛd]
to miss (fail to catch)	at lade gå ind	[at 'læːðə gɔː en]
to miss the ball	at lade et mål gå ind	[at 'læːðə ed mɔːl gɔː en]
ball	bold (c)	[bɒld]
pass	aflevering (c)	['awleˌveɒeŋ]
kick	skud (n)	[skuð]
to kick (~ the ball)	at sparke	[at 'sbaːkə]
free kick	frispark (n)	['fʁiˌsbaːk]
corner kick	hjørnespark (c)	['jœɒneˌsbaːk]
attack	angreb (n)	['anˌgʁɛːb]
counterattack	modangreb (n)	['moðˌangʁɛb]
combination	kombination (c)	[kɒmbina'ɕoːn]
referee	dommer (c)	['dɒmʌ]
to whistle (vi)	at fløjte	[at 'flɒjdə]
whistle (sound)	fløjte (c)	['flɒjdə]
foul, misconduct	forseelse (c)	[fɒ'seːəlsə]
to commit a foul	at begå en forseelse	[at be'gɔː en fʌ'seəlsə]
to send off	at udvise	[at 'uðˌviːsə]

yellow card	**gult kort** (c)	[gu:ld kɒ:d]
red card	**rødt kort** (n)	['ʁœd kɒ:d]
disqualification	**diskvalifikation** (c)	[diskvalifika'ɕo:n]
to disqualify (vt)	**at diskvalificere**	[at 'diskvalifi‚seɒ]
penalty kick	**straffespark** (n)	['sdʁɑfəsbɑ:k]
wall	**mur** (c)	['muɒ]
to score (vi, vt)	**at score**	[at 'sgo:ɒ]
goal (score)	**mål** (n)	[mɔ:l]
to score a goal	**at score et mål**	[at 'sgo:ɒ ed mɔ:l]
replacement	**udskiftning** (c)	['uð‚sgifdneŋ]
to replace (vt)	**at udskifte**	[at 'uð‚skifdə]
rules	**regler** (pl)	['ʁɛjəlʌ]
tactics	**taktik** (c)	[tɑk'tik]
stadium	**stadion** (n)	['sdædjʌn]
stand (at stadium)	**tribune** (c)	[tʁi'by:nə]
fan, supporter	**fan** (c)	[fan]
to shout (vi, vt)	**at råbe**	[at 'ʁɔ:bə]
scoreboard	**lystavle** (c)	['lys‚tɑulə]
score	**score** (c)	['sgo:ʌ]
defeat	**nederlag** (n)	['neðɒlæ:]
to lose (not win)	**at tabe**	[at 'tæ:bə]
draw	**uafgjorte resultat** (n)	['uɑw‚gjoɒde ʁɛsultæd]
to draw (vi)	**at spille uafgjort**	[at sbelə 'uɑu‚gjoɒd]
victory	**sejr** (c)	['sɑjʌ]
to win (vi, vt)	**at vinde**	[at 'venə]
champion	**mester** (c)	['mɛsdʌ]
the best	**bedst**	['bɛsd]
to congratulate (vt)	**at lykønske**	[at 'løk‚ønskə]
commentator	**kommentator** (c)	[kɔmən'tæ:tʌ]
to commentate (vi, vt)	**at kommentere**	[at kɔmən'teʌ]
broadcast	**transmission** (c)	[tʁɑnsmi'ɕon]

137. Alpine skiing

skis	**ski** (pl)	[ski:]
to ski (vi)	**at stå på ski**	[at sdɔ: pɔ ski:]
mountain-ski resort	**alpint ski resort** (n)	[al'pi:nd ski ʁi'sɒ:d]
ski lift	**hejseværk** (c)	['hɑjsəv‚væɒk]
ski poles	**skistave** (pl)	['ski:‚sdæwə]
slope	**skråning** (c)	['sgʁɔ:neŋ]
slalom	**slalom** (c)	['slæ:lɔm]

138. Tennis. Golf

golf	**golf** (c)	[gɒlf]
golf club	**golfklub** (c)	['gɒlf klub]
golfer	**golfspiller** (c)	['gɒlf ˌsbelʌ]
hole	**hule** (c)	['hu:lə]
club	**kølle** (c)	['køllə]
golf trolley	**golfvogn** (c)	['gɒlf 'vɒwn]
tennis	**tennis** (c)	['tɛnis]
court (for tennis)	**tennisbane** (c)	['tɛnisˌbæ:nə]
serve	**serv** (c)	['sæɒv]
to serve (vt)	**at serve**	[at 'saɒuə]
racket	**ketsjer** (c)	['kədɕʌ]
net	**net** (n)	[nɛd]
ball	**bold** (c)	[bɒld]

139. Chess

chess	**skak** (c)	[skɑk]
chessmen	**skakbrikker** (pl)	['skɑkˌbʁɛkkʌ]
chess player	**skakspiller** (c)	['skɑkˌsbelʌ]
chessboard	**skakbræt** (n)	['skɑkˌbʁad]
chessman	**brik** (c)	[bʁɛk]
White (white pieces)	**Hvid**	[við]
Black (black pieces)	**sort**	['sɒ:d]
pawn	**bonde**	['bɔnə]
bishop	**løber** (c)	['lø:bʌ]
knight	**springer** (c)	['sbʁɛŋʌ]
castle	**tårn** (n)	[tɒ:n]
queen	**dronning** (c)	['dʁɒnen]
king	**konge** (c)	['kʌŋə]
move	**træk** (n)	[tʁak]
to move (vi, vt)	**at trække**	[at 'tʁakə]
to sacrifice	**at ofre**	[at 'ɒfʁɒ]
castling	**rokade** (c)	[ʁo'kæ:ðə]
check	**skak** (c)	[skɑk]
checkmate	**mat** (c)	[mæ:d]
chess tournament	**skakturnering** (c)	['sgɑgˌtuɒneɒeŋ]
Grand Master	**stormester** (c)	['sdɒ:ˌmɛsdʌ]
combination	**kombination** (c)	[kɒmbina'ɕo:n]
game (in chess)	**parti** (n)	[pɑ'ti:]
checkers	**dam** (c)	[dɑm]

140. Boxing

boxing	**boksning** (c)	['bɒgsneŋ]
fight	**kamp** (c)	[kɑmb]
boxing match	**tvekamp** (c)	['tvekɑmb]
round (in boxing)	**runde** (c)	['ʁɔndə]

| ring | **ring** (c) | [ʁɛŋ] |
| gong | **gongong** (c) | [gʌŋ'gʌŋ] |

punch	**stød** (n)	['sdøð]
knock-down	**knockdown** (n)	['nɒk,dawn]
knockout	**knockout** (c)	['nɒk,kaud]
to knock out	**at knockoute**	[at nɒ'kkaudə]

| boxing glove | **boksehandske** (c) | ['bɒksə ,hanskə] |
| referee | **dommer** (c) | ['dɒmʌ] |

lightweight	**letvægt** (c)	['lɛd,vɛgd]
middleweight	**mellemvægt** (c)	['mɛləm,vɛgd]
heavyweight	**sværvægt** (c)	['svɛɒ,vɛgd]

141. Sports. Miscellaneous

Olympic Games	**De Olympiske Lege**	[di o'lømpisgə 'lɑjə]
winner	**vinder** (c)	['venʌ]
to be winning	**at vinde**	[at 'venə]
to win (vi)	**at sejre**	[at 'sɑjʁʌ]

| leader | **leder** (c) | ['le:ðʌ] |
| to lead (vi) | **at føre** | [at 'fø:ɒ] |

first place	**førstepladsen** (c)	['fœɒsdɛ 'plasən]
second place	**andenplads** (c)	['anən,plas]
third place	**tredjeplads** (c)	['tʁɛðjə,plas]

medal	**medalje** (c)	[me'daljə]
trophy	**trofæ** (c)	[tʁo'fɛ:]
cup (trophy)	**pokal** (c)	[po'kæ:l]
prize (in game)	**pris** (c)	[pʁi:s]
main prize	**førstepris** (c)	['fœɒsdɛ,pʁi:s]

| record | **rekord** (c) | [ʁɛ'kɒ:d] |
| to set a record | **at sætte rekord** | [at 'sɛdə ʁɛ'kɒ:d] |

final	**finale** (c)	[fi'næ:lə]
final (adj)	**finale-**	[fi'næ:lə]
champion	**mester** (c)	['mɛsdʌ]
championship	**mesterskab** (n)	['mɛsdʌ,skæ:b]

stadium	**stadion** (n)	['sdædjʌn]
stand (at stadium)	**tribune** (c)	[tʁi'by:nə]
fan, supporter	**fan** (c)	[fan]
opponent, rival	**modstander** (c)	['moð,sdanʌ]
start	**start** (c)	[sdɑ:d]
finish	**mål** (c)	[mɔ:l]
defeat	**nederlag** (n)	['neðɒlæ:]
to lose (not win)	**at tabe**	[at 'tæ:bə]
referee	**dommer** (c)	['dɒmʌ]
judges	**jury** (c)	['dju:əi]
score	**score** (c)	['sgo:ʌ]
draw	**uafgjorte resultat** (n)	['uaw,gjoɒde ʁɛsultæd]
to draw (vi)	**at spille uafgjort**	[at sbelə 'uɑu,gjoɒd]
point	**point** (n)	[po'ɛŋ]
result (of match)	**resultat** (n)	[ʁɛsul'tæ:d]
half-time	**pause** (c)	['pɑusə]
dope (for athlete, horse)	**doping** (c)	['dowpeŋ]
to penalize (vt)	**at straffe**	[at 'sdʁɑfə]
to disqualify (vt)	**at diskvalificere**	[at 'diskvalifi,seɒ]
apparatus	**redskab** (n)	['ʁɛð,skæb]
javelin	**spyd** (n)	[sbyð]
shot (metal ball)	**kugle** (c)	['ku:lə]
ball (in snooker, croquet)	**kugle** (c)	['ku:lə]
target (objective)	**mål** (n)	[mɔ:l]
target (e.g., for archery)	**skive** (c)	['ski:və]
to shoot (vi)	**at skyde**	[at 'sky:ðə]
precise (shot)	**præcis**	[pʁɛ'si:s]
trainer, coach	**træner** (c)	['tʁɛ:nʌ]
to train sb	**at træne**	[at 'tʁɛ:nə]
to train (vi)	**at træne sig**	[at 'tʁɛ:nə sɑj]
training	**træning** (c)	['tʁɛ:neŋ]
gym	**sportshal** (c)	['sbɒ:dshal]
exercise (physical)	**øvelse** (c)	['ø:vəlsə]
warm-up (of athlete)	**opvarmning** (c)	[ʌb'vɑ:mneŋ]

Education

142. School

school	**skole** (c)	['sko:lə]
headmaster	**skoleinspektør** (c)	['sko:lə ensbɛk'tøɒ]
pupil (boy)	**elev** (c)	[e'lew]
pupil (girl)	**elev** (c)	[e'lew]
schoolboy	**skoleelev** (c)	['sko:læe'lew]
schoolgirl	**skoleelev** (c)	['sko:læe'lew]
to teach (sb)	**at undervise**	[at 'ɔnɒ‚vi:səi]
to learn (language etc.)	**at lære**	[at 'lɛ:ɒ]
to learn by heart	**at lære udenad**	[at 'lɛ:ɒ 'uðən'að]
to study (vi)	**at studere**	[at 'sdude:ɒ]
to be in school	**at gå i skole**	[at gɔ: i 'sgo:lə]
to go to school	**at gå i skole**	[at gɔ: i 'sgo:lə]
alphabet	**alfabet** (n)	[alfa'be:ð]
subject (at school)	**fag** (n)	['fæj]
classroom	**klasse** (c)	['klasə]
recess	**frikvarter** (n)	['fʁikvɑ‚teʌ]
school bell	**klokke** (c)	['klɒkə]
desk (for pupil)	**skolebord** (n)	['sko:lə‚boɒ]
chalkboard	**tavle** (c)	['tɑwlə]
grade	**karakter** (c)	[kɑɑk'teʌ]
good grade	**høj karakter** (c)	[hɒj kɑɑk'teʌ]
bad grade	**dårlig karakter** (c)	['dɒ:li kɑɑ'gtʌ]
to give a grade	**at give karakter**	[at gi: kɑɑg'tɒə]
mistake	**fejl** (n)	[fɑjl]
to make mistakes	**at lave fejl**	[at 'læ:uə fɑjl]
to correct (vt)	**at rette**	[at 'ʁadə]
cheat sheet	**snydeseddel** (c)	['sny:ðə‚sɛðəl]
homework	**hjemmeopgave** (c)	['jɛmə‚ɒbgæ:uə]
exercise (in education)	**øvelse** (c)	['ø:vəlsə]
to be present	**at være til stede**	[at 'vɛ:ɒ tel 'sdɛ:ðə]
to be absent	**at være fraværende**	[at 'vɛ:ɒ fʁɑ'vɛ:ɒ nə]
to miss classes	**at forsømme**	[at fʌ'sœmə]
to punish (vt)	**at straffe**	[at 'sdʁɑfə]

| punishment | **straf** (c) | [sdʁɑf] |
| conduct (behavior) | **opførsel** (c) | [ʌbˈføɒsəl] |

report card	**karakterbog** (c)	[kɑɑˈteɒˌbɒu]
pencil	**blyant** (c)	[ˈblyand]
eraser	**viskelæder** (n)	[ˈveskəˌlɛðʌ]
chalk	**kridt** (n)	[kʁid]
pencil case	**penalhus** (n)	[peˈnæːlˌhuːs]

schoolbag	**skoletaske** (c)	[ˈskoːləˌtaskə]
pen	**kuglepen** (c)	[ˈkuːləˌpen]
school notebook	**hæfte** (n)	[ˈhɛfdə]
textbook	**lærebog** (c)	[ˈlɛːɒˌbou]
compasses	**passer** (c)	[ˈpasʌ]

| to draw (a blueprint etc.) | **at tegne** | [at ˈtɑjnə] |
| technical drawing | **teknisk tegning** (c) | [ˈtɛgnisg ˈtɑjneŋ] |

poem	**digt** (n)	[degd]
by heart	**udenad**	[ˈuðeˈnɑð]
to learn by heart	**at lære udenad**	[at ˈlɛːɒ ˈuðenˈɑð]

school vacation	**ferie** (c)	[ˈfeɒjə]
to be on vacation	**at holde ferie**	[at ˈhɒlə ˈfeɒjə]
to spend one's vacation	**at tilbringe ferien**	[at telˈbʁɛŋə ˈfeɒjən]

quiz (at school)	**test** (c)	[tɛsd]
essay (composition)	**stil** (c)	[sdiːl]
dictation	**diktat** (c)	[dikˈtæːd]
exam	**prøve** (c), **eksamen** (c)	[ˈpʁœːwəˌɛkˈsæːmən]
to take an exam	**at aflægge en eksamen**	[at auˈlɛgə en ɛgˈsæːmən]
experiment (chemical ~)	**forsøg** (n)	[fɒˈsøː]

143. College. University

academy	**akademi** (n)	[akadeˈmiː]
university	**universitet** (n)	[univæɒsiˈteːd]
faculty (section)	**fakultet** (n)	[fakulˈteːð]

student (man)	**studerende** (c)	[sduˈdeʌnə]
student (woman)	**studerende** (c)	[sduˈdeʌnə]
lecturer (teacher)	**underviser** (c)	[ˈɔnɒˌviːsʌ]
professor	**professor** (c)	[pʁoˈfɛsɒ]

lecture hall, room	**klasseværelse** (n)	[ˈklasəˌvæːɒlsə]
graduate (of high school)	**afgangsstudent** (c)	[auˈgaŋs sduˈdɛnd]
diploma	**diplom** (n)	[dipˈlɒm]
dissertation	**afhandling** (c)	[auˈhanleŋ]
study (report)	**afhandling** (c)	[auˈhanleŋ]
laboratory	**laboratorium** (n)	[laboʁɑˈtooɒjɔm]

lecture	forelæsning (c)	['fo:ɒˌlɛ:snen]
schoolmate	studiekammerat (c)	['sdu:djəkɑməˌʁɑ:d]
stipend	Statens Uddannelsesstøtte (c)	['sdæ:dəns 'uðˌdanəlsə'sdødə]
academic degree	akademisk grad (c)	[aka'de:misg gʁɑ:ð]

144. Sciences. Disciplines

mathematics	matematik (c)	[madəma'tik]
algebra	algebra (c)	['aljəbʁɑ]
geometry	geometri (c)	[geome'tʁi:]
astronomy	astronomi (c)	[asdʁono'mi:]
biology	biologi (c)	[biolo'gi:]
geography	geografi (c)	[geogʁɑ'fi:]
geology	geologi (c)	[geolo'gi:]
history	historie (c)	[hi'sdo:ʁiə]
medicine	lægevidenskab (c)	['lɛ:jə 'viðənˌsgæb]
pedagogy	pædagogik (c)	[pɛdago'gig]
law (e.g., student of ~)	jura (c)	['ju:ʁɑ]
physics	fysik (c)	[fy'sik]
chemistry	kemi (c)	[ke'mi:]
philosophy	filosofi (c)	[filoso'fi:]
psychology	psykologi (c)	[sygolo'gi:]

145. Writing system. Orthography

grammar	grammatik (c)	[gʁama'tig]
vocabulary	ordforråd (n)	['oɒfɒˌʁɒð]
phonetics	fonetik (c)	[fɒnə'tik]
noun	substantiv (n)	['subsdanˌtiw]
adjective	adjektiv (n)	['aðjɛktiu]
verb	verbum (n)	['væɒbɔm]
adverb	biord (n)	['bioɒd]
pronoun	pronomen (n)	[pʁo'no:mən]
interjection	udråbsord (n)	['uðʁobsˌoɒ]
preposition	præposition (c)	[pʁɛposi'ɕo:n]
root (base form)	rod (c)	[ʁoð]
ending	endelse (c)	['ɛndəlsə]
prefix	præfiks (n)	[pʁɛ'fiks]
syllable	stavelse (c)	['sdæ:vəlsə]
suffix	suffiks (n)	[su'fiks]
stress mark	betoning (c)	[be'to:nen]

apostrophe	apostrof (c)	[ɑpo'sdʁɒf]
period, dot	punktum (n)	['pɔŋtɔm]
comma	komma (n)	['kɒma]
semicolon	semikolon (n)	[semi'ko:lʌn]
colon	kolon (n)	['kolɒn]
ellipsis	udeladelsesprikker (c pl)	['u:ðəˌlæːðəlsə 'sbʁɛkʌ]

| question mark | spørgsmålstegn (n) | ['sbɒœɒsmɔlˌstɑjn] |
| exclamation point | udråbstegn (n) | ['uðʁɔbsˌtɑjn] |

quotation marks	anførselstegn (n)	['anføɒsəlstɑjn]
in quotation marks	i anførselstegn	[i 'anˌføɒsəlstɑjn]
parenthesis	parenteser (pl)	[pɑɑn'te:sʌ]
in parenthesis	i parentes	[i pɑɑn'təs]

| hyphen | bindestreg (c) | ['benəˌsdʁɑj] |
| dash | tankestreg (c) | ['tɑŋgəˌsdʁɑj] |

| space (between words) | hul (n) | [hɔl] |
| hyphen (end of a line) | bindestreg (c) | ['benəˌsdʁɑj] |

| letter | bogstav (n) | ['bɒgˌsdæːu] |
| capital letter | stort bogstav (n) | ['sdoɒd 'bɒgsdæw] |

| vowel (noun) | vokal (c) | [vo'kæːl] |
| consonant (noun) | konsonant (c) | [kʌnso'nand] |

sentence	sætning (c)	['sɛdneŋ]
subject	subjekt (n)	['subjɛkd]
predicate	prædikat (n)	[pʁɛdi'kæːd]

line (in writing)	linje (c)	['linjə]
on a new line	med ny linje	[mɛð ny: 'linjə]
paragraph	afsnit (n)	[ɑu'snid]

word	ord (n)	['oɒ]
word group	ordforbindelse (c)	['oɒfʌˌbenəlsə]
expression	udtryk (n)	['uðtʁœk]

| synonym | synonym (n) | [syno'ny:m] |
| antonym | antonym (n) | [antɔ'ny:m] |

rule	regel (c)	['ʁɛjəl]
exception	undtagelse (c)	['ɔnˌtæːəlsə]
right (correct)	rigtig	['ʁɛgdi]

conjugation	bøjning (c)	['bɒjneŋ]
declension	bøjning (c)	['bɒjneŋ]
nominal case	kasus (c)	['kæːsus]
question	spørgsmål (n)	['sbɒœɒsˌmɔl]
to underline (vt)	at understrege	[at 'ɔnɒˌsdʁɑjə]
dotted line	punkteret linje (c)	[pɔŋ'te:ɒð 'linjə]

146. Foreign languages

language	**sprog** (n)	['sbʁɔw]
foreign	**fremmed**	['fʁaməð]
to study (vt)	**at studere**	[at 'sdude:ɒ]
to learn (language etc.)	**at lære**	[at 'lɛ:ɒ]
to read (vi, vt)	**at læse**	[at 'lɛ:sə]
to speak (vi, vt)	**at tale**	[at 'tæ:lə]
to understand (vt)	**at forstå**	[at fʌ'sdɔ:]
to write (vi, vt)	**at skrive**	[at 'skʁiuə]
fast	**hurtigt**	['huɒdid]
slowly	**langsomt**	['laŋsɒmd]
fluently	**frit**	[fʁid]
rules	**regler** (pl)	['ʁɛjəlʌ]
grammar	**grammatik** (c)	[gʁama'tig]
vocabulary	**ordforråd** (n)	['ɒɒfɒˌʁɔð]
phonetics	**fonetik** (c)	[fɒnə'tik]
textbook	**lærebog** (c)	['lɛ:ɒˌbou]
dictionary	**ordbog** (c)	['ɒɒˌbɒw]
teach-yourself book	**lærebog til selvstudium**	['lɛ:ɒˌbou tel 'sɛlˌsdu:djɒm]
phrasebook	**parlør** (c)	[pa'lœ:ɒ]
cassette	**kassette** (c)	[ka'sɛdə]
videotape	**videokassette** (c)	['vi:deo ka'sɛdə]
CD (compact disc)	**CD** (c)	[se'de]
DVD	**DVD** (c)	[deve'de]
alphabet	**alfabet** (n)	[alfa'be:ð]
pronunciation	**udtale** (c)	['uðtæ:lə]
accent	**accent** (c)	[ag'saŋd]
with an accent	**med accent**	[mɛð ag'saŋd]
without an accent	**uden accent**	['uðən a'gsaŋd]
word	**ord** (n)	['ɒɒ]
meaning	**mening** (c)	['me:neŋ]
course (e.g., a French ~)	**kursus** (pl)	['kuɒsus]
to sign up	**at indskrive sig**	[at enˌsgʁive saj]
teacher	**lærer** (c)	['lɛ:ʌ]
translation (process)	**oversættelse** (c)	['ɒwʌsɛdəlsə]
translation (text etc.)	**oversættelse** (c)	['ɒwʌsɛdəlsə]
translator	**tolk** (c), **oversætter** (c)	[tɒlk], ['ɒwʌˌsɛdʌ]
interpreter	**tolk** (c)	[tɒlk]
polyglot	**polyglot** (c)	[poly'glʌd]
memory	**hukommelse** (c)	[hu'kʌməlsə]

147. Fairy tale characters

Santa Claus	**Julemand** (c)	['ju:lə‚man]
Cinderella	**Askepot**	['askəpɒd]
mermaid	**havfrue** (c)	['hɑufʁu:ə]
Neptune	**Neptun**	['nəbdu:n]
magician, wizard	**troldmand** (c)	['tʁɒlman]
good witch	**troldkvinde** (c)	['tʁɒl‚kvenə]
magic	**trylle-**	['tʁylə]
magic wand	**tryllestav** (c)	['tʁylə‚sdæw]
fairy tale	**eventyr** (n)	['ɛ:vən‚typ]
miracle	**under** (n)	['ɔnʌ]
dwarf	**gnom** (c)	[gnɒm]
to turn into …	**at forvandles til …**	[at fʌ'vanləs tel]
ghost	**spøgelse** (n)	['sbø:jəlsə]
phantom	**fantom** (n)	[fan'tɒm]
monster	**uhyre** (n)	['u‚hy:ɒ]
dragon	**drage** (c)	['dʁɑ:uə]
giant	**kæmpe** (c)	['kɛmbə]

148. Zodiac Signs

Aries	**Vædderen**	['vɛðɒn]
Taurus	**Tyren**	['ty:ʁɒn]
Gemini	**Tvillingerne**	['tvileŋɒnə]
Cancer	**Krebsen**	['kʁabsən]
Leo	**Løven**	['lø:uən]
Virgo	**Jomfruen**	['jʌmfʁu:ən]
Libra	**Vægten**	['vɛgdən]
Scorpio	**Skorpionen**	[skɒbi'onən]
Sagittarius	**Skytten**	['skytən]
Capricorn	**Stenbukken**	['sde:nbukn]
Aquarius	**Vandmanden**	['van‚manən]
Pisces	**Fiskene**	['feskənə]
character	**karakter** (c)	[kɑɑk'teʌ]
features of character	**karaktertrækkene** (pl)	[kɑɑk'teɒ ‚tʁakkənə]
behavior	**opførsel** (c)	[ʌb'føɒsəl]
to tell fortunes	**at spå**	[at sbɔ:]
fortune-teller	**spåkone** (c)	['sbʌ‚ko:ne]
horoscope	**horoskop** (n)	[hoo'skob]

Arts

149. Theater

theater	teater (n)	[te'ædʌ]
opera	opera (c)	['oːbɐʁɑ]
operetta	operette (c)	[oːbə'ʁadə]
ballet	ballet (c)	[ba'lɛd]

playbill	plakat (c)	[pla'kæːd]
company	trup (c)	[tʁɔb]
tour	gæstespil (n)	['gɛsdəˌsbel]
to be on tour	at være på gæstespil	[at 'vɛːɒ pɔ 'gɛsdəˌsbel]
to rehearse (vi, vt)	at prøve	[at 'pʁœːuə]
rehearsal	prøve (c)	['pʁœːwə]
repertoire	repertoire (n)	[ʁɛbæɒto'ɑː]

performance	forestilling (c)	['fɒːɒˌsdeleŋ]
show, play	teaterforestilling (c)	[te'ædʌ 'fɒːɒˌsdeleŋ]
play	skuespil (n)	['skuəˌsbel]

ticket	billet (c)	[bi'lɛd]
ticket office	billetsalg (n)	[bi'lɛd ˌsalj]
lobby, foyer	lobby (c)	['lɔbi]
coat check	garderobe (c)	[gɑdə'ʁoːbə]
coat check tag	mærke (n)	['mæɒkə]
binoculars	kikkert (c)	['kikʌd]
usher	kontrollør (c)	[kʌntʁo'løɒ]

orchestra seats	parket (n)	[pɑ'kɛd]
balcony	balkon (c)	[bal'kɒŋ]
dress circle	balkon (c)	[bal'kɒŋ]
box	loge (c)	['loːɕə]
row	række (c)	['ʁakə]
seat	plads (c)	[plas]

audience	publikum (n)	['publikɔm]
spectator	tilskuer (c)	[tel'skuːʌ]
to clap (vi, vt)	at klappe ad	[at 'klɑbə að]
applause	klapsalve (c)	['klɑbsalvə]
ovation	bifald (c)	['bifal]

stage	scene (c)	['seːnə]
curtain	tæppe (n)	['tɛbə]
scenery	dekoration (c)	[dekoʁɑ'ɕon]
backstage	kulisser (pl)	[ku'lisʌ]

scene (e.g., the last ~)	**scene** (n)	['se:nə]
act	**akt** (c)	[ɑkd]
intermission	**pause** (c)	['pɑusə]

150. Cinema

| actor | **skuespiller** (c) | ['skuə,sbelʌ] |
| actress | **skuespillerinde** (c) | [,sku:əsbelʌ'ene] |

movies (industry)	**filmkunst** (c)	['film,kɔnsd]
movie	**film** (c)	[film]
episode	**del** (c)	[de:l]

detective	**krimi** (c)	['kʁi:mi:]
action movie	**actionfilm** (c)	['ɑgɕən 'film]
adventure movie	**eventyrfilm** (c)	['ɛ:uən,tyɒ film]
science fiction movie	**science fiction film** (c)	[sɑjəns'fegɕən film]
horror movie	**gyser** (c)	['gy:sʌ]

comedy movie	**lystspil** (n)	['løsd,sbel]
melodrama	**melodrama** (n)	[melo'dʁɑ:ma]
drama	**drama** (n)	['dʁɑ:ma]

fictional movie	**spillefilm** (c)	['sbelə,film]
documentary	**dokumentar** (c)	[dokumɛn'ta]
cartoon	**tegnefilm** (c)	['tɑjnə,film]
silent movies	**stumfilm** (c)	['sdɔm,film]

role	**rolle** (c)	['ʁɒlə]
leading role	**hovedrolle** (c)	['ho:əð ,ʁɒlə]
to play (vi, vt)	**at spille**	[at 'sbelə]

movie star	**filmstjerne** (c)	['film,sdjɑɒnə]
well-known	**kendt**	[kɛnd]
famous	**berømt**	[be'ʁœmd]
popular	**populær**	[popu'lɛɒ]

script (screenplay)	**manuskript** (n)	[manu'skʁɛbd]
scriptwriter	**manuskriptforfatter** (c)	[manu'skʁɛbd fʌ'fadʌ]
movie director	**filminstruktør** (c)	['film ensdʁuk'tøɒ]
producer	**producer** (c)	[pʁo'dju:sʌ]
assistant	**assistent** (c)	[asi'sdɛnd]
cameraman	**kameramand** (c)	['kæ:məʁɑ,man]
stuntman	**stuntmand** (c)	['sdɔnd,man]

to shoot a movie	**at optage en film**	[at 'ɒb,tæ:ə ən film]
audition, screen test	**prøver** (pl)	['pʁœ:wəʌ]
shooting	**filmoptagelse** (c)	['film,ɒbtæ:əlsə]
movie crew	**filmoptagelseshold** (n)	['film,ɒbtæ:əlsəshɒl]
movie set	**filmoptagelsessted** (n)	['film,ɒbtæ:əlsəsdɛð]

camera	filmkamera (c)	['film,kæ:meʁɑ]
movie theater	biograf (c)	[bio'gʁɑ:f]
screen (e.g., big ~)	skærm (c)	['skæʊm]
to show a movie	at vise en film	[at 'vi:sə en film]

soundtrack	lydspor (n)	['lyð,sboɒ]
special effects	filmtrick (n)	['film,tʁek]
subtitles	undertekster (pl)	['ɔnɒ,tɛksdʌ]
credits	rulletekster (c pl)	['ʁulə,dɛksdʌ]
translation	oversættelse (c)	['ɒwʌsɛdəlsə]

151. Painting

art	kunst (c)	[kɔnsd]
fine arts	de skønne kunster	[di 'skœnə 'kɔnsdɒ]
art gallery	galleri (n)	[galə'ʁi:]
art exhibition	kunstudstilling (c)	['kɔnsd,uðsdelen]

painting	maleri (n)	[mæ:lə'ʁi:]
graphic art	grafik (c)	[gʁɑ'fig]
abstract art	abstrakt kunst (c)	[ɑbsd'ʁɑkd kɔnsd]
impressionism	impressionisme (c)	[empʁɛɑçʊ'nismə]

picture (painting)	billede (n)	['beləðə]
drawing	tegning (c)	['tɑjnen]
poster	plakat (c)	[pla'kæ:d]

illustration (picture)	illustration (c)	[ilusdʁɑ'çʊ:n]
miniature	miniature (c)	[miniæ:'tu:ɒ]
copy (of painting etc.)	kopi (c)	[ko'pi:]
reproduction	reproduktion (c)	[ʁɛpʁɒduk'çʊ:n]

mosaic	mosaik (c)	[mosa'ik]
stained glass	glasmaleri (n)	['glasmæ:lə'ʁi:]
fresco	fresko (c)	['fʁasko]
engraving	gravure (c)	[gʁɑ'vy:ʌ]

bust (sculpture)	buste (c)	['bysdə]
sculpture	skulptur (c)	[skulb'tuɒ]
statue	statue (c)	['sdætuə]
plaster of Paris	gips (c)	[gibs]
plaster (e.g., ~ statue)	af gips	[a gibs]

portrait	portræt (n)	[pɒ'tʁad]
self-portrait	selvportræt (n)	['sɛl,pɒtʁad]
landscape	landskabsmaleri (n)	['lanskæ:bs mæ:lə'ʁi:]
still life	stilleben (n)	['sdelə,be:n]
caricature	karikatur (c)	[kɑʁikæ:'tuɒ]
paint	farve (c)	['fɑ:uə]
watercolor	akvarel (c)	[ɑkvɑ'ʁal]

oil (paint)	**olie** (c)	[ˈoːljə]
pencil	**blyant** (c)	[ˈblyand]
Indian ink	**tusch** (c)	[tuɕ]
charcoal	**tegnekul** (n)	[ˈtɑjneˌkɔl]
to draw (vi, vt)	**at tegne**	[at ˈtɑjnə]
to paint (vi, vt)	**at male**	[at ˈmæːlə]
to pose (vi)	**at posere**	[at poːˈseːɒ]
artist's model (man)	**model** (c)	[moˈdɛl]
artist's model (woman)	**model** (c)	[moˈdɛl]
artist (painter)	**kunstmaler** (c)	[ˈkɔnsdˌmæːlʌ]
work of art	**værk** (n)	[ˈvæɒk]
masterpiece	**mesterværk** (n)	[ˈmɛsdʌˌvɑɒk]
workshop (of artist)	**atelier** (n)	[atəlˈje]
canvas (cloth)	**lærred** (n)	[ˈlæɒʌð]
easel	**staffeli** (n)	[sdɑfəˈliː]
palette	**palet** (c)	[paˈləð]
frame (of picture etc.)	**ramme** (c)	[ˈʁɑmə]
restoration	**restauration** (c)	[ʁɛsdoʁɑˈɕoːn]
to restore (vt)	**at restaurere**	[at ʁɛsdɑuˈʁɛːɒ]

152. Literature & Poetry

literature	**litteratur** (c)	[lidəʁɑˈtuɒ]
author (writer)	**forfatter** (c)	[foˈfadʌ]
pseudonym	**pseudonym** (n)	[sœwdoˈnym]
book	**bog** (c)	[ˈbɔu]
volume	**bind** (n)	[ben]
contents list	**indhold** (n)	[ˈenhɒl]
page	**side** (c)	[ˈsiːðə]
main character	**hovedperson** (c)	[ˈhoːəð paɒˈsoːn]
autograph	**autograf** (c)	[ɑutoˈgʁɑːf]
short story	**fortælling** (c)	[foˈtɛlen]
story (novella)	**novelle** (c)	[noˈvɛlə]
novel	**roman** (c)	[ʁoˈmæːn]
work (writing)	**værk** (n)	[ˈvæɒk]
fable	**fabel** (c)	[ˈfæːbəl]
detective novel	**kriminalroman** (c)	[kʁimiˈnæl ʁoˈmæn]
poem (verse)	**digt** (n)	[degd]
poetry	**poesi** (c)	[poeˈsiː]
poem (epic, ballad)	**poem** (n)	[poˈɛm]
poet	**digter** (c)	[ˈdegdʌ]
fiction	**skønlitteratur** (c)	[ˈskœnlidəʁɑˌtuɒ]

science fiction	science fiktion (c)	[sɑjəns'fekɕən]
adventures	eventyr (pl)	['ɛ:vən,tyɒ]
educational literature	undervisningslitteratur	['ɔnʊ,vesneŋs lidəʁɑ'tuɒ]
children's literature	børnelitteratur (c)	['bœɒnə 'li:dəʁɑ,tuɒ]

153. Circus

circus	cirkus (n)	['siɒkus]
big top (circus)	cirkustelt (n)	['siɒkus,dɛld]
program	program (n)	[pʁo'gʁɑm]
performance	forestilling (c)	['fɒ:ɒ,sdeleŋ]

| act (circus ~) | nummer (n) | ['nɔmʌ] |
| circus ring | arena (c) | [ɑ'ʁɛ:na] |

| pantomime (act) | pantomime (c) | [panto'mi:mə] |
| clown | klovn (c) | ['klɒwn] |

acrobat	akrobat (c)	[akʁo'bad]
acrobatics	akrobatik (c)	[akʁoba'tik]
gymnast	gymnast (c)	[gym'nasd]
gymnastics	gymnastik (c)	[gymna'sdig]
somersault	salto (c)	['salto]

athlete	atlet (c)	[ad'led]
animal-tamer	dyretæmmer (c)	['dy:ɒ,tɛmʌ]
rider	rytter (c)	['ʁydʌ]
assistant	assistent (c)	[asi'sdɛnd]

stunt	trick (n)	[tʁek]
conjuring trick	kunststykke (n)	['kɔnsd,sdøkə]
conjurer, magician	tryllekunstner (c)	['tʁylə,kɔnsdnʌ]

juggler	jonglør (c)	[ɕɒŋg'løɒ]
to juggle (vi, vt)	at jonglere	[at ɕʌŋ'leʌ]
animal trainer	domptør (c)	[dɒmb'tøɒ]
animal training	dressur (c)	[dʁɛ'suɒ]
to train (animals)	at dressere	[at dʁɛ'seɒ]

154. Music. Pop music

music	musik (c)	[mu'sik]
musician	musiker (c)	['musikʌ]
musical instrument	musikinstrument (n)	['musikensdʁu'mɛnd]
to play ...	at spille ...	[at 'sbelə ...]

| guitar | guitar (c) | ['gitɑ:] |
| violin | violin (c) | [vio'li:n] |

cello	**cello** (c)	[ˈsɛlo]
double bass	**kontrabas** (c)	[ˈkʌntʁɑˌbas]
harp	**harpe** (c)	[ˈhɑːbə]
piano	**klaver** (n)	[klaˈveʌ]
grand piano	**flygel** (n)	[ˈflyːəl]
organ	**orgel** (n)	[ˈɒwəl]
wind instruments	**blæseinstrumenter** (pl)	[ˈblɛːsˌensdʁuˌmɛndʌ]
oboe	**obo** (c)	[oːˈboː]
saxophone	**saxofon** (c)	[sɑgsoˈfon]
clarinet	**klarinet** (c)	[klɑiˈnɛd]
flute	**fløjte** (c)	[ˈflɒjdə]
trumpet	**trompet** (c)	[tʁɔmˈped]
accordion	**akkordeon** (c)	[aˈkɒːdəɒn]
drum	**tromme** (c)	[ˈtʁɔmə]
duo	**duet** (c)	[duˈɛd]
trio	**trio** (c)	[tʁiːo]
quartet	**kvartet** (c)	[kvɑˈtɛd]
choir	**kor** (n)	[koɒ]
orchestra	**orkester** (n)	[ɒˈkɛsdʌ]
pop music	**pop musik** (c)	[ˈpɒbmuˌsik]
rock music	**rock musik** (c)	[ʁɒkmuˈsik]
rock group	**rockgruppe** (c)	[ʁɒgˈgʁubə]
jazz	**jazz** (c)	[ˈdjas]
idol	**afgud** (c)	[ˈɑuguð]
admirer, fan	**beundrer** (c)	[beˈɔndʁʌ]
concert	**koncert** (c)	[kɔnˈsæɒd]
symphony	**symfoni** (c)	[symfoːˈniː]
composition	**musikstykke** (n)	[muˈsikˌsdøkə]
to compose (write)	**at komponere**	[at kɒmpoˈneːɒ]
singing	**sang** (c)	[sɑŋ]
song	**sang** (c)	[sɑŋ]
tune (melody)	**melodi** (c)	[meloˈdiː]
rhythm	**rytme** (c)	[ˈʁydmə]
blues	**blues** (c)	[ˈbluːs]
sheet music	**noder** (pl)	[ˈnoːðʌ]
baton	**taktstok** (c)	[ˈtɑkdˌsdɒk]
bow	**bue** (c)	[ˈbuːə]
string	**streng** (c)	[sdʁaŋ]
case (e.g., for guitar)	**kasse** (c)	[ˈkasə]

Rest. Entertainment. Travel

155. Trip. Travel

tourism	turisme (c)	[tuˈʁismə]
tourist	turist (c)	[tuˈʁisd]
trip, voyage	rejse (c)	[ˈʁɑjsə]

| adventure | eventyr (n) | [ˈɛːvənˌtyɒ] |
| trip, journey | rejse (c) | [ˈʁɑjsə] |

vacation	ferie (c)	[ˈfeɒjə]
to be on vacation	at holde ferie	[at ˈhɒlə ˈfeɒjə]
rest	afslapning (c)	[ɑuˈslɑbnɛŋ]

train	tog (n)	[ˈtow]
by train	med toget	[mɛð ˈtɔːwəð]
airplane	fly (c)	[flyː]
by airplane	med fly	[mɛð flyː]

| by car | med bil | [mɛð biːl] |
| by ship | på skib | [pɔ skiːb] |

luggage	bagage (c)	[baˈgæːɕə]
suitcase, luggage	kuffert (c)	[ˈkɔfɒd]
luggage cart	bagagevogn (c)	[baˈgæːɕəˌvɒwn]

| passport | pas (n) | [pas] |
| visa | visum (n) | [ˈviːsɔm] |

| ticket | billet (c) | [biˈlɛd] |
| air ticket | flybillet (c) | [ˈflyːˌbiləð] |

| guidebook | rejsehåndbog (c) | [ˈʁɑjsəˌhɒnbow] |
| map | kort (n) | [kɒːd] |

| area (place) | egn (c) | [ɑjn] |
| place, site | sted (n) | [sdɛð] |

exotica	eksotisme (c)	[ɛgsoˈtismə]
exotic	eksotisk	[ɛˈgsoːtisk]
amazing	forunderlig	[fɒˈɒnɒli]

group	gruppe (c)	[ˈgʁubə]
excursion	udflugt (c)	[ˈuðflɒgd]
guide (person)	guide (c)	[ˈgɑjd]

156. Hotel

hotel, inn	**hotel** (n)	[ho'tɛl]
motel	**motel** (n)	[mo'tɛl]
three-star	**tre stjerner**	[tʁɛ: 'sdjɑɒnɒ]
five-star	**fem stjerner**	[fɛm 'sdjɑɒnɒ]
to stay (in hotel etc.)	**at bo (på hotel)**	[at bo: pɒ ho'tɛl]
room	**værelse** (n)	['væːɒlsə]
single room	**enkeltværelse** (n)	['ɛŋkəld‚væːɒlsə]
double room	**dobbeltværelse** (n)	['dɒbəld ‚væːɒlsə]
to book a room	**at booke**	[at 'bukə]
half board	**halvpension** (c)	['halpɑŋ‚ɕoːn]
full board	**fuldpension** (c)	['fulpɑŋ‚ɕoːn]
with bath	**med bad**	[mɛð bað]
with shower	**med brusebad**	[mɛð 'bʁusə‚bað]
satellite television	**satellit-tv** (n)	[sadə'lid 'te‚ve]
air-conditioner	**klimaanlæg** (n)	['kliːman‚lɛːg]
towel	**håndklæde** (n)	['hɒn‚klɛːðə]
key	**nøgle** (c)	['nɒjlə]
administrator	**forretningsfører** (c)	[fɒ'ʁadneŋs ‚føːʌ]
chambermaid	**stuepige** (c)	['sduə‚piːə]
porter, bellboy	**drager** (c)	['dʁɑːuʌ]
doorman	**portier** (c)	[pɒ'tje]
restaurant	**restaurant** (c)	[ʁɛsdo'ʁɑŋ]
pub, bar	**bar** (c)	[bɑ:]
café	**cafe** (c)	[ka'fe]
breakfast	**morgenmad** (c)	['mɒːɒn‚mað]
dinner	**aftensmad** (c)	['ɑfdənsmað]
buffet	**tagselvbord** (n)	[ta'sɛl‚bɒɒ]
lobby	**forhal** (c)	[fɒ'hal]
elevator	**elevator** (c)	[elə'væːtɒ]
DO NOT DISTURB	**VIL IKKE FORSTYRRES**	[vel 'ekə fɒ'sdyɒɒs]
NO SMOKING	**RYGNING FORBUDT**	['ʁyːneŋ fɒ:'bud]

157. Books. Reading

book	**bog** (c)	['bɒu]
author	**forfatter** (c)	[fɒ'fadʌ]
writer	**forfatter** (c)	[fɒ'fadʌ]
to write (e.g., ~ a book)	**at skrive**	[at 'skʁiuə]
reader	**læser** (c)	['lɛːsʌ]

| to read (vi, vt) | at læse | [at 'lɛ:sə] |
| reading (activity) | læsning (c) | ['lɛ:snen] |

| silently | for sig selv | [fɒ sɑj sɛl] |
| aloud | højt | [hɒjd] |

to publish (vt)	at udgive	[at 'uð‚giuə]
publication	udgave (c)	['uð‚gæ:və]
publisher	forlægger (c)	[fɒ'lɛ:gʌ]
publishing house	forlag (n)	['fɒlæ:]

to come out	at udkomme	[at 'uð‚kɒmə]
publication	udgivelse (c)	['uð‚givəlsə]
print run	oplag (n)	['ʌb‚læj]

| bookstore | boghandel (c) | ['bou‚hanəl] |
| library | bibliotek (n) | [biblio'te:k] |

story (novella)	novelle (c)	[no'vɛlə]
short story	fortælling (c)	[fɒ'tɛlen]
novel	roman (c)	[ʁo'mæ:n]
detective novel	kriminalroman (c)	[kʁimi'næl ʁo'mæn]

memoirs	erindringer (pl)	[e'ʁendʁɛŋʌ]
legend	sagn (n)	['sɑun]
myth	myte (c)	['mydə]

poetry, poems	digte (n)	['degdə]
autobiography	selvbiografi (c)	[‚sɛlbiogʁa'fi:]
collected works	udvalgte værker (pl)	['uðvaldə 'væɒgʌ]
science fiction	science fiction (c)	[sɑjəns'fegɕən]

title	titel (c)	['tidəl]
introduction	indledning (c)	[en'leðnen]
title page	titelblad (n)	['tidəl‚blɑð]

chapter	kapitel (c)	[ka'pidəl]
extract	fragment (n)	[fʁɑu'mɛnd]
episode	episode (c)	[epi'so:ðə]

thread (of story)	plot (n)	[plɒd]
contents	indhold (n)	['enhɒl]
table of contents	indhold (n)	['enhɒl]
main character	hovedperson (c)	['ho:əð paɒ'so:n]

volume	bind (n)	[ben]
cover	omslag (n)	['ʌmslæ:]
binding	bind (n)	[ben]
bookmark	bogmærke (n)	['bou‚maɒgə]

| page | side (c) | ['si:ðə] |
| to flick through | at bladre | [at 'blɑðʁʌ] |

margins	**marginer** (pl)	['mɑ:gi:nʌ]
note (in margins)	**notits** (c)	[no'tids]
annotation	**anmærkning** (c)	['an̩mɑɒgneŋ]
text	**tekst** (c)	[tɛksd]
type, font	**skrift** (c)	[skʁɛfd]
misprint, typo	**trykfejl** (c)	['tʁɶk̩fɑjl]
translation	**oversættelse** (c)	['ɒwʌsɛdəlsə]
to translate (vi, vt)	**at oversætte**	[at ɒuɒ'sɛdə]
original (read in the ~)	**original** (c)	[ɒigi'næl]
famous	**berømt**	[be'ʁɶmd]
unknown	**ukendt**	['u̩kɛnd]
interesting	**interessant**	[entʁɵ'sand]
bestseller	**bestseller** (c)	['bɛsd̩sɛlʌ]
dictionary	**ordbog** (c)	['ɒɒ̩bɒw]
textbook	**lærebog** (c)	['lɛ:ɒ̩bɒu]
encyclopedia	**encyklopædi** (c)	[ɛnsyklɒpə'di]

158. Hunting. Fishing

hunt (of animal)	**jagt** (c)	['jɑgd]
to hunt (vi, vt)	**at jage**	[at 'jæ:jə]
hunter	**jæger** (c)	['jɛ:jʌ]
to shoot (vi)	**at skyde**	[at 'sky:ðə]
rifle	**gevær** (n)	[ge'vɛɒ]
bullet (cartridge)	**patron** (c)	[pa'tʁo:n]
shotgun pellets	**hagl** (n)	[hɑul]
trap (e.g., bear ~)	**fælde** (c)	['fɛlə]
snare (for birds etc.)	**snare** (c)	['snɑ:ɑ]
to lay a trap	**at sætte en fælde**	[at 'sɛdə en 'fɛlə]
poacher	**krybskytte** (c)	['kʁyb̩skødə]
game (in hunting)	**fuglevildt** (n)	['fu:ləvild]
hound	**jagthund** (c)	['jɑgd̩hun]
safari	**safari** (c)	[sa'fɑ:i]
mounted animal	**udstoppet dyr** (n)	['uðsdɒbəð ̩dyɒ]
fisherman	**fisker** (c)	['feskʌ]
fishing	**fiskefangst** (c)	['fesgə̩fɑŋsd]
to fish (vi)	**at fiske**	[at 'feskə]
fishing rod	**fiskestang** (c)	['fesgə̩sdɑŋ]
fishing line	**fiskesnøre** (c)	['feskə̩snɶɒ]
hook	**krog** (c)	['kʁou]
float	**flyder** (c)	['flyðʌ]

bait	**lokkemad** (c)	['lɒkəmað]
to cast a line	**at kaste en line ud**	[at 'kasdə en 'li:nə uð]
to bite (about fish)	**at bide (på)**	[at 'bi:ðə pɔ]
catch (of fish)	**fangst** (c)	[faŋsd]
ice-hole	**hul** (n) **i isen**	['hɔl i ˌisən]
net	**net** (n)	[nɛd]
boat	**båd** (c)	[bɔð]
to net (catch with net)	**at fiske med net**	[at 'feskə mɛð nɛd]
to cast the net	**at kaste net ud**	[at 'kasdə nɛd uð]
to haul in the net	**at tage net ind**	[at 'tæ:ə nɛd en]
to fall into the net	**at blive fanget i nettet**	[at 'bli:ə 'faŋəð i 'nɛdəð]
whaler (person)	**hvalfanger** (c)	['væ:lˌfaŋʌ]
whaleboat	**hvalfangerbåd** (c)	['væ:lˌfaŋɒbɔð]
harpoon	**harpun** (c)	[hɑ:'pu:n]

159. Games. Billiards

billiards	**billard** (n)	['biliˌɑd]
billiard room, hall	**billardsalon** (c)	['biliˌɑd sa'lʌŋ]
ball	**billardkugle** (c)	['biliˌɑd 'ku:lə]
to pocket a ball	**at skyde en bal i hul**	[at 'sky:ðə en bal i hɔl]
cue	**billardkø** (c)	['kø:]
pocket	**hul** (n)	[hɔl]

160. Games. Playing cards

diamonds	**ruder** (c)	['ʁu:ðʌ]
spades	**spar** (c)	[sbɑ:]
hearts	**hjerter** (pl)	['jæɒdʌ]
clubs	**klør** (pl)	[kløɒ]
ace	**es** (n)	[ɛs]
king	**konge** (c)	['kʌŋə]
queen	**dame** (c)	['dæ:mə]
jack, knave	**knægt** (c)	[knɛgd]
playing card	**spillekort** (n)	['sbeləˌkɒ:d]
cards	**spillekort** (pl)	['sbeləˌkɒ:d]
trump	**trumf** (c)	[tʁɔmf]
deck of cards	**sæt** (n) **spillekort**	[sɛd 'sbeləˌkɒ:d]
point	**point** (n)	[po'ɛŋ]
to deal (vi, vt)	**at give**	[at gi:]
to shuffle (in card games)	**at blande kort**	[at 'blanə kɒ:d]
lead, turn (noun)	**træk** (n)	[tʁak]
card sharp	**falskspiller** (c)	['falskˌsbelʌ]

161. Casino. Roulette

casino	**kasino** (n)	[ka'si:no]
roulette (game)	**roulette** (c)	[ʁu'lɛdə]
bet, stake	**indsats** (c)	['enˌsads]
to place bets	**at satse**	[at 'sadsə]

red (in roulette)	**rødt** (n)	[ʁœd]
black	**sort**	['sɒːd]
to bet on red	**at satse på rødt**	[at 'sadsə pɔ ʁœd]
to bet on black	**at satse på sort**	[at 'sadsə pɔ 'soɒd]

croupier	**croupier** (c)	[kʁu'pje]
to turn the wheel	**at dreje hjulet**	[at 'dʁɑjə 'ju:ləð]
rules (of game)	**spilleregler** (pl)	['sbeləˌʁɛjəlʌ]
chip	**jeton** (c)	[jɛ'tɒn]

| to win (vi, vt) | **at vinde** | [at 'venə] |
| winnings | **gevinst** (n) | [ge'vensd] |

| to lose (not win) | **at tabe** | [at 'tæːbə] |
| loss | **tab** (n) | [tæːb] |

player	**spiller** (c)	['sbelʌ]
blackjack (card game)	**blackjack** (c)	['blakˌdjak]
game of dice	**terningspil** (n)	['tæɒnɐŋˌspiːl]
dice	**terninger** (pl)	['tæɒnɐŋʌ]
slot machine	**spilleautomat** (c)	['sbeləɑwto'mæd]

162. Rest. Games. Miscellaneous

to walk, to stroll (vi)	**at spadsere**	[at 'sbaseːɒ]
walk, stroll	**spadseretur** (c)	[sba'seːɒˌtuɒ]
pleasure-ride, trip	**køretur** (c)	['køːɒˌtuɒ]
adventure	**eventyr** (n)	['ɛ:vənˌtyɒ]
picnic	**picnic** (c)	['pignig]

game (chess etc.)	**spil** (n)	[sbel]
player	**spiller** (c)	['sbelʌ]
game (one ~ of chess)	**parti** (n)	[pɑ'tiː]

collector (e.g., philatelist)	**samler** (c)	['samlʌ]
to collect (vt)	**at samle på**	[at 'samlə pɒ]
collection	**samling** (c)	['samleŋ]

crossword	**krydsord** (n)	['kʁysɒɒ]
dominoes	**domino** (n, c)	[domi'no]
racecourse (for horses)	**travbane** (c)	['tʁɑwˌbæːnə]
disco (place)	**diskotek** (n)	[disko'teːk]

sauna	**sauna** (c)	['sɑuna]
lottery	**lotteri** (n)	[lɒdə'ʁi:]
camping trip	**camping** (c)	['kæːmpeŋ]
camp	**lejr** (c)	['lɑjɒ]
tent (for camping)	**telt** (n)	[tɛld]
compass	**kompas** (n)	[kɔm'pas]
camper	**turist** (c)	[tu'ʁisd]
to watch (movie etc.)	**at se fjernsyn**	[at seː 'fjɑɒnsyːn]
viewer	**seer** (c)	['seʌ]
TV show	**tv-udsendelse** (c)	['teˌve 'uðˌsɛnəlsə]

163. Photography

camera (photo)	**fotografiapparat** (n)	[fotoɡʁɑ'fiɑpɑʁɑːd]
photo, picture	**fotobillede** (n)	['fotoˌbiləðə]
photographer	**fotograf** (c)	[foto'ɡʁɑːf]
photo studio	**fotoatelier** (n)	['fotoæːˌtəljejʌ]
photo album	**fotoalbum** (n)	['fotoˌalbɔm]
camera lens	**objektiv** (n)	[ɒbjɛk'tiu]
telephoto lens	**teleobjektiv** (n)	['tele ʌbjək'tiw]
filter	**filter** (n)	['fildʌ]
lens	**linse** (c)	['lensə]
set of lenses	**optik** (c)	[ʌb'tik]
diaphragm (aperture)	**blænder** (c)	['blɛnʌ]
exposure time	**eksponering** (c)	[ɛgspo'neːʁeŋ]
viewfinder	**søger** (c)	['søːʌ]
digital camera	**digital kamera** (n)	[digi'tæːl 'kæːməʁa]
tripod	**stativ** (n)	[sda'tiw]
flash	**blitz** (c)	[blids]
to photograph (vt)	**at fotografere**	[at fotoɡʁɑːˈfeːɒ]
to take pictures	**at fotografere**	[at fotoɡʁɑːˈfeːɒ]
to be photographed	**lade sig fotografere**	['læːðə saj fotoɡʁɑːˈfeːɒ]
focus	**fokusering** (c)	[foɡu'seɒeŋ]
to adjust the focus	**at fokusere**	[at foku'seʌ]
sharp, in focus	**skarp**	[skɑːb]
sharpness	**skarphed** (c)	['skɑːpˌheð]
contrast	**kontrast** (c)	[kʌn'tʁɑsd]
contrasty	**kontrast-**	[kʌn'tʁɑsd]
picture (photo)	**billede** (n)	['beləðə]
negative (noun)	**negativ** (n)	[nega'tiu]

film (e.g., a roll of ~)	film (c)	[film]
shot, frame	filmbillede (n)	['film,bileðe]
to print (photos)	at kopiere	[at ko'pjeʌ]

164. Beach. Swimming

beach	badestrand (c)	['bæ:ðe,sdʁɑn]
sand	sand (n)	[san]
deserted (beach)	øde	[ø:ðe]

suntan	solbrændthed (c)	['so:l,bʁandheð]
to get a tan	at solbade	[at 'so:l,bæ:ðe]
tan (adj)	solbrændt	['so:l,bʁand]
sunscreen	solcreme (c)	['so:l,kʁɛ:m]

bikini	bikini (c)	[bi'ki:ni]
bathing suit	badedragt (c)	['bæ:ðe,dʁagd]
swim briefs	badebukser (pl)	['bæ:ðe,boksʌ]

swimming pool	svømmebassin (n)	['svœmeba,sɛn]
to swim (vi)	at svømme	[at 'svœme]
shower	brusebad (n)	['bʁuse,bað]
to change (one's clothes)	at klæde sig om	[at 'klɛ:ðe saj ɒm]
towel	håndklæde (n)	['hɒn,klɛ:ðe]

| boat | båd (c) | [bɔð] |
| motorboat | motorbåd (c) | ['mo:tʌ,bɔð] |

water ski	vandski (pl)	['vanski]
pedal boat	vandcykel (c)	['van,sykel]
surfing	surfing (c)	['sœ:feŋ]
surfer	surfer (c)	['sœ:fʌ]

scuba set	SCUBA	['sku:be]
flippers	svømmefødder (pl)	['svœme,føðʌ]
mask	maske (c)	['maske]
diver, snorkeler	dykker (c)	['døkʌ]
to dive (vi)	at dykke	[at 'døke]
underwater (adv)	under vandet	['ɔnʌ 'vaneð]

beach umbrella	parasol (c)	[pɑɑ'sʌl]
beach chair	liggestol (c)	['lege,sdo:l]
sunglasses	solbriller (pl)	['so:l,bʁɛlʌ]
air mattress	luftmadras (c)	['lɔfdma'dʁɑs]

| to play (amuse oneself) | at spille | [at 'sbele] |
| to go for a swim | at bade | [at 'bæ:ðe] |

| beach ball | bold (c) | [bɒld] |
| to inflate (vt) | at blæse op | [at 'blɛ:se ɔp] |

inflatable, air	**oppustelig**	[ʌbˈpusdəli]
wave	**bølge** (c)	[ˈbøljə]
buoy	**bøje** (c)	[bɒjə]
to drown (ab. person)	**at drukne**	[at ˈdʁɔknə]
to save, to rescue	**at redde**	[at ˈʁɛðə]
life vest	**redningsvest** (c)	[ˈʁɛðneŋsˌvesd]
to observe, to watch	**at betragte**	[at beˈtʁɑgdə]
lifeguard	**livredder** (c)	[ˈliːuˌʁɛðʌ]

TECHNICAL EQUIPMENT. TRANSPORT

Technical equipment

165. Computer

computer	computer (c)	[kɒm'pju:dʌ]
notebook, laptop	bærbar (c), laptop (c)	['bɛɒˌbɑ:], ['labˌtʌb]
to switch on (vt)	at tænde	[at 'tɛnə]
to turn off	at slukke for	[at 'slɔkə fɒ]
keyboard	tastatur (n, c)	[tasdaˈtuɒ]
key	tast (c)	[tasd]
mouse	mus (c)	[mu:s]
mouse pad	musemåtte (c)	['museˌmɒdə]
button	knap (c)	[knɑb]
cursor	cursor (c)	['kœ:sʌ]
monitor	monitor (c)	['mʌnitʌ]
screen	skærm (c)	['skæɒm]
hard disk	harddisk (c)	['hɑ:dˌdesk]
hard disk volume	harddisk kapacitet (c)	['hɑ:dˌdesk kabasi'ted]
memory	hukommelse (c)	[hu'kʌmelsə]
random access memory	RAM (n), arbejdslager (n)	['ʁam], ['ɑ:bɑjdsˌlæjʌ]
file	fil (c)	[fi:l]
folder	mappe (c)	['mɑbə]
to open (a file)	at åbne	[at 'ɔ:bnə]
to close (vt)	at lukke	[at 'lɔkə]
to save (vt)	at bevare	[at be'vɑ:ɑ]
to delete (vt)	at slette	[at 'slɛdə]
to copy (vt)	at kopiere	[at ko'pjeʌ]
to sort (vt)	at sortere	[at sɒ'teʌ]
to copy (vt)	at kopiere	[at ko'pjeʌ]
program	program (n)	[pʁo'gʁam]
software	programmel (n)	[pʁogʁa'məl]
programmer	programmør (c)	[pʁogʁa'møɒ]
to program (vi)	at programmere	[at pʁogʁa'meʌ]
hacker	hacker (c)	['hakʌ]
password	password (n)	['pasvɒɒd]

| virus | **virus** (n, c) | ['viːʁus] |
| to find, to detect | **at opdage** | [at 'ʌbˌdæjə] |

| byte | **byte** (c) | ['bɑjd] |
| megabyte | **megabyte** (c) | ['meːgaˌbɑjd] |

| data | **data** (n) | ['dæːta] |
| database | **database** (c) | ['dæːtaˌbæːsə] |

cable (wire)	**kabel** (n)	['kæːbəl]
to disconnect (vt)	**at koble fra**	[at 'kɒblə fʁɑ]
to connect (sth to sth)	**at forbinde**	[at fɒ'benə]

166. Internet. E-mail

Internet	**Internet** (n)	['entʌˌnɛd]
browser	**browser** (c)	['bʁɑwsʌ]
search engine	**søgemaskine** (c)	['søːmaˌsgiːnə]
provider	**udbyder** (c)	['uðˌbyðʌ]

web master	**webmaster** (c)	['wɛbˌmɑːsdʌ]
website	**website** (n)	['wɛbˌsɑjd]
web page	**webside** (c)	['wɛbˌsiːðə]

| address | **e-mail adresse** (c) | ['iːˌmɛjl a'dʁasə] |
| address book | **adressebog** (c) | [a'dʁasəˌbɔw] |

mailbox	**postkasse** (c)	['pɒsdˌkasə]
mail	**e-mail** (c)	['iːˌmɛjl]
overfull	**overfyldt**	['ɒwʌfyld]

message	**meddelelse** (c)	['mɛðˌdeləlsə]
incoming messages	**indgående e-mails** (pl)	[en'gɔːənə 'iːˌmɑjls]
outgoing messages	**udgående e-mails** (pl)	['uðgɔːənə 'iːˌmɛjls]

sender	**afsender** (c)	[ɑu'sɛnʌ]
to send (vt)	**at afsende**	[at ɑu'sɛnə]
sending (of mail)	**afsendelse** (c)	[ɑu'sɛnəlsə]

| receiver | **adressat** (c) | [adʁɛ'sæd] |
| to receive (vt) | **at få** | [at fɔː] |

| correspondence | **brevveksling** (c) | ['bʁeuˌvɛgsleŋ] |
| to correspond (vi) | **at korrespondere** | [at kɒɒsbʌn'deʌ] |

file	**fil** (c)	[fiːl]
to download (vt)	**at downloade**	[at 'dɑwnˌlɔwdə]
to create (vt)	**at skabe**	[at 'skæːbə]
to delete (vt)	**at slette**	[at 'slɛdə]
deleted	**slettet**	['slɛdəð]

connection (good, bad ~)	forbindelse (c)	[fɒ'benəlsə]
speed	hastighed (c)	['hasdiˌheð]
modem	modem (n)	['moːˌdɛm]
access	adgang (c)	['aðgɑŋ]
port (e.g., input ~)	port (c)	['poɒd]

connection	forbindelse (c)	[fɒ'benəlsə]
to connect to … (vi)	at oprette	[at 'ʌbˌʁadə
	forbindelse til …	fʌ'benəlsə tel …]

| to choose (vt) | at vælge | [at 'vɛljə] |
| to search for … | at søge efter … | [at 'søːə 'ɛfdɒ] |

167. Electricity

electricity	elektricitet (c)	[elɛktʁisi'ted]
electrical	elektrisk	[e'lɛktʁisk]
electric power station	el-værk (n)	['ɛlˌvaɒk]
energy	energi (c)	[enɑɒ'giː]
electric power	elkraft (c)	['ɛlkʁɑfd]

light bulb	pære (c)	['pɛːɒ]
flashlight	lommelygte (c)	['lʌməˌløgdə]
street light	gadelygte (c)	['gæːðəˌløgdə]

light	lys (n)	[lyːs]
to turn on	at tænde	[at 'tɛnə]
to turn off	at slukke for	[at 'slɔkə fɒ]
to turn off the light	at slukke lyset	[at 'slɔkə 'lyːsəð]

to burn out (vi)	at brænde over	[at 'bʁanə 'ɒuɒ]
short circuit	kortslutning (c)	['kɒːdˌsludnen]
broken wire	brud (n)	[bʁuð]
contact	kontakt (c)	[kɔn'takd]

switch (for light)	afbryder (c)	[ɑu'bʁyðʌ]
wall socket	stikkontakt (c)	['sdekkɔn'takd]
plug	stik (n)	[sdek]
extension cord	stikdåse (c)	['sdekˌdɔːsə]

fuse	sikring (c)	['segʁɛŋ]
cable, wire	ledning (c)	['leðnen]
wiring	elinstallation (c)	['eːl ensdala'çoːn]

ampere	ampere (c)	[ɑm'pɒɒ]
amperage	strømstyrke (c)	['sdʁœmˌsdyɒkə]
volt	volt (c)	[vɔld]
voltage	spænding (c)	['sbɛnen]
electrical device	el-apparat (n)	['ɛlɑpɑ'ʁɑːd]
indicator	indikator (c)	[endi'kæːtɒ]

electrician	**elektriker** (c)	[eˈlɛktʁikʌ]
to solder (vt)	**at lodde**	[at ˈlʌðə]
soldering iron	**loddekolbe** (c)	[ˈlʌðəˌkʌlbə]
current	**strøm** (c)	[sdʁœm]

168. Tools

tool, instrument	**redskab** (n)	[ˈʁɛðˌskæb]
tools	**værktøj** (pl)	[ˈvæɒkˌtøj]
equipment (factory ~)	**udstyr** (n)	[ˈuðsdyɒ]

hammer	**hammer** (c)	[ˈhamʌ]
screwdriver	**skruetrækker** (c)	[ˈskʁuːəˌtʁakʌ]
ax	**økse** (c)	[ˈøksə]

saw	**sav** (c)	[ˈsæv]
to saw (vt)	**at save**	[at ˈsæːuə]
plane (tool)	**høvl** (c)	[ˈhœwl]
to plane (vt)	**at høvle**	[at ˈhœulə]
soldering iron	**loddekolbe** (c)	[ˈlʌðəˌkʌlbə]
to solder (vt)	**at lodde**	[at ˈlʌðə]

file (for metal)	**fil** (c)	[fiːl]
carpenter pincers	**knibtang** (c)	[ˈkniwˌtɑŋ]
lineman's pliers	**fladtang** (c)	[ˈfladɑŋ]
chisel	**stemmejern** (n)	[ˈsdɛməˌjæɒn]

drill bit	**bor** (n)	[ˈboɒ]
electric drill	**drilbor** (c)	[ˈdʁɛlbɒ]
to drill (vi, vt)	**at bore**	[at ˈboːɒ]

knife	**kniv** (c)	[ˈkniu]
pocket knife	**lommekniv** (c)	[ˈlʌməˌkniu]
folding (knife etc.)	**klap-**	[klɑb]
blade	**æg** (c)	[ɛːg]

sharp (knife)	**skarp**	[skɑːb]
blunt	**sløv**	[ˈsløw]
to become blunt	**at blive sløv**	[at ˈbliːə sløu]
to sharpen (vt)	**at hvæsse**	[at ˈvɛsə]

bolt	**bolt** (c)	[bʌld]
nut	**møtrik** (c)	[ˈmøtʁɛk]
thread (of a screw)	**gevind** (n)	[geˈven]
screw (for wood)	**skrue** (c)	[ˈskʁuːə]

nail	**søm** (n)	[sœm]
nailhead	**hoved** (n)	[ˈhoːəð]
ruler (for measuring)	**lineal** (c)	[lineˈæːl]
tape measure	**målebånd** (n)	[ˈmɔːləˌbɒn]

level (tool)	**niveau** (n)	[ni'vo]
magnifying glass	**lup** (c)	[lɔb]
measuring instrument	**måleapparat** (n)	['mɔːleaba'ʁad]
to measure (vt)	**at måle**	[at 'mɔːle]
scale (of thermometer etc.)	**skala** (c)	['skæːla]
readings	**måling** (c)	['mɔːleŋ]
compressor	**kompressor** (c)	[kɔmpʁa'sɒ]
microscope	**mikroskop** (n)	[mikʁɔ'skoːb]
pump (e.g., water ~)	**pumpe** (c)	['pɔmbə]
robot	**robot** (c)	[ʁo'bɒd]
laser	**laser** (c)	['lɛjsʌ], ['læːsʌ]
wrench	**skruenøgle** (c)	['sgʁuə̩nɒjlə]
adhesive tape	**klisterbånd** (n), **tape** (c)	['klisdɒ̩bɒn], ['tɛjb]
glue	**lim** (c)	[liːm]
emery paper	**sandpapir** (n)	['sanpa̩piɒ]
spring	**springfjeder** (c)	['sbʁɛŋ̩fjeðʌ]
magnet	**magnet** (c)	[maw'ned]
gloves	**gummihandsker** (pl)	['gomi̩hanskʌ]
rope	**snor** (c)	['snoɒ]
cord	**snor** (c)	['snoɒ]
wire (e.g., telephone ~)	**ledning** (c)	['leðneŋ]
cable	**kabel** (n)	['kæːbəl]
sledgehammer	**forhammer** (c)	['fɒhamʌ]
crowbar	**brækjern** (n)	['bʁakjæɒn]
ladder	**stige** (c)	['sdiːə]
stepladder	**trappestige** (c)	['tʁabə̩sdiə]
to screw (tighten)	**at skrue fast**	[at 'skʁuːə fasd]
to unscrew (vt)	**at skrue af**	[at 'skʁuːə a]
to tighten (vt)	**at klemme**	[at 'klɛmə]
to glue, to stick	**at klæbe**	[at 'klɛːbə]
to cut (vt)	**at skære**	[at 'skɛːɒ]
malfunction (fault)	**fejl** (n)	[fajl]
fault, problems	**defekter** (pl)	[de'fɛkdʌ]
repair (mending)	**reparation** (c)	[ʁɛbʁa'ɕon]
to repair, to mend (vt)	**at istandsættelse**	[at i'sdan̩sɛdəlsə]
to adjust (machine etc.)	**at regulere**	[at ʁɛgu'leːɒ]
to check (to examine)	**at kontrollere**	[at kʌntʁo'leʌ]
checking	**kontrol** (c)	[kʌn'tʁɔl]
readings	**måling** (c)	['mɔːleŋ]
to reduce (vt)	**at formindske**	[at fʌ'menskə]
reduction	**reduktion** (c)	[ʁɛduk'ɕoːn]
reliable (machine)	**pålidelig**	[pʌ'liðəli]

complicated	**kompliceret**	[kʌmbliˈseʌð]
to rust (vi)	**at ruste**	[at ˈʁɔsdə]
rusty, rusted	**rusten**	[ˈʁɔsdən]
rust	**rust** (c)	[ʁɔsd]

Transport

169. Airplane

airplane	**fly** (c)	[fly:]
air ticket	**flybillet** (c)	['fly:ˌbiləð]
airline	**luftfartsselskab** (n)	['lɔfdfɑds 'sɛlˌskæb]
airport	**lufthavn** (c)	['lɔfdˌhɑun]
supersonic	**overlyds-**	['ɒwʌˌlyðs]
captain	**kaptajn** (c)	[kɑb'tɑjn]
crew	**besætning** (c)	[be'sɛdnen]
pilot	**pilot** (n)	[pi'lo:d]
flight attendant	**stewardesse** (c)	[sdjuɑ'dɛsə]
navigator	**styrmand** (c)	['sdyɒˌman]
wings	**vinger** (pl)	['veŋʌ]
tail	**hale** (c)	['hæ:lə]
cockpit	**cockpit** (n)	['kɒkpid]
engine	**motor** (c)	['mo:tʌ]
undercarriage	**chassis** (n)	[ɕa'si]
turbine	**turbine** (c)	[tuɒ'bi:nə]
propeller	**propel** (c)	[pʁo'pəl]
black box	**sort boks** (c)	['sɒɒdə 'bʌgs]
control column	**rat** (n)	[ʁɑd]
fuel	**brændstof** (n)	['bʁanˌsdɒf]
instructions	**instruks** (c)	[en'sdʁuks]
oxygen mask	**iltmaske** (c)	['ildmaskə]
uniform	**uniform** (c)	[uni'fɒ:m]
life vest	**redningsvest** (c)	['ʁɛðneŋsˌvesd]
parachute	**faldskærm** (c)	['falˌskɑɒm]
takeoff	**take-off**	[tɛjg'ɒ:f]
to take off (vi)	**at lette**	[at 'lɛdə]
runway	**startbane** (c)	['sdɑ:dˌbæ:nə]
visibility	**sigtbarhed** (c)	['segdbɑˌheð]
flight (act of flying)	**flyvning** (c)	['fly:uneŋ]
altitude	**højde** (c)	['hɒjdə]
air pocket	**lufthul** (n)	['lɔfdˌhɔl]
seat	**plads** (c)	[plas]
headphones	**hovedtelefoner** (pl)	['ho:əð deləˌfo:nʌ]
folding tray	**klapbord** (n)	['klɑbˌbɒɒ]

window (in plane)	**koøje** (n)	['koːˌɒjə]
No smoking!	**RYGNING FORBUDT!**	['ʁyːneŋ fɒːˈbud]
aisle	**midtergang** (c)	['medʌˌgɑŋ]

170. Train

train	**tog** (n)	['tɔw]
suburban train	**S-tog** (n)	['ɛsˌtɔw]
fast train	**lyntog** (n)	['lyːnˌtɔw]
diesel locomotive	**diesellokomotiv** (n)	['diːsɛl lokomoˈtiu]
steam engine	**lokomotiv** (n)	[lokomoˈtiu]

| passenger car | **vogn** (c) | [vɒwn] |
| dining car | **spisevogn** (c) | ['sbiseˌvɒwn] |

rails	**skinner** (pl)	['skenʌ]
railroad	**jernbane** (c)	['jæɒnˌbæːnə]
railway tie	**svelle** (c)	['svɛllə]

platform (railway ~)	**perron** (c)	[paˈʁʌŋ]
track (e.g., ~ 1, 2 etc.)	**vej** (c)	[vɑj]
semaphore	**semafor** (c)	[semaˈfɒ]
station	**station** (c)	[sdaˈɕoːn]

engineer	**togfører** (c)	['tɔwˌføːʌ]
porter (of luggage)	**drager** (c)	['dʁɑːuʌ]
train steward	**konduktør** (c)	[kʌndɔˈkdøɒ]
passenger	**passager** (c)	[pasaˈɕeʌ]
conductor	**kontrollør** (c)	[kʌntʁoˈløɒ]

| corridor (in train) | **gang** (c) | [gɑŋ] |
| emergency break | **nødbremse** (c) | ['nøðˌbʁeːmsə] |

compartment	**kupe** (c)	[kuˈpe]
berth	**køje** (c)	['kɒjə]
upper berth	**overkøje** (c)	['ɒwʌkɒjə]
lower berth	**underkøje** (c)	['ɔnɒˌkʌjə]
linen	**linned** (n)	['lenəð]

ticket	**billet** (c)	[biˈlɛd]
schedule	**køreplan** (c)	['køːɒˌplæːn]
timetable	**lystavle** (c)	['lysˌtɑulə]

to leave, to depart	**at afgå**	[at ɑuˈgɔː]
departure	**afgang** (c)	[ɑuˈgɑŋ]
to arrive (about train)	**at ankomme**	[at 'anˌkʌmə]
arrival	**ankomst** (c)	['anˌkɒmsd]

| to be late (about train) | **at forsinke** | [at fʌˈsenkə] |
| to arrive by train | **at komme med toget** | [at 'kɒmə mɛð 'tɔːuəð] |

to get on the train	at stå på toget	[at sdɔ: pɔ 'to:uəð]
to get off the train	at stige af toget	[at 'sdi:ə a 'to:uəð]
train wreck	jernbaneulykke (c)	['jæɒn‚bæ:nuløkə]
to be derailed	at blive afsporet	[at 'bli:ə ɑus'bo:ɒð]
steam engine	lokomotiv (n)	[lokomo'tiu]
stoker, fireman	fyrbøder (c)	['fyɒbø:ðʌ]
firebox	fyr (n)	[fyɒ]
coal	kul (n)	[kɔl]

171. Ship

ship	skib (n)	[ski:b]
vessel	skib (n)	[ski:b]
steamship	dampbåd (c)	['dɑmb‚bɔð]
riverboat	motorskib (n)	['mo:tʌski:b]
ocean liner	liner (c)	['lɑjnʌ]
cruiser	krydser (c)	['kʁyðsʌ]
yacht	lystbåd (c)	['løsd‚bɔð]
tug	bugserbåd (c)	[bug'sɒbɔð]
barge	pram (c)	[pʁɑm]
ferry	færge (c)	['fæɒwə]
sailing ship	sejlbåd (c)	['sɑjl‚bɔð]
brigantine	brigantine (c)	[bʁigan'ti:nə]
ice breaker	isbryder (c)	['isbʁyðʌ]
submarine	u-båd (c)	['u:‚bɔð]
boat	båd (c)	[bɔð]
dinghy	jolle (c)	[jɒlə]
lifeboat	redningsbåd (c)	['ʁɛðneŋs‚bɔð]
motorboat	motorbåd (c)	['mo:tʌ‚bɔð]
captain	kaptajn (c)	[kɑb'tɑjn]
seaman	matros (c)	[ma'tʁos]
sailor	sømand (c)	['søman]
crew	besætning (c)	[be'sɛdneŋ]
boatswain	bådsmand (c)	['bɔðs‚man]
ship's boy	skibsdreng (c)	['sgibs‚dʁaŋ]
cook	skibskok (c)	['skibs‚kɒk]
ship's doctor	skibslæge (c)	['sgibs‚lɛ:jə]
deck	dæk (n)	[dɛk]
mast	mast (c)	[masd]
sail	sejl (n)	['sɑjl]

hold	**lastrum** (n)	['lasdˌʁɔm]
bow	**bov** (c)	['bɒu]
stern	**agterende** (c)	['agdɒʁɒnə]
oar	**åre** (c)	['ɒːɒ]
propeller	**propel** (c)	[pʁo'pəl]

cabin	**kahyt** (c)	[ka'hyd]
wardroom	**officersmesse** (c)	[ɒfi'sɒs ˌmɛsə]
engine room	**maskinrum** (n)	[ma'skiːnˌʁɔm]
the bridge	**kommandobro** (c)	[ko'mandoˌbʁoː]
radio room	**radiorum** (n)	['ʁɑːdioˌʁɔm]
wave (radio)	**radiobølge** (c)	['ʁɑːdioˌbøljə]
logbook	**skibsjournal** (c)	['skibs ɕɒɒ'næl]

spyglass	**kikkert** (c)	['kikʌd]
bell	**klokke** (c)	['klɒkə]
flag	**flag** (n)	[flæː]

| rope (mooring ~) | **reb** (n) | [ʁɛːb] |
| knot (bowline etc.) | **knob** (c) | [knoːb] |

| handrail | **gelænder** (pl) | [ge'lɛnʌ] |
| gangway | **landgang** (c) | ['lanˌgaŋ] |

| anchor | **anker** (n) | ['aŋkʌ] |
| to weigh anchor | **at lette anker** | [at 'lɛdə 'aŋkɒ] |

| to drop anchor | **at kaste anker** | [at 'kasdə 'aŋkɒ] |
| anchor chain | **ankerkæde** (c) | ['aŋkɒˌkɛːðə] |

| port (harbor) | **havn** (c) | [haun] |
| wharf, quay | **kaj** (c) | [kɑj] |

| to berth (moor) | **at lægge til** | [at 'lɛgə tel] |
| to cast off | **at lægge fra** | [at 'lɛgə fʁɑ] |

| trip (voyage) | **rejse** (c) | ['ʁɑjsə] |
| cruise (sea trip) | **krydstogt** (n) | ['kʁystɒgd] |

| course (route) | **kurs** (c) | [kuɒs] |
| route (itinerary) | **rute** (c) | ['ʁuːdə] |

fairway	**farvand** (n)	['fɑːvan]
shallows (shoal)	**sandbanke** (c)	['sanˌbaŋkə]
to run aground	**at gå på grund**	[at gɒː pɔ gʁɒn]

storm	**storm** (c)	[sdɒːm]
signal	**signal** (n)	[si'næːl]
to sink (about boat)	**at synke**	[at 'søŋkə]
Man overboard!	**Mand over bord!**	[man 'ɒuɒ ˌbɒɒ]
SOS	**SOS**	[ɛso'ɛs]
life buoy	**redningsbælte** (n)	['ʁɛðneŋsˌbɛldə]

172. Airport

airport	**lufthavn** (c)	['lɔfd̥ˌhɑun]
airplane	**fly** (c)	[fly:]
airline	**luftfartsselskab** (n)	['lɔfd̥fɑds 'sɛlˌskæb]
air-traffic controller	**flyveleder** (c)	['fly:uəˌleːð̩ʌ]
departure	**afgang** (c)	[ɑu'gɑŋ]
arrival	**ankomst** (c)	['anˌkɔmsd̥]
to arrive (vi)	**at ankomme**	[at 'anˌkʌmə]
departure time	**afgangstid** (c)	[ɑu'gɑŋstið]
arrival time	**ankomsttid** (c)	['anˌkɔmsdtið]
to be delayed	**at forsinke**	[at fʌ'seŋkə]
flight delay	**afgangs forsinkelse** (c)	['ɑwˌgɑŋs fʌ'seŋgəlsə]
information board	**informationstavle** (c)	[enfɔma'ɕoːns ˌd̥ɑulə]
information	**information** (c)	[enfɔma'ɕoːn]
to announce (vt)	**at meddele**	[at 'mɛð̩ˌde:lə]
flight (e.g., next ~)	**flight** (c)	[flɑjd̥]
customs	**told** (c)	[tɔl]
customs officer	**toldbetjent** (c)	['tɔl be'tjɛnd̥]
declaration	**tolddeklaration** (c)	['tɔl dəklɑɑ'ɕoːn]
to fill out a declaration	**at udfylde**	[at 'uð̩ˌfylə
	en toldangivelse	en 'tɔldˌagiuəlsə]
passport control	**paskontrol** (c)	['paskɔnˌtʁɔl]
luggage	**bagage** (c)	[ba'gæːɕə]
hand luggage	**håndbagage** (c)	['hɔn ba'gæːɕə]
LOST-AND-FOUND	**bagageeftersøgning** (c)	[ba'gæːɕə 'ɛfdɒ 'søːneŋ]
luggage cart	**bagagevogn** (c)	[ba'gæːɕəˌvɒwn]
landing	**landing** (c)	['laneŋ]
runway	**landingsbane** (c)	['laneŋsˌbæːnə]
to land (vi)	**at lande**	[at 'lanə]
airstairs	**trappe** (c)	['tʁɑbə]
check-in	**check-in** (c)	['ɕɛk-en]
check-in desk	**check-in-skranke** (c)	['ɕɛk-en-ˌskʁɑŋkə]
to check-in (vi)	**at registrere sig**	[at ʁɛgi'sdʁɛːɒ saj]
boarding pass	**boardingkort** (n)	['bɒːdeŋˌkɒːd̥]
departure gate	**gate** (c)	[gɛjd̥]
transit	**transit** (c)	[tʁɑn'sid̥]
to wait (vi, vt)	**at vente (på ...)**	[at 'vɛndə pɔ]
departure lounge	**ventesal** (c)	['vɛndəˌsæːl]
to see off	**at sende af sted**	[at 'sɛnə a sdɛð]
to say goodbye	**at sige farvel**	[at 'siːə fɑ'vɛl]

173. Bicycle. Motorcycle

bicycle	**cykel** (c)	['sykəl]
scooter	**scooter** (c)	['sgu:dʌ]
motorcycle, bike	**motorcykel** (c)	['mo:tʌˌsykəl]
to go by bicycle	**at cykle**	[at 'syklə]
handlebars	**styr** (n)	['sdø]
pedal	**pedal** (c)	[peˈdæːl]
brake	**bremse** (c)	['bʁamsə]
bicycle seat	**sadel** (c)	['saðəl]
pump	**pumpe** (c)	['pɔmbə]
rack	**bagagekurv** (c)	[baˈgæːɕə ˌkuɒw]
front lamp	**lygte** (c)	['løgdə]
helmet	**hjelm** (c)	[jɛlm]
wheel	**hjul** (n)	[ju:l]
mudguard	**skærm** (c)	['skæɒm]
rim	**hjulfælg** (c)	['ju:lˌfɛlj]
spoke	**eger** (c)	['ejʌ]

Cars

174. Types of cars

automobile, car	**bil** (c)	[biːl]
sports car	**sportsbil** (c)	[ˈsbɒːdsˌbiːl]
limousine	**limousine** (c)	[limuˈsiːnə]
off-road vehicle	**terrænbil** (c)	[taˈʁaŋˌbiːl]
convertible	**cabriolet** (c)	[kabʁioˈlɛd]
minibus	**minibus** (c)	[ˈminiˌbus]
ambulance	**ambulance** (c)	[ɑmbuˈlɑŋsə]
snowplow	**sneryddemaskine** (c)	[ˈsneʁyðə maˈskiːnə]
truck	**lastbil** (c)	[ˈlasdˌbiːl]
tank truck	**tankvogn** (c)	[ˈtɑŋgˌvɒwn]
van	**varevogn** (c)	[ˈvɑːɑˌvɒwn]
road tractor	**truck** (c)	[ˈtʁʌk]
trailer	**påhængsvogn** (c)	[ˈpɒhɛŋsˌvɒwn]
comfortable	**komfortabel**	[kɒmfoˈtæːbəl]
second hand	**brugt**	[bʁɔgd]

175. Cars. Bodywork

hood	**motorhjelm** (c)	[ˈmoːtʌjɛlm]
fender	**skærm** (c)	[ˈskæɒm]
roof	**tag** (n)	[tæː]
windshield	**forrude** (c)	[ˈfɒːʁuːðə]
rear-view mirror	**bagspejl** (n)	[ˈbɑuˌsbɑjl]
windshield washer	**sprinkler** (c)	[ˈsbʁɛŋklʌ]
windshield wipers	**vinduesviskere** (pl)	[ˈvendusˌveskɒɒ]
side window	**sidevindue** (n)	[ˈsiːðəˌvendu]
window crank	**rudeoptræk** (n)	[ˈʁuːðə ˈɒbˌtʁak]
antenna	**antenne** (c)	[anˈtɛnə]
sun roof	**soltag** (n)	[ˈsoːlˌtæj]
bumper	**kofanger** (c)	[ˈkoːfɑŋʌ]
trunk	**bagagerum** (n)	[baˈgæːɕəˌʁɔm]
door	**dør** (c)	[dœɒ]
door handle	**dørgreb** (n)	[ˈdœɒˌgʁɛːb]

door lock	lås (c)	[lɔ:s]
license plate	nummerplade (c)	['nɔmʌˌplæ:ðə]
muffler	lyddæmper (c)	['lyðˌdɛmbʌ]
gas tank	benzintank (c)	[bɛn'si:nˌtɑŋk]
tail pipe	udstødningsrør (n)	['uðsdø:ðneŋs ˌʁœɒ]

gas, accelerator	gas (c)	[gas]
pedal	pedal (c)	[pe'dæ:l]
gas pedal	gaspedal (c)	['gaspeˌdæ:l]

brake	bremse (c)	['bʁamsə]
brake pedal	bremsepedal (c)	['bʁamsə peˌdæ:l]
to slow down (to brake)	at bremse op	[at 'bʁamsə ɔp]
parking brake	parkeringsbremse (c)	[pɑ'keʁeŋ 'bʁamsə]

clutch	kobling (c)	['kɒbleŋ]
clutch pedal	koblingspedal (c)	['kɒbleŋspeˌdæ:l]
clutch plate	skivekobling (c)	['sgi:vəˌkɒbleŋ]
shock absorber	støddæmper (c)	['sdøðˌdɛmbʌ]
wheel	hjul (n)	[ju:l]
spare tire	reservehjul (n)	[ʁɛ'sæɒvəˌju:l]
wheel cover (hubcap)	hjulkapsel (c)	['ju:lˌkɑbsəl]

driving wheels	drivhjul (n)	['dʁi:uju:l]
front-wheel drive	forhjulstrukket	['fɒ:jlsˌtʁɔkəð]
rear-wheel drive	baghjulstrukket	['bawjulsˌtʁɔgəð]
all-wheel drive	firehjulstrukket	['fi:ɒjulsˌtʁɔkəð]

gearbox	gearkasse (c)	['giɒkasə]
automatic	automatisk	[ɑuto'matisk]
mechanical	mekanisk	[me'kænisk]
gear shift	gearstang (c)	['giɒsdɑŋ]

| headlight | billygte (c) | ['bi:lˌløgdə] |
| headlights | billygter (pl) | ['bi:lˌløgdʌ] |

low beam	nærlys (n)	['nɛɒly:s]
high beam	fjernlys (n)	['fjaɒnly:s]
brake light	bremselygte (c)	['bʁamsə ˌløgdə]

parking lights	positionslys	[posi'ɕo:nsˌly:s]
hazard lights	havariblink (n pl)	[hɑvɑ'ʁi ˌbleŋk]
fog lights	tågelygter (pl)	['tɔ:wəˌløgdʌ]
turn signal	blinklys (n)	['bleŋkˌly:s]
back-up light	baglys (n)	['bɑuˌlys]

176. Cars. Passenger compartment

| car inside | salon (c) | [sa'lɒn] |
| leather (attr) | læder- | ['lɛðɒ] |

velour (attr)	fløjl-	[flɒjl]
upholstery	betræk (n)	[beˈtʁak]
instrument (gage)	instrument (n)	[ensdʁuˈmɛnd]
dashboard	panel (n)	[paˈneːl]
speedometer	speedometer (c)	[sbidoˈmedʌ]
needle (pointer)	viser (c)	[ˈviːsʌ]
odometer	taxameter (n)	[tɑgsaˈmedʌ]
indicator	indikator (c)	[endiˈkæːtɒ]
level	niveau (n)	[niˈvo]
indicator light	elpære (c)	[ˈɛlbɛːɒ]
steering wheel	rat (n)	[ʁɑd]
horn	signalhorn (n)	[siˈnæːlˌhoɒn]
button	knap (c)	[knɑb]
switch	omskifter (c)	[ʌmˈskifdʌ]
seat	sæde (n)	[ˈsɛːðə]
seat back	ryglæn (n)	[ˈʁɒegˌlɛːn]
headrest	nakkestøtte (c)	[ˈnɑkəˌsdødə]
seat belt	sikkerhedssele (c)	[ˈsekʌˌheðs ˈseːlə]
to fasten the belt	at spænde sikkerhedsselen	[at ˈsbɛnə ˈsekɒheðˌselən]
adjustment (of seats)	regulering (c)	[ʁɛguˈleːʁeŋ]
airbag	luftpude (c)	[ˈlɔfdˌpuːðə]
air-conditioner	klimaanlæg (n)	[ˈkliːmanˌlɛːg]
radio	radio (c)	[ˈʁɑːdio]
CD player	cd-afspiller (c)	[seˈde ˈauˌsbelʌ]
to turn on	at tænde	[at ˈtɛnə]
antenna	antenne (c)	[anˈtɛnə]
glove box	handskerum (c)	[ˈhanskəˌʁɔm]
ashtray	askebæger (n)	[ˈasgəˌbɛːʌ]

177. Cars. Engine

engine	motor (c)	[ˈmoːtʌ]
motor	motor (c)	[ˈmoːtʌ]
diesel (e.g., ~ engine)	diesel-	[ˈdiːsəl]
gasoline (e.g., ~ engine)	benzin-	[bɛnˈsiːn]
engine volume	motor størrelse (c)	[ˈmoːtʌ ˈsdœɒʌlsə]
power	kapacitet (c)	[kapasiˈteːd]
horsepower	hestekraft (c)	[ˈhɛsdəˌkʁɑfd]
piston	stempel (n)	[ˈsdɛmbəl]
cylinder	cylinder (c)	[syˈlenʌ]
valve	ventil (c)	[vɛnˈtiːl]
injector	injektor (c)	[enˈjɛkdɒ]

generator	generator (c)	[genə'ʁɑːtɒ]
carburetor	karburator (c)	[kɑbu'ʁɑːtʌ]
engine oil	motorolie (c)	['moːtʌˌoːljə]

radiator	køler (c)	['køːlʌ]
cooling liquid	kølervæske (c)	['køːlɒˌvɛskə]
cooling fan	ventilator (c)	[vɛnti:'lɑtɒ]

battery (accumulator)	batteri (n)	[badə'ʁiː]
starter	starter (c)	['sdɑːdʌ]
ignition	tænding (c)	['tɛneŋ]
spark plug	tændrør (n)	['tɛnˌʁœɒ]

terminal (of battery)	terminal (c)	[tæɒmi'næl]
plus (positive terminal)	plus (n)	[plus]
minus (negative terminal)	minus (n)	['miːnus]
fuse	sikring (c)	['segʁɛŋ]

air filter	luftfilter (c)	['lɔfdˌfildʌ]
oil filter	oliefilter (n)	['oːljəˌfildʌ]
fuel filter	brændselsfilter (n)	['bʁansəls ˌfildʌ]

178. Cars. Crash. Repair

car accident	ulykke (c)	['uˌløkə]
road accident	færdselsuheld (n)	['faɒsɛlˌsuhɛl]
to run into …	at køre ind i …	[at 'køːɒ en i]
to have an accident	at have et uheld	[at 'hæːvə ed 'uˌhɛl]
damage	beskadigelse (c)	[be'sgæːðiːəlsə]
intact	uskadt	['uˌskad]

| to break down (vi) | at gå i stykker | [at gɔː i 'sdøgɒ] |
| towrope | slæbetrosse (c) | ['slɛːbəˌtʁɒssə] |

puncture	punktering (c)	[pɔŋ'deːʁeŋ]
to be flat	at være fladt	[at 'vɛːɒ flat]
to pump up	at pumpe	[at 'pɔmbə]
pressure	tryk (n)	[tʁœk]
to check (to examine)	at kontrollere	[at kʌntʁo'leʌ]

repair	reparation (c)	[ʁɛbʁɑ'ɕon]
auto repair shop	bilværksted (n)	['bil 'vaɒkˌsdɛð]
spare part	reservedel (c)	[ʁɛ'sæɒuəˌdeːl]
part	maskindel (c)	[ma'skiːnˌdəl]

bolt	bolt (c)	[bɒld]
screw bolt	skrue (c)	['skʁuːə]
nut	møtrik (c)	['møtʁɛk]
washer	skive (c)	['skiːvə]
bearing	leje (n)	['lɑjə]

tube	rør (n)	[ʁœɒ]
gasket, washer	pakning (c)	['pɑgneŋ]
cable, wire	ledning (c)	['leðneŋ]

jack	donkraft (c)	['dɔnkʁɑfd]
wrench	skruenøgle (c)	['sgʁuəˌnɒjlə]
hammer	hammer (c)	['hɑmʌ]
pump	pumpe (c)	['pɔmbə]
screwdriver	skruetrækker (c)	['skʁu:əˌtʁɑkʌ]

| fire extinguisher | brandslukker (c) | ['bʁɑnˌslɔkʌ] |
| warning triangle | advarselstrekant (c) | [að'vɑ:səlstʁɛ'kand] |

to stall (vi)	at gå i stå	[at gɔ: i sdɔ:]
stall	standsning (c)	['sdɑnsneŋ]
to be broken	at være ødelagt	[at 'vɛ:ɒ 'ø:ðəˌlɑgd]

to overheat (vi)	at være overophedet	[at 'vɛ:ɒ 'ɒuɒɒˌbhe:ðəð]
to be clogged up	at blive tilstoppet	[at 'bli:ə tel'sdɒbəð]
to freeze (about pipe etc.)	at fryse	[at 'fʁy:sə]
to burst (vi)	at briste	[at 'bʁɛsdə]

pressure	tryk (n)	[tʁœk]
level	niveau (n)	[ni'vo]
slack (e.g., ~ belt)	svag	[svæ:]

dent	bule (c)	['bu:lə]
knock (in motor)	banken (c)	['bɑŋkən]
crack	revne (c)	['ʁɑwnə]
scratch	skramme (c)	['skʁɑmə]

179. Cars. Road

road	vej (c)	[vɑj]
highway, freeway	motorvej (c)	['mo:tʌvɑj]
freeway	motorvej (c)	['mo:tʌvɑj]
direction (way)	retning (c)	['ʁɑdneŋ]
distance	afstand (c)	[ɑu'sdan]

bridge	bro (c)	[bʁo:]
parking lot	parkeringsplads (c)	[pɑ'ke:ʁeŋsˌplas]
square	plads (c)	[plas]
interchange	til- og frakørsel (c)	[tel ɒu 'fʁɑˌkøɒsəl]
tunnel	tunnel (c)	['tɔnəl]

gas station	tankstation (c)	['taŋk sda'çon]
parking lot	parkeringsplads (c)	[pɑ'ke:ʁeŋsˌplas]
gas pump	benzin pumpe (c)	[bɛn'si:n 'pɔmbə]
auto repair shop	bilværksted (n)	['bil 'vɑɒkˌsdɛð]
to get gas	at tanke op	[at 'taŋkə ɒb]

| fuel | brændstof (n) | [ˈbʁanˌsdɒf] |
| jerrycan | dunk (c) | [dɔŋk] |

asphalt	asfalt (c)	[ˈasˌfald]
road markings	vejafmærkning (c)	[ˈvajɑuˌmæɒgneŋ]
curb	kantsten (c)	[ˈkandˌsdeːn]
guardrail	afspærring (c)	[ɑuˈsbaɒeŋ]
ditch	vejgrøft (c)	[ˈvajˌgʁœfd]
roadside	vejkant (c)	[ˈvajˌkand]
street light	pæl (c)	[pɛːl]

to drive (a car)	at føre	[at ˈføːɒ]
to turn (steering wheel)	at dreje	[at ˈdʁajə]
to turn (left, right etc.)	at dreje	[at ˈdʁajə]
to make a U-turn	at vende om	[at ˈvɛnə ʌm]
reverse	baglænskørsel (c)	[ˈbaulɛnˌsgøɒsəl]

to honk (about car)	at dytte	[at ˈdydə]
honk (sound)	dyt (n)	[ˈdyd]
to get stuck	at sætte sig fast	[at ˈsɛdə saj fasd]
to spin (in the mud)	at skride ud	[at ˈskʁiːðə uð]
to cut, to turn off	at standse motoren	[at ˈsdanseː moːtɒɒn]

speed	hastighed (c)	[ˈhasdiˌheð]
to exceed the speed limit	at overskride	[at ɒuɒˈskʁiːðə]
to give sb a ticket	at straffe med bøde	[at ˈsdʁafə mɛð ˈbøːðə]
traffic lights	lyskurv (n)	[ˈlysˌkuɒu]
driver's license	kørekort (n)	[ˈkøːɒˌkɒːd]

grade crossing	jernbaneoverskæring (c)	[ˈjæɒnˌbæːnə ˈɒuɒˌsgɛːʁen]
intersection	gadekryds (n)	[ˈgæːðəˌkʁys]
crosswalk	fodgængerovergang (c)	[ˈfoðgɛn ˈɒuʌˌgaŋ]
turn (curve in road)	kurve (c)	[ˈkuɒwə]
pedestrian zone	gågade (c)	[ˈgɔːˌgæːðə]

180. Traffic signs

rules of the road	færdseldregler (pl)	[ˈfaɒsəlˌdʁɛːlʌ]
traffic sign	tegn (n)	[tajn]
passing (overtaking)	overhaling (c)	[ɒuʌˈhæːleŋ]
curve	vejsving (n)	[ˈvajsveŋ]
U-turn	vending (c)	[ˈvɛnen]
traffic circle	rundkørsel (c)	[ˈʁɒnˌkøɒsəl]

No entry	al indkørsel forbudt	[al enˈkøɒsəl fɒːˈbud]
No vehicles allowed	al kørsel forbudt	[al ˈkøɒsəl fɒːˈbud]
No passing	overhaling forbudt	[ɒuʌˈhæːleŋ fɒːˈbud]
No parking	parkering forbudt	[paˈkeːʁen fɒːˈbud]
No stopping	stopforbud	[ˈsdɒbfɒːˌbuð]
dangerous turn	farligt sving (n)	[ˈfaːlid sveŋ]

steep descent	**brat skråning**	[bʁɑd ˈskʁɔːneŋ]
one-way traffic	**ensrettet trafik** (c)	[ˈeːnsʁɑdeð tʁɑˈfik]
pedestrian crossing	**fodgængerovergang** (c)	[ˈfoðgɛŋ ˈɒwʌˌgɑŋ]
slippery road	**glat vej**	[ˈglat ˌvɑj]
YIELD	**giv forkørselsret**	[giu ˈfɒːˌkøɒsəlsʁad]

PEOPLE. LIFE EVENTS

Life events

181. Holidays. Event

celebration, holiday	**fest** (c)	[fɛsd]
national day	**national fest** (c)	[naɕo'næːl fɛsd]
public holiday	**festdag** (c)	['fɛsdˌdæː]
to celebrate (vi, vt)	**at fejre**	[at 'fɑjʁʌ]
event (happening)	**begivenhed** (c)	[be'givənˌheð]
event (organized activity)	**arrangement** (n)	[ɑɑɕə'mɑŋd]
banquet (party)	**banket** (c)	['bɑŋkəð]
reception (formal party)	**reception** (c)	[ʁɛsəb'ɕon]
feast	**gilde** (n)	['gilə]
anniversary	**årsdag** (c)	['ɒːsˌdæ]
jubilee	**jubilæum** (n)	[jubi'lɛːɔm]
to celebrate (jubilee etc.)	**at fejre**	[at 'fɑjʁʌ]
New Year	**Nytår**	['nydɒː]
Happy New Year!	**Godt nytår!**	[gɒd ny'dɒː]
Santa Claus	**Julemand** (c)	['juːləˌman]
Christmas tree	**Juletræ** (n)	['juːləˌtʁɛː]
Christmas	**Jul** (c)	[juːl]
Merry Christmas!	**God Jul!**	[goð juːl]
Christmas tree	**Juletræ** (n)	['juːləˌtʁɛː]
fireworks	**salut** (c)	[sa'lud]
wedding	**bryllup** (n)	['bʁœlʌb]
groom	**brudgom** (c)	['bʁuðˌgɒm]
bride	**brud** (c)	[bʁuð]
to invite (vt)	**at invitere**	[at envi'teːɒ]
invitation	**invitation** (c)	[envita'ɕoːn]
guest	**gæst** (c)	[gɛsd]
to visit with sb	**at tage på besøg**	[at 'tæːə pɒ 'besøː]
to greet the guests	**at møde gæster**	[at 'møːðə 'gɛsdɒ]
gift, present	**gave** (c)	['gæːvə]
to give (sth as present)	**at forære**	[at fʌ'ɛʌ]
to receive gifts	**at få gaver**	[at fɒː 'gæːvɒ]

bouquet (of flowers)	**buket** (c)	[bu'kɛd]
congratulations	**lykønskning** (c)	['løg̩ønsknen]
to congratulate (vt)	**at lykønske**	[at 'løk̩ønskə]
greeting card	**lykønskningskort** (n)	['løg̩ønsknens kɒːd]
to send a postcard	**at sende et kort**	[at 'sɛnə ed kɒːd]
to get a postcard	**at få et postkort**	[at fɔ: et 'pʌsd̩kɒːd]
toast	**skål** (c)	[skɔːl]
to offer (a drink etc.)	**at beværte**	[at be'vaɒdə]
champagne	**champagne** (c)	[ɕɑm'panjə]
to have fun	**at more sig**	[at 'moːɒ saj]
fun, merriment	**morskab** (c)	['moɒskæːb]
joy	**glæde** (c)	['glɛːðə]
dance	**dans** (c)	[dans]
to dance (vi, vt)	**at danse**	[at 'dansə]
waltz	**vals** (c)	['vals]
tango	**tango** (c)	['tɑŋgo]

182. Funerals. Burial

cemetery	**kirkegård** (c)	['kiɒgə̩gɒ:]
grave, tomb	**grav** (c)	['gʁɑːu]
cross	**kors** (n)	[kɒːs]
gravestone	**gravsten** (c)	['gʁɑːusdən]
fence	**hegn** (n)	[hɑjn]
chapel	**kapel** (n)	[ka'pəl]
death	**død** (c)	[døð]
to die (vi, vt)	**at dø**	[at dø:]
the deceased	**den afdøde** (c)	[dɛn au'dø:ðə]
mourning	**sorg** (c)	['sɒw]
to bury (vt)	**at begrave**	[at be'gʁɑːuə]
funeral home	**begravelseskontor** (n)	[be'gʁɑːuəlsəs̩gɒntoɒ]
funeral	**begravelse** (c)	[be'gʁɑːuəlsə]
wreath	**krans** (c)	[kʁɑns]
casket	**ligkiste** (c)	['liː̩kiːsdə]
hearse	**rustvogn** (c)	['ʁɔsd̩vɒwn]
shroud	**ligklæde** (n)	['liːklɛːðə]
procession	**procession** (c)	[pʁɔsɛ'ɕoːn]
funeral procession	**sørgetog** (n)	['sœɒwə̩tɒw]
cremation urn	**begravelse urne** (c)	[be'gʁɑwəlsə 'uɒnə]
crematory	**krematorium** (n)	[kʁɛma'toːʁɔm]
obituary	**nekrolog** (c)	[nekʁo'loː]

| to cry (weep) | at græde | [at 'gʁaðə] |
| to sob (vi) | at hulke | [at 'hulkə] |

183. War. Soldiers

platoon	deling (c)	['de:leŋ]
company	kompagni (n)	[kɒmpa'ni:]
regiment	regiment (n)	[ʁɛgi'mɛnd]
army	hær (c)	['hɛɒ]
division	division (c)	[divi'ɕo:n]

| detachment | afdeling (c) | [ɑu'de:leŋ] |
| host (army) | hær (c) | ['hɛɒ] |

| soldier | soldat (c) | [sɔl'dæ:d] |
| officer | officer (c) | [ɒfi'seʌ] |

private	en menig (c)	[en 'me:ni]
sergeant	sergent (c)	[sæɒ'ɕand]
lieutenant	løjtnant (c)	['lʌjd‚nand]
captain	kaptajn (c)	[kɑb'tɑjn]
major	major (c)	[ma'joɒ]
colonel	oberst (c)	['o:bɒsd]
general	general (c)	[genə'ʁɑ:l]

sailor	sømand (c)	['søman]
captain	kaptajn (c)	[kɑb'tɑjn]
boatswain	bådsmand (c)	['bɔðs‚man]

artilleryman	artillerist (c)	[ɑtilə'ʁisd]
paratrooper	faldskærmsjæger (c)	['fal‚sgaɒmɕɑʌ]
pilot	pilot (c)	[pi'lo:d]
navigator	styrmand (c)	['sdyɒ‚man]
mechanic	mekaniker (c)	[me'kænikʌ]

pioneer (sapper)	pioner (c)	[pio'neʌ]
parachutist	faldskærmsudspringer (c)	['falsgaɒmsuð ‚sbʁɛŋʌ]
scout	spejder (c)	['sbɑjdʌ]
sniper	snigskytte (c)	['sni‚sgødə]

patrol (group)	patrulje (c)	[pa'tʁuljə]
to patrol (vi, vt)	at patruljere	[at patʁu'lje:ɒ]
sentry, guard	vagt (c)	[vɑgd]

warrior	kriger (c)	['kʁi:ʌ]
hero	helt (c)	[hɛld]
heroine	heltinde (c)	[hɛld'enə]
patriot	patriot (c)	[patʁi:'ɒd]
traitor	forræder (c)	[fɒ'ʁaðʌ]
betrayer	forræder (c)	[fɒ'ʁaðʌ]

deserter	**desertør** (c)	[desæɒ'tøɒ]
to desert (vi)	**at desertere**	[at desɛ:ɒ'te:ɒ]
mercenary	**lejesoldat** (c)	['lɑjə sɔlˌdæ:d]
recruit	**rekrut** (c)	[ʁɛ'kʁud]
volunteer	**frivillig** (c)	[fʁi'vili]
dead	**dræbt** (c)	['dʁabd]
wounded	**en såret**	[en 'sɒ:ɒð]
prisoner of war	**fange** (c)	['fɑŋə]

184. War. Military actions. Part 1

war	**krig** (c)	[kʁi:]
to be at war	**at føre krig**	[at 'fø:ɒ kʁi:]
civil war	**borgerkrig** (c)	['bɒːuɒˌkʁi:]
treacherously	**listigt**	['lesdid]
declaration (~ of war)	**krigserklæring** (c)	[ˌkʁisæ'klɛɒeŋ]
to declare (~ war)	**at erklære**	[at aɒ'klɛ:ɒ]
aggression	**aggression** (c)	[agʁɛ'ɕo:n]
to attack (invade)	**at angribe**	[at 'anˌgʁi:bə]
to invade (vt)	**at erobre**	[at e'ʁobʁɒ]
invader	**erobrer** (c)	[e'ʁobʁʌ]
conqueror	**erobrer** (c)	[e'ʁobʁʌ]
defense	**forsvar** (n)	['fɒsvɑ:]
to defend (a country etc.)	**at forsvare**	[at fʌ'svɑ:ɑ]
to defend oneself	**at forsvare sig**	[at fʌ'svɑ:ɑ sɑj]
enemy, hostile	**fjende** (c)	['fjɛnə]
hostile (attr)	**fjendtlig**	['fjɛndli]
strategy	**strategi** (c)	[sdʁɑdə'gi:]
tactics	**taktik** (c)	[tɑk'tik]
order	**ordre** (c)	['ɒ:dʁɒ]
command (order)	**befaling** (c)	[be'fæ:leŋ]
to order (vi, vt)	**at beordre**	[at be'ɒ:dʁɒ]
mission	**opgave** (c)	['ʌbˌgæ:və]
secret (adj)	**hemmelig**	['hɛməli]
battle, combat	**slag** (n)	[slæ:]
combat	**kamp** (c)	[kɑmb]
attack	**angreb** (n)	['anˌgʁɛ:b]
storming (assault)	**storm** (c)	[sdɒ:m]
to storm (vt)	**at storme**	[at 'sdɒ:mə]
siege (to be under ~)	**belejring** (c)	[be'lɑjʁɛŋ]

offensive (noun)	angreb (n)	['anˌgʁɛːb]
to go on the offensive	at angribe	[at 'anˌgʁiːbə]
retreat	tilbagetog (n)	['tebæːəˌtɔw]
to retreat (vi)	at trække sig tilbage	[at 'tʁagə sɑj te'bæːjə]

| encirclement | omringning (c) | [ʌm'ʁɛŋneŋ] |
| to encircle (vt) | at omringe | [at ɒm'ʁɛŋə] |

bombing (by aircraft)	bombardement (n)	[bɔmbɑdə'maŋ]
to drop a bomb	at kaste en bombe	[at 'kasdə en 'bɔmbə]
to bomb (vt)	at bombardere	[at bɔmba'deʌ]
explosion	eksplosion (c)	[ɛksblo'ɕon]

shot	skud (n)	[skuð]
to fire a shot	at skyde	[at 'skyːðə]
shooting	skydning (c)	['sgyðneŋ]

to take aim (at ...)	at sigte (på ...)	[at 'segdə pɔ]
to point (a gun)	at sigte på	[at 'segdə pɔ]
to hit (the target)	at ramme	[at 'ʁamə]

to sink (e.g., ~ a ship)	at sænke	[at 'sɛŋkə]
hole (in a ship)	læk (c)	[lɛk]
to founder, to sink	at synke	[at 'søŋkə]

front (at war)	front (c)	[fʁɒnd]
rear (noun)	bagland (n)	['baulan]
evacuation	evakuering (c)	[evaku'eːʁeŋ]
to evacuate (vt)	at evakuere	[at eva'kueːɒ]

trench	skyttegrav (c)	['sgødeˌgʁaːu]
barbwire	pigtråd (c)	['pigtʁɔð]
barrier	afspærring (c)	[au'sbaɒeŋ]
watchtower	tårn (n)	[tɒːn]

hospital	military hospital (n)	['miliˌtæɒi hɔsbi'tæːl]
to wound (vi, vt)	at såre	[at 'sɒːɒ]
wound	sår (n)	['sɒː]
wounded (noun)	en såret	[en 'sɒːɒð]
to be injured	at blive såret	[at 'bliːə 'sɔɒ]
serious	alvorlig	[al'vɒːliː]

185. War. Military actions. Part 2

captivity	fangenskab (n)	['faŋenˌsgæb]
to take sb captive	at tage til fange	[at 'tæːə tel 'faŋə]
to be in captivity	at være i fangenskab	[at 'vɛːɒ i 'faŋenskæːb]
to be taken prisoner	at blive taget til fange	[at 'bliːə 'tauəð tel 'faŋə]
concentration camp	kz-lejr (c)	[kɔ'sɛdˌlajʌ]
prisoner of war	fange (c)	['faŋə]

to escape (vi)	**at flygte**	[at 'fløgdə]
to betray (vt)	**at forråde**	[at fʌ'ʁɔðə]
betrayer	**forræder** (c)	[fɔ'ʁaðʌ]
betrayal	**forræderi** (n)	[fɔʁaðə'ʁi:]
to execute (shoot)	**at nedskyde**	[at 'neð̩sky:ðə]
execution (shooting)	**nedskydning** (c)	[neð'sgyðnen]
uniform	**uniform** (c)	[uni'fɔ:m]
shoulder board	**skulderstrop** (c)	['skulɒ̩sdʁɒb]
gas mask	**gasmaske** (c)	['gas̩masgə]
radio transmitter	**radio** (c)	['ʁɑ:dio]
cipher, code	**kodeskrift** (c)	['ko:ðə̩skʁɛfd]
conspiracy	**konspiration** (c)	[kʌnsbiɑ'ɕon]
password	**feltråb** (n)	['fɛldʁɔ:b]
mine (explosive)	**mine** (c)	['minə]
to mine (road etc.)	**at minere**	[at mi'ne:ɒ]
minefield	**minefelt** (n)	['minəfɛld]
air-raid warning	**luftalarm** (c)	['lofd̩alɑ:m]
alarm (warning)	**alarm** (c)	[a'lɑ:m]
signal	**signal** (n)	[si'næ:l]
signal flare	**signalraket** (c)	[si'næ:l ʁɑ'kɛd]
headquarters	**stab** (c)	[sdæ:b]
reconnaissance	**rekognoscering** (c)	[ʁɛkʌno'se:ʁen]
situation	**forhold** (n)	['fɔ:hɒl]
report	**rapport** (c)	[ʁɑ'pɒ:d]
ambush	**baghold** (n)	['bɑuhɒl]
reinforcement (of army)	**forstærkning** (c)	[fʌ'sdæɒgnen]
target	**skive** (c)	['ski:və]
shooting ground	**skydeplads** (c)	['sky:ðə̩plas]
military exercise	**manøvre** (pl)	[ma'nøwʁʌ]
panic	**panik** (c)	[pa'nik]
devastation	**ødelæggelse** (c)	['ø:ðə̩lɛgəlsə]
destruction, ruins	**ødelæggelser** (pl)	['ø:ðəlɛgəlsʌ]
to destroy (vt)	**at ødelægge**	[at 'ø:ðə̩lɛgə]
to survive (vi, vt)	**at overleve**	[at 'ɒuɒle:uə]
to disarm (vt)	**at afvæbne**	[at ɑu'vɛ:bnə]
to handle (e.g., ~ a gun)	**at håndtere**	[at hɒn'te:ɒ]
Attention!	**Stå ret!**	[sdɔ: ʁad]
At ease!	**Rør!**	[ʁɶɒ]
feat (of courage)	**bedrift** (c)	[be'dʁɛfd]
oath (vow)	**ed** (c)	[eð]
to swear (an oath)	**at sværge (på ...)**	[at 'svaɒuə pɔ]

decoration (medal etc.)	udmærkelse (c)	['uð‚mæɒkəlsə]
to award (give medal to)	at dekorere	[at deko'ʁɛɒ]
medal	medalje (c)	[me'daljə]
order (e.g., ~ of Merit)	orden (c)	['ɒdən]

victory	sejr (c)	['sɑjʌ]
defeat	nederlag (n)	['neðɒlæ:]
armistice	våbenhvile (c)	['vɔ:bən‚vi:lə]

banner (flag)	fane (c)	['fæ:nə]
glory (honor, fame)	ære (c)	['ɛ:ɒ]
parade	parade (c)	[pɑ'ʁɑ:ðə]
to march (on parade)	at marchere	[at mɑ'çeʌ]

186. Weapons

weapons	våben (n)	['vɔ:bən]
firearm	skydevåben (n)	['sky:ðə‚vɔ:bən]
cold weapons (knives etc.)	blanke våben (n)	['blɑŋkə 'vɔ:bən]

chemical weapons	kemiske våben (n)	['ke:miskə ‚vɔ:bən]
nuclear	atom-	[a'to:m]
nuclear weapons	atomvåben (n)	[a'to:m 'vɔ:bən]

| bomb | bombe (c) | ['bɔmbə] |
| atomic bomb | atombombe (c) | [a'to:m 'bɔmbə] |

pistol (gun)	pistol (c)	[pi'sdo:l]
rifle	gevær (n)	[ge'vɛɒ]
submachine gun	maskinpistol (c)	[ma'ski:npi‚sdo:l]
machine gun	maskingevær (n)	[ma'sgi:ŋɛ:vɛɒ]

muzzle	munding (c)	['monɐŋ]
barrel	løb (n)	[lø:b]
caliber	kaliber (c)	[kæ:'libʌ]

trigger	aftrækker (c)	['ɑutʁakʌ]
sight (aiming device)	sigte (n)	['segdə]
magazine	magasin (n)	[mɑgɑ'si:n]
butt (of rifle)	skæfte (n)	['sgɛfdə]

| hand grenade | håndgranat (c) | ['hɒn gʁɑ'næd] |
| explosive | sprængstof (n) | ['sbʁaŋ‚sdʌf] |

bullet	kugle (c)	['ku:lə]
cartridge	patron (c)	[pa'tʁo:n]
charge	ladning (c)	['lɑðnɐŋ]
ammunition	ammunition (c)	[ɑmuni'ço:n]
bomber (aircraft)	bombefly (n)	['bɔmbe‚fly:]
fighter	jagerfly (n)	['jɛ:jə‚fly:]

helicopter	**helikopter** (c)	[hɛli'kʌbdʌ]
anti-aircraft gun	**luftværnskanon** (c)	['lɔfdvɑɒnskaˌnɒn]
tank	**kampvogn** (c)	['kɑmbˌvɒwn]
tank gun	**kanon** (c)	[ka'nɒn]
artillery	**artilleri** (n)	[ɑtilə'ʁi:]
cannon	**kanon** (c)	[ka'nɒn]
to take aim (at …)	**at sigte efter …**	[at 'segdə 'ɛfdɒ]
shell (projectile)	**projektil** (n)	[pʁɒɡɛk'til]
mortar bomb	**mortérgranat** (c)	[mɒ'teə gʁɑ'næd]
mortar	**mortér** (c)	[mɒ'teə]
splinter (of shell)	**splint** (c)	[sblend]
submarine	**u-båd** (c)	['u:ˌbɒð]
torpedo	**torpedo** (c)	[tɒ'pe:do]
missile	**missil** (n)	[mi'sil]
to load (gun)	**at lade**	[at 'læ:ðə]
to shoot (vi)	**at skyde**	[at 'sky:ðə]
to take aim (at …)	**at sigte (på …)**	[at 'segdə pɔ]
bayonet	**bajonet** (c)	[bɑjo'nɛd]
epee	**kårde** (c)	['kɒ:ɒ]
saber (e.g., cavalry ~)	**sabel** (c)	['sæ:bəl]
spear (weapon)	**spyd** (n)	[sbyð]
bow	**bue** (c)	['bu:ə]
arrow	**pil** (c)	[pi:l]
musket	**musket** (c)	[mu'skəð]
crossbow	**armbrøst** (c)	['ɑ:mˌbʁœsd]

187. Ancient people

primitive (prehistoric)	**forhistorisk**	['fɒˌhisdo:ʁisk]
prehistoric	**forhistorisk**	['fɒˌhisdo:ʁisk]
ancient (civilization etc.)	**oldtids-**	['ɒltiðs]
Stone Age	**Stenalderen** (c)	['sde:nˌalən]
Bronze Age	**Bronzealder** (c)	['bʁɒŋsə ˌalʌ]
Ice Age	**Istiden** (c)	['isdiðən]
tribe	**folkestamme** (c)	['fɒlkəˌsdɑmə]
cannibal	**kannibal** (c)	[kani'bal]
hunter	**jæger** (c)	['jɛ:jʌ]
to hunt (vi, vt)	**at jage**	[at 'jæ:jə]
mammoth	**mammut** (c)	[mɑ'mud]
cave	**grotte** (c)	['gʁɒdə]
fire	**ild** (c)	[il]
campfire	**bål** (n)	[bɔ:l]

rock painting	**helleristning** (c)	['hɛlə‿ʁisdnɜŋ]
tool (e.g., stone ax)	**redskab** (n)	['ʁɛð‿skæb]
spear	**spyd** (n)	[sbyð]
stone ax	**stenøkse** (c)	['sde:n‿øksə]
to be at war	**at føre krig**	[at 'fø:ɒ kʁi:]
to domesticate (tame)	**at tæmme**	[at 'tɛmə]
idol	**idol** (n)	[i'do:l]
to worship (vt)	**at tilbede**	[at tel'be:ðə]
superstition	**overtro** (c)	['ɒwʌtʁo:]
rite	**ritual** (n)	[ʁitu'æ:l]
evolution	**evolution** (c)	[evolu'ɕo:n]
development	**udvikling** (c)	['uðveglɜŋ]
disappearance	**forsvinden** (c)	[fɒ'svenən]
to adapt oneself	**at tilpasse sig**	[at 'tel‿pasə sɑj]
archeology	**arkæologi** (c)	[ɑkɛolo'gi:]
archeologist	**arkæolog** (c)	[ˌɑ:kɛo'lo]
archeological	**arkæologisk**	[ˌɑkɛo'lo:isg]
excavation site	**udgravningssted** (n)	['uð‿gʁɑ:unɜŋsˌsdɛð]
excavations	**udgravninger** (pl)	['uð‿gʁɑ:unɜŋʌ]
find (object)	**fund** (n)	[fɔn]
fragment	**fragment** (n)	[fʁɑu'mɛnd]

188. Middle Ages

people (nation)	**folk** (n)	[fɔlk]
peoples	**folkene** (pl)	['fɔlkənə]
tribe	**folkestamme** (c)	['fɔlkəˌsdɑmə]
tribes	**folkestammer** (pl)	['fɔlkəˌsdɑmɒ]
barbarians	**barbarer** (pl)	[bɑ'bɑ:ɑ]
Gauls	**gallere** (pl)	['galle:ɒ]
Goths	**gotere** (pl)	[go'te:ɒ]
Slavs	**slaver** (pl)	['slæ:vʌ]
Vikings	**vikinger** (pl)	['vikɜŋʌ]
Romans	**romere** (pl)	['ʁo:me:ɒ]
Roman	**romersk**	['ʁomʌsk]
Byzantines	**byzantinere** (pl)	[bysan'ti:ne:ɒ]
Byzantium	**Byzans**	[by'sans]
Byzantine	**byzantinsk**	[bysan'tensk]
emperor	**kejser** (c)	['kɑjsʌ]
leader, chief	**høvding** (c)	['hœwdɜŋ]
powerful (e.g., ~ king)	**magtfuld**	['mɑgdful]
king	**konge** (c)	['kʌŋə]

ruler (sovereign)	**hersker** (c)	['hæɒskʌ]
knight	**ridder** (c)	['ʁiðʌ]
knightly	**ridder-**	['ʁiðɒ]
feudal lord	**feudalherre** (c)	[fœw'dæl,hæːɒ]
feudal (adj)	**feudal**	[fœw'dæl]
vassal	**vasal** (c)	[va'sal]
duke	**hertug** (c)	['hæɒtu]
earl	**greve** (c)	['gʁɛːvə]
baron	**baron** (c)	[bɑ'ʁoːn]
bishop	**biskop** (c)	['biskʌb]
armor	**rustning** (c)	['ʁɔsdneŋ]
shield	**skjold** (n)	['skjʌl]
sword	**sværd** (n)	[svɛɒ]
visor	**visir** (n)	[vi'siɒ]
chain armor	**ringbrynje** (c)	['ʁɛŋ,bʁynjə]
crusade	**korstog** (n)	['kɒːs,tou]
crusader	**korsfarer** (c)	['kɒːs,faːɑ]
territory	**territorium** (n)	[tæɒi'toojɒm]
to attack (invade)	**at angribe**	[at 'an,gʁiːbə]
to conquer (vt)	**at erobre**	[at e'ʁobʁɒ]
to occupy (invade)	**at erobre**	[at e'ʁobʁɒ]
siege (to be under ~)	**belejring** (c)	[be'lɑjʁɛŋ]
besieged	**belejret**	[be'lɑjʁʌð]
to besiege (vt)	**at belejre**	[at be'lɑjʁʌ]
inquisition	**inkvisition** (c)	[enkvisi'ɕon]
inquisitor	**inkvisitor** (c)	[eŋkvi'sitɒ]
torture	**tortur** (c)	[tɒ'tuɒ]
cruel	**grusom**	['gʁuːsɒm]
heretic	**kætter** (c)	['kɛdʌ]
heresy	**kætteri** (n)	[kɛdə'ʁiː]
seafaring	**søfart** (c)	['sø,faːd]
pirate	**pirat** (c)	[pi'ʁɑːd]
piracy	**sørøveri** (n)	[søʁœːə'ʁiː]
boarding (attack)	**entring** (c)	['antʁɛŋ]
loot	**fangst** (c)	[faŋsd]
treasures	**skatte** (pl)	['skadə]
discovery	**opdagelse** (c)	['ʌb,dæjəlsə]
to discover (new land etc.)	**at opdage**	[at 'ʌb,dæjə]
expedition (noun)	**ekspedition** (c)	[ɛksbədi'ɕoːn]
musketeer	**musketer** (c)	[muskə'tɒə]
cardinal	**kardinal** (c)	[kɑdi'næːl]
heraldry	**heraldik** (c)	[heal'dik]
heraldic	**heraldisk**	[he'ʁaldisk]

189. Leader. Chief. Authorities

king	**konge** (c)	['kʌŋə]
queen	**dronning** (c)	['dʁɒneŋ]
royal	**kongelig**	['kʌŋəli]
kingdom	**kongerige** (n)	['kʌŋəˌʁi:ə]
prince	**prins** (c)	[pʁɛns]
princess	**prinsesse** (c)	[pʁɛn'sɛsə]
president	**præsident** (c)	[pʁɛsi'dɛnd]
vice-president	**vicepræsident** (c)	['visɛ pʁɛsi'dɛnd]
senator	**senator** (c)	[se'natɒ]
monarch	**monark** (c)	[mo'nɑ:k]
ruler (sovereign)	**styrer** (c)	['sdyːʌ]
dictator	**diktator** (c)	[diktæ:'tɒ]
tyrant	**tyran** (c)	[ty'ʁan]
magnate	**magnat** (c)	[mɑw'næd]
director	**direktør** (c)	[diɒek'tøɒ]
chief	**chef** (c)	[ɕɛ:f]
manager (director)	**forretningsfører** (c)	[fɒ'ʁadneŋs ˌføːʌ]
boss	**chef** (c)	[ɕɛ:f]
owner	**ejer** (c)	['ɑjʌ]
head (~ of delegation)	**leder** (c)	['le:ðʌ]
authorities	**myndigheder** (pl)	['møndihe:ðʌ]
management (of hotel etc.)	**ledelse** (c)	['le:ðəlsə]
governor	**guvernør** (c)	[guvʌ'nøɒ]
consul	**konsul** (c)	['kʌnˌsul]
diplomat	**diplomat** (c)	[diplo'mad]
mayor	**borgmester** (c)	[bɒw'mɛsdʌ]
sheriff	**sherif** (c)	[ɕe'ʁif]
emperor	**kejser** (c)	['kɑjsʌ]
tsar, czar	**tsar** (c)	[sɑ:]
Pharaoh	**farao** (c)	['fɑ:ʁao]
khan	**khan** (c)	[kæ:n]

190. Road. Way. Directions

road	**vej** (c)	[vɑj]
way	**vej** (c)	[vɑj]
freeway	**motorvej** (c)	['mo:tʌvɑj]
highway, freeway	**motorvej** (c)	['mo:tʌvɑj]
interstate	**fjerntrafikvej** (c)	['fjaɒn tʁɑ'fikˌvɑj]

| main road | **hovedvej** (c) | [ˈhoːəð ˌvɑj] |
| dirt road | **bivej** (c) | [ˈbiːˌvɑj] |

| pathway | **sti** (c) | [sdiː] |
| footpath | **gangsti** (c) | [ˈgæːŋsdiː] |

Where?	**Hvor?**	[vɒː]
Where (to)?	**Hvorhen?**	[vɒˈhɛn]
Where … from?	**Hvorfra?**	[vɒˈfʁɑː]

| direction (way) | **retning** (c) | [ˈʁadnɛŋ] |
| to point (e.g., ~ the way) | **at pege** | [at ˈpɑjə] |

to the left	**til venstre**	[tel ˈvɛnsdʁɒ]
to the right	**til højre**	[tel ˈhʌjʁʌ]
straight ahead	**lige frem**	[ˈliːə fʁam]
back (e.g., to turn ~)	**tilbage**	[teˈbæːjə]

turn, curve	**kurve** (c)	[ˈkuɒwə]
to turn (left, right etc.)	**at dreje**	[at ˈdʁɑjə]
to make a U-turn	**at vende om**	[at ˈvɛnə ʌm]

| to be visible | **at være synlig** | [at ˈvɛːɒ ˈsyːnli] |
| to appear (come into view) | **at vise sig** | [at ˈviːsə sɑj] |

stop, halt (in journey)	**ophold** (n)	[ˈʌbˌhʌl]
to rest, to halt (vi)	**at hvile (sig)**	[at ˈviːlə sɑj]
rest (pause)	**pause** (c)	[ˈpɑusə]

| to lose one's way | **at fare vild** | [at ˈfɑːɑ vil] |
| to lead to … (about road) | **at føre til …** | [at ˈføːɒ tel] |

| to reach … (arrive at) | **at nå frem til …** | [at nɒː fʁam tel …] |
| stretch (of road) | **strækning** (c) | [ˈsdʁagnɛŋ] |

asphalt	**asfalt** (c)	[ˈasˌfald]
curb	**kantsten** (c)	[ˈkandˌsdeːn]
ditch	**grøft** (c)	[gʁœfd]
manhole	**kloakdæksel** (c)	[ˈkloɑkˌdɛksəl]

| roadside | **vejkant** (c) | [ˈvɑjˌkand] |
| pit, pothole | **hul** (n) | [hɔl] |

| to go (on foot) | **at gå** | [at gɔː] |
| to pass (overtake) | **at overhale** | [at ˈɒuɒhæːlə] |

| step (footstep) | **skridt** (n) | [skʁid] |
| on foot | **til fods** | [tel ˈfoðs] |

to block (road)	**at spærre**	[at ˈsbæːɒ]
boom barrier	**bom** (c)	[bɒm]
dead end	**blindgyde** (c)	[ˈblenˌgyːðə]

191. Breaking the law. Criminals. Part 1

bandit	**bandit** (c)	[ban'did]
crime	**forbrydelse** (c)	[fɒ'bʁyðəlsə]
criminal (person)	**forbryder** (c)	[fɒ'bʁyðʌ]
thief	**tyv** (c)	[tyw]
to steal (vi, vt)	**at stjæle**	[at 'sdjɛ:lə]
stealing, theft	**tyveri** (n)	[tywʌ'ʁi]
to kidnap (vt)	**at kidnappe**	[at 'kid,nɑbə]
kidnapping	**kidnapning** (c)	['kidnɑbnɐŋ]
kidnapper	**kidnapper** (c)	['kidnɑbʌ]
ransom	**løsepenge** (pl)	['lø:sə,pɛŋə]
to ask for ransom	**at forlange løsepenge**	[at fʌ'lɑŋə 'lø:sə,pɛŋə]
to rob (vt)	**at røve**	[at 'ʁœ:wə]
robbery	**røveri** (n)	[ʁœ:wʌ'ʁi]
robber	**røver** (c)	['ʁœ:wə]
to extort (vt)	**at afpresse**	[at ɑu'pʁasə]
extortionist	**afpresser** (c)	[ɑu'pʁasʌ]
extortion	**afpresning** (c)	[ɑu'pʁasnɐŋ]
to murder, to kill	**at myrde**	[at 'myɒdə]
murder	**mord** (n)	['moɒ]
murderer	**morder** (c)	['moɒdʌ]
gunshot	**skud** (n)	[skuð]
to fire a shot	**at skyde**	[at 'sky:ðə]
to shoot down	**at skyde ned**	[at 'sky:ðə neð]
to shoot (vi)	**at skyde**	[at 'sky:ðə]
shooting	**skydning** (c)	['sgyðnɐŋ]
incident (fight etc.)	**hændelse** (c)	['hɛnəlsə]
fight, brawl	**slagsmål** (n)	['slaws,mɔl]
Help!	**Hjælp!**	[jɛlb]
victim	**offer** (n)	['ɒfʌ]
to damage (vt)	**at beskadige**	[at be'sgæ:ðiə]
damage	**tab** (n)	[tæ:b]
dead body	**lig** (n)	[li:]
grave (e.g., ~ crime)	**alvorlig**	[al'vɒ:li:]
to attack (vi, vt)	**at overfalde**	[at 'ɒuɒfalə]
to beat (dog, person)	**at slå**	[at slɔ:]
to beat sb up	**at tæske**	[at 'tɛskə]
to take (snatch)	**at fratage**	[at fʁɑ'tæ:ə]
to stab to death	**at slagte**	[at 'slɑgdə]
to maim (vt)	**at lemlæste**	[at lɛm'lɛsdə]

to wound (vi, vt)	at såre	[at ˈsɒːɒ]
blackmail	afpresning (c)	[ɑuˈpʁasneŋ]
to blackmail (vt)	at afpresse	[at ɑuˈpʁasə]
blackmailer	afpresser (c)	[ɑuˈpʁasʌ]

racketeering	pengeafpresning (c)	[ˈpɛŋə ˈɑuˌpʁasneŋ]
racketeer	pengeafpresser (c)	[ˈpɛŋə ˈɑuˌpʁasʌ]
gangster	gangster (c)	[ˈgæːŋsdʌ]
mafia, Mob	mafia (c)	[ˈmɑfija]

pickpocket	lommetyv (c)	[ˈlʌməˌtyu]
burglar	indbrudstyv (c)	[ˈenbʁuðstyu]
smuggling	smugleri (n)	[smuləˈʁiː]
smuggler	smugler (c)	[ˈsmuːlʌ]

forgery	forfalskning (c)	[fɒˈfalsknen]
to forge (counterfeit)	at forfalske	[at fɒˈfalskə]
fake, forged (adj)	falsk	[ˈfalsk]

192. Breaking the law. Criminals. Part 2

rape	voldtægt (c)	[ˈvʌlˌtɛgd]
to rape (vt)	at voldtage	[at ˈvɒltæːə]
rapist	voldsmand (c)	[ˈvɒlsˌman]
maniac	maniker (c)	[ˈmanikʌ]

prostitute (woman)	prostitueret (c)	[pʁosdituˈeʌð]
prostitution	prostitution (c)	[pʁɒstituˈɕoːn]
pimp	alfons (c)	[alˈfɒŋs]

| drug addict | narkoman (c) | [nɑkoˈmæn] |
| drug dealer | narkohandler (c) | [ˈnɑːkoˌhanlʌ] |

to blow up (bomb)	at sprænge	[at ˈsbʁaŋə]
explosion	eksplosion (c)	[ɛksbloˈɕon]
to set fire	at sætte ild	[at ˈsɛdə il]
incendiary (arsonist)	brandstifter (c)	[ˈbʁanˌsdefdʌ]

terrorism	terrorisme (c)	[tæʁɒˈʁismə]
terrorist	terrorist (c)	[tæʁɒˈʁisd]
hostage	gidsel (c)	[ˈgisəl]

to swindle (vt)	at snyde	[at ˈsnyːðə]
swindle	bedrag (n)	[beˈdʁɑw]
swindler	svindler (c)	[ˈsvenlʌ]

to bribe (vt)	at bestikke	[at beˈsdekə]
bribery	bestikkelse (c)	[beˈsdekəlsə]
bribe	bestikkelse (c)	[beˈsdekəlsə]
poison	gift (c)	[gifd]

| to poison (vt) | at forgifte | [at fɒ'gifdə] |
| to poison oneself | at tage gift | [at 'tæːə gifd] |

| suicide (act) | selvmord (n) | ['sɛlmɒɒ] |
| suicide (person) | selvmorder (c) | ['sɛlˌmɒɒdʌ] |

to threaten (vt)	at true	[at 'tʁuːə]
threat	trussel (c)	['tʁusəl]
to make an attempt	at begå attentat	[at be'gɔː adən'tæd]
attempt (attack)	attentat (n)	[adən'tæːd]

| to steal (a car) | at stjæle | [at 'sdjɛːlə] |
| to hijack (a plane) | at kapre | [at 'kæːbʁʌ] |

| revenge | hævn (c) | ['hɛwn] |
| to avenge (vt) | at hævne | [at 'hɛunə] |

to torture (vt)	at torturere	[at tɒtu'ʁɛʌ]
torture	tortur (c)	[tɒ'tuɒ]
to abuse (treat cruelly)	at plage	[at 'plæːjə]

pirate	pirat (c)	[pi'ʁɑːd]
hooligan	bølle (c)	['bølə]
armed	bevæbnet	[be'vɛːbnəð]
violence	vold (n)	[vɒl]

| spying (noun) | spionage (c) | [sbio'næːɕə] |
| to spy (vi) | at spionere | [at sbio:'neːɒ] |

193. Police. Law. Part 1

| justice | dom (c), kendelse (c) | [dɒm], ['kɛnəlsə] |
| court (court room) | domstol (c) | ['dɒmˌsdoːl] |

judge	dommer (c)	['dɒmʌ]
jurors	nævninger (pl)	['nɛunenʌ]
jury trial	nævningedomstol (c)	['nɛunen 'dʌmˌsdol]
to judge (vt)	at dømme	[at 'dœmə]

lawyer, attorney	advokat (c)	[aðvo'kæːd]
accused	anklagede (c)	[an'klæːəðə]
dock	anklagebænk (c)	['anˌklæːjəɛŋg]

| charge | sigtelse (c) | ['segdəlsə] |
| accused | anklagede (c) | [an'klæːəðə] |

sentence	dom (c)	[dɒm]
to sentence (vt)	at idømme	[at i'dœmə]
guilty (e.g., ~ of murder)	den skyldige (c)	[dɛn 'sgyldiə]
to punish (vt)	at afstraffe	[at au'sdʁɑfə]

punishment	**afstraffelse** (c)	[ɑuˈsdʁɑfəlsə]
fine (penalty)	**bøde** (c)	[ˈbøːðə]
life imprisonment	**fængsel** (c) **på livstid**	[ˈfɛŋsəl pɔ ˈliwsˌtið]
death penalty	**dødsstraf** (c)	[ˈdøðsˌsdʁɑf]
electric chair	**elektrisk stol** (c)	[eˈlɛktʁisk sdoːl]
gallows	**galge** (c)	[ˈgaljə]
to execute (vt)	**at henrette**	[at hɛnˈʁɑdə]
execution	**henrettelse** (c)	[ˈhɛnˌʁadəlsə]
prison, jail	**fængsel** (n)	[ˈfɛŋsəl]
cell	**celle** (c)	[ˈsɛlə]
escort	**konvoj** (c)	[kʌnˈvɒj]
prison guard	**fangevogter** (c)	[ˈfɑŋəˌvɒgdʌ]
prisoner	**fange** (c)	[ˈfɑŋə]
handcuffs	**håndjern** (pl)	[ˈhɒnˌjæːn]
to handcuff (vt)	**at lægge i håndjern**	[at ˈlɛgə i ˈhɒnjaɒn]
escape	**flugt** (c)	[flɔgd]
to escape (vi, vt)	**at flygte**	[at ˈfløgdə]
to disappear (vi)	**at forsvinde**	[at fʌˈsvenə]
to release (from prison)	**at løslade**	[at ˈløsˌlæːðə]
amnesty	**amnesti** (n)	[ɑmnəˈsdi]
police	**politi** (n)	[poliˈtiː]
policeman	**politibetjent** (c)	[poliˈtibeˌtjɛnd]
police station	**politistation** (c)	[poliˈtisdaˌɕoːn]
billy club	**gummiknippel** (c)	[ˈgomiˌknebəl]
loudspeaker	**talerør** (c)	[ˈtæːləˌʁœɒ]
patrol car	**patruljebil** (c)	[paˈtʁuljəˌbiːl]
siren	**sirene** (c)	[siˈʁɛːnə]
to turn on the siren	**at tænde for sirene**	[at ˈtɛnə fɒ siɒˈɛːnə]
siren call	**sirene hyl** (n)	[siˈʁɛːnə ˈhyl]
scene of the crime	**gerningssted** (n)	[ˈgaɒneŋssdɛð]
witness	**vidne** (n)	[ˈviðnə]
freedom	**frihed** (c)	[ˈfʁihəð]
accomplice	**medskyldig** (c)	[ˈmɛðˌsgyldi]
to flee	**at gemme sig**	[at ˈgɛmə saj]
footprint	**spor** (n)	[ˈsboɒ]

194. Police. Law. Part 2

search (for a criminal)	**eftersøgning** (c)	[ˈɛfdɒsøːnen]
to look for ...	**at søge efter ...**	[at ˈsøːə ˈɛfdɒ]
suspicion	**mistanke** (c)	[miˈstaŋkə]
suspicious (suspect)	**mistænksom**	[misˈtɛŋkˌsʌm]

| to stop (cause to halt) | **at standse** | [at 'sdanse:] |
| to detain (keep in custody) | **at anholde** | [at an'hɒlə] |

case (trial)	**sag** (c)	[sæ:]
investigation	**undersøgelse** (c)	['ɔnɒˌsø:əlsə]
detective	**detektiv** (c)	[detɛ'ktiu]
investigator	**forhørsdommer** (c)	[fɒ'hœɒˌsdɒmʌ]
version	**version** (c)	[væɒ'ɕo:n]

motive	**motiv** (n)	[mo'tiu]
interrogation	**forhør** (n)	[fɒ'høɒ]
to interrogate (vt)	**at forhøre**	[at fʌ'hø:ɒ]
to question (interrogate)	**at afhøre**	[at ɑu'hø:ɒ]
questioning	**afhøring** (c)	['ɑuhɒɒeŋ]
checking (police ~)	**kontrol** (c)	[kʌn'tʁɔl]

round-up	**razzia** (c)	['ʁadsia]
search (by police)	**ransagning** (c)	['ʁanˌsæjneŋ]
chase (pursuit)	**forfølgelse**	[fɒ'føljəlsə]
to pursue, to chase	**at forfølge**	[at fɒ'føljə]
to track (a criminal)	**at overvåge**	[at 'ɒuɒˌvɔ:uə]

arrest	**arrestation** (c)	[aɑsda'ɕon]
to arrest (sb)	**at arrestere**	[at aɑ'sdeʌ]
to catch (thief etc.)	**at fange**	[at 'fɑŋə]
capture	**pågribelse** (c)	[pɒ'gʁi:bəlsə]

document	**dokument** (n)	[doku'mɛnd]
proof (evidence)	**bevis** (n)	[be'vi:s]
to prove (vt)	**at bevise**	[at be'vi:sə]
footprint	**spor** (n)	['sbɒɒ]
fingerprints	**fingeraftryk** (n)	['feŋɒˌɑutʁœg]
piece of evidence	**bevis** (n)	[be'vi:s]

alibi	**alibi** (n)	['æ:libi:]
innocent (not guilty)	**uskyldig**	['uˌsgyldi]
injustice (unjust act)	**uretfærdighed** (c)	[uʁad'fæɒdiˌheð]
unjust, unfair	**uretfærdig**	[uʁad'fæɒdi]

crime (e.g., ~ reporter)	**kriminel**	[kʁimi'nɛ:l]
to confiscate (vt)	**at konfiskere**	[at kɒnfe'skɒɒ]
drug (illegal substance)	**narkotikum** (n)	[nɑ'kotikɒm]
weapon, gun	**våben** (n)	['vɔ:bən]
to disarm (vt)	**at afvæbne**	[at ɑu'vɛ:bnə]
to order (command)	**at befale**	[at be'fæ:lə]
to disappear (vi)	**at forsvinde**	[at fʌ'svenə]

law	**lov** (c)	['lɒw]
legal	**lovlig**	['lɒuli]
illegal	**ulovlig**	[u'lɒwli]
responsibility	**ansvar** (n)	['ansvɑ:]
responsible	**ansvarlig**	[an'svɑ:li]

NATURE

The Earth. Part 1

195. Outer space

cosmos	**kosmos** (n)	['kʌsmʌs]
space (e.g., ~ flight)	**rum-**	[ʁɔm]
outer space	**ydre rum** (n)	['yðʁɒ ʁɔm]
world	**univers** (n)	[uni'væɒs]
galaxy	**galakse** (c)	[ga'lɑgsə]
star	**stjerne** (c)	['sdjæɒnə]
constellation	**stjernebillede** (n)	['sdjæɒnəˌbeləðə]
planet	**planet** (c)	[pla'ned]
satellite	**satellit** (c)	[sadə'lid]
meteorite	**meteorit** (c)	[meteo'ʁid]
comet	**komet** (c)	[ko'məð]
asteroid	**asteroide** (c)	[asdəʁo'i:ðə]
orbit	**bane** (c)	['bæ:nə]
to rotate (vi)	**at dreje rundt**	[at 'dʁɑjə ʁɔnd]
atmosphere	**atmosfære** (c)	[admos'fɛ:ʌ]
the Sun	**Solen**	['so:lən]
solar system	**Solsystem** (n)	['so:lsyˌsde:m]
solar eclipse	**solformørkelse** (c)	['so:l fʌ'mœʁkəlsə]
the Earth	**Jorden**	['jjo:ɒn]
the Moon	**Månen**	['mɔ:nən]
Mars	**Mars**	[mɑ:s]
Venus	**Venus**	['ve:nus]
Jupiter	**Jupiter**	['jupidɒ]
Saturn	**Saturn**	['sæ:ˌtuɒn]
Mercury	**Merkur**	[maɒ'kuɒ]
Uranus	**Uranus**	[u'ʁanus]
Neptune	**Neptun**	['nəbdu:n]
Pluto	**Pluto**	['pluto]
Milky Way	**Mælkevejen**	['mɛlkəˌvɑjən]
Great Bear	**Karlsvognen**	['kɑ:lsˌvɒwnən]
Pole Star	**Polarstjern**	[po'lɑ:ˌsdjæɒnə]

Martian	**marsboer** (c)	['mɑ:sbo:ʌ]
extraterrestrial	**rumvæsen** (n)	['ʁɔmˌvɛsən]
alien	**fremmed** (c)	['fʁaməð]
flying saucer	**flyvende tallerken** (c)	['fly:uənə taˈlaɒkən]

spaceship	**rumskib** (n)	['ʁɔmˌski:b]
space station	**rumstation** (c)	['ʁɔmsdaˌɕo:n]
blast-off	**start** (c)	[sdɑ:d]

engine	**motor** (c)	['mo:tʌ]
nozzle	**dyse** (c)	['dysə]
fuel	**brændsel** (n)	['bʁansəl]

cockpit, flight deck	**cockpit** (n)	['kɒkpid]
antenna	**antenne** (c)	[an'tɛnə]
porthole	**koøje** (n)	['ko:ˌɒjə]
solar battery	**solbatteri** (n)	['so:lbadʌ'ʁi]
spacesuit	**rumdragt** (c)	['ʁɔmˌdʁagd]

| weightlessness | **vægtløshed** (c) | ['vɛgdˌlø:sheð] |
| oxygen | **ilt** (c) | [ild] |

| docking (in space) | **sammenkobling** (c) | ['sɑmənˌkɒblen] |
| to dock (vi, vt) | **at sammenkoble** | [at 'sɑmənˌkɒblə] |

observatory	**observatorium** (n)	[ɒbsaɒvæ:'to:ʁɔm]
telescope	**teleskop** (n)	[telə'skob]
to observe (vt)	**at observere**	[at ʌbsæɒ'vʌ]
to explore (vt)	**at forske**	[at 'fɒ:skə]

196. The Earth

the Earth	**Jorden**	['jjo:ɒn]
globe	**jordklode** (c)	['jɒɒˌklo:ðə]
planet	**planet** (c)	[pla'ned]

atmosphere	**atmosfære** (c)	[admos'fɛ:ʌ]
geography	**geografi** (c)	[geogʁa'fi:]
nature	**natur** (c)	[na'tuɒ]

globe (model of Earth)	**globus** (c)	['glo:bus]
map	**landkort** (n)	['lanˌkɒ:d]
atlas	**atlas** (n)	['adlas]

Europe	**Europa**	[œw'ʁo:pa]
Asia	**Asien**	['æ:ɕən]
Africa	**Afrika**	['ɑfʁika]
Australia	**Australien**	[ɑu'sdʁɑ:ljən]
America	**Amerika**	[a'meɒika]
North America	**Nordamerika**	['noɒ a'meɒika]

South America	**Sydamerika**	['syðɑˌmeʁika]
Antarctica	**Antarktis**	[an'tɑːktis]
the Arctic	**Arktis**	['ɑːktis]

197. Cardinal directions

north	**nord** (n)	['noɒ]
to the north	**mod nord**	[moð 'noɒ]
in the north	**i norden**	[i 'noːɒn]
northern	**nordlig**	['noɒli]
south	**syd** (c)	[syð]
to the south	**mod syd**	[moð syð]
in the south	**i syden**	[i 'syːðən]
southern	**sydlig**	['syðli]
west	**vest** (c)	[vɛsd]
to the west	**mod vest**	[moð vɛsd]
in the west	**i vesten**	[i 'vɛsdən]
western	**vestlig**	['vɛsdli]
east	**øst** (c)	[øsd]
to the east	**mod øst**	[moð øsd]
in the east	**i østen**	[i 'øsdən]
eastern	**østlig**	['øsdli]

198. Sea. Ocean

sea	**hav** (n)	[hɑu]
ocean	**ocean** (c)	[ose'æːn]
gulf (bay)	**havbugt** (c)	['hɑubɒgd]
straits	**stræde** (n)	['sdʁɛːðə]
continent (mainland)	**kontinent** (n)	[kʌnti'nɛnd]
island	**ø** (c)	[øː]
peninsula	**halvø** (c)	['halˌø]
archipelago	**øhav** (n)	[ø'hɑu]
bay	**bugt** (c)	[bɒgd]
harbor	**havn** (c)	[hɑun]
lagoon	**lagune** (c)	[la'guːnə]
cape	**kap** (n)	[kɑb]
atoll	**atol** (c)	[a'toːl]
reef	**rev** (n)	['ʁɛu]
coral	**koral** (c)	[ko'ʁal]
coral reef	**koralrev** (n)	[ko'ʁalˌʁɛu]
deep	**dyb**	[dyːb]

depth (deep water)	**dybde** (c)	['dybdə]
abyss	**dyb** (n)	[dy:b]
trench (e.g., Mariana ~)	**fordybning** (c)	[fɒ'dy:bnɛn]

| current | **strøm** (c) | [sdʁœm] |
| to surround (vt) | **at omgive** | [at 'ʌm,givə] |

| shore | **kyst** (c) | [køsd] |
| coast | **kyst** (c) | [køsd] |

high tide	**højvande** (n)	['hɒjvanə]
low tide	**lavvande** (n)	['lɑu,vanə]
sandbank	**banke** (c)	['baŋkə]
bottom	**bund** (c)	[bɔn]

wave	**bølge** (c)	['bøljə]
crest (~ of a wave)	**bølgekam** (c)	['bøljəkɑm]
foam	**skum** (n)	[skɔm]

storm	**storm** (c)	[sdɒ:m]
hurricane	**orkan** (c)	[ɒ'kæn]
tsunami	**tsunami** (c)	[tsu'na:mi]
calm	**vindstille** (n)	['vensdelə]
quiet (e.g., ~ ocean)	**stille**	['sdelə]

| pole | **pol** (c) | [po:l] |
| polar | **polar-** | [po'la:] |

latitude	**bredde** (c)	['bʁɛ:də]
longitude	**længde** (c)	['lɛŋdə]
parallel	**breddegrad** (c)	['bʁɛ:də,gʁa:ð]
equator	**ækvator** (c)	[ɛk'væ:tɒ]

sky	**himmel** (c)	['heməl]
horizon	**horisont** (c)	[hɒi'sʌnd]
air	**luft** (c)	[lɔfd]

lighthouse	**fyrtårn** (n)	['fyɒ,tɒn]
to dive (vi)	**at dykke**	[at 'døkə]
to sink (about boat)	**at synke**	[at 'søŋkə]
treasures	**skatte** (pl)	['skadə]

199. Seas' and Oceans' names

Atlantic Ocean	**Atlanterhavet**	[ad'lantɒ 'hævəð]
Indian Ocean	**Det Indiske Ocean**	[de 'endiskə ose'æ:n]
Pacific Ocean	**Stillehavet**	['sdelə 'hævəð]
Arctic Ocean	**Nordlige Ishav**	['nɒɒliə i'shɑu]
Black Sea	**Sortehavet**	['sɒɒdə 'hævəð]
Red Sea	**Rødehavet**	['ʁœ:ðə 'hævəð]

| Yellow Sea | Gule hav | ['gu:lə 'hɑu] |
| White Sea | Hvidehavet | ['vi:ðə 'hæveð] |

Caspian Sea	Kaspiske Hav	['kasbi:skə 'hɑu]
Dead Sea	Døde Hav	['dø:ðə 'hɑu]
Mediterranean Sea	Middelhavet	['miðəl 'hæveð]

| Aegean Sea | Ægæerhavet | [ɛ'gɛ:ɒ 'hæveð] |
| Adriatic Sea | Adriaterhavet | [æ:dʁi'æ:dɒ 'hæveð] |

Arabian Sea	Det Arabiske Hav	[de ɑ'ʁɑ:biskə 'hɑu]
Sea of Japan	Japanske Hav	[ja'pæ:nskə 'hɑu]
Bering Sea	Beringshavet	['be:ʁeŋs 'hæveð]
South China Sea	Sydkinesiske Hav	['syðki,ne:siskə hɑw]

Coral Sea	Koralhavet	[ko'ʁɑl 'hæveð]
Tasman Sea	Tasmanske hav	[tas'manskə hɑu]
Caribbean Sea	Caribiske Hav	[kɑ'ʁibiskə ,hɑu]

| Barents Sea | Barentshavet | ['bɑ:ænds 'hæveð] |
| Kara Sea | Karahavet | ['kɑɑ 'hæveð] |

North Sea	Nordsøen	['noɒsø:ən]
Baltic Sea	Østersøen	['øsdɒ,sø:ən]
Norwegian Sea	Norskehavet	['nɒ:skə 'hæveð]

200. Mountains

mountain	bjerg (c)	['bjɑɒ]
mountain range	bjergkæde (c)	['bjɑɒu,kɛ:ðə]
mountain ridge	bjergkæde (c)	['bjɑɒu,kɛ:ðə]

summit, top	bjergtop (c)	['bjɑɒu,tɒb]
peak	bjergtinde (c)	['bjɑɒu,tenə]
foot (of mountain, hill)	fod (c)	[foð]
slope (mountainside)	skråning (c)	['sgʁɔ:neŋ]

volcano	vulkan (c)	[vul'kæ:n]
active volcano	aktiv vulkan (c)	[ɑk'tiu vul'kæ:n]
dormant volcano	udslukt vulkan (c)	['uðslɒkd vul'kæ:n]

eruption	udbrud (n)	['uðbʁuð]
crater	krater (n)	['kʁɑ:dʌ]
magma	magma (c)	['mɑwma]
lava	lava (c)	['læ:va]
molten (~ lava)	glødende	['glø:ðənə]

canyon	canyon (c)	['kanyɒn]
gorge	bjergkløft (c)	['bjɑɒu,kløfd]
crevice	revne (c)	['ʁawnə]

pass, col	**bjergpas** (n)	['bjɑɒuˌpas]
plateau	**højslette** (c)	['hɒjˌslɛdə]
cliff	**klippe** (c)	['klebə]
hill	**bakke** (c)	['bɑkə]

glacier	**gletscher** (c)	['glɛdɕʌ]
waterfall	**vandfald** (n)	['vanˌfal]
geyser	**gejser** (c)	['gɑjsʌ]
lake	**sø** (c)	[sø:]

plain	**slette** (c)	['slɛdə]
landscape	**landskab** (n)	['lanskæ:b]
echo	**ekko** (n)	['ɛko]

alpinist	**alpinist** (c)	[alpi:'nisd]
rock climber	**bjergbestiger** (c)	['bjɑɒubeˌsdi:ʌ]
conquer (in climbing)	**at bestige**	[at be'sdiə]
climb (e.g., an easy ~)	**opstigning** (c)	['ʌbsdi:neŋ]

201. Mountains names

Alps	**Alperne**	['albɒnə]
Mont Blanc	**Mont Blanc**	['mɒnblejn]
Pyrenees	**Pyrenæerne**	['py:ɒnɛ:ɒnə]

Carpathians	**Karpaterne**	[kɑ:'padɒnə]
Ural Mountains	**Uralbjergene**	[u:'ʁæ:l 'bjæɒwənə]
Caucasus	**Kaukasus**	['kɑukasus]
Elbrus	**Elbrus**	[ɛl'bʁu:s]

Altai	**Altaj**	[al'tɑj]
Tien Shan	**Tien-Shan**	['ti:ən ɕæn]
Pamir Mountains	**Pamir**	[pæ:'miɒ]
Himalayas	**Himalaya**	[hima'lɑja]
Everest	**Mount Everest**	['maunt 'ɛ:vʁɛsd]

Andes	**Andesbjergene**	['anəsbjɑɒuənə]
Cordilleras	**Cordillerene**	[kɒdil'lɒɒenə]
Kilimanjaro	**Kilimanjaro**	[kiliman'jaʁo:]

202. Rivers

river	**flod** (c)	[floð]
spring (natural source)	**vandkilde** (c)	['vankilə]
bed (of the river)	**flodseng** (c)	['floðˌsɛŋ]
basin	**flodbækken** (c)	['floðˌbɛkən]
to flow into ...	**at munde ud ...**	[at 'mɔnə uð]
tributary	**biflod** (c)	['bifloð]

bank (of river)	**bred** (c)	[bʁɛð]
current, stream	**strøm** (c)	[sdʁœm]
downstream	**ned ad floden**	[neð að 'flo:ðən]
upstream	**op ad floden**	[ɒb að 'flo:ðən]
flood	**oversvømmelse** (c)	['ɒwʌˌsvœməlsə]
flooding	**højvande** (n)	['hɒjvanə]
to flood (vt)	**at oversvømme**	[at 'ɒʊɒˌsvœmə]
shallows (shoal)	**sandbanke** (c)	['sanˌbaŋkə]
rapids	**strømfald** (n)	['sdʁœmˌfal]
dam	**dæmning** (c)	['dɛmnen]
canal	**kanal** (c)	[ka'næ:l]
reservoir, artificial lake	**kunstig sø** (n)	['kʊnsdi sø:]
sluice, lock	**sluse** (c)	['slu:sə]
reservoir (water body)	**bassin** (n)	[ba'sɛn]
marsh, swamp	**sump** (c)	[sɔmb]
bog	**hængedynd** (n)	['hɛŋəˌdøn]
whirlpool	**malstrøm** (c)	['mæ:lsdʁœm]
stream (brook)	**bæk** (c)	[bɛk]
drinking (about water)	**drikke-**	['dʁɛkə]
fresh (not salt)	**fersk**	['faɒsk]
ice	**is** (c)	[i:s]
to ice over	**at fryse til**	[at 'fʁy:sə tel]

203. Rivers' names

Seine	**Seinen**	['sɛ:nən]
Loire	**Loire**	[lo'ɒʁ]
Thames	**Themsen**	['tɛmsən]
Rhine	**Rhinen**	['ʁi:nən]
Danube	**Donau**	['dɒnɑʊo]
Volga	**Volga**	['vɔʊga]
Don	**Don**	[dɒn]
Lena	**Lena**	['le:na]
Yellow River	**Huang He**	[hu'ɑng ˌhe:]
Yangtze	**Yangtze**	['jɑŋdsə]
Mekong	**Mekong**	[me'kɒŋ]
Ganges	**Ganges**	['gɑ:ŋəs]
Nile River	**Nilen**	['ni:lən]
Congo	**Congo**	['kɒngo]
Okavango	**Okavango**	[ɔuka'vɑngo]

| Zambezi | **Zambezi** | [sɑmˈbɛsi] |
| Limpopo | **Limpopo** | [liːmˈpopo] |

204. Forest

| forest | **skov** (c) | [ˈskɒw] |
| forest (attr) | **skov-** | [ˈskɒw] |

thick forest	**skovtykning** (c)	[ˈsgɒwˌtygnen]
grove	**lund** (c)	[lɔn]
clearing	**skovlysning** (c)	[ˈsgɒwˌlyːsnen]

| thicket | **bevoksning** (c) | [beˈvɒgsnen] |
| scrubland | **buskads** (n) | [buˈskæːs] |

pathway	**sti** (c)	[sdiː]
footpath	**gangsti** (c)	[ˈgæːŋsdiː]
gully	**slugt** (c)	[slugd]

tree	**træ** (n)	[tʁɛː]
leaf	**blad** (n)	[blað]
leaves	**løv** (n)	[ˈløu]

falling leaves	**løvfald** (n)	[ˈløːuˌfal]
to fall (about leaves)	**at falde**	[at ˈfalə]
top (of the tree)	**trætop** (c)	[ˈtʁadɒb]

branch	**gren** (c)	[gʁɛn]
bough	**gren** (c)	[gʁɛn]
bud (on shrub, tree)	**knop** (c)	[knɒb]
needle (of pine tree)	**nål** (n)	[nɔːl]
cone (of pine, fir)	**knogle** (c)	[ˈknɒwlə]

hollow (in a tree)	**hul** (n)	[hɔl]
nest	**rede** (c)	[ˈʁɛːðə]
burrow, animal hole	**hul** (n)	[hɔl]

trunk (of a tree)	**stamme** (c)	[ˈsdɑmə]
root	**rod** (c)	[ʁoð]
bark (of a tree)	**bark** (c)	[bɑːk]
moss	**mos** (n)	[moːs]

to uproot (vt)	**at rykke op med rode**	[at ˈʁœkə ɒb mɛð ˈʁoːðə]
to chop down	**at hugge**	[at ˈhɒgə]
to deforest (vt)	**at skove, at rydde**	[at ˈskɒuə], [at ˈʁyðə]
tree stump	**træstub** (c)	[ˈtʁɛsdub]

campfire	**bål** (n)	[bɔːl]
forest fire	**brand** (c)	[bʁɑn]
to extinguish (vt)	**at slukke**	[at ˈslɔkə]

forest ranger	**skovløber** (c)	[ˈskɒwˌløːbʌ]
protection	**fredning** (c)	[ˈfʁɛðneŋ]
to protect (e.g., ~ nature)	**at værn om skov**	[at ˈvaɒn ɒm ˈskɒu]
poacher	**krybskytte** (c)	[ˈkʁybˌskødə]
trap (e.g., bear ~)	**fælde** (c)	[ˈfɛlə]
to pick (mushrooms)	**at plukke**	[at ˈplɔkə]
to pick (berries)	**at plukke**	[at ˈplɔkə]
to lose one's way	**at fare vild**	[at ˈfɑːɒ vil]

205. Natural resources

natural resources	**naturressourcer** (pl)	[naˈtuɒ ʁɛˈsuɒsʌ]
minerals	**mineralske ressourcer** (pl)	[mineˈʁɑːlskə ʁɛˈsuɒsʌ]
deposit (e.g., coal ~)	**forekomster** (pl)	[ˈfɒːɒkɒmsdʌ]
field (e.g., oilfield)	**forekomst** (c)	[ˈfɒːɒkɒmsd]
to mine (extract)	**at udvinde**	[at ˈuðˌvenə]
mining (extraction)	**udvinding** (c)	[ˈuðveneŋ]
ore	**malm** (c)	[ˈmalm]
mine (e.g., for coal)	**mine** (c)	[ˈminə]
mine shaft, pit	**grube** (c)	[ˈgʁuːbə]
miner	**minearbejder** (c)	[ˈmineˌɑːbɑjdʌ]
gas	**gas** (c)	[gas]
gas pipeline	**gasledning** (c)	[ˈgasˌleːðneŋ]
oil (petroleum)	**råolie** (c)	[ˈʁɒˌoːljə]
oil pipeline	**olieledning** (c)	[ˈoːljəˌleːðneŋ]
oil rig	**boreplatform** (c)	[ˈboːɒˌpladfɒːm]
derrick	**boretårn** (c)	[ˈboːɒˌtɒːn]
tanker	**tankskib** (n)	[ˈtɑŋkˌskiːb]
sand	**sand** (n)	[san]
limestone	**kalksten** (c)	[ˈkalksdən]
gravel	**grus** (n)	[gʁuːs]
peat	**tørv** (c)	[ˈtœɒw]
clay	**ler** (n)	[leʌ]
coal	**kul** (n)	[kɔl]
iron	**jern** (n)	[ˈjæɒn]
gold	**guld** (n)	[gul]
silver	**sølv** (n)	[søl]
nickel	**nikkel** (n)	[ˈnekəl]
copper	**kobber** (n)	[ˈkɒwʌ]
zinc	**zink** (n, c)	[seŋk]
manganese	**mangan** (c)	[mɑŋˈgæn]
mercury	**kviksølv** (n)	[ˈkvikˌsøl]
lead	**bly** (n)	[blyː]

mineral	**mineral** (n)	[minəˈʁɑːl]
crystal	**krystal** (c)	[kʁyˈsdal]
marble	**marmor** (n)	[ˈmɑːmoɒ]
uranium	**uran** (n)	[uˈʁɑn]
diamond (stone)	**diamant** (c)	[diaˈmand]

The Earth. Part 2

206. Weather

weather	**vejr** (n)	['vɛɒ]
weather forecast	**vejrudsigt** (c)	['vɛɒˌuðsegd]
temperature	**temperatur** (c)	[tɛmbəʁɑ'tuɒ]
thermometer	**termometer** (n)	[taɒmo'me:dʌ]
barometer	**barometer** (n)	[bɑo'medʌ]
humidity	**fugtighed** (c)	['fɒgdiheð]
heat (of summer)	**hede** (c)	['he:ðə]
hot (torrid)	**varm**	[vɑ:m]
it's hot	**meget varmt**	['mɑɒð vɑ:md]
it's warm	**varmt**	[vɑ:md]
warm (moderately hot)	**varm**	[vɑ:m]
it's cold	**koldt**	[kɒld]
cold	**kold**	[kɒl]
sun	**sol** (c)	[so:l]
to shine	**at skinne**	[at 'skenə]
sunny (day)	**sol-**	[so:l]
to come up (vi)	**at stå op**	[at sdɔ: ɒb]
to set (vi)	**at gå ned**	[at gɔ: neð]
cloud	**sky** (c)	[sky:]
cloudy	**skyet**	['sky:əð]
rain cloud	**mørk sky** (c)	['mœɒk sky:]
somber (gloomy)	**mørk**	['mœɒk]
rain	**regn** (c)	[ʁɑjn]
it's raining	**det regner**	[de 'ʁɑjnɒ]
rainy (day)	**regnfuld**	['ʁɑjnˌful]
to drizzle (vi)	**at småregne**	[at 'smɒʁɑjnə]
pouring rain	**styrtregn** (c)	['sdyɒdˌʁɑjn]
downpour	**skylregn** (c)	['sgylˌʁɑjn]
heavy (e.g., ~ rain)	**silende regn**	['si:lənə ʁɑjn]
puddle	**pyt** (c)	[pyd]
to get wet (in rain)	**at blive våd**	[at 'bli:ə vɔð]
mist (fog)	**tåge** (c)	['tɔ:wə]
misty	**tåget**	['tɔ:wəð]
snow	**sne** (c)	[sne:]
it's snowing	**det sner**	[de 'sne:ɒ]

207. Severe weather. Natural disasters

thunderstorm	**tordenvejr** (n)	['toɒdən‚vɛɒ]
lightning (~ strike)	**lyn** (n)	[ly:n]
to flash (vi)	**at lyne, at glimte**	[at 'ly:nə], [at 'glemdə]
thunder	**torden** (c)	['toɒdən]
to thunder (vi)	**at tordne**	[at 'toɒdnə]
it's thundering	**det tordner**	[de 'toɒdnɒ]
hail	**hagl** (n)	[haul]
it's hailing	**det hagler**	[de 'haulɒ]
to flood (vt)	**at oversvømme**	[at 'ɒuɒ‚svœmə]
flood	**oversvømmelse** (c)	['ɒwʌ‚svœməlsə]
earthquake	**jordskælv** (n)	['joɒ‚skɛlv]
tremor, quake	**skælv** (n)	['skɛlv]
epicenter	**epicenter** (n)	[epi'sɛndʌ]
eruption	**udbrud** (n)	['uðbʁuð]
lava	**lava** (c)	['læ:va]
whirlwind, tornado	**skypumpe** (c)	['sky:‚pɔmbə]
tornado	**tornado** (c)	[tɒ'næ:do]
typhoon	**tyfon** (c)	[ty'fo:n]
hurricane	**orkan** (c)	[ɒ'kæn]
storm	**storm** (c)	[sdɒ:m]
tsunami	**tsunami** (c)	[tsu'na:mi]
cyclone (e.g., tropical ~)	**cyklon** (c)	[sy'klon]
bad weather	**uvejr** (n)	['u‚vɛɒ]
fire (e.g., house on ~)	**brand** (c)	[bʁɑn]
disaster	**katastrofe** (c)	[kata'sdʁo:fə]
meteorite	**meteorit** (c)	[meteo'ʁid]
avalanche	**lavine** (c)	[la'vi:nə]
snowslide	**sneskred** (n)	['sne‚skʁɛð]
blizzard	**snestorm** (c)	['sne‚sdɒ:m]
snowstorm	**snefog** (c)	['sne‚fɔw]

208. Noises. Sounds

quiet, silence	**stilhed** (c)	['sdel‚heð]
sound	**lyd** (c)	[lyð]
noise	**larm** (n)	[lɑ:m]
to make noise	**at larme**	[at 'lɑ:mə]
noisy	**larmende**	['lɑ:mənə]

loudly (to speak etc.)	**højt**	[hɒjd]
loud (voice etc.)	**høj**	[hɒj]
constant (continuous)	**stadig**	['sdæːð]
shout (noun)	**skrig** (n)	[sgʁiː]
to shout (vi)	**at råbe**	[at 'ʁɔːbə]
whisper	**hvisken** (c)	['veskən]
to whisper (vi, vt)	**at hviske**	[at 'veskə]
barking (of dog)	**gøen** (c)	['gøːən]
to bark (vi)	**at gø**	[at gøː]
groan (of pain)	**støn** (n)	[sdœn]
to groan (vi)	**at stønne**	[at 'sdœnnə]
cough	**hoste** (c)	['hoːsdə]
to cough (vi)	**at hoste**	[at 'hoːsdə]
whistle	**fløjt** (n)	[flɒjd]
to whistle (vi)	**at fløjte**	[at 'flɒjdə]
knock (at the door)	**banken** (c)	['baŋkən]
to knock (vi)	**at banke**	[at 'baŋkə]
to crackle (vi)	**at knitre**	[at 'knidʁʌ]
crackle	**knæk** (n)	['knɛg]
siren	**sirene** (c)	[si'ʁɛːnə]
whistle (factory's ~)	**fløjten** (c)	['flɒjdən]
to whistle (ship, train)	**at hyle**	[at 'hyːlə]
honk (signal)	**signal** (n)	[si'næːl]
to honk (about car)	**at dytte**	[at 'dydə]

209. Winter

winter (noun)	**vinter** (c)	['vendʌ]
winter (attr)	**vinter-**	['vendɒ]
in the winter	**om vinteren**	[ɒm 'vendɒɒn]
snow	**sne** (c)	[sneː]
it's snowing	**det sner**	[de 'sneːɒ]
snowfall	**snefald** (n)	['snefal]
snowdrift	**snedrive** (c)	['sneˌdʁiːvə]
snowflake	**snefnug** (n)	['snefnug]
snowball	**snebold** (c)	['snebɒld]
snowman	**snemand** (c)	['sneˌman]
icicle	**istap** (c)	['istɒb]
December	**december** (c)	[de'sɛmbʌ]
January	**januar** (c)	['januɑː]
February	**februar** (c)	['febʁuɑː]

New Year	**Nytår**	['nydɒ:]
Christmas tree	**Juletræ** (n)	['ju:ləˌtʁɛ:]
Christmas	**Jul** (c)	[ju:l]

heavy frost	**frost** (c)	[fʁɒsd]
frosty (weather, air)	**frost-**	[fʁɒsd]
below zero	**under nul**	['ɔnʌ 'nol]
light frost	**let frost** (c)	[lɛd 'fʁɒsd]
hoarfrost	**rim** (c)	[ʁɛm]

| cold (cold weather) | **kulde** (c) | ['kulə] |
| it's cold | **koldt** | [kɒld] |

| fur coat | **pelskåbe** (c) | ['pɛlsˌkɔ:bə] |
| mittens | **vanter** (c pl) | ['vandə] |

to get sick	**at blive syg**	[at 'bli:ə sy:]
cold (illness)	**forkølelse** (c)	[fɒ'kø:ləlsə]
to catch a cold	**at blive forkølet**	[at 'bli:ə fɒ'kø:ləð]

ice	**is** (c)	[i:s]
black ice	**isslag** (n)	['isˌslæj]
to ice over	**at fryse til**	[at 'fʁy:sə tel]
ice floe	**isflage** (c)	['isflæ:jə]

skis	**ski** (pl)	[ski:]
skier	**skiløber** (c)	['skilø:bʌ]
to ski (vi)	**at stå på ski**	[at sdɔ: pɔ ski:]
to skate (vi)	**at skøjte**	[at 'skɒjdə]

Fauna

210. Mammals. Predators

predator	**rovdyr** (n)	['ʁɒwˌdyɒ]
tiger	**tiger** (c)	['tiːʌ]
lion	**løve** (c)	['løːuə]
wolf	**ulv** (c)	[ulv]
fox	**ræv** (c)	['ʁɛu]
jaguar	**jaguar** (c)	[jaguˈɑː]
leopard	**leopard** (c)	[leoˈpɑːd]
cheetah	**gepard** (c)	[geˈpɑːd]
black panther	**panter** (c)	[panˈdʌ]
puma	**puma** (c)	['puma]
snow leopard	**sneleopard** (c)	['sneleoˌpɑːd]
lynx	**los** (c)	[lɒs]
coyote	**prærieulv** (c)	['pʁɛjəɒ 'ulv]
jackal	**sjakal** (c)	[ɕaˈkæːl]
hyena	**hyæne** (c)	[hyˈɛːnə]

211. Wild animals

animal	**dyr** (n)	['dyɒ]
beast (animal)	**dyr** (n)	['dyɒ]
squirrel	**egern** (n)	['ejʌn]
hedgehog	**pindsvin** (n)	['penˌsviːn]
hare	**hare** (c)	['hɑːɒ]
rabbit	**kanin** (c)	[kaˈniːn]
badger	**grævling** (c)	['gʁaulen]
raccoon	**vaskebjørn** (c)	['vaskəˌbjœɒn]
hamster	**hamster** (c)	['hɑmsdʌ]
marmot	**murmeldyr** (n)	['muɒmɛldyɒ]
mole	**muldvarp** (c)	['mulvɑːb]
mouse	**mus** (c)	[muːs]
rat	**rotte** (c)	['ʁɒdə]
bat	**flagermus** (c)	['flɑwʌˌmus]
ermine	**hermelin** (c)	[hæɒməˈlin]
sable	**zobel** (c)	['sobəl]

marten	mår (c)	[mɒ:]
weasel	væsel (c)	['vɛ:səl]
mink	mink (c)	[meŋk]
beaver	bæver (n)	['bɛvʌ]
otter	odder (c)	['ɒðʌ]
horse	hest (c)	[hɛsd]
moose	elg (c)	['ɛlj]
deer	hjort (c)	[jɒ:d]
camel	kamel (c)	[ka'me:l]
bison	bison (c)	['bisɒn]
aurochs	urokse (c)	['uɒ,ʁʌksə]
buffalo	bøffel (c)	['bøfəl]
zebra	zebra (c)	['se:bʁɑ]
antelope	antilope (c)	[anti'lo:bə]
roe deer	rå (c)	[ʁɔ:]
fallow deer	dådyr (n)	['dɒ,dyɒ]
chamois	gemse (c)	['gamsə]
wild boar	vildsvin (n)	['vil,svi:n]
whale	hval (c)	[væ:l]
seal	sæl (c)	[sɛ:l]
walrus	hvalros (c)	['valʁɒs]
fur seal	sæl (c)	[sɛ:l]
dolphin	delfin (c)	[dɛl'fi:n]
bear	bjørn (c)	['bjœɒn]
polar bear	isbjørn (c)	['isbjœɒn]
panda	panda (c)	['panda]
monkey	abe (c)	['æ:bə]
chimpanzee	chimpanse (c)	[ɕim'pansə]
orangutan	orangutang (c)	[o'ʁɑŋgu,taŋ]
gorilla	gorilla (c)	[go'ʁila]
macaque	makak (c)	[mæ'kɑk]
gibbon	gibbon (c)	['gibʌn]
elephant	elefant (c)	[elə'fand]
rhinoceros	næsehorn (n)	['nɛ:səhoɒn]
giraffe	giraf (c)	[gi'ʁɑf]
hippopotamus	flodhest (c)	['floð,hɛsd]
kangaroo	kænguru (c)	[kɛŋ'gu:ʁu]
koala (bear)	koala (c)	[ko'æ:la]
mongoose	desmerdyr (n)	['dɛsmɒdyɒ]
chinchilla	chinchilla (c)	[tjen'tjila]
skunk	skunk (c)	[skɔŋk]
porcupine	hulepindsvin (n)	['hu:lə ,pensvi:n]

212. Domestic animals

cat	**kat** (c)	[kad]
tomcat	**kat** (c)	[kad]
horse	**hest** (c)	[hɛsd]
stallion	**hingst** (c)	[heŋsd]
mare	**hoppe** (c)	['hɒbə]
cow	**ko** (c)	[ko:]
bull	**okse** (c)	['ɒksə]
ox	**stud** (c)	[sduð]
sheep	**får** (n)	[fɒ:]
ram	**vædder**	['vɛðʌ]
goat	**ged** (c)	[geð]
billy goat, he-goat	**gedebuk** (c)	['ge:ðəbɔg]
donkey	**æsel** (n)	['ɛsəl]
mule	**muldyr** (n)	['muldyɒ]
pig	**svin** (n)	[svi:n]
piglet	**gris** (c)	[gʁi:s]
rabbit	**kanin** (c)	[ka'ni:n]
hen (chicken)	**høne** (c)	['hœ:nə]
rooster	**hane** (c)	['hæ:nə]
duck	**and** (c)	[an]
drake	**andrik** (c)	['anʁɛk]
goose	**gås** (c)	[gɔ:s]
turkey cock	**kalkunsk hane** (c)	[kal'ku:nsk 'hæ:nə]
turkey (hen)	**kalkun** (c)	[kal'ku:n]
domestic animals	**husdyr** (pl)	['hus͵dyɒ]
tame (e.g., ~ hamster)	**tam**	[tɑm]
to tame (vt)	**at tæmme**	[at 'tɛmə]
to breed (vt)	**at avle**	[at 'ɑulə]
farm	**farm** (c)	[fɑ:m]
poultry	**fjerkræ** (n)	['fjeɒkʁɛ:]
cattle	**kvæg** (n)	[kvɛ:]
herd (of cattle, goats)	**hjord** (c)	['joɒ]
stable	**hestestald** (c)	['hɛsdə͵sdal]
pigpen	**svinesti** (c)	['svi:nəsdi]
cowshed	**kostald** (c)	['ko:sdal]
rabbit hutch	**kaninhus** (n)	[ka'ni:n͵hu:s]
hen house	**hønsehus** (n)	['hœnsə͵hu:s]

213. Dogs. Dog breeds

dog	**hund** (c)	[hun]
sheepdog	**schæferhund** (c)	[ˈɕɛːfɒˌhun]
poodle	**puddel(hund)** (c)	[ˈpuðəl]
dachshund	**gravhund** (c)	[ˈgʁɑːuˌhun]
bulldog	**buldog** (c)	[ˈbuldɒu]
boxer	**bokser** (c)	[ˈbɒksʌ]
mastiff	**mastiff** (c)	[masˈdif]
rottweiler	**rottweiler** (c)	[ˈʁʌdˌvɑjlʌ]
Doberman	**dobermann** (c)	[ˈdʌbʌˌman]
basset	**basset** (c)	[ˈbasɛd]
bobtail	**bobtail** (c)	[ˈbɒbtɛjl]
Dalmatian	**dalmatiner** (c)	[dæːlmæːˈtiːnʌ]
cocker spaniel	**cockerspaniel** (c)	[ˈkɒkɒ ˈsbænjəl]
Newfoundland	**newfoundlænder** (c)	[njuˈfɑwndˌlɛnʌ]
Saint Bernard	**sanktbernhardshund** (c)	[ˈsɑɲdˌbɒnhɑːdsˌhun]
husky	**husky** (c)	[ˈhʌski]
chow-chow	**chowchow** (c)	[ˌɕɔːu ˈɕɔːu]
spitz	**spidshund** (c)	[ˈsbesˌhun]
pug	**moppe, mops** (c)	[mɒbbə], [mɒbs]

214. Sounds made by animals

barking (noun)	**gøen** (c)	[ˈgøːən]
to bark (vi)	**at gø**	[at gøː]
to meow (vi)	**at mjave**	[at ˈmjæːuə]
to purr (vi)	**at spinde**	[at ˈsbenə]
to moo (vi)	**at brøle**	[at ˈbʁœːlə]
to bellow (bull)	**at brøle**	[at ˈbʁœːlə]
to growl (vi)	**at brøle**	[at ˈbʁœːlə]
howl (noun)	**hyl** (n)	[hyːl]
to howl (vi)	**at hyle**	[at ˈhyːlə]
to whine (vi)	**at klynke**	[at ˈkløŋkə]
to bleat (sheep)	**at bræge**	[at ˈbʁɛːə]
to oink, to grunt (pig)	**at grynte**	[at ˈgʁœndə]
to squeal (vi)	**at hyle**	[at ˈhyːlə]
to croak (frog)	**at kvække**	[at ˈkvɛkə]
to buzz (insect)	**at brumme**	[at ˈbʁɔmə]
to stridulate (vi)	**at synge**	[at ˈsøŋə]

215. Young animals

cub	dyreunge (c)	['dy:ɒˌɔŋə]
kitten	kattekilling (c)	['kadeːkeleŋ]
baby mouse	museunge (c)	['musɛːɔŋə]
pup, puppy	hvalp (c)	[valb]
leveret	harekilling (c)	['hɑːɑˌkeleŋ]
baby rabbit	kaninunge (c)	[ka'ninˌɔŋə]
wolf cub	ulveunge (c)	['ulvəˌɔŋə]
fox cub	ræveunge (c)	['ʁɛːuə ˌɔŋə]
bear cub	bjørneunge (c)	['bjɶɒnəˌɔŋə]
lion cub	løveunge (c)	['løːuəˌɔŋə]
tiger cub	tigerunge (c)	['tiːɒˌɔŋə]
elephant calf	elefantunge (c)	[eləˈfantˌɔnŋə]
piglet	gris (c)	[gʁiːs]
calf (young cow, bull)	kalv (c)	[kalv]
kid (young goat)	gedekid (n)	['gəðəkið]
lamb	lam (n)	[lɑm]
fawn (deer)	kid (n)	[kið]
young camel	kamelføl (n)	[ka'məlˌføl]
baby snake	slangeunge (c)	['slɑŋəˌɔŋə]
baby frog	frøunge (c)	['fʁøˌɔnŋə]
nestling	fugleunge (c)	['fuːləɔŋə]
chick (of chicken)	kylling (c)	['kyleŋ]
duckling	ælling (c)	['ɛleŋ]

216. Birds

bird	fugl (c)	[fuːl]
pigeon	due (c)	['duːə]
sparrow	spurv (c)	['sbuɒw]
tit	blåmejse (c)	[blɒ'mɑjsə]
magpie	skade (c)	['skæːðə]
raven	ravn (c)	['ʁɑwn]
hooded crow	krage (c)	['kʁɑːuə]
jackdaw	allike (c)	['alikə]
rook	råge (c)	['ʁɔːwə]
duck	and (c)	[an]
goose	gås (c)	[gɔːs]
pheasant	fasan (c)	[fa'san]
eagle	ørn (c)	['ɶɒn]
hawk	høg (c)	[høː]

falcon	**falk** (c)	[falk]
vulture	**grib** (c)	[gʁi:b]
condor	**kondor** (c)	[ˈkʌndoɒ]
swan	**svane** (c)	[ˈsvæ:nə]
crane	**trane** (c)	[ˈtʁɑ:nə]
stork	**stork** (c)	[sdɒ:k]
parrot	**papegøje** (c)	[pɑbəˈgʌjə]
hummingbird	**kolibri** (c)	[koˈliˈbʁi:]
peacock	**påfugl** (c)	[ˈpɒfu:l]
ostrich	**struds** (c)	[ˈsdʁus]
heron	**hejre** (c)	[ˈhɑjʁʌ]
flamingo	**flamingo** (c)	[flaˈmeŋgo]
pelican	**pelikan** (c)	[pəliˈkæ:n]
nightingale	**nattergal** (c)	[ˈnadʌˌgæl]
swallow	**svale** (c)	[ˈsvæ:lə]
fieldfare	**drossel** (c)	[ˈdʁɔssəl]
song thrush	**sangdrossel** (c)	[ˈsɑŋˌdʁɔssəl]
blackbird	**solsort** (c)	[ˈso:lsɒːd]
swift	**mursejler** (c)	[ˈmuɒsɑjlʌ]
lark	**lærke** (c)	[ˈlæɒkə]
quail	**vagtel** (c)	[ˈvɑgdəl]
woodpecker	**spætte** (c)	[ˈsbɛdə]
cuckoo	**gøg** (c)	[gɒj]
owl	**ugle** (c)	[ˈu:lə]
eagle owl	**hornugle** (c)	[ˈhoɒnu:lə]
wood grouse	**tjur** (c)	[ˈtjuɒ]
black grouse	**urfugl** (c)	[ˈuɒfu:l]
partridge	**agerhøne** (c)	[ˈæːɒhœ:nə]
starling	**stær** (c)	[sdɛɒ]
canary	**kanariefugl** (c)	[kaˈnɑʁiəˌfu:l]
hazel grouse	**hjerpe** (c)	[ˈjæɒbə]
chaffinch	**bogfinke** (c)	[ˈbɔufeŋgə]
bullfinch	**dompap** (c)	[ˈdɒmpɑb]
gull (seagull)	**måge** (c)	[ˈmɔ:uə]
albatross	**albatros** (c)	[ˈalbaˈtʁɒs]
penguin	**pingvin** (c)	[ˈpeŋvi:n]

217. Birds. Singing and sounds

| to sing (vi) | **at synge** | [at ˈsøŋə] |
| to call (shout) | **at råbe** | [at ˈʁɔ:bə] |

to crow (rooster)	**at gale kykeliky**	[at 'gæ:lə kygəli'ky:]
cock-a-doodle-doo	**kykeliky**	[kykli'ky:]
to cluck (hen)	**at kagle**	[at 'kɑulə]
to caw (vi)	**at skrige**	[at 'sgʁi:ə]
to quack (duck)	**at rappe**	[at 'ʁabə]
to cheep (vi)	**at pippe**	[at 'pigə]
to chirp, to twitter	**at pippe**	[at 'pigə]

218. Fish. Marine animals

bream	**brasen** (c)	['bʁɑ:sən]
carp	**karpe** (c)	['ka:bə]
perch	**aborre** (c)	['ɑˌbɒ:ɒ]
catfish	**malle** (c)	['mallə]
pike	**gedde** (c)	['geðə]
salmon	**laks** (c)	[lɑks]
sturgeon	**stør** (c)	['sdøɒ]
herring	**sild** (c)	[sil]
Atlantic salmon	**laks** (c)	[lɑks]
mackerel	**makrel** (c)	[mɑ'kʁal]
flatfish	**rødspætte** (c)	['ʁœðˌsbɛdə]
zander, pike perch	**sandart** (c)	['sanˌɑ:d]
cod	**torsk** (c)	[tɒ:sk]
tuna	**tunfisk** (c)	['tu:nˌfesk]
trout	**forel** (c)	[fo'ʁal]
eel	**ål** (c)	[ɔ:l]
electric ray	**elektrisk rokke** (c)	[e'lɛktʁisk 'ʁɒkə]
moray eel	**muræne** (c)	[mu'ʁɛ:nə]
piranha	**piratfisk** (c)	[pi'ʁɑdˌfesk]
shark	**haj** (c)	[hɑj]
dolphin	**delfin** (c)	[dɛl'fi:n]
whale	**hval** (c)	[væ:l]
crab	**krabbe** (c)	['kʁabə]
jellyfish	**vandmand** (c)	['vanˌman]
octopus	**blæksprutte** (c)	['blɛkˌsbʁudə]
starfish	**søstjerne** (c)	['søˌsdjæɒnə]
sea urchin	**søpindsvin** (n)	['søˌpensvi:n]
seahorse	**søhest** (c)	['søˌhɛsd]
oyster	**østers** (c)	['øsdɒs]
shrimp	**reje** (c)	['ʁajə]
lobster	**hummer** (c)	['hɔmʌ]
spiny lobster	**languster** (c)	[lɑ'gɔsdʌ]

219. Amphibians. Reptiles

| snake | **slange** (c) | ['slaŋə] |
| poisonous | **giftig** | ['gifdi] |

viper	**hugorm** (c)	['hɔgoɒm]
cobra	**kobra** (c)	['ko:bʁɑ]
python	**pyton** (c)	['pytɒn]
boa	**kvælerslange** (c)	['kvɛ:lɒˌslaŋə]

grass snake	**snog** (c)	[sno:]
rattle snake	**klapperslange** (c)	['klabɒˌslaŋə]
anaconda	**anakonda** (c)	[anɑ'kɒnda]

lizard	**firben** (n)	[fiɒ'be:n]
iguana	**leguan** (c)	[legu'æn]
monitor lizard	**varan** (c)	[vɑ'ʁan]
salamander	**salamander** (c)	[sala'mandʌ]
chameleon	**kamæleon** (c)	[kamɛle'o:n]
scorpion	**skorpion** (c)	[skɒbi'on]

turtle	**skildpadde** (c)	['skelˌpaðə]
frog	**frø** (c)	[fʁœ:]
toad	**skrubtudse** (c)	['skʁɔbˌtuse]
crocodile	**krokodille** (c)	[kʁokə'dilə]

220. Insects

insect, bug	**insekt** (n)	[en'sɛkd]
butterfly	**sommerfugl** (c)	['sɒmɒˌfu:l]
ant	**myre** (c)	['my:ɒ]
fly	**flue** (c)	['flu:ə]
mosquito	**myg** (c)	[myg]
beetle	**bille** (c)	['belə]

wasp	**hveps** (c)	[vɛbs]
bee	**bi** (c)	[bi:]
bumblebee	**humlebi** (c)	['hɔmləˌbi:]
gadfly	**bremse** (c)	['bʁamsə]

| spider | **edderkop** (c) | ['eðɒkɒb] |
| spider's web | **spindelvæv** (n) | ['sbenəlˌvɛw] |

dragonfly	**guldsmed** (c)	['gulˌsmeð]
grasshopper	**græshoppe** (c)	['gʁasˌhɒbə]
moth (night butterfly)	**sommerfugl** (c)	['sɒmɒˌfu:l]

| cockroach | **kakerlak** (c) | [kɑkʌ'lɑk] |
| tick | **mide** (c) | ['mi:ðə] |

| flea | **loppe** (c) | [lɒbə] |
| midge | **myg** (c) | [myg] |

locust	**skadelig græsshoppe** (c)	['sgæːðəlig 'gʁasˌhʌbə]
snail	**snegl** (c)	[snɑjl]
cricket	**fårekylling** (c)	['fɒːɒkyleŋ]

lightning bug	**ildflue** (c)	['ilfluːə]
ladybug	**mariehøne** (c)	[mɑ'ʁiːəˌhœːnə]
cockchafer	**oldenborre** (c)	['ʌlənˌbɒːɒ]

leech	**lægeigle** (c)	['lɛːjəˌiːlə]
caterpillar	**larve** (c)	['lɑːvə]
worm	**orm** (c)	['oɒm]
larva	**larve** (c)	['lɑːvə]

221. Animals. Body parts

beak	**næb** (n)	[nɛːb]
wings	**vinger** (pl)	['veŋʌ]
foot (of bird)	**fod** (c)	[foð]
feathering	**fjerbeklædning** (c)	['fjeðʌˌklɛðneŋ]

| feather | **fjeder** (c) | ['fjeðʌ] |
| crest | **fjertop** (c), **kam** (c) | ['fjeɒtɒb], [kɑm] |

gill	**gælle** (c)	[gɛlə]
spawn	**æg** (n), **æg** (pl)	[ɛːg]
larva	**larve** (c)	['lɑːvə]

| fin | **finne** (c) | ['fenə] |
| scales (of fish, reptile) | **skæl** (n) | [skɛl] |

fang (of wolf etc.)	**hugtand** (c)	['hɔgtan]
paw (e.g., cat's ~)	**pote** (c)	['poːdə]
muzzle	**mule** (c)	['muːlə]
mouth (of cat, dog)	**gab** (n)	[gæːb]

| tail | **hale** (c) | ['hæːlə] |
| whiskers | **knurhår** (n) | ['knuɒˌhɒː] |

| hoof | **klov** (c), **hov** (c) | ['klɒw], ['hɒw] |
| horn | **horn** (n) | [hoɒn] |

carapace	**rygskjold** (n)	['ʁœgˌsgjɒl]
shell (of mollusk)	**skal** (c)	[skal]
shell (of egg)	**skal** (c)	[skal]

| hair (e.g., dog's ~) | **dyrehår** (n) | ['dyːɒˌhɒː] |
| skin (of animal) | **skind** (n) | [skenj] |

222. Actions of animals

to fly (bird, insect)	at flyve	[at 'fly:və]
to make circles	at kredse	[at 'kʁɛ:sə]
to fly away	at flyve bort	[at 'fly:və bɔ:d]
to flap (~ the wings)	at baske	[at 'bɑ:skə]
to peck (vi)	at pikke	[at 'pikə]
to incubate (vt)	at udruge	[at 'uð̞ʁu:ə]
to hatch out (vi)	at udklækkes	[at 'uð̞ˌklɛkəs]
to build (nest)	at bygge rede	[at 'bygə 'ʁɛ:ðə]
to slither, to crawl	at kravle	[at 'kʁɑulə]
to sting, to bite (insect)	at stikke	[at 'sdekə]
to bite (about animal)	at bide	[at 'bi:ðə]
to sniff (vt)	at snuse	[at 'snu:sə]
to bark (vi)	at gø	[at gø:]
to hiss (snake)	at hvæse	[at 'vɛ:sə]
to scare (vt)	at forskrække	[at fʌ'skʁakə]
to attack (vt)	at angribe	[at 'anˌgʁi:bə]
to gnaw (bone etc.)	at gnave	[at 'gnæ:uə]
to scratch (with claws)	at skramme	[at 'skʁɑmə]
to hide (vi)	at skjule sig	[at 'sgju:lə saj]
to play (kittens etc.)	at lege	[at 'lɑjə]
to hunt (vi, vt)	at jage	[at 'jæ:jə]
to hibernate (vi)	at ligge i dvale	[at 'legə i 'dvæ:lə]
to become extinct	at uddø	[at 'uð̞ˌdø:]

223. Animals. Habitats

habitat	miljø (n)	[mil'jø]
migration	migration (c)	[migʁɑ'ɕon]
mountain	bjerg (c)	['bjaɒ]
reef	rev (n)	['ʁɛu]
cliff	klippe (c)	['klebə]
forest	skov (c)	['skɒw]
jungle	jungle (c)	['djɔŋlə]
savanna	savanne (c)	[sa'vannə]
tundra	tundra (c)	['tɔndʁɑ]
steppe	steppe (c)	['sdɛbə]
desert	ørken (c)	['œɒkən]
oasis	oase (c)	[o'æ:sə]
sea	hav (n)	[hɑu]

| lake | **sø** (c) | [sø:] |
| ocean | **ocean** (c) | [ose'æ:n] |

wetland	**sump** (c)	[sɔmb]
freshwater	**ferskvands-**	['faɒskˌvans]
pond	**dam** (c)	[dɑm]
river	**flod** (c)	[floð]

den	**hule** (c)	['hu:lə]
nest	**rede** (c)	['ʁɛ:ðə]
hollow (in tree)	**hul** (n)	[hɔl]
burrow (animal hole)	**hul** (n)	[hɔl]
anthill	**myretue** (c)	['my:ɒtu:ə]

224. Animal care

| zoo | **zoologisk have** (c) | [soo'lo:isg 'hæ:və] |
| nature preserve | **naturpark** (c) | [na'tuɒˌpɑ:k] |

breeder, breed club	**opdrætter** (c)	['ɒbˌdʁadʌ]
open-air cage	**voliere** (c)	[vʌl'jɛ:ʌ]
cage	**bur** (n)	['buɒ]
doghouse	**hundehus** (n)	['hunəˌhu:s]

dovecot	**dueslag** (n)	['duəslæ:]
aquarium	**akvarium** (n)	[a'kva:iɒm]
dolphinarium	**delfinarium** (n)	[dɛlfi'na:iɒm]

to breed (animals)	**at opdrætte**	[at 'ɒbdʁadə]
brood, litter	**afkom** (n)	['aukɒm]
to tame (vt)	**at tæmme**	[at 'tɛmə]
feed (for animal)	**foder** (n)	['foðʌ]
to feed (vt)	**at fodre**	[at 'foðʁʌ]
to train (animals)	**at dressere**	[at dʁɛ'seɒ]

pet store	**dyrehandel** (c)	['dy:ɒˌhanəl]
muzzle (for dog)	**mundkurv** (c)	['mɔnkuɒu]
collar (for animal)	**hundehalsbånd** (n)	['hunəˌhalsbɒn]
name (of animal)	**navn** (n)	['naun]
pedigree (of dog)	**stamtavle** (c)	['sdɑmˌtɑwlə]

225. Animals. Miscellaneous

pack (wolves)	**ulveflok** (c)	['ulvəˌflɒk]
flock (birds)	**fugleflok** (c)	['fu:ləflɒg]
shoal (fish)	**stime** (c)	['sdi:mə]
herd	**hjord** (c)	['joɒ]
male (noun)	**handyr** (n)	['handyɒ]

female (noun)	**hundyr** (n)	['hunyɒ]
hungry	**sulten**	['suldən]
wild	**vild**	[vil]
dangerous	**farlig**	['fɑ:li]

226. Horses

| horse | **hest** (c) | [hɛsd] |
| breed (race) | **race** (c) | ['ʁɑ:sə] |

| foal (of horse) | **føl** (n) | [føl] |
| mare | **hoppe** (c) | ['hɒbə] |

mustang	**mustang** (c)	['musdɑŋ]
pony (small horse)	**pony** (c)	['pʌni]
draft horse	**bryggerhest** (c)	['bʁygɒˌhɛsd]

| mane | **manke** (c) | ['mɑŋkə] |
| tail | **hale** (c) | ['hæ:lə] |

hoof	**hov** (c)	['hɒw]
horseshoe	**hestesko** (c)	['hɛsdəˌsko:]
to shoe (vt)	**at beslå**	[at be'slɔ:]
blacksmith	**smed** (c)	[smeð]

saddle	**sadel** (c)	['saðəl]
stirrup	**stigbøjle** (c)	['sdiˌbʌjlə]
bridle	**tøjle** (c)	['tɒjlə]
reins	**tømmen** (pl)	['tœmən]
whip (for riding)	**pisk** (c)	[pisk]

rider	**rytter** (c)	['ʁydʌ]
to break in (horse)	**at afrette (en hest)**	[at 'afˌʁadə en hɛsd]
to saddle (vt)	**at sadle**	[at 'saðlə]
to mount (a horse)	**at stige til hest**	[at 'sdi:ə tel hɛsd]

gallop	**galop** (c)	[ga'lɒb]
to gallop (vi)	**at galopere**	[at galo'pe:ɒ]
trot (noun)	**trav** (n)	['tʁɑw]
at a trot	**i trav**	[i 'tʁɑu]

| racehorse | **travhest** (c) | ['tʁɑwˌhɛsd] |
| races | **travløb** (n) | ['tʁɑwˌlø:b] |

stable	**hestestald** (c)	['hɛsdəˌsdal]
to feed (vt)	**at fodre**	[at 'foðʁʌ]
hay	**hø** (n)	[hø:]
to water (animals)	**at vande**	[at 'vanə]
to wash (horse)	**at børste**	[at 'bœɒsdə]
to hobble (vt)	**at binde benene sammen**	[at 'benə 'be:nənə 'samən]

horse-drawn wagon	**hestevogn** (c)	['hɛsdə̩vɒwn]
to graze (vi)	**at græsse**	[at 'gʁasə]
to neigh (vi)	**at vrinske**	[at 'vʁɛnskə]
to kick (horse)	**at sparke**	[at 'sbɑːkə]

Flora

227. Trees

tree	**træ** (n)	[tʁɛ:]
deciduous	**løv-**	['løu]
coniferous	**nåle-**	['nɔ:lə]
evergreen	**stedsegrøn**	['sdɛðsə,gʁœn]
apple tree	**æbletræ** (n)	['ɛ:blətʁɛ:]
pear tree	**pæretræ** (n)	['pɛ:ɒ,tʁɛ:]
cherry tree (sweet)	**moreltræ** (n)	[mo:'ɒltʁɛ:]
cherry tree (sour)	**kirsebærtræ** (n)	['kiɒsəbæɒ,tʁɛ:]
plum tree	**blommetræ** (n)	['blɒmə,tʁɛ:]
birch	**birketræ** (n)	['biɒkətʁɛ:]
oak	**eg** (c)	[e:]
linden tree	**lind** (c)	[len]
aspen	**asp** (c)	[asb]
maple	**ahorn** (c)	['ahoɒn]
fir tree	**grantræ** (n)	['gʁɑn,tʁɛ:]
pine	**fyrretræ** (n)	['fœɒtʁɛ:]
larch	**lærk** (c)	['læɒk]
silver fir	**ædelgran** (c)	['ɛ:ðəlgʁɑn]
cedar	**ceder** (n)	['se:ðʌ]
poplar	**poppel** (c)	['pɒbəl]
rowan	**rønnebærtræ** (n)	['ʁœnəbæɒ,tʁɛ:]
willow	**pil** (c)	[pi:l]
alder	**elletræ** (n)	['ɛlətʁɛ:]
beech	**bøg** (c)	[bø:]
elm	**elm** (c)	[ɛlm]
ash (tree)	**asketræ** (n)	['askə,tʁɛ:]
chestnut	**kastanietræ** (n)	[ka'sdanjə,tʁɛ:]
magnolia	**magnolie** (c)	[mɑun'o:ljə]
palm tree	**palme** (c)	['palmə]
cypress	**cypres** (c)	[sy'pʁas]
baobab	**baobabtræ** (n)	[bao'bab ,tʁɛ]
eucalyptus	**eukalyptus** (c)	[œwka'lybtus]
redwood	**rødtræ** (n)	['ʁœð,tʁɛ]

228. Shrubs

| bush | busk (c) | [busk] |
| shrub | buskads (n) | [bu'skæ:s] |

| grapevine | vin (c) | [vi:n] |
| vineyard | vingård (c) | ['vi:ngɒ:] |

raspberry bush	hindbær (n)	['henbaɒ]
blackcurrant bush	solbær (n)	['so:l,bæɒ]
redcurrant bush	ribs (n)	[ʁɛbs]
gooseberry bush	stikkelsbær (n)	['sdekəls,bæɒ]

acacia	akacie (c)	[a'kæ:ɕə]
barberry	berberis (c)	['bæɒbʌʁis]
jasmine	jasmin (c)	[ɕas'min]

juniper	enebær (c)	['e:nəbaɒ]
rosebush	rosenbusk (c)	['ʁo:sən,busk]
dog rose	vild rosenbusk (c)	[vil 'ʁo:sən,busk]

229. Mushrooms

mushroom	svamp (c)	[svɑmb]
edible mushroom	spiselig svamp (c)	['sbi:səli 'svɑmb]
toadstool	giftig svamp (c)	['gifdi svɑmb]
cap (of mushroom)	hat (c)	[had]
foot (of mushroom)	stok (c)	[sdɒk]

boletus	karljohan (n)	[,kɑ:ljo'han]
orange-cap boletus	skælstokket rørhat (c)	['skɛl,sdɒkəð 'ʁœɒhad]
brown-cap boletus	galderørhat (c)	['galəʁœɒhad]
chanterelle	kantarel (c)	[kanta'ʁal]
russula	skørhat (c)	['skøɒ,had]

morel	morkel (c)	['mɒkəl]
fly agaric	fluesvamp (c)	['flu:ə,svɑmb]
death cap	giftsvamp (c)	['gifd,svɑmb]

230. Fruits. Berries

| fruit | frugt (c) | [fʁɔgd] |
| fruits | frugter (pl) | ['fʁɔgdʌ] |

apple	æble (n)	['ɛ:blə]
pear	pære (c)	['pɛ:ɒ]
plum	blomme (c)	['blɒmə]

strawberry	jordbær (n)	['joɒˌbaɒ]
cherry (sour cherry)	kirsebær (n)	['kiɒsəˌbæɒ]
cherry (sweet cherry)	morel (c)	[mo:'ɒl]
grapes	vindrue (c)	['vi:nˌdʁu:ə]

raspberry	hindbær (n)	['henbaɒ]
blackcurrant	solbær (n)	['so:lˌbæɒ]
redcurrant	ribs (n)	[ʁɛbs]
gooseberry	stikkelsbær (n)	['sdekəlsˌbæɒ]
cranberry	tranebær (n)	['tʁɑːnəbaɒ]

orange	appelsin (c)	[ɑpəl'si:n]
mandarin	mandarin (c)	[mandɑ'ʁi:n]
pineapple	ananas (c)	['ananas]
banana	banan (c)	[ba'næ:n]
date	daddel (c)	['daðəl]

lemon	citron (c)	[si'tʁo:n]
apricot	abrikos (c)	[ɑbʁi'ko:s]
peach	fersken (c)	['faɒskən]
kiwi	kiwi (c)	['ki:vi]
grapefruit	grapefrugt (c)	['gʁɑpəˌfʁɔgd]

berry	bær (n)	[baɒ]
berries	bær (pl)	[baɒ]
cowberry	tyttebær (n)	['tydəˌbæɒ]
field strawberry	skovjordbær (n)	['skɒwjoɒˌbæɒ]
bilberry	blåbær (n)	['blɒbaɒ]

231. Flowers. Plants

| flower | blomst (c) | [blɒmsd] |
| bouquet (of flowers) | buket (c) | [bu'kɛd] |

rose (flower)	rose (c)	['ʁo:sə]
tulip	tulipan (c)	[tuli'pæ:n]
carnation	nellike (c)	['nelikə]
gladiolus	gladiolus (c)	[glɑ:di'olus]

cornflower	kornblomst (c)	['koɒnˌblɒmsd]
bluebell	klokkeblomst (c)	['klɒkəˌblɒmsd]
dandelion	mælkebøtte (c)	['mɛlkəˌbødə]
camomile	kamille (c)	[ka'milə]

aloe	aloe (c)	[a'lo:ə]
cactus	kaktus (c)	['kɑktus]
rubber plant	gummitræ (n)	['gomiˌtʁɛ:]

| lily | lilje (c) | ['liljə] |
| geranium | geranie (c) | [ge'ʁani] |

hyacinth	**hyacint** (c)	[hya'send]
mimosa	**mimose** (c)	[mi'mo:sə]
narcissus	**narcis** (c)	[nɑ'si:s]
nasturtium	**nasturtie** (c)	[na'sdupti:ə]
orchid	**orkide** (c)	[ɒki'de]
peony	**pæon** (c)	[pɛ'on]
violet	**viol** (c)	[vi'o:l]
pansy	**stedmoderblomster**	['sdɛð,moɒ ,blɒmsdɒ]
forget-me-not	**forglemmigej** (c)	[fʌ'glɛmmɑ,ɑj]
daisy	**tusindfryd** (c)	['tu:sən,fʁyð]
poppy	**valmue** (c)	['valmu:ə]
hemp	**hamp** (c)	[hɑmb]
mint	**pebermynte** (c)	['pewʌ,møndə]
lily of the valley	**liljekonval** (c)	['liljə kɔn'val]
snowdrop	**vintergæk** (c)	['vendɒ,gɛg]
nettle	**brændenælde** (c)	['bʁɑnə,nɛlə]
sorrel	**syre** (c)	['sy:ɒ]
water lily	**åkande** (c)	['ɔ:kanə]
fern	**bregne** (c)	['bʁɑjnə]
lichen	**lav** (c)	['læ:u]
greenhouse (tropical ~)	**drivhus** (n)	['dʁi:u,hu:s]
lawn	**græsplæne** (c)	['gʁas,plɛ:nə]
flowerbed	**blomsterbed** (n)	['blɒmsdɒ,beð]
plant	**plante** (c)	['plandə]
grass	**græs** (n)	[gʁas]
blade (of grass)	**græsstrå** (n)	['gʁas,dʁɔ:]
leaf	**blad** (n)	[blað]
petal (of flower)	**blomsterblad** (n)	['blɒmsdɒ,blað]
stem (of plant)	**stilk** (c)	[sdelk]
tuber	**rodknold** (c)	['ʁoðknɒl]
young plant (shoot)	**spire** (c)	['sbi:ʌ]
thorn	**torn** (c)	[toɒn]
to blossom (vi)	**at blomstre**	[at 'blɒmsdʁɒ]
to fade, to wither	**at visne**	[at 'vesnə]
smell (odor)	**duft** (c)	[dɒfd]
to cut (flowers)	**at skære**	[at 'skɛ:ɒ]
to pick (a flower)	**at plukke**	[at 'plɔkə]

232. Cereals, grains

grain	**korn** (n)	['koɒn]
cereals	**kornsorter** (c pl)	['koɒn,sɒ:dʌ]

ear (of grain)	aks (n)	[ɑks]
wheat	hvede (c)	[ˈveːðə]
rye	rug (c)	[ʁuː]
oats	havre (c)	[ˈhɑwʁʌ]
millet	hirse (c)	[ˈhiɒsə]
barley	byg (c)	[byg]

corn	majs (c)	[mɑjs]
rice	ris (c)	[ʁiːs]
buckwheat	boghvede	[ˈbouveðə]

pea	ærter (pl)	[ˈɑɒdʌ]
kidney beans	bønne (c)	[ˈbœnə]
soy beans	soja	[ˈsʌja]
lentil	linse (c)	[ˈlensə]
beans	bønner (c pl)	[ˈbœnʌ]

233. Vegetables. Greens

| vegetables | grønsager (pl) | [ˈgʁœnˌsæːʌ] |
| greens | grønt (n) | [gʁœnd] |

tomato	tomat (c)	[toˈmæːd]
cucumber	agurk (c)	[aˈguɒg]
carrot	gulerod (c)	[ˈguləˌʁoð]
potato	kartoffel (c)	[kɑˈtɒfəl]
onion	løg (n)	[lɒj]
garlic	hvidløg (n)	[ˈviðˌlɒj]

cabbage	kål (c)	[kɔːl]
cauliflower	blomkål (c)	[ˈblʌmˌkɔl]
Brussels sprouts	rosenkål (c)	[ˈʁoːsənˌkɔːl]
broccoli	broccoli (c)	[ˈbʁɒkoli]

beetroot	rødbede (c)	[ˈʁœðˌbeːðə]
eggplant	aubergine (c)	[obæɒˈɕiːnə]
zucchini	squash (c)	[ˈsgwʌɕ]
pumpkin	græskar (n)	[ˈgʁasgɑ]
turnip	roe (c)	[ˈʁoːə]

parsley	persille (c)	[paɒˈsilə]
dill	dild (c)	[dil]
lettuce	salat (c)	[saˈlæːd]
celery	selleri (c)	[sɛləˈʁiː]
asparagus	asparges (c)	[aˈsbɑːɑəs]
spinach	spinat (c)	[sbiˈnæːd]

pea	ærter (pl)	[ˈɑɒdʌ]
beans	bønner (c pl)	[ˈbœnʌ]
corn (maize)	majs (c)	[mɑjs]

kidney beans	**bønne** (c)	['bœnə]
bell pepper	**peber** (n)	['pewʌ]
radish	**radiser** (c)	[ʁɑ'disə]
artichoke	**artiskok** (c)	[ɑti'skɒk]

REGIONAL GEOGRAPHY

Countries. Nationalities

234. Western Europe

Europe	**Europa**	[œw'ʁoːpa]
European Union	**Den Europæiske Union**	[dɛn œuʁo'pɛːiskə uni'oːn]
European (noun)	**europæer** (c)	[œwʁo'pɛːʌ]
European (adj)	**europæisk**	[œwʁo'pɛːisk]
Austria	**Østrig**	['øsdʁi]
Austrian (man)	**østriger** (c)	['ø‚sdʁiʌ]
Austrian (woman)	**østriger** (c)	['ø‚sdʁiʌ]
Austrian (adj)	**østrigsk**	['øsdʁisg]
Great Britain	**Storbritannien**	['sdɔːbʁi‚taniən]
England	**England**	['ɛŋlan]
British (man)	**englænder** (c)	['ɛŋ‚lɛnʌ]
British (woman)	**englænder** (c)	['ɛŋ‚lɛnʌ]
English, British (adj)	**engelsk**	['ɛŋəlsg]
Belgium	**Belgien**	['bɛlgjən]
Belgian (man)	**belgier** (c)	['bɛlgjʌ]
Belgian (woman)	**belgier** (c)	['bɛlgjʌ]
Belgian (adj)	**belgisk**	['bɛlgisg]
Germany	**Tyskland**	['tysklan]
German (man)	**tysker** (c)	['tyskʌ]
German (woman)	**tysker** (c)	['tyskʌ]
German (adj)	**tysk**	['tysk]
Netherlands	**Nederlandene**	['neːðʌ‚lɛnnə]
Holland	**Holland**	['hɔlan]
Dutchman	**hollænder** (c)	['hɔ‚lɛnʌ]
Dutchwoman	**hollænder** (c)	['hɔ‚lɛnʌ]
Dutch (adj)	**hollandsk**	['hɔ‚lansk]
Greece	**Grækenland**	['gʁɛːgənlan]
Greek (man)	**græker** (c)	['gʁɛːgʌ]
Greek (woman)	**græker** (c)	['gʁɛːgʌ]
Greek (adj)	**græsk**	[gʁasg]
Denmark	**Danmark**	['dænmɑk]
Dane (man)	**dansker** (c)	['dænskʌ]

Dane (woman)	**dansker** (c)	['dænskʌ]
Danish (adj)	**dansk**	[dænsk]
Ireland	**Irland**	['iɒlan]
Irishman	**irlænder** (c)	['iɒˌlɛnʌ]
Irishwoman	**irlænder** (c)	['iɒˌlɛnʌ]
Irish (adj)	**irsk**	['iɒsk]
Iceland	**Island**	['islan]
Icelander (man)	**islænding** (c)	[is'lɛneŋ]
Icelander (woman)	**islænding** (c)	[is'lɛneŋ]
Icelandic (adj)	**islandsk**	['islɛnsk]
Spain	**Spanien**	['sbæːnjən]
Spaniard (man)	**spanier** (c)	['sbænjʌ]
Spaniard (woman)	**spanier** (c)	['sbænjʌ]
Spanish (adj)	**spansk**	['sbænsk]
Italy	**Italien**	[i'taljən]
Italian (man)	**italiener** (c)	[ital'jɛnʌ]
Italian (woman)	**italiener** (c)	[ital'jɛnʌ]
Italian (adj)	**italiensk**	[ital'jɛnsk]
Cyprus	**Cypern**	['kybɒn]
Cypriot (man)	**cypriot** (c)	[kypʁi'o:d]
Cypriot (woman)	**cypriot** (c)	[kypʁi'o:d]
Cypriot (adj)	**cypriotisk**	[kypʁi'o:tisk]
Malta	**Malta**	['malta]
Maltese (man)	**malteser** (c)	[mal'te:sʌ]
Maltese (woman)	**malteser** (c)	[mal'te:sʌ]
Maltese (adj)	**maltesisk**	[mal'təsisk]
Norway	**Norge**	['nɒ:uə]
Norwegian (man)	**nordmand** (c)	['noɒman]
Norwegian (woman)	**nordmand** (c)	['noɒman]
Norwegian (adj)	**norsk**	[nɒ:sk]
Portugal	**Portugal**	['pɒ:tugəl]
Portuguese (man)	**portugiser** (c)	[pɒtu'gisʌ]
Portuguese (woman)	**portugiser** (c)	[pɒtu'gisʌ]
Portuguese (adj)	**portugisisk**	[pɒtu'gisisk]
Finland	**Finland**	[fenlan]
Finn (man)	**finne** (c)	['fenə]
Finn (woman)	**finne** (c)	['fenə]
Finnish (adj)	**finsk**	[fensk]
France	**Frankrig**	['fʁaŋkʁi]
Frenchman	**franskmand** (c)	['fʁansk,man]
Frenchwoman	**franskmand** (c)	['fʁansk,man]
French (adj)	**fransk**	[fʁansk]

Sweden	**Sverige**	[ˈsvɛɒi]
Swede (man)	**svensker** (c)	[ˈsvɛnskʌ]
Swede (woman)	**svensker** (c)	[ˈsvɛnskʌ]
Swedish (adj)	**svensk**	[svɛnsk]

Switzerland	**Schweiz**	[ˈsvɑjds]
Swiss (man)	**schweizer** (c)	[ˈsvɑjdsʌ]
Swiss (woman)	**schweizer** (c)	[ˈsvɑjdsʌ]
Swiss (adj)	**schweizisk**	[ˈsvɑjdsisk]

Scotland	**Skotland**	[ˈskɒdlan]
Scottish (man)	**skotte** (c)	[ˈskʌdə]
Scottish (woman)	**skotte** (c)	[ˈskʌdə]
Scottish (adj)	**skotsk**	[ˈskʌdsk]

Vatican	**Vatikanstaten**	[vateˈkæːnˌsdæːdən]
Liechtenstein	**Liechtenstein**	[liːˈɛːgdənˌsdɑjn]
Luxembourg	**Luxembourg**	[ˈlygsɑŋnbɒː]
Monaco	**Monaco**	[moˈnɑko]

235. Central and Eastern Europe

Albania	**Albanien**	[alˈbæːnjən]
Albanian (man)	**albaner** (c)	[alˈbæːnʌ]
Albanian (woman)	**albaner** (c)	[alˈbæːnʌ]
Albanian (adj)	**albansk**	[alˈbæːnsk]

Bulgaria	**Bulgarien**	[bulˈgɑːiən]
Bulgarian (man)	**bulgarer** (c)	[bulˈgɑːɑ]
Bulgarian (woman)	**bulgarer** (c)	[bulˈgɑːɑ]
Bulgarian (adj)	**bulgarsk**	[bulˈgɑːsg]

Hungary	**Ungarn**	[ˈɔŋgɑːn]
Hungarian (man)	**ungarer** (c)	[ˈɔŋˌgɑːɑ]
Hungarian (woman)	**ungarer** (c)	[ˈɔŋˌgɑːɑ]
Hungarian (adj)	**ungarsk**	[ˈɔŋgɑːsg]

Latvia	**Letland**	[ˈlɛdlan]
Latvian (man)	**lette** (c)	[ˈlɛdə]
Latvian (woman)	**lette** (c)	[ˈlɛdə]
Latvian (adj)	**lettisk**	[ˈlɛdtisk]

Lithuania	**Litauen**	[ˈliˌtɑuən]
Lithuanian (man)	**litauer** (c)	[ˈliˌtɑwʌ]
Lithuanian (woman)	**litauer** (c)	[ˈliˌtɑwʌ]
Lithuanian (adj)	**litauisk**	[ˈliˌtɑwisk]

Poland	**Polen**	[ˈpoːlæn]
Pole (man)	**polak** (c)	[poˈlɑk]
Pole (woman)	**polak** (c)	[poˈlɑk]

Polish (adj)	polsk	[po:lsk]
Romania	Rumænien	[ʁuˈmɛ:njən]
Romanian (man)	rumæner (c)	[ʁuˈmɛnʌ]
Romanian (woman)	rumæner (c)	[ʁuˈmɛnʌ]
Romanian (adj)	rumænsk	[ʁuˈmɛ:nsk]

Serbia	Serbien	[ˈsæɒbiən]
Serbian (man)	serber (c)	[ˈsæɒbʌ]
Serbian (woman)	serber (c)	[ˈsæɒbʌ]
Serbian (adj)	serbisk	[ˈsæɒbisk]

Slovakia	Slovakiet	[slovaˈki:əð]
Slovak (man)	slovak (c)	[sloˈvɑk]
Slovak (woman)	slovak (c)	[sloˈvɑk]
Slovak (adj)	slovakisk	[sloˈvɑkisk]

Croatia	Kroatien	[kʁoˈæ:tiən]
Croatian (man)	kroat (c)	[kʁoˈæ:d]
Croatian (woman)	kroat (c)	[kʁoˈæ:d]
Croatian (adj)	kroatisk	[kʁoˈæ:tisk]

The Czech Republic	Tjekkiet	[tjɛˈkiəð]
Czech (man)	tjekke (c)	[ˈtjɛkə]
Czech (woman)	tjekke (c)	[ˈtjɛkə]
Czech (adj)	tjekkisk	[ˈtjɛkisk]

Estonia	Estland	[ˈɛsdlan]
Estonian (man)	ester (c)	[ˈɛsdʌ]
Estonian (woman)	ester (c)	[ˈɛsdʌ]
Estonian (adj)	estisk	[ˈɛsdisk]

Bosnia-Herzegovina	Bosnien-Herzegovina	[ˈbɒsniən hɒsəgɒuˈvi:na]
Macedonia	Makedonien	[mɑkeˈdo:njən]
Slovenia	Slovenien	[sloˈve:njən]
Montenegro	Montenegro	[ˈmɒntəˌnɛgʁə]

236. Former USSR countries

Azerbaijan	Aserbajdsjan	[asæɒbɑjˈdjæn]
Azerbaijani (man)	aserbajdsjaner (c)	[asæɒbɑjˈdjænʌ]
Azerbaijani (woman)	aserbajdsjaner (c)	[asæɒbɑjˈdjænʌ]
Azerbaijani (adj)	aserbajdsjansk	[asæɒbɑjˈdjænsk]

Armenia	Armenien	[ɑːˈme:njən]
Armenian (man)	armenier (c)	[ɑːˈme:niʌ]
Armenian (woman)	armenier (c)	[ɑːˈme:niʌ]
Armenian (adj)	armensk	[ɑːˈmənsk]

| Belarus | Hviderusland | [ˈvi:ðəˌʁuslan] |
| Belarusian (man) | hviderusser (c) | [ˈvi:ðəˌʁusʌ] |

Belarusian (woman)	hviderusser (c)	['viːðəˌʁusʌ]
Belarusian (adj)	hviderussisk	['viːðəˌʁusisk]

Georgia	Georgien	[geɒˈgiən]
Georgian (man)	georgier (c)	[geɒˈgiʌ]
Georgian (woman)	georgier (c)	[geɒˈgiʌ]
Georgian (adj)	georgisk	['geɒgisg]
Kazakhstan	Kasakhstan	[kasɑkˈsdan]
Kazakh (man)	kasakher (c)	[kaˈsɑkʌ]
Kazakh (woman)	kasakher (c)	[kaˈsɑkʌ]
Kazakh (adj)	kasakhisk	[kaˈsɑkisk]

Kirghizia	Kirgisistan	[kiɒˈgisisdan]
Kirghiz (man)	kirgiser (c)	[kiɒˈgisʌ]
Kirghiz (woman)	kirgiser (c)	[kiɒˈgisʌ]
Kirghiz (adj)	kirgisisk	[kiɒˈgisisk]

Moldavia	Moldova	[mɒlˈdɒuva]
Moldavian (man)	moldover (c)	[mʌlˈdovʌ]
Moldavian (woman)	moldover (c)	[mʌlˈdovʌ]
Moldavian (adj)	moldovisk	[mʌlˈdovisk]
Russia	Rusland	['ʁuslan]
Russian (man)	russer (c)	['ʁusʌ]
Russian (woman)	russer (c)	['ʁusʌ]
Russian (adj)	russisk	['ʁusisk]

Tajikistan	Tadsjikistan	[taˈdɕikiːsdan]
Tajik (man)	tadsjiker (c)	[taˈdɕikʌ]
Tajik (woman)	tadsjiker (c)	[taˈdɕikʌ]
Tajik (adj)	tadsjikisk	[taˈdɕikisk]

Turkmenistan	Turkmenistan	[tuɒkˈmeːnisdan]
Turkmen (man)	turkmener (c)	[tuɒkˈmənʌ]
Turkmen (woman)	turkmener (c)	[tuɒkˈmənʌ]
Turkmenian (adj)	turkmensk	[tuɒkˈmənsk]

Uzbekistan	Usbekistan	[usˈbekiːsdan]
Uzbek (man)	usbeker (c)	[usˈbekʌ]
Uzbek (woman)	usbeker (c)	[usˈbekʌ]
Uzbek (adj)	usbekisk	[usˈbekisk]

Ukraine	Ukraine	[ukʁɑˈiːnə]
Ukrainian (man)	ukrainer (c)	[ukʁɑˈinʌ]
Ukrainian (woman)	ukrainer (c)	[ukʁɑˈinʌ]
Ukrainian (adj)	ukrainsk	[ukʁɑˈiːnsk]

237. Asia

Asia	Asien	['æːɕən]
Asian	asiatisk	[asiˈæːtisk]

Vietnam	**Vietnam**	['vjɛdnɑm]
Vietnamese (man)	**vietnameser** (c)	[vjɛdnɑ'mesʌ]
Vietnamese (woman)	**vietnameser** (c)	[vjɛdnɑ'mesʌ]
Vietnamese (adj)	**vietnamesisk**	[vjɛdnɑ'mesisk]
India	**Indien**	['endjən]
Indian (man)	**inder** (c)	['endʌ]
Indian (woman)	**inder** (c)	['endʌ]
Indian (adj)	**indisk**	['endisk]
Israel	**Israel**	['isʁɑ:l]
Israeli (man)	**israeler** (c)	[isʁɑ'e:lʌ]
Israeli (woman)	**israeler** (c)	[isʁɑ'e:lʌ]
Israeli (adj)	**israelsk**	[isʁɑ'e:lsk]
Jew (noun)	**jøde** (c)	['jø:ðə]
Jewess (noun)	**jøde** (c)	['jø:ðə]
Jewish (adj)	**jødisk**	['jø:ðisk]
China	**Kina**	['ki:na]
Chinese (man)	**kineser** (c)	[ki'ne:sʌ]
Chinese (woman)	**kineser** (c)	[ki'ne:sʌ]
Chinese (adj)	**kinesisk**	[ki'ne:sisk]
Korean (man)	**koreaner** (c)	[koʁe'æ:nʌ]
Korean (woman)	**koreaner** (c)	[koʁe'æ:nʌ]
Korean (adj)	**koreansk**	[koʁe'æ:nsk]
Lebanon	**Libanon**	['li:banɒn]
Lebanese (man)	**libaneser** (c)	[li:ba'ne:sʌ]
Lebanese (woman)	**libaneser** (c)	[li:ba'ne:sʌ]
Lebanese (adj)	**libanesisk**	[li:ba'ne:sisk]
Mongolia	**Mongoliet**	[mɒŋgo:'lieð]
Mongolian (man)	**mongol** (c)	[mɒŋ'go:l]
Mongolian (woman)	**mongol** (c)	[mɒŋ'go:l]
Mongolian (adj)	**mongolsk**	[mɒŋ'go:lsg]
Malaysia	**Malaysia**	[ma'lɑjçiʌ]
Malaysian (man)	**malaj** (c)	[ma'lɑj]
Malaysian (woman)	**malaj** (c)	[ma'lɑj]
Malaysian (adj)	**malajisk**	[ma'lɑjisk]
Pakistan	**Pakistan**	['pɑkisdan]
Pakistani (man)	**pakistaner** (c)	[pɑki'sdænʌ]
Pakistani (woman)	**pakistaner** (c)	[pɑki'sdænʌ]
Pakistani (adj)	**pakistansk**	[pɑki'sdænsk]
Saudi Arabia	**Saudi-Arabien**	['saudi ɑ'ʁɑ:bjən]
Arab (man)	**araber** (c)	[ɑ'ʁɑ:bʌ]
Arab (woman)	**araber** (c)	[ɑ'ʁɑ:bʌ]
Arabian (adj)	**arabisk**	[ɑ'ʁɑ:bisk]

Thailand	**Thailand**	['tɑjlɛn]
Thai (man)	**thailænder** (c)	['tɑj‚lɛnʌ]
Thai (woman)	**thailænder** (c)	['tɑj‚lɛnʌ]
Thai (adj)	**thailandsk**	['tɑj‚lansk]

Taiwan	**Taiwan**	['tɑj‚væ:n]
Taiwanese (man)	**taiwaner** (c)	[tɑj'vænʌ]
Taiwanese (woman)	**taiwaner** (c)	[tɑj'vænʌ]
Taiwanese (adj)	**taiwansk**	[tɑj'vænsk]

Turkey	**Tyrkiet**	[tyɒ'ki:əð]
Turk (man)	**tyrker** (c)	['tyɒkʌ]
Turk (woman)	**tyrker** (c)	['tyɒkʌ]
Turkish (adj)	**tyrkisk**	['tyɒkisk]

Japan	**Japan**	['japan]
Japanese (man)	**japaner** (c)	[ja'pæ:nʌ]
Japanese (woman)	**japaner** (c)	[ja'pæ:nʌ]
Japanese (adj)	**japansk**	[ja'pæ:nsk]

Afghanistan	**Afghanistan**	[ɑu'gɑnisdan]
Bangladesh	**Bangladesh**	[bɑŋla'dɛɕ]
Indonesia	**Indonesien**	[endo'ne:ɕən]
Jordan	**Jordan**	['joɒdan]

Iraq	**Irak**	['iʁɑk]
Iran	**Iran**	[i'ʁɑ:n]
Cambodia	**Cambodja**	[kæ:m'boðjɑa]
Kuwait	**Kuwait**	[ku'vɑjd]

Laos	**Laos**	['læ:ɒs]
Myanmar	**Myanmar**	[my'anmɑ]
Nepal	**Nepal**	['nepal]
United Arab Emirates	**Forenede Arabiske Emirater**	[fɒ'e:nəðə ɑ'ʁɑ:biskə emi'ʁɑ:dɒ]

Syria	**Syrien**	['syʁiən]
Palestine	**Det Palæstinensiske selvstyre**	[de palɛ:sdi:'nənsiskə 'sɛlsdy:ɒ]
South Korea	**Sydkorea**	['syð ko'ʁɛ:a]
North Korea	**Nordkorea**	['noɒ koɒ'ɛ:a]

238. North America

United States of America	**De Forenede Stater**	[di fɒ'e:nəðə 'sdæ:dɒ]
American (man)	**amerikaner** (c)	[ɑmeɒi'kæ:nʌ]
American (woman)	**amerikaner** (c)	[ɑmeɒi'kæ:nʌ]
American (adj)	**amerikansk**	[ɑmeɒi'kæ:nsk]
Canada	**Canada**	['kanada]
Canadian (man)	**canadier** (c)	[ka'næ:di:ʌ]

Canadian (woman)	**canadier** (c)	[ka'næ:di:ʌ]
Canadian (adj)	**canadisk**	[ka'næ:disk]
Mexico	**Mexiko**	['mɛksiko]
Mexican (man)	**mexikaner** (c)	[mɛksi'kænʌ]
Mexican (woman)	**mexikaner** (c)	[mɛksi'kænʌ]
Mexican (adj)	**mexikansk**	[mɛksi'kænsk]

239. Central and South America

Argentina	**Argentina**	[agɛn'ti:na]
Argentinian (man)	**argentiner** (c)	[agɛn'ti:nʌ]
Argentinian (woman)	**argentiner** (c)	[agɛn'ti:nʌ]
Argentinian (adj)	**argentinsk**	[agɛn'tensk]
Brazil	**Brasilien**	[bʁa'siljən]
Brazilian (man)	**brasilianer** (c)	[bʁasil'jænʌ]
Brazilian (woman)	**brasilianer** (c)	[bʁasil'jænʌ]
Brazilian (adj)	**brasiliansk**	[bʁasil'jæ:nsk]
Colombia	**Colombia**	[ko'lombia]
Colombian (man)	**colombianer** (c)	[kolombi'anʌ]
Colombian (woman)	**colombianer** (c)	[kolombi'anʌ]
Colombian (adj)	**colombiansk**	[kolombi'æ:nsk]
Cuba	**Cuba**	['ku:ba]
Cuban (man)	**cubaner** (c)	[ku'bæ:nʌ]
Cuban (woman)	**cubaner** (c)	[ku'bæ:nʌ]
Cuban (adj)	**cubansk**	[ku'bæ:nsk]
Chile	**Chile** (n)	['tji:lə]
Chilean (man)	**chilener** (c)	[tji'lenʌ]
Chilean (woman)	**chilener** (c)	[tji'lenʌ]
Chilean (adj)	**chilensk**	[tji'lensk]
Bolivia	**Bolivia**	[bo'livia]
Venezuela	**Venezuela**	[venəsu'e:la]
Paraguay	**Paraguay**	[paagu'aj]
Peru	**Peru**	[pe'ʁu:]
Surinam	**Surinam**	['suʁi:‚nam]
Uruguay	**Uruguay**	[uʁug'waj]
Ecuador	**Ecuador**	[ekua'doɒ]
Bahamas	**Bahamas**	[ba'hamas]
Haiti	**Haiti**	[iti:]
Dominican Republic	**Dominikanske Republik**	[domini'kæ:nskə ʁepu'blik]
Panama	**Panama**	['panamæ:]
Jamaica	**Jamaica**	[ɕa'majka]

240. Africa

Egypt	**Egypten**	[ε'gybdən]
Egyptian (man)	**egypter** (c)	[ε'gybdʌ]
Egyptian (woman)	**egypter** (c)	[ε'gybdʌ]
Egyptian (adj)	**egyptisk**	[ε'gybtisk]
Morocco	**Marokko**	[mɑ'oko]
Moroccan (man)	**marokkaner** (c)	[mɑo'kænʌ]
Moroccan (woman)	**marokkaner** (c)	[mɑo'kænʌ]
Moroccan (adj)	**marokkansk**	[mɑo'kænsk]
Tunisia	**Tunis**	['tu:nis]
Tunisian (man)	**tuneser** (c)	[tu'nesʌ]
Tunisian (woman)	**tuneser** (c)	[tu'nesʌ]
Tunisian (adj)	**tunesisk**	[tu'nesisk]
Ghana	**Ghana**	['ganə]
Zanzibar	**Zanzibar**	['sa:nsibɑ:]
Kenya	**Kenya**	['kɛnja]
Libya	**Libyen**	['li:byən]
Madagascar	**Madagaskar**	[mada'gæsgɑ]
Namibia	**Namibia**	[na'mibia]
Senegal	**Senegal**	['se:nəgæ:l]
Tanzania	**Tanzania**	['tansa,niæ]
South Africa	**Sydafrika**	['syð,afʁika]
African (man)	**afrikaner** (c)	[afʁi'kæ:nʌ]
African (woman)	**afrikaner** (c)	[afʁi'kæ:nʌ]
African (adj)	**afrikansk**	[afʁi'kæ:nsk]

241. Australia. Oceania

Australia	**Australien**	[au'sdʁɑ:ljən]
Australian (man)	**australier** (c)	[au'sdʁɑ:ljjʌ]
Australian (woman)	**australier** (c)	[au'sdʁɑ:ljjʌ]
Australian (adj)	**australsk**	[au'sdʁɑ:lsk]
New Zealand	**New Zealand**	[nju: 'zi:lan]
New Zealander (man)	**newzealænder** (c)	[nju'se:,lɛnʌ]
New Zealander (woman)	**newzealænder** (c)	[nju'se:,lɛnʌ]
New Zealand (attr)	**newzealandsk**	[nju'se:,lansk]
Tasmania	**Tasmanien**	[tas'mani:ən]
French Polynesia	**Fransk Polynesien**	[fʁansk poly'ne:çən]

242. Cities

Amsterdam	**Amsterdam**	['ɑmsdɒˌdɑm]
Ankara	**Ankara**	['ɑnkɑːʁɑ]
Athens	**Athen**	[a'teːn]
Baghdad	**Bagdad**	['bɑudɑð]
Bangkok	**Bangkok**	['bɑŋkɒg]
Barcelona	**Barcelona**	[bɑsə'loːnæː]
Beijing	**Beijing**	['bɛjdʒiŋ]
Beirut	**Beirut**	['bæiːˌʁud]
Berlin	**Berlin**	['bæɒliːn]
Bombay	**Bombay**	['bɒmbəj]
Bonn	**Bonn**	[bɒn]
Bordeaux	**Bordeaux**	['boːdoː]
Bratislava	**Bratislava**	[bʁɑːti'slæːva]
Brussels	**Bruxelles**	['bʁysɛl]
Bucharest	**Bukarest**	['bokɑːɒsd]
Budapest	**Budapest**	['budɑpɛsd]
Cairo	**Cairo**	['kɑjʁo]
Calcutta	**Calcutta**	['kalkɒta]
Chicago	**Chicago**	[ɕi'kɑːgo]
Copenhagen	**København**	['købənˌhɑun]
Dar-es-Salaam	**Dar es-Salaam**	['dɑːɛs saˌlɑm]
Delhi	**Delhi**	[dɛ'li]
Dubai	**Dubai**	[dɒ'bɑj]
Dublin	**Dublin**	[dɒ'blin]
Düsseldorf	**Düsseldorf**	['dysəlˌdɒːf]
Florence	**Firenze**	[fi'ʁansə]
Frankfurt	**Frankfurt**	['fʁɑŋkfuɒd]
Geneva	**Geneve**	[gje'nɛːvə]
Hamburg	**Hamburg**	['hɑmbuɒg]
Hanoi	**Hanoi**	['hanɒj]
Havana	**Havanna**	[hæ'vana]
Helsinki	**Helsingfors**	['hɛlseŋˌfɒːs]
Hiroshima	**Hiroshima**	[hiʁo'ɕiːma]
Hong Kong	**Hongkong**	['hɒŋkɒn]
Istanbul	**Istanbul**	[isdan'bul]
Jerusalem	**Jerusalem**	[je'ʁusalɛm]
Kiev	**Kijev**	['kijəw]
Kuala Lumpur	**Kuala Lumpur**	[ku'ala lɒm'puɒ]
Lisbon	**Lissabon**	['lisabɒn]
London	**London**	['lɒnˌdɒn]
Los Angeles	**Los Angeles**	[lɒs 'æŋʒələləs]
Lyons	**Lyon**	[li'ɒn]

Madrid	**Madrid**	[ma'dʁið]
Marseille	**Marseille**	[mɑː'səi]
Mexico	**Mexico City**	['mɛgsiko 'siti]
Miami	**Miami**	[miː'ami]
Montréal	**Montreal**	['mɒntʁeeːl]
Moscow	**Moskva**	[mɒ'skvə]
Munich	**München**	['mynɕən]
Nairobi	**Nairobi**	[nɑj'ʁoːbi]
Naples	**Neapel**	[nə'apəl]
New York	**New York**	[njuː 'jɒːk]
Nice	**Nice**	[niːs]
Oslo	**Oslo**	['oslu]
Ottawa	**Ottawa**	['ɔːtəwə]
Paris	**Paris**	[pɑ'ʁiːs]
Prague	**Prag**	['pʁɑːu]
Rio de Janeiro	**Rio de Janeiro**	['ʁiːo di ʒa'neːiʁo]
Rome	**Rom**	[ʁɒm]
Saint Petersburg	**Sankt-Petersborg**	[sɑŋd 'piːdɒsbɒː]
Seoul	**Seoul**	[sœ'uːl]
Shanghai	**Shanghai**	['ɕɑŋhɑj]
Singapore	**Singapore**	['seŋapɒː]
Stockholm	**Stockholm**	['sdɒkhɒlm]
Sydney	**Sydney**	['sidni]
Taipei	**Taipei**	['taj‚pæj]
The Hague	**Haag**	[hæː'ɑj]
Tokyo	**Tokyo**	['tokjo]
Toronto	**Toronto**	['toːɒnto]
Venice	**Venedig**	[ve'neːdi]
Vienna	**Wien**	[viːn]
Warsaw	**Warszawa**	[vɑ'ɕæːva]
Washington	**Washington**	['wɒɕentɒn]

243. Politics. Government. Part 1

politics	**politik** (c)	[poli'tik]
political	**politisk**	[po'litisk]
politician	**politiker** (c)	[po'litikʌ]
state (country)	**stat** (c)	[sdæːd]
citizen	**statsborger** (c)	['sdæːds‚bɒːwʌ]
citizenship	**borgerskab** (n)	['bɒːwʌ‚sgæb]
national emblem	**rigsvåben** (n)	['ʁis‚voːbən]
national anthem	**nationalsang** (c)	[naɕo'næːl‚sɑŋ]
government	**regering** (c)	[ʁɛ'geːʁen]

head of state	**statsoverhoved** (n)	['sdæ:ds 'ɒwʌˌho:əð]
parliament	**folketing** (n), **parlament** (n)	['fɒlgəteŋ], [pɑlɑ'mɛnd]
party	**parti** (n)	[pɑ'ti:]
capitalism	**kapitalisme** (c)	[kapita'lismə]
capitalist (adj)	**kapitalistisk**	[kapita'lisdisk]
socialism	**socialisme** (c)	[soɕa'lismə]
socialist (adj)	**socialistisk**	[soɕa'lisdisk]
communism	**kommunisme** (c)	[komu'nismə]
communist (adj)	**kommunistisk**	[komu'nisdisk]
communist (noun)	**kommunist** (c)	[komu'nisd]
democracy	**demokrati** (n)	[demokʁɑ'ti:]
democrat	**demokrat** (c)	[demo'kʁɑ:d]
democratic (adj)	**demokratisk**	[demo'kʁɑ:tisk]
Democratic party	**demokratisk parti** (n)	[demo'kʁɑ:tisk pɑ'ti:]
liberal (noun)	**liberal** (c)	[libə'ʁɑ:l]
liberal (adj)	**liberal**	[libə'ʁɑ:l]
conservative (noun)	**konservativ** (c)	[kʌn'sæɒvatiu]
conservative (adj)	**konservativ**	[kʌn'sæɒvatiu]
republic (noun)	**republik** (c)	[ʁɛpu'blik]
republican (noun)	**republikaner** (c)	[ʁɛpubli'kæ:nʌ]
Republican party	**republikansk parti** (n)	[ʁɛpubli'kæ:nsk pɑ'ti:]
poll, elections	**valg** (n)	[valj]
to elect (vt)	**at vælge**	[at 'vɛljə]
elector, voter	**vælger** (c)	['vɛljʌ]
election campaign	**valgkampagne** (c)	['valj kɑm'panjə]
voting (noun)	**afstemning** (c)	['ɑusdɛmneŋ]
to vote (vi, vt)	**at stemme**	[at 'sdɛmə]
suffrage, right to vote	**stemmeret** (c)	['sdɛməɒð]
candidate	**kandidat** (c)	[kandi'dæ:d]
to be a candidate	**at stile op til valget**	[at 'sdi:lə ɒb tel 'valjəð]
campaign	**kampagne** (c)	[kɑm'panjə]
opposition (attr)	**oppositions-**	[oposi'ɕo:ns]
opposition (noun)	**opposition** (c)	[obosi'ɕon]
visit	**besøg** (n)	[be'søj]
official visit	**officielt besøg** (n)	[ɒfiɕ'ɛld be'søj]
international	**international**	['entʌnaɕoˌnæl]
negotiations	**forhandlinger** (pl)	[fɒ'hanleŋʌ]
to negotiate (vi)	**at forhandle**	[at fʌ'hanlə]

244. Politics. Government. Part 2

society	samfund (n)	['samfɔn]
constitution	forfatning (c)	[fɔ'fadnen]
power (political control)	magt (c)	[magd]
corruption	korruption (c)	[kɔʁub'ɕo:n]

| law (justice) | lov (c) | ['lɒw] |
| legal (legitimate) | lovlig | ['lɒuli] |

| justice (fairness) | retfærdighed (c) | [ʁad'fæɒdiheð] |
| just (fair) | retfærdig | [ʁad'fæɒdi] |

committee	komite (c)	[komi'te:]
bill (draft of law)	lovforslag (n)	['lɒuˌfɔ:slæ:]
budget	budget (n)	[by'ɕɛd]
policy	politik (c)	[poli'tik]
reform	reform (c)	[ʁɛ'fɔ:m]
radical (adj)	radikal	[ʁadi'kæ:l]

power (strength, force)	magt (c)	[magd]
powerful	stærk	['sdæɒk]
supporter (follower)	tilhænger (c)	[tel'hɛŋʌ]
influence	indflydelse (c)	[en'flyðəlsə]

regime (e.g., military ~)	regime (n)	[ʁɛ'ɕi:mə]
conflict	konflikt (c)	[kʌn'flikd]
conspiracy (plot)	sammensværgelse (c)	['samənˌsvæɒwəlsə]
provocation	provokation (c)	[pʁovoka'ɕo:n]

to overthrow (regime etc.)	at styrte	[at 'sdyɒdə]
overthrow (of government)	afsættelse (c)	[au'sɛdəlsə]
revolution	revolution (c)	[ʁɛvolu'ɕo:n]

| coup d'état | kup (n) | [kub] |
| military coup | militærkup (n) | [mili'tɛɒˌku:b] |

crisis	krise (c)	['kʁi:sə]
economic recession	økonomisk nedgang (c)	[økono:'misg 'neðgaŋ]
demonstrator (protester)	demonstrant (c)	[demɒn'sdʁand]
demonstration	demonstration (c)	[demɒnsdʁa'ɕo:n]
martial law	krigstilstand (c)	['kʁis 'delˌsdan]
military base	militærbase (c)	[mili'tɛɒˌbæ:sə]

| stability | stabilitet (c) | [sdabili'te:d] |
| stable | stabil | [sda'bi:l] |

exploitation	udbytning (c)	['uðˌbydnen]
to exploit (workers)	at udbytte	[at 'uðˌbydə]
racism	racisme (c)	[ʁa'sismə]
racist	racist (c)	[ʁa'sisd]

| fascism | **fascisme** (c) | [fa'sismə] |
| fascist | **fascist** (c) | [fa'sisd] |

245. Countries. Miscellaneous

foreigner	**udlænding** (c)	['uð‚lɛneŋ]
foreign (adj)	**udenlandsk**	['uðen‚lansk]
abroad (overseas)	**i udlandet**	[i 'uðlanəð]

emigrant	**emigrant** (c)	[emi'gʁɑnd]
emigration	**emigration** (c)	[emigʁɑ'ɕo:n]
to emigrate (vi)	**at emigrere**	[at emi'gʁɛ:ɒ]

the West	**Vesten**	['vɛsdən]
the East	**Østen**	['øsdən]
the Far East	**Fjernøsten**	['fjaɒn‚øsdən]

civilization	**civilisation** (c)	[sivilisa'ɕon]
humanity (mankind)	**menneskehed** (c)	['mɛnəskə‚heð]
world (earth)	**verden** (c)	['væɒdən]
peace	**fred** (c)	[fʁɛð]
worldwide (adj)	**verdens-**	['væɒdəns]

homeland (native country)	**fædreland** (n)	['fɛðɒ‚lan]
people	**folk** (n)	[fɒlk]
population	**befolkning** (c)	[be'fɒlgneŋ]
people (e.g., a lot of ~)	**folk** (pl)	[fɒlk]

| nation (people) | **nation** (c) | [na'ɕo:n] |
| generation | **generation** (c) | [genəʁɑ'ɕo:n] |

territory (area)	**territorium** (n)	[tæɒi'toɒjom]
region	**region** (c)	[ʁɛgi'o:n]
state (part of a country)	**stat** (c)	[sdæ:d]

tradition	**tradition** (c)	[tʁɑdi'ɕo:n]
custom (tradition)	**skik** (c)	[skik]
ecology	**økologi** (c)	[økolo'gi:]

| Indian (Native American) | **indianer** (c) | [endi'ænʌ] |
| Gipsy (man) | **sigøjner** (c) | [si'gɒjnʌ] |

| Gipsy (woman) | **sigøjner** (c) | [si'gɒjnʌ] |
| Gipsy (adj) | **sigøjner-** | [si'gɒjnɒ] |

empire	**imperium** (n)	[em'pe:ʁiɔm]
colony	**koloni** (c)	[kolo'ni:]
slavery	**slaveri** (n)	[slæwʌ'ʁi]
invasion	**invasion** (c)	[enva'ɕo:n]
famine	**hungersnød** (c)	['hɔŋɒs‚nøð]

246. Major religious groups. Confessions

religion	**religion** (c)	[ʁɛliˈgjoːn]
religious	**religiøs**	[ʁɛliˈgjøːs]
belief (in God)	**tro** (c)	[tʁoː]
to believe (vi)	**at tro på Gud**	[at tʁoː pɔ guð]
believer	**troende** (c)	[ˈtʁoːənə]
atheism	**ateisme** (c)	[ateˈismə]
atheist	**ateist** (c)	[ateˈisd]
Christianity	**kristendom** (c)	[ˈkʁɛsdənˌdɒm]
Christian (noun)	**kristen** (c)	[ˈkʁɛsdən]
Christian (adj)	**kristen**	[ˈkʁɛsdən]
Catholicism	**Katolicisme** (c)	[katoliˈsismə]
Catholic (noun)	**katolik** (c)	[katoˈlik]
Catholic (adj)	**katolsk**	[kaˈtoːlsk]
Protestantism	**Protestantisme** (c)	[pʁotɛsdanˈtismə]
Protestant Church	**Protestantisk kirke** (c)	[pʁotɛsdantisk ˈkiɒkə]
Protestant	**protestant** (c)	[pʁotɛˈsdand]
Orthodoxy	**Ortodokse tro** (c)	[ɒtoˈdɒksə tʁoː]
Orthodox Church	**Ortodokse kirke** (c)	[ɒtoˈdɒksə ˈkiɒkə]
Orthodox	**ortodoks** (c)	[ɒtoˈdɒks]
Presbyterianism	**Presbyterianisme** (c)	[pʁɛsbytæɒiæˈnismə]
Presbyterian Church	**Presbyteriansk kirke** (c)	[pʁɛsbytæɒiˈænsk ˈkiɒkə]
Presbyterian (noun)	**presbyterianer** (c)	[pʁɛsbytæɒiˈæːnʌ]
Lutheranism	**Lutheransk kirke** (c)	[ludeˈʁansk ˈkiɒkə]
Lutheran	**lutheraner** (c)	[ludeˈʁɑnʌ]
Baptist Church	**Baptisme** (c)	[bɑbˈtismə]
Baptist	**baptist** (c)	[bɑbˈtisd]
Anglican Church	**Anglikansk kirke**	[aŋleˈkæːnsk ˈkiɒgə]
Anglican	**anglikaner** (c)	[aŋleˈkæːnʌ]
Mormonism	**Mormonisme** (c)	[mɒːmoːˈnismə]
Mormon	**mormon** (c)	[mɒːˈmoːn]
Judaism	**Jødedom** (c)	[ˈjøːðəˌdɒm]
Jew	**jøde** (c)	[ˈjøːðə]
Buddhism	**Buddhisme** (c)	[buˈdismə]
Buddhist	**buddhist** (c)	[buˈdisd]
Hinduism	**Hinduisme** (c)	[henduˈismə]
Hindu	**hinduist** (c)	[henduˈisd]

Islam	**Islam**	[is'lɑːm], ['islɑm]
Muslim (noun)	**muslim**	[mu'sliːm]
Muslim (adj)	**muslimsk**	[mu'sliːmsk]
Shiism	**Shiisme** (c)	[ɕi'ismə]
Shiite (noun)	**shiit** (c)	[ɕi'id]
Sunni (religion)	**Sunnisme** (c)	[su'nismə]
Sunnite (noun)	**sunnit** (c)	[su'nid]

247. Religions. Priests

priest	**præst** (c)	['pʁasd]
the Pope	**Pave** (c)	['pæːu]
monk, friar	**munk** (c)	[mɔŋk]
nun	**nonne** (c)	['nɒnə]
pastor	**pastor** (c)	['pasdɒ]
abbot	**abbed** (c)	['abəð]
vicar	**vikar** (c)	[vi'kɑː]
bishop	**biskop** (c)	['biskʌb]
cardinal	**kardinal** (c)	[kɑdi'næːl]
pope (orthodox priest)	**pave** (c)	['pæːu]
preacher	**prædiker** (c)	['pʁɛðikʌ]
preaching	**prædiken** (c)	['pʁɛðəkən]
parishioners	**sogneborn** (pl)	['sɒwnəˌbœɒn]
believer	**troende** (c)	['tʁoːənə]
atheist	**ateist** (c)	[ate'isd]

248. Faith. Christianity. Islam

Adam	**Adam**	['æːdɑm]
Eve	**Eva**	['eːva]
God	**Gud** (c)	[guð]
the Lord	**Gud, Herren** (c)	[guð], ['hæːɒn]
the Almighty	**Almægtig**	['almɛgdi]
sin	**synd** (c)	[søn]
to sin (vi)	**at synde**	[at 'sønə]
sinner (man)	**synder** (c)	['sønʌ]
sinner (woman)	**synder** (c)	['sønʌ]
hell	**helvede** (n)	['hɛlvəðə]
paradise	**paradis** (n)	['pɑːɑˌdis]
Jesus	**Jesus**	['jeːsus]

Jesus Christ	**Jesus Kristus**	[ˈjeːsus ˈkʁɛsdus]
Christ	**Kristus**	[ˈkʁɛsdus]
the Holy Spirit	**Hellige Ånd**	[ˈhɛli ˌʌn]
the Savior	**Frelseren**	[ˈfʁalsʌ]
the Virgin Mary	**Jomfru Maria** (c)	[ˈjʌmfʁu maˌʁiːa]
the Devil	**Djævel** (c)	[ˈdjɛːvəl]
devil's	**djævel-**	[ˈdjɛːvəl]
Satan	**Satan** (c)	[ˈsæːtan]
Satan's	**satanisk**	[saˈtæːnisk]
angel	**engel** (c)	[ˈɛŋəl]
guardian angel	**skytsengel** (c)	[ˈsgødsˌɛŋəl]
angelic	**engle-**	[ˈɛŋlə]
apostle	**apostel** (c)	[ɑˈpɒsdɛl]
archangel	**ærkeengel** (c)	[ˈɑŋeːiːŋəl]
the Antichrist	**antikrist** (c)	[ˈantiˌkʁiːsd]
the Church	**Kirke**	[ˈkiɒkə]
Bible	**bibel** (c)	[ˈbiːbəl]
biblical	**bibelsk**	[ˈbiːbəlsk]
Old Testament	**Det Gamle Testamente**	[de ˈgamlə tɛsdaˈmɛndə]
New Testament	**Det Nye Testamente**	[de ˈnyːə tɛsdaˈmɛndə]
Gospel	**Evangelium** (n)	[evɑŋˈgeljɔm]
Holy Scripture	**Den Hellige Skrift**	[dɛn ˈhɛliə ˌsgʁɛfd]
Heaven	**Himlen**	[ˈhemlən]
Commandment	**bud** (n)	[buð]
prophet	**profet** (c)	[pʁoˈfeːd]
prophecy	**profeti** (c)	[pʁofeˈti]
Allah	**Allah**	[ˈala]
Mohammed	**Muhammed**	[muˈhaməð]
the Koran	**Koranen**	[koˈʁanən]
mosque	**moske** (c)	[moˈske]
mullah	**mullah** (c)	[ˈmula]
prayer	**bøn** (c)	[bœn]
to pray (vi, vt)	**at bede**	[at ˈbeːðə]
pilgrimage	**pilgrimsrejse** (c)	[ˈpiːlgʁemsˌʁɑjsə]
pilgrim	**pilgrim** (c)	[ˈpiːlgʁɛm]
Mecca	**Mekka**	[ˈmɛka]
church	**kirke** (c)	[ˈkiɒkə]
temple	**tempel** (n)	[ˈtɛmbəl]
cathedral	**katedral** (c)	[kadəˈdʁɑːl]
Gothic	**gotisk**	[ˈgoːtisk]
synagogue	**synagoge** (c)	[synaˈgoːə]

mosque	moske (c)	[mo'ske]
chapel	kapel (n)	[ka'pəl]
abbey	abbedi (n)	[abə'di:]
convent	nonnekloster (n)	['nɒnəklɒsdʌ]
monastery	munkekloster (n)	['mɔŋkəklɒsdʌ]

bell (in church)	klokke (c)	['klɒkə]
bell tower	klokketårn (n)	['klɒkə͵tɔ:n]
to ring (about bells)	at ringe	[at 'ʁɛŋə]

cross	kors (n)	[kɒ:s]
cupola (roof)	kuppel (c)	['kubəl]
icon	ikon (n)	[i'kɒn]

soul	sjæl (c)	[ɕɛ:l]
fate (destiny)	skæbne (c)	['skɛ:bnə]
evil (noun)	det onde (n)	[de 'ɔnə]
good (noun)	det gode (n)	[de 'go:ðə]

vampire	vampyr (c)	[vɑm'pyɒ]
witch (sorceress)	heks (c)	[hɛks]
demon	dæmon (c)	['dɛmo:ŋ]
devil	djævel (c)	['djɛ:vəl]
spirit	ånd (c)	[ɒn]

| redemption | soning (c) | ['sɒneŋ] |
| to redeem (vt) | at sone | [at 'so:nə] |

church service, mass	gudstjeneste (c)	['guð͵stjɛnəsdə]
to say mass	at holde messe	[at 'hɒlə 'mɛsə]
confession	bekendelse (c)	[be'kɛnəlsə]
to confess (vi)	at bekende	[at be'kɛnə]

saint (noun)	helgen (c)	['hɛljən]
sacred (holy)	hellig	['hɛli]
holy water	vievand (n)	['vi:ə͵van]

ritual (noun)	ritual (n)	[ʁitu'æ:l]
ritual (adj)	ritual-	[ʁitu'æ:l]
sacrifice (offering)	ofring (c)	['ʌfʁʌɛŋ]

superstition	overtro (c)	['ɒwʌtʁo:]
superstitious	overtroisk	['ɒwʌtʁo:isk]
afterlife	liv (n) efter døden	['liu 'ɛfdɒ 'dø:ðən]
eternal life	det evige liv (n)	[de 'e:viə liu]

MISCELLANEOUS

249. Various useful words

background (green ~)	**baggrund** (c)	['baugʁɔn]
balance (of situation)	**balance** (c)	[ba'laŋsə]
barrier (obstacle)	**forhindring** (c)	[fɔ'hendʁɛŋ]
base (basis)	**basis** (c)	['bæ:sis]
beginning	**begyndelse** (c)	[be'gønəlsə]
category	**kategori** (c)	[kadego'ʁi]
cause (reason)	**grund** (c)	[gʁɔn]
choice	**udvalg** (n)	['uðvalj]
coincidence	**sammenfald** (n)	['samən̩fal]
comfortable (~ chair)	**bekvem**	[be'kvɛm]
comparison	**sammenligning** (c)	['samən̩linəŋ]
compensation	**kompensation** (c)	[kɔmpɛnsa'ɕo:n]
degree (extent, amount)	**grad** (c)	[gʁɑ:ð]
development	**udvikling** (c)	['uðvegləŋ]
difference	**forskel** (c)	['fɔ:skɛl]
effect (e.g., of drug)	**effekt** (c)	[ɛ'fɛkd]
effort (exertion)	**anstrengelse** (c)	['an̩sdʁaŋəlsə]
element	**element** (n)	[ele'maŋd]
end (finish)	**ende** (c)	['ɛnə]
example (illustration)	**eksempel** (n)	[ɛ'ksɛmbəl]
fact	**faktum** (n)	['faktɔm]
frequent	**hyppig**	['hybi]
growth (development)	**vækst** (c)	[vɛksd]
help	**hjælp** (c)	[jɛlb]
ideal	**ideal** (n)	[ide'æ:l]
kind (sort, type)	**slags** (c)	[slags]
labyrinth	**labyrint** (c)	[laby'ʁɛnd]
mistake	**fejl** (n)	[fajl]
moment	**øjeblik** (n)	['ɒjə̩blek]
object (thing)	**objekt** (n)	[ɒb'jɛkd]
obstacle	**hindring** (c)	['hendʁɛŋ]
original (original copy)	**original** (c)	[ɒigi'næl]
part (~ of sth)	**del** (c)	[de:l]
particle, small part	**partikel** (c)	[pɑ'tikəl]
pause (break)	**pause** (c)	['pausə]

position	**position** (c)	[posi'ɕoːn]
principle	**princip** (n)	[pʁin'sib]
problem (is there any ~?)	**problem** (n)	[pʁo'bleːm]
process	**proces** (c)	[pʁo'sɛs]
progress	**fremskridt** (n)	['fʁamskʁid]
property (quality)	**egenskab** (n)	['ejənˌsgæb]
reaction	**reaktion** (c)	[ʁɛak'ɕoːn]
risk	**risiko** (c)	['ʁisiko]
secret	**hemmelighed** (c)	['hɛməliˌheð]
section (sector)	**sektion** (c)	[sɛk'ɕoːn]
series	**serie** (c)	['seɒjə]
shape (outer form)	**form** (c)	[fɒːm]
situation	**situation** (c)	[situa'ɕoːn]
solution	**løsning** (c)	['løːsneŋ]
standard (adj)	**standard-**	[sdan'dɑːd]
standard (level of quality)	**standard** (c)	[sdan'dɑːd]
stop (pause)	**pause** (c)	['pɑusə]
style	**stil** (c)	[sdiːl]
system	**system** (n)	[sys'deːm]
table (chart)	**tabel** (c)	[ta'bɛl]
tempo, rate	**tempo** (n)	['tɛmpo]
term (word, expression)	**fagudtryk** (n)	['fɑuuðˌtʁœg]
thing (object)	**genstand** (c)	['gɛnsdan]
thing (object, item)	**ting** (c)	[teŋ]
truth	**sandhed** (c)	['sanheð]
turn (please, wait your ~)	**tur** (c)	[tuɒ]
type (sort, kind)	**type** (c)	['tyːbə]
urgent	**haster**	['hasdə]
urgently	**omgående**	[ɒmˈgɔːənə]
use (usefulness)	**nytte** (c)	['nødə]
variant	**variant** (c)	[vɑi'and]
way (means, method)	**måde** (c)	['mɔːðə]
zone	**zone** (c)	['soːnə]

250. Modifiers. Adjectives. Part 1

additional	**ekstra**	['ɛksdʁɑ]
ancient (civilization etc.)	**oldtids-**	['ɒltiðs]
artificial	**kunstig**	['kɔnsdi]
back, rear	**bag-**	[bæː]
bad	**dårlig**	['dɒːli]
beautiful	**smuk**	[smɔk]
beautiful (e.g., ~ palace)	**skøn**	[skœn]

big (in size)	**stor**	[ˈsdoɒ]
bitter (taste)	**bitter**	[ˈbedɒ]
blind (sightless)	**blind**	[blen]
calm	**rolig**	[ˈʁoːli]
calm, quiet	**rolig**	[ˈʁoːli]
careless (negligent)	**efterladende**	[ˈɛfdɒˌlæːðənə]
caring (kindly)	**omsorgsfuld**	[ˈʌmsɒwsful]
central (in location)	**central-**	[sɛnˈtʁɑːl]
cheap (inexpensive)	**billig**	[ˈbili]
children's	**børne-**	[ˈbœɒnə]
civil (of community)	**borgerlig**	[ˈbɒːwʌli]
clandestine (secret)	**illegal**	[ˈilegæːl]
clean (free from dirt)	**ren**	[ʁɛːn]
clear (thinking, argument)	**klar**	[klɑː]
clever (smart)	**klog**	[ˈklɔu]
close (near in space)	**nær**	[ˈnɛɒ]
closed	**lukket**	[ˈlɔkəð]
cloudless (sky)	**skyfri**	[ˈskyfʁiː]
cold (drink, weather)	**kold**	[kɒl]
compatible	**forenelig**	[fɒˈeːnəli]
contented	**tilfreds**	[teˈfʁɛs]
continuous	**langvarig**	[ˈlɑŋvɑːi]
continuous (uninterrupted)	**uafbrudt**	[ˈuɑwˈbʁud]
cool (weather)	**kølig**	[ˈkøːli]
dangerous	**farlig**	[ˈfɑːli]
dark (room)	**mørk**	[ˈmœɒk]
dead (not alive)	**død**	[døð]
dense (fog, smoke)	**tæt**	[tɛd]
difficult (decision)	**vanskelig**	[ˈvanskəli]
difficult (problem, task)	**kompliceret**	[kʌmbliˈseʌð]
dim, faint (light)	**svag**	[svæː]
dirty (not clean)	**snavset**	[ˈsnɑusəð]
distant (faraway)	**fjern**	[ˈfjaɒn]
dry (climate, clothing)	**tør**	[ˈtœɒ]
easy (not difficult)	**enkel**	[ˈɛŋkəl]
empty (glass, room)	**tom**	[tom]
exact (amount)	**præcis**	[pʁɛˈsiːs]
excellent	**udmærket**	[ˈuðˌmæɒkəð]
excessive (demand)	**umådelig**	[uˈmɔðəli]
expensive	**dyr, kostbar**	[ˈdyɒ], [ˈkʌsdˌbɑ]
exterior	**ydre**	[ˈyðʁɒ]
far (distant in space)	**fjern**	[ˈfjaɒn]
fast (quick)	**hurtig**	[ˈhuɒdi]

fatty (food)	**fed**	[feð]
fertile (land, soil)	**frugtbar**	[ˈfʁɔgdˌbɑː]
flat (e.g., ~ panel display)	**flad**	[flæːð]
flat (e.g., ~ surface)	**jævn**	[ˈjɛun]
foreign (country, language)	**udenlandsk**	[ˈuðənˌlansk]
fragile (china, glass)	**skør**	[ˈskøɒ]
free (at no cost)	**gratis**	[ˈgʁɑtiːs]
free (unrestricted)	**fri**	[fʁiː]
fresh (~ water)	**fersk**	[ˈfaɒsk]
fresh (e.g., ~ bred)	**frisk**	[fʁɛsk]
frozen (food)	**frossen**	[ˈfʁɔən]
full (completely filled)	**fuld**	[ful]
good (book etc.)	**god**	[goð]
good, kind	**god**	[goð]
grateful	**taknemmelig**	[tɑgˈnɛməli]
happy	**lykkelig**	[ˈløgəli]
hard (not soft)	**hård**	[hɒː]
heavy (in weight)	**tung**	[tɔŋ]
hostile	**fjendtlig**	[ˈfjɛndli]
hot (high in temperature)	**varm**	[vɑːm]
huge	**enorm**	[eˈnɒːm]
humid	**fugtig**	[ˈfɔgdi]
hungry	**sulten**	[ˈsuldən]
ill (sick, unwell)	**syg**	[syː]
illegible	**uforståelig**	[ufʌˈsdɔəli]
immobile	**ubevægelig**	[ˈubeˌvɛːəli]
important	**vigtig**	[ˈvegdi]
impossible (not possible)	**umulig**	[uˈmuːli]
indispensable	**nødvendig**	[nøðˈvɛndi]
inexperienced	**uerfaren**	[uænˈfɑːɑn]
insignificant (unimportant)	**ubetydelig**	[ˈubeˌtyðəli]
interior	**indre**	[ˈendʁɒ]
joint (~ decision)	**fælles**	[ˈfɛləs]
last (e.g., ~ week)	**forleden**	[fɒˈleːðən]
last (final)	**sidste**	[ˈsisdə]
left (e.g., ~ side)	**venstre**	[ˈvɛnsdʁʌ]
legal (legitimate)	**lovlig**	[ˈlɒuli]
light (in weight)	**let**	[lɛd]
light (pale color)	**lys**	[lyːs]
limited (restricted)	**begrænset**	[beˈgʁansəð]
liquid (fluid)	**flydende**	[ˈflyːˌðənə]
long (e.g., ~ way)	**lang**	[lɑŋ]
loud (voice etc.)	**høj**	[hɒj]
low (voice)	**stille**	[ˈsdelə]

251. Modifiers. Adjectives. Part 2

main (principal)	hoved-	['ho:əð]
matt	mat-	['mad]
merry, cheerful	glad	[glað]
meticulous (job)	omhyggelig	[ʌm'hygəli]
mysterious	gådefuld	['gɔ:ðəful]
narrow (street, passage)	smal	[smal]
native (of country)	hjem-	[jɛm]
near (in space)	nær	['nɛɒ]
near-sighted	nærsynet	['nɛɒsy:nəð]
necessary (indispensable)	nødvendig	[nøð'vɛndi]
negative	negativ	[nega'tiu]
neighboring	nabo-	['næ:bo]
nervous	nervøs	[næɒ'vø:s]
new	ny	[ny:]
next (e.g., ~ week)	næste	['nɛsdə]
nice (kind)	kær	[kɛɒ]
nice (voice)	rar	[ʁɑ:]
normal (common, typical)	normal	[nɒ'mæ:l]
not big	lille	['lilə]
not clear	uklar	['u̯klɑ]
not difficult	let	[lɛd]
obligatory	obligatorisk	[ɒbliga'to:ʁisg]
old (house)	gammel	['gɑməl]
open	åben	['ɔ:bən]
opposite	modsat	['moðsad]
ordinary (usual, normal)	almindelig	[al'menəli]
original (unusual)	original	[ɒigi'næl]
past (recent)	forrige	['fɒ:iə]
permanent	fast	[fasd]
personal (message, letter)	personlig	[pɑɒ'so:nli]
polite	høflig	['høfli]
poor (not rich)	fattig	['fadi]
possible	mulig	['mu:li]
poverty-stricken	fattig	['fadi]
present (in time)	nu	[nu]
principal (main)	hoved-	['ho:əð]
private (not for the public)	privat	[pʁi'væ:d]
private (personal)	privat	[pʁi'væ:d]
probable (likely)	sandsynlig	[san'sy:nli]
public (open to all)	offentlig	['ɒfəndli]
punctual (person)	punktlig	['pɒŋdli]
rare (uncommon)	sjælden	['ɕɛlən]

raw (uncooked)	**rå**	[ʁɔ:]
right	**højre**	['hɒjʁɒ]
right, correct	**rigtig**	['ʁɛgdi]
ripe (fruit)	**moden**	['mo:ðən]
risky	**risikabel**	[ʁisi'kæbəl]
sad (depressing)	**sørgelig**	['sœɒwəli]
sad (unhappy)	**sørgelig**	['sœɒwəli]
safe (not dangerous)	**sikker**	['sekɒ]
salty (food)	**saltet**	['saldəð]
satisfied (customer)	**tilfreds**	[te'fʁɛs]
second hand	**brugt**	[bʁɔgd]
shallow (water)	**lavvandet**	['lɑu̯ˌvanəð]
sharp (blade, scissors)	**skarp**	[skɑ:b]
short (in length)	**kort**	[kɒ:d]
short, short-lived	**kortvarig**	['kɒdvɑ:i]
significant (notable)	**betydelig**	[be'tyðəli]
similar	**lignende**	['li:nənə]
simple (easy)	**enkel**	['ɛŋkəl]
skinny (too thin)	**mager**	['mæjʌ], ['mægʌ]
slim (person)	**tynd**	[tøn]
small (in size)	**lille**	['lilə]
smooth (surface)	**glat**	[glad]
soft (to touch)	**blød**	[bløð]
somber, gloomy	**mørk**	['mœɒk]
sour (flavor, taste)	**sur**	['suɒ]
spacious (house, room)	**rummelig**	['ʁɔməli]
special	**speciel**	[sbe'ɕɛl]
straight (line, road)	**lige**	['li:ə]
strong (construction)	**holdbar**	['hɒlˌbɑ:]
strong (person)	**kraftig**	['kʁɑfdi]
stupid (foolish)	**dum**	[dɔm]
suitable	**brugbar**	['bʁuˌbɑ:]
sunny (day)	**solrig**	['so:lʁi:]
superb, perfect	**fortræffelig**	[fo'tʁafəli]
swarthy	**mørklødet**	['mœɒklø:ðət]
sweet (in taste)	**sød**	[søð]
tan	**solbrændt**	['so:lˌbʁand]
tasty	**lækker**	['lɛkɒ]
tender (affectionate)	**øm, blid**	[œm], ['blið]
the highest	**den øverste**	[dɛn 'ø:vɒsdə]
the most important	**den vigtigste**	[dɛn 'vegdisdə]
the nearest	**nærmest**	['næɒməsd]
the same, equal	**identisk**	[i'dɛntisk]
thick (e.g., ~ fog)	**tyk**	[tyk]

thick (wall, slice)	**tyk**	[tyk]
tired (exhausted)	**træt**	[tʁad]
tiring	**trættende**	['tʁadənə]
transparent	**gennemsigtig**	['gɛnəmˌsegdi]
unique (exceptional)	**enestående**	['eːnəsdɔːənə]
warm (moderately hot)	**varm**	[vɑːm]
wet (e.g., ~ clothes)	**gennemvåd**	['gɛnəmvɔð]
whole (entire, complete)	**hel**	[heːl]
wide (e.g., ~ road)	**bred**	[bʁɛð]
young	**ung**	[ɔŋ]

MAIN 500 VERBS

252. Verbs A-C

to accompany (vt)	at følge	[at 'føljə]
to accuse (vt)	at beskylde	[at be'skylə]
to act (take action)	at virke	[at 'viɒkə]
to add (put together)	at tilføje	[at tel'fojə]
to address (speak to)	at henvende sig til ...	[at 'hɛnˌvɛnə sɑj tel]
to admire (vi)	at beundre	[at be'ondʁʌ]
to advertise (vt)	at reklamere	[at ʁɛklæː'meːɒ]
to advise (give advice to)	at råde	[at 'ʁɔːðə]
to affirm (vt)	at påstå	[at pɒ'sdɔː]
to agree (say yes)	at enes	[at 'eːnəs]
to allow (sb to do sth)	at tillade	[at 'teˌlæðə]
to amputate (vt)	at amputere	[at ɑmpu'teʌ]
to anger (vt)	at gøre vred	[at 'gœːɒ vʁɛð]
to answer (vi, vt)	at svare	[at 'svɑːɑ]
to apologize (vi)	at undskylde sig	[at 'ɔnˌsgylə sɑj]
to appear (come into view)	at dukke op	[at 'dɔkə ɒb]
to applaud (vi, vt)	at applaudere	[at aplɑw'deʌ]
to appoint (assign)	at udnævne	[at 'uðˌnɛunə]
to approach (come nearer)	at nærme sig	[at 'naɒmə sɑj]
to arrive (about train)	at ankomme	[at 'anˌkʌmə]
to ask (~ sb to do sth)	at bede om	[at 'beːðə ɒm]
to aspire (vi)	at bestræbe sig på	[at be'sdʁɛːbə sɑj pɔ]
to assist (help)	at assistere	[at asi'sdeʌ]
to attack (military)	at angribe	[at 'anˌgʁiːbə]
to attain (objectives)	at opnå	[at 'ɒbˌnɔː]
to avenge (vt)	at hævne	[at 'hɛunə]
to avoid (danger, task)	at undgå	[at 'ɔnˌgɔː]
to award (give medal to)	at dekorere	[at deko'ʁɛɒ]
to bathe (~ one's baby)	at bade (ngn.)	[at 'bæːðə]
to battle (vi)	at kæmpe	[at 'kɛmbə]
to be (on the table etc.)	at ligge	[at 'legə]
to be able to ...	kunne ...	['kunə]
to be afraid (of ...)	at frygte (for ...)	[at 'fʁɒegdə fʌ ...]
to be angry (with ...)	at blive vred (på ...)	[at 'bliːə vʁɛð pɔ ...]

to be at war	**at føre krig**	[at 'fø:ɒ kʁi:]
to be based (on …)	**at basere (på …)**	[at bæːˈseːɒ pɒ …]
to be bored	**at kede sig**	[at 'keːðə saj]
to be convinced	**at være overbevist**	[at 'vɛːɒ 'ɒwʌbeˌvisd]
to be enough	**at være nok**	[at 'vɛːɒ nɒk]
to be envious	**at misunde**	[at 'miˌsɔnə]
to be in a hurry	**at skynde sig**	[at 'sgønə saj]
to be indignant	**at være forarget**	[at 'vɛːɒ 'fɒɑːuəð]
to be interested in …	**at interessere sig (for …)**	[at entʁəˈseʌ saj fɒ …]
to be needed	**at være behøvet**	[at 'vɛːɒ beˈhøːuəð]
to be perplexed	**at være i vildrede**	[at 'vɛːʌ i 'vilˌʁɛːðə]
to be preserved	**at bevare**	[at beˈvɑːɑ]
to be required	**at være nødvendig**	[at 'vɛːɒ nøðˈvɛndi]
to be surprised	**at blive forbavset**	[at 'bliːə fɒˈbɑusəð]
to be worried	**at bekymre sig**	[at beˈkømɒ saj]
to beat (dog, person)	**at slå**	[at slɔ:]
to become (e.g., ~ old)	**at blive**	[at 'bliːə]
to become pensive	**at falde i tanker**	[at 'falə i 'taŋkɒ]
to behave (vi)	**at opføre sig**	[at 'ɒbˌføːɒ saj]
to believe (think)	**at tro**	[at tʁo:]
to belong to …	**at tilhøre**	[at telˈhøːɒ]
to berth (moor)	**at lægge til**	[at 'lɛgə tel]
to blind (of flash of light)	**at blænde**	[at 'blɛnə]
to blow (wind)	**at blæse**	[at 'blɛːsə]
to blush (vi)	**at rødme**	[at 'ʁœðmə]
to boast (vi)	**at prale**	[at 'pʁɑːlə]
to borrow (money)	**at låne**	[at 'lɔːnə]
to break (branch, toy etc.)	**at brække**	[at 'bʁakə]
to breathe (vi)	**at ånde**	[at 'ɒnə]
to bring sth	**at bringe**	[at 'bʁɛŋə]
to burn (paper, logs)	**at brænde**	[at 'bʁanə]
to burst (vi)	**at rive over**	[at 'ʁiːuə 'ɒuɒ]
to buy (purchase)	**at købe**	[at 'kø:bə]
to call (for help)	**at tilkalde**	[at 'telˌkalə]
to call (with one's voice)	**at kalde**	[at 'kalə]
to calm down (vt)	**at berolige**	[at beˈʁoːliə]
to cancel (call off)	**at annullere**	[at anuˈleʌ]
to cast off	**at lægge fra**	[at 'lɛgə fʁɑ]
to catch (e.g., ~ a ball)	**at fange**	[at 'faŋə]
to catch sight (of …)	**at bemærke**	[at beˈmæɒkə]
to cause …	**at være årsag til …**	[at 'vɛːɒ 'ɒːsæː tel]
to change (~ one's opinion)	**at ændre**	[at 'ɛndʁɒ]
to change (exchange)	**at veksle**	[at 'vɛkslə]

to charm (please, delight)	at fortrylle	[at fʌ'tʁylə]
to choose (select)	at vælge	[at 'vɛljə]
to chop off (vt)	at hugge af	[at 'hɔgə a]
to clean (from dirt)	at børste	[at 'bœɒsdə]
to clean (shoes etc.)	at rense	[at 'ʁansə]
to clean (tidy)	at rydde op	[at 'ʁyðə ɒb]
to close (window, shop)	at lukke	[at 'lɔkə]
to comb hair	at rede	[at 'ʁɛ:ðə]
to come down (the stairs)	at stige ned	[at 'sdi:ə neð]
to come in (enter)	at gå ind	[at gɔ: en]
to come out (book)	at udkomme	[at 'uðˌkɒmə]
to compare (vt)	at sammenligne	[at 'samənˌli:nə]
to compensate (vt)	at kompensere	[at kɒmpɛn'se:ɒ]
to compete (vi)	at konkurrere	[at kʌŋko'ʁɛʌ]
to compile, to make (a list)	at skrive en liste	[at 'skʁiuə en 'lesdə]
to complain (vi, vt)	at klage	[at 'klæ:jə]
to complicate (vt)	at komplicere	[at kʌmpli'seʌ]
to compose (music etc.)	at komponere	[at kɒmpo'ne:ɒ]
to compromise (vt)	at kompromittere	[at kɒmpʁomi'de:ɒ]
to concentrate (vi)	at koncentrere sig	[at konsɛn'tʁɛ:ɒ saj]
to confess (criminal)	at vedkende sig	[at 'veðˌkɛnə saj]
to congratulate (vt)	at lykønske	[at 'løkˌønskə]
to consult (doctor, expert)	at konsultere	[at konsul'te:ɒ]
to continue (~ to do sth)	at fortsætte	[at fʌ:'dsɛdə]
to control (verify)	at kontrollere	[at kʌntʁo'leʌ]
to convince (vt)	at overbevise	[at ɒuɒbe'vi:sə]
to cooperate (with)	at samarbejde	[at 'samaˌbɑjdə]
to coordinate (vt)	at koordinere	[at koɒdi'ne:ɒ]
to correct (rectify)	at rette	[at 'ʁadə]
to cost (vt)	at koste	[at 'kɒsdə]
to count (add up)	at regne	[at 'ʁɑjnə]
to count on ...	at regne med ...	[at 'ʁɑjnə mɛð]
to crack (ab. ceiling, wall)	at sprække	[at 'sbʁakə]
to create (vt)	at skabe	[at 'skæ:bə]
to cry (weep)	at græde	[at 'gʁaðə]
to cut off (vt)	at afskære	[at ɑu'skɛ:ɒ]

253. Verbs D-G

to dare (e.g., ~ to do sth)	at vove sig	[at 'vɔ:uə saj]
to date from	at datere sig	[at da'te:ɒ saj]
to deceive (vi, vt)	at snyde	[at 'sny:ðə]
to decide (e.g., ~ to do sth)	at beslutte	[at be'sludə]

to decorate (tree, street)	**at pynte**	[at ˈpøndə]
to dedicate (book etc.)	**at tilegne**	[at teˈlɑjnə]
to defend (a country etc.)	**at forsvare**	[at fʌˈsvɑːɑ]
to defend oneself	**at forsvare sig**	[at fʌˈsvɑːɑ sɑj]
to demand (request firmly)	**at kræve**	[at ˈkʁɛːuə]
to denounce (vt)	**at tage afstand (fra)**	[at ˈtæːə ˈɑwˌsdan]
to deny (declare untrue)	**at nægte**	[at ˈnɛgdə]
to depend on ...	**at afhænge af ...**	[at ɑuˈhɛŋə a ...]
to deprive (vt)	**at fratage**	[at fʁɑˈtæːə]
to deserve (vt)	**at fortjene**	[at fʌˈtjɛːnə]
to design (machine etc.)	**at projektere**	[at pʁoɕəkˈteʌ]
to desire (want, wish)	**at ønske**	[at ˈønskə]
to despise (vt)	**at foragte**	[at foˈagdə]
to destroy (documents etc)	**at tilintetgøre**	[at teˈendəðˌgœʌ]
to differ (from sth)	**at adskille sig (fra ...)**	[at ˈaðˌsgelə sɑj fʁɑ ...]
to dig (tunnel etc.)	**at grave**	[at ˈgʁɑːuə]
to direct (point the way)	**at rette**	[at ˈʁadə]
to disappear (vi)	**at forsvinde**	[at fʌˈsvenə]
to discover (new land etc.)	**at opdage**	[at ˈʌbˌdæjə]
to discuss (talk about)	**at drøfte**	[at ˈdʁœfdə]
to dismiss (from job)	**at fritage**	[at ˈfʁitæːə]
to distribute (leaflets etc.)	**at uddele**	[at ˈuðˌdeːlə]
to disturb (vt)	**at forstyrre**	[at fʌˈsdyʁɒ]
to dive (vi)	**at dykke**	[at ˈdøkə]
to divide (math)	**at dividere**	[at diviˈdeɒ]
to do (vt)	**at gøre**	[at ˈgœːɒ]
to do the laundry	**at vaske**	[at ˈvaskə]
to double (increase)	**at fordoble**	[at fʌˈdʌblə]
to doubt (have doubts)	**at tvivle**	[at ˈtviulə]
to draw a conclusion	**at konkludere**	[at kɒŋkluˈdeːɒ]
to dream (daydream)	**at drømme**	[at ˈdʁœmə]
to dream (in sleep)	**at drømme**	[at ˈdʁœmə]
to drink (vi, vt)	**at drikke**	[at ˈdʁɛkə]
to drive (a car)	**at føre**	[at ˈføːɒ]
to drive sb away	**at jage bort**	[at ˈjæːjə bɒːd]
to drop (let fall)	**at tabe**	[at ˈtæːbə]
to drown (ab. person)	**at drukne**	[at ˈdʁɔknə]
to dry (clothes, hair)	**at tørre**	[at ˈtœɒ]
to eat (vi, vt)	**at spise**	[at ˈsbiːsə]
to eavesdrop (vi)	**at smuglytte**	[at ˈsmueˌødə]
to emit (smell)	**at udsprede**	[at ˈuðˌsbʁɛːðə]
to enter (on list)	**at indskrive**	[at enˈskʁiuə]
to entertain (amuse)	**at underholde**	[at ˈɒnɒˌhɒlə]

to equip (fit out)	at installere	[at ensda'le:ɒ]
to examine (proposal)	at undersøge	[at 'ɔnɒˌsø:ə]
to exchange sth	at udveksle	[at 'uðˌvɛkslə]
to exclude, to expel	at ekskludere	[at ɛksklu'de:ɒ]
to excuse (forgive)	at undskylde	[at 'ɔnˌskylə]
to exist (vi)	at eksistere	[at ɛksi'sdeɒ]
to expect (anticipate)	at forvente	[at fʌ'vɛndə]
to expect (foresee)	at forudse	[at 'fɒuðˌse]
to explain (vi, vt)	at forklare	[at fʌ'klɑ:ɑ]
to express (vt)	at udtrykke	[at 'uðˌtʁɶkə]
to extinguish (a fire)	at slukke	[at 'slɔkə]
to fall in love (with ...)	at forelske sig i ...	[at fɒ:'ɛlsgə sɑj i]
to feed (provide food)	at give mad	[at gi: mað]
to feel (fear, regret)	at føle	[at 'fø:lə]
to fight (against the enemy)	at kæmpe	[at 'kɛmbə]
to fight (vi)	at slås	[at slɒs]
to fill (glass, bottle)	at fylde	[at 'fylə]
to find (~ lost items)	at finde	[at 'fenə]
to find out (make enquiries)	at erfare	[at ɑɒ'fɑ:ɑ]
to finish (vt)	at afslutte	[at ɑu'sludə]
to fish (with a line)	at fiske	[at 'feskə]
to fit (about dress etc.)	at passe	[at 'pasə]
to flatter (vi, vt)	at smigre	[at 'smi:ɒ]
to fly (bird, plane)	at flyve	[at 'fly:və]
to follow ... (come after)	at følge efter ...	[at 'føljə 'ɛfdʌ]
to forbid (not allow)	at forbyde	[at fʌ'byðə]
to force (compel)	at påtvinge	[at 'pɒˌtvenə]
to forget (vi, vt)	at glemme	[at 'glɛmə]
to forgive (pardon)	at tilgive	[at 'telˌgiuə]
to form (constitute)	at danne	[at 'danə]
to get dirty (vi)	at blive beskidt	[at 'bli:ə be'skid]
to get infected (with ...)	at blive smittet	[at 'bli:ə 'smedəð]
to get irritated	at blive irriteret	[at 'bli:ə iɒi'teʌð]
to get married	at gifte sig	[at 'gifdə sɑj]
to get rid of ...	at blive fri for ...	[at 'bli:ə fʁi: fɒ]
to get tired	at være træt	[at 'vɛ:ɒ tʁat]
to get up (arise from bed)	at stå op	[at sdɔ: ɒb]
to give a hug, to hug (vt)	at omfavne	[at ɒm'fɑunə]
to give in (yield to)	at stå tilbage (for ...)	[at sdɔ: te'bæ:jə fɒ]
to go (by car, train etc.)	at køre	[at 'kø:ɒ]
to go (to walk)	at gå	[at gɔ:]
to go for a swim	at bade	[at 'bæ:ðə]
to go out (for dinner etc.)	at gå ud af	[at gɔ: uð a]

to go to bed	at gå i seng	[at gɔ: i sɛŋ]
to greet (vt)	at hilse	[at 'hilsə]
to grow (plants)	at dyrke	[at 'dyɒkə]
to guarantee (assure)	at garantere	[at gɑɑn'te:ɒ]
to guess right	at gætte	[at 'gɛdə]

254. Verbs H-M

to hand out (distribute)	at fordele	[at fʌ'delə]
to hang (curtains etc.)	at hænge	[at 'hɛŋə]
to have (vt)	at have	[at 'hæ:və]

to have a try	at forsøge	[at fʌ'sø:ə]
to have breakfast	at spise morgenmad	[at 'sbi:sə 'mɒ:ɒn,mað]
to have dinner	at spise aftensmad	[at 'sbi:sə 'ɑfdəns,mað]
to have fun	at more sig	[at 'mo:ɒ saj]
to have lunch	at spise frokost	[at 'sbi:sə 'fʁɔkʌsd]

to head (group etc.)	at stå i spidsen	[at sdɔ: i 'sbesən]
to hear (vi, vt)	at høre	[at 'hø:ɒ]
to heat (vt)	at opvarme	[at ɒb'vɑ:mə]
to help (assist, aid)	at hjælpe	[at 'jɛlbə]
to hide (e.g., ~ something)	at gemme	[at 'gɛmə]

to hint (vi)	at antyde	[at an'tyðə]
to hire (e.g., ~ a boat)	at leje	[at 'lɑjə]
to hire (staff)	at engagere	[at ɑŋga'ɕeɒ]
to hope (vi, vt)	at håbe	[at 'hɔ:bə]
to hunt (for food, sport)	at jage	[at 'jæ:jə]
to hurry sb	at skynde på	[at 'skønə pɔ]

to imagine (to picture)	at forestille sig	[at fɒ:ɒ'sdelə saj]
to imitate (vt)	at imitere	[at imi'te:ɒ]
to implore (vt)	at bede	[at 'be:ðə]
to import (vt)	at importere	[at empɒ'te:ɒ]
to increase (vi)	at blive forhøjet	[at 'bli:ə fʌ'hʌjet]
to increase (vt)	at forøge	[at fʌ'øjə]

to infect (vt)	at smitte	[at 'smedə]
to influence (vt)	at have indflydelse (på)	[at 'hæ:və 'en,flyðəlsə]
to inform (~ sb about ...)	at meddele	[at 'mɛð,de:lə]
to inform (vi, vt)	at informere	[at enfɒ'me:ɒ]
to inherit (property, right)	at arve	[at 'ɑ:uə]

to insist (vi, vt)	at insistere (på ...)	[at ensi'sdeʌ pɔ ...]
to inspire (vt)	at inspirere	[at ensbi'ʁɛ:ɒ]
to instruct (teach)	at instruere	[at ensdʁu'eʌ]
to insult (offend)	at fornærme	[at fʌ'naɒmə]
to interest (vt)	at interessere	[at entʁə'seʌ]
to intervene (vi)	at blande sig	[at 'blanə saj]

to introduce (present)	**at gøre bekendt**	[at 'gœːɒ beˈkɛnd]
to invent (machine etc.)	**at opfinde**	[at ˈʌbˌfenə]
to invite (ask to come)	**at invitere**	[at enviˈteːɒ]
to iron (laundry)	**at stryge**	[at 'sdʁyːə]
to irritate (annoy)	**at irritere**	[at iɒiˈteːɒ]
to isolate (vt)	**at isolere**	[at isoˈleːɒ]
to join (political party etc.)	**at tilslutte sig**	[at 'telsludə sɑj]
to joke (be kidding)	**at spøge**	[at 'sbøːjə]
to keep (old letters etc.)	**at opbevare**	[at 'ɒbbeˌvɑːɑ]
to keep silent	**at tie**	[at 'tiːə]
to kill (vt)	**at dræbe**	[at 'dʁɛːbə]
to knock (at the door)	**at banke (på døren)**	[at 'bɑŋkə pɔ 'dœɒn]
to know (sb)	**at kende**	[at 'kɛnə]
to know (sth)	**at vide**	[at 'viːðə]
to laugh (at the joke)	**at grine**	[at 'gʁiːnə]
to launch (start up)	**at starte**	[at 'sdɑːdə]
to leave (abandon)	**at forlade**	[at fʌˈlæːðə]
to leave (e.g., ~ for Mexico)	**at rejse bort**	[at 'ʁɑjsə bɒːd]
to leave (forget)	**at glemme**	[at 'glɛmə]
to liberate (vt)	**at befri**	[at beˈfʁiː]
to lie (be in lying position)	**at ligge**	[at 'legə]
to lie (tell untruth)	**at lyve**	[at 'lyːvə]
to light (e.g., a campfire)	**at tænde**	[at 'tɛnə]
to light up (illuminate)	**at belyse**	[at beˈlyːsə]
to like (e.g., I like ...)	**at holde af ...**	[at 'holə a]
to like (enjoy)	**at holde af ...**	[at 'holə a]
to limit (vt)	**at begrænse**	[at beˈgʁɑnsə]
to listen (vi)	**at høre**	[at 'høːɒ]
to live (e.g., ~ in France)	**at bo**	[at boː]
to live (exist)	**at leve**	[at 'leːuə]
to load (gun)	**at oplade**	[at 'ɒbˌlæːðə]
to load (vehicle etc.)	**at laste**	[at 'lasdə]
to look (out of the window)	**at se**	[at seː]
to look for ... (search)	**at søge ...**	[at 'søːə]
to look like (resemble)	**at ligne**	[at 'liːnə]
to lose (umbrella etc.)	**at tabe**	[at 'tæːbə]
to love (sb)	**at elske**	[at 'ɛlskə]
to lower (blind, head)	**at nedsænke**	[at neðˈsɛŋkə]
to make (e.g., ~ dinner)	**at lave**	[at 'læːuə]
to make a mistake	**at tage fejl**	[at 'tæːə fɑjl]
to make copies	**at kopiere**	[at koˈpjeʌ]
to make easier	**at lette**	[at 'lɛdə]
to make use (of ...)	**at benytte ...**	[at beˈnødə]

to manage (business)	at lede	[at 'le:ðə]
to mark (make a mark)	at mærke	[at 'maɒkə]
to mean (signify)	at betyde	[at be'tyðə]
to meet (get acquainted)	at stifte bekendtskab	[at 'sdefdə be'kɛndˌskæb]
to memorize (vt)	at huske	[at 'huskə]
to mention (talk about)	at omtale	[at ɒm'tæ:lə]
to miss (school etc.)	at forsømme	[at fʌ'sœmə]
to mix (combine, blend)	at blande	[at 'blanə]
to mix up (confuse)	at blande sammen	[at 'blanə 'samən]
to mock (deride)	at håne, at spotte	[at 'hɔ:nə], [at 'sbʌdə]
to move (wardrobe etc.)	at forflytte	[at fo'flødə]
to multiply (math)	at gange	[at 'gaŋə]
must	måtte	['mʌdə]

255. Verbs N-S

to name, to call (vt)	at kalde	[at 'kalə]
to negotiate (vi)	at forhandle	[at fʌ'hanlə]
to note (write down)	at notere	[at no'te:ɒ]
to notice (see)	at bemærke	[at be'mæɒkə]
to obey (vi, vt)	at underordne sig	[at 'ɔnɒˌɒ:dnə sɑj]
to object (vi, vt)	at indvende	[at en'vɛnə]
to observe (see)	at observere	[at ʌbsæɒ'vʌ]
to offend (person)	at fornærme	[at fʌ'naɒmə]
to omit (word, phrase)	at springe over	[at 'sbʁɛŋə 'ɒwʌ]
to open (vt)	at åbne	[at 'ɔ:bnə]
to order (in restaurant)	at bestille	[at be'sdelə]
to order (military)	at beordre	[at be'ɒ:dʁɒ]
to organize (concert, party)	at arrangere	[at aaŋ'ɕeʌ]
to overestimate (vt)	at overvurdere	[at 'ɒuɒvuɒˌde:ɒ]
to own (possess)	at eje	[at 'ɑjə]
to participate (vi)	at deltage	[at 'delˌtæ]
to pass (go beyond)	at passere	[at pa'seʌ]
to pay (vi, vt)	at betale	[at be'tæ:lə]
to peep, spy on	at lure	[at 'lu:ɒ]
to penetrate (vi)	at trænge ind i	[at 'tʁaŋə en i]
to permit (allow)	at tillade	[at 'teˌlæðə]
to pick (flowers)	at plukke	[at 'plɔkə]
to place (put, set)	at placere	[at pla'se:ɒ]
to plan (~ to do sth)	at planlægge	[at 'plæ:nˌlɛ:gə]
to play (actor)	at spille	[at 'sbelə]
to play (children)	at lege	[at 'lɑjə]

to point (e.g., ~ the way)	**at pege**	[at 'pɑjə]
to pour (liquid)	**at skænke**	[at 'skɛŋkə]
to pray (vi, vt)	**at bede**	[at 'be:ðə]
to predominate (vi)	**at dominere**	[at domi'ne:ɒ]
to prefer (like better)	**at foretrække**	[at fɒ:ɒ'tʁakə]
to prepare (~ a plan)	**at forberede**	[at 'fɒ:beˌʁɛðə]
to present (sb to sb)	**at præsentere**	[at pʁɛsən'te:ɒ]
to preserve (peace, life)	**at beholde**	[at be'hɒlə]
to progress (move forward)	**at fremme**	[at 'fʁamə]
to promise (vt)	**at love**	[at 'lɔ:uə]
to pronounce (say)	**at udtale**	[at 'uðˌtæ:lə]
to propose (vt)	**at foreslå**	[at fɒ:ɒ'slɔ:]
to protect (e.g., ~ nature)	**at beskytte**	[at be'skødə]
to protest (vi)	**at protestere**	[at pʁotɛ'sde:ɒ]
to prove (vt)	**at bevise**	[at be'vi:sə]
to provoke (vt)	**at provokere**	[at pʁovo'ke:ɒ]
to pull (e.g., ~ the rope)	**at trække**	[at 'tʁakə]
to punish (vt)	**at straffe**	[at 'sdʁɑfə]
to push (e.g., ~ the door)	**at skubbe**	[at 'skɔbə]
to put away (vt)	**at gemme**	[at 'gɛmə]
to put in (insert, include)	**at indsætte**	[at en'sɛdə]
to put in order	**at bringe i orden**	[at 'bʁɛŋə i 'ɒ:dn]
to put, to place	**at lægge**	[at 'lɛgə]
to quote (cite)	**at citere**	[at si'teɒ]
to reach (arrive at)	**at nå**	[at nɔ:]
to read (vi, vt)	**at læse**	[at 'lɛ:sə]
to realize (achieve)	**at gennemføre**	[at 'gɛnəmfø:ɒ]
to recall (~ one's name)	**at komme i tanke om**	[at 'kɒmə i 'tɑŋkə ɔm]
to recognize (admit)	**at erkende**	[at ɒ'kɛnə]
to recognize (identify sb)	**at genkende**	[at gɛn'kɛnə]
to recommend (vt)	**at anbefale**	[at anbe'fæ:lə]
to recover (~ from flu)	**at blive rask**	[at 'bli:ə ʁɑsk]
to redo (vt)	**at lave om**	[at 'læ:uə ɒm]
to reduce (speed etc.)	**at formindske**	[at fʌ'menskə]
to refuse (~ sb)	**at afsige**	[at ɑu'seə]
to regret (be sorry)	**at fortryde**	[at fʌ'tʁyðə]
to reinforce (position)	**at styrke**	[at 'sdyɒkə]
to remember (not forget)	**at huske**	[at 'huskə]
to remind (vt)	**at påminde**	[at pɔ'menə]
to remove (~ an obstacle)	**at fjerne**	[at 'fjæɒnə]
to remove (e.g., ~ a stain)	**at fjerne**	[at 'fjæɒnə]
to rent (of a tenant)	**at leje**	[at 'lɑjə]
to repair (mend)	**at reparere**	[at ʁɛpɑ'ʁɛ:ɑ]
to repeat (say again)	**at gentage**	[at gɛn'tæ:ə]

to report (make a report)	at rapportere	[at ʁabɒˈteʌ]
to reproach (vt)	at bebrejde	[at beˈbʁɑjdə]
to reserve, to book	at reservere	[at ʁɛsaɒˈveːɒ]
to restrain (hold back)	at afholde fra	[at auˈhɒlə fʁɑ]
to return (come back)	at komme tilbage	[at ˈkɒmə teˈbæːjə]
to risk, to take a risk	at risikere	[at ʁisiˈkeʌ]
to rub off (erase)	at viske ud	[at ˈveskə uð]
to run (move fast)	at løbe	[at ˈløːbə]
to satisfy (please)	at tilfredsstille	[at ˈtefʁɛðsˌsdelə]
to save (rescue)	at redde	[at ˈʁɛðə]
to say (e.g., ~ thank you)	at sige	[at ˈsiːə]
to scold (vt)	at skælde	[at ˈskɛlə]
to scratch (with claws)	at skramme	[at ˈskʁɑmə]
to select (to pick)	at udvælge	[at ˈuðˌvɛljə]
to sell (goods)	at sælge	[at ˈsɛljə]
to send (a letter)	at afsende	[at auˈsɛnə]
to send back (vt)	at tilbagesende	[at ˈtebæːəˌsɛnə]
to sentence (vt)	at idømme	[at iˈdœmə]
to serve (in restaurant)	at betjene	[at beˈtjɛːnə]
to settle (a conflict)	at ordne	[at ˈɒːdnə]
to shake (vt)	at ryste	[at ˈʁœsdə]
to shave (vi)	at barbere sig	[at bɑˈbeːɒ sɑj]
to shine (vi)	at stråle	[at ˈsdʁɔːlə]
to shoot (vi)	at skyde	[at ˈskyːðə]
to shout (vi)	at råbe	[at ˈʁɔːbə]
to show (to display)	at vise	[at ˈviːsə]
to shudder (vi)	at skælve	[at ˈskɛlvə]
to sigh (vi)	at sukke	[at ˈsɔkə]
to sign (document)	at underskrive	[at ˈɔnɒˌskʁiuə]
to signify (mean)	at betyde	[at beˈtyðə]
to simplify (vt)	at forenkle	[at fɒˈʁɛŋklə]
to sin (vi)	at synde	[at ˈsønə]
to sit (be seated)	at sidde	[at ˈseðə]
to smash (~ a bug)	at knuse	[at ˈknuːsə]
to smell (have odor)	at lugte, at dufte	[at ˈlɔgdə], [at ˈdɔfdə]
to smell (sniff at)	at lugte til ...	[at ˈlɔgdə tel]
to smile (vi)	at smile	[at ˈsmiːlə]
to solve (problem)	at løse	[at ˈløːsə]
to sow (seed, crop)	at så	[at sɒ]
to spill (liquid)	at spilde	[at ˈsbilə]
to spill out (vi, flour etc.)	at blive spildt	[at ˈbliːə sbild]
to spit (vi)	at spytte	[at ˈsbødə]

| to stand (toothache, cold) | at tåle | [at 'tɔ:lə] |
| to start (begin) | at starte | [at 'sdɑ:də] |

to steal (money, property)	at stjæle	[at 'sdjɛ:lə]
to stop (cease)	at standse	[at 'sdansə:]
to stop (for pause etc.)	at opholde sig	[at 'ʌbˌhʌlə sɑj]
to stop talking	at tie stille	[at ti:ə 'sdelə]

to stroke (caress)	at kærtegne	[at 'kɛɒtɑjnə]
to study (vt)	at studere	[at 'sdude:ɒ]
to suffer (feel pain)	at lide	[at 'liðə]

to support (cause, idea)	at støtte	[at 'sdødə]
to suppose (assume)	at forudsætte	[at fʌ:uð'sɛdə]
to surface (ab. submarine)	at dykke ud	[at 'døkə uð]
to surprise (amaze)	at forundre	[at fʌ'ɔndʁʌ]
to suspect (of wrongdoing)	at mistænke	[at mi'stɛŋkə]
to swim (vi)	at svømme	[at 'svœmə]
to switch on (vt)	at tænde	[at 'tɛnə]

256. Verbs T-W

to take (get hold of)	at tage	[at 'tæ:ə]
to take a bath	at vaske sig	[at 'vasgə sɑj]
to take a rest	at hvile ud	[at 'vi:lə uð]
to take a seat	at sætte sig ned	[at 'sɛdə sɑj neð]
to take aim (at the target)	at sigte (på ...)	[at 'segdə pɔ]

to take away	at tage med sig	[at 'tæ:ə mɛð sɑj]
to take off (airplane)	at lette	[at 'lɛdə]
to take off (remove)	at fjerne	[at 'fjæɒnə]
to take pictures	at fotografere	[at fotogʁɑ:'fe:ɒ]

to talk to ...	at tale med ...	[at 'tæ:lə mɛð]
to teach (give lessons)	at oplære	[at 'ɒbˌlɛ:ɒ]
to tear off (vt)	at rive af	[at 'ʁi:uə a]
to tell (story, joke)	at fortælle	[at fʌ'tɛlə]

to thank (vt)	at takke	[at 'tɑkə]
to think (believe)	at mene	[at 'me:nə]
to think (vi, vt)	at tænke	[at 'tɛŋkə]
to threaten (vt)	at true	[at 'tʁu:ə]
to throw (stone)	at kaste	[at 'kasdə]

to tie (~ sb to a tree)	at binde	[at 'benə]
to tie up (prisoner)	at forbinde	[at fɒ'benə]
to tire (exhaust)	at trætte	[at 'tʁadə]
to touch (one's arm etc.)	at røre	[at 'ʁœ:ɒ]
to tower (over ...)	at rejse sig	[at 'ʁɑjsə sɑj]
to train (animals)	at dressere	[at dʁɛ'seɒ]

to train (vi)	at træne sig	[at 'tʁɛ:nə saj]
to train sb	at træne	[at 'tʁɛ:nə]
to transform (vt)	at transformere	[at tʁɑnsfɒ'me:ɒ]
to translate (word, text)	at oversætte	[at ɒuɒ'sɛdə]
to treat (patient, illness)	at behandle	[at be'hanlə]
to tremble (with cold)	at ryste	[at 'ʁœsdə]
to trust (vt)	at stole på	[at 'sdo:lə pɔ]
to try (attempt)	at prøve	[at 'pʁœ:uə]
to turn (change direction)	at dreje	[at 'dʁɑjə]
to turn away (vi)	at vende sig bort	[at 'vɛnə saj bɒ:d]
to turn off (the light)	at slukke lyset	[at 'slɔkə 'ly:səð]
to turn over (stone etc.)	at vende op	[at 'vɛnə ʌp]
to underestimate (vt)	at undervurdere	[at 'ɔnaɒvuɒ,de:ɒ]
to underline (vt)	at understrege	[at 'ɔnɒ,sdʁɑjə]
to understand (vi, vt)	at forstå	[at fʌ'sdɔ:]
to undertake (vt)	at foretage	[at fɒ:ɒ'tæ:ə]
to unite (join)	at forene	[at fʌ'enə]
to untie (vt)	at binde op	[at 'benə ɔp]
to use (phrase, word)	at bruge	[at 'bʁuə]
to vaccinate (vt)	at vaccinere	[at vɑgsi:'ne:ɒ]
to vote (vi)	at stemme	[at 'sdɛmə]
to wait (vi, vt)	at vente (på ...)	[at 'vɛndə pɔ]
to wake sb (vt)	at vække	[at 'vɛkə]
to want (wish, desire)	at ville	[at 'vilə]
to warn (of the danger)	at advare	[at að'va:ɑ]
to wash (clean)	at vaske	[at 'vaskə]
to water (plants)	at vande	[at 'vanə]
to wave (the hand)	at vinke	[at 'veŋkə]
to weigh (have weight)	at veje	[at 'vɑjə]
to work (vi)	at arbejde	[at 'ɑ:bɑjdə]
to worry (make anxious)	at bekymre	[at be'kømɒ]
to worry (vi)	at bekymre sig	[at be'kømɒ saj]
to wrap (goods, parcel)	at pakke	[at 'pɑkə]
to wrestle (sport)	at kæmpe	[at 'kɛmbə]
to write (letter etc.)	at skrive	[at 'skʁiuə]
to write down	at skrive ned	[at 'skʁiuə neð]

Made in the USA
Lexington, KY
10 March 2013